D1512167

1.00

Greek terracotta figures

R. A. Higgins

GREEK TERRACOTTA FIGURES

Published by The Trustees of The British Museum
LONDON 1963

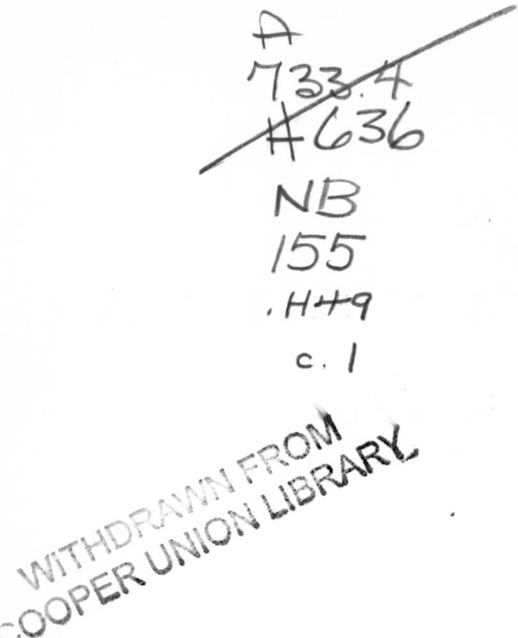

Printed by Eyre and Spottiswoode Limited, Her Majesty's Printers, at the Grosvenor Press, Portsmouth

Contents

Introduction

The chief use of fired clay – or terracotta – in antiquity was for domestic pottery. At a very early time, however, we may imagine a potter taking a spare piece of clay, making a model of one of his gods, his friends, or his animals, and firing it with his pots. For many centuries terracotta figures were no more than a by-product of the potter's craft, but eventually their manufacture achieved the status of a craft in its own right.

This booklet attempts to trace the history of Greek terracotta figures – commonly known as terracottas – with illustrations taken from the British Museum collections. Although the term terracotta is generally used to include large statues, architectural ornament, and decorative reliefs of this material, it is here restricted to statuettes, which form a distinct class, and are best considered alone.

The purpose of terracottas

I

Terracottas were made in Greek lands from the Neolithic period down to the Roman Empire – a span of some 4,000 years – but they were by no means common before the second half of this long period. In Classical times we know that they were held in very low esteem beside major works of art, and this was probably their position at all times; but they are well worth our study today.

Terracottas were used in antiquity for several purposes. We learn from literary sources that many were made to serve as dolls and toys. Surviving examples are indeed frequently in this form, and Athenian tomb-monuments often depict women holding the toys of their childhood, which look very like surviving examples of terracotta. We learn also that statuettes were commonly dedicated in rustic shrines. The evidence of excavation gives a more complete picture; it reveals that terracottas were kept in private houses, were dedicated in shrines and temples, and were buried with the dead. As the subjects are at all periods predominantly religious, we may suppose that when found in houses they had frequently belonged to domestic shrines. Their function as votive offerings needs little comment, since most surviving examples are eminently suitable for this purpose. They were dedicated in temples and sanctuaries; when these places became too full, they were taken out and ceremoniously buried in trenches nearby, being frequently broken before burial to avoid being salvaged and re-used. As for those found in tombs, it would probably in general be correct to say that they were buried not for any specifically religious purpose, but as being the treasured possessions of the dead, like his (or her) pottery, jewellery, or weapons.

Most terracottas were equally suitable for domestic, votive, or funerary use, but certain exceptional varieties seem to have been specially designed for one purpose only. Some were made at temple-workshops for offering on the spot; and certain other types seem to have had an exclusively funerary purpose, such as the mourner on pl. 2.

Yet another use of terracotta statuettes may be noted in passing; they occasionally served as scent-bottles. Objects of this kind have in general been disregarded in this survey as being by nature vases rather than statuettes. One class has, however, been included as a vital stage in the evolution of the Greek terracotta. (See pl. 4.)

Technical processes

The clay, which is the basis of the terracotta, was (and is) so abundant in Greece that almost every community had its own clay-beds and made its own terracottas – a fact of great importance for the archaeologist, since the origin of a terracotta can frequently be determined by the clay of which it is made. The natural clay is refined and mixed with some other substance, such as sand, to reduce shrinkage during the drying and firing.

There are several ways in which statuettes could be fashioned. Hand-modelling is the simplest, was for a long time the only method, and needs no further comment. Another way is to make a hollow figure such as a cone or a cylinder on the potter's wheel, and to adapt it by hand to human or animal shape.

By far the most effective method, and the commonest from about 500 B.C. onwards, is moulding. The first requirement for this process is an original model, of wax or fired clay, from which a clay mould is taken. As a general rule a mould was needed only for the front, but occasionally the back was also moulded. The mould is touched up by hand, if necessary, and fired; it is then ready for use.

To make a statuette, wet clay is pressed into the mould. If a solid figure is wanted, the mould is completely filled with clay; but if, as was more usual in antiquity, a hollow figure is envisaged, the clay forms only a thin layer. When it has dried and is 'leather-hard', the clay impression is removed from the mould. The figure is built up from a number of separately made parts, stuck together with liquid clay. For a simple piece, all that is required is to attach the front and the back, which latter may be moulded like the front, or may be a piece of clay roughly shaped to fit.

A more ambitious piece is assembled from any number of separate parts. In a hollow piece, to avoid the risk of a 'blow-out' in the firing, the bottom is usually left open and in addition a vent is cut in the back.

These three methods of making terracottas could be used in combination, and were so used. For example, in the seventh and sixth centuries B.C. hand-made and wheel-made bodies were often equipped with moulded heads, and Hellenistic moulded figures frequently have hand-made additions.

When all was ready, the figures were fired in a potter's kiln, to a temperature ranging between 750 and 950 degrees Centigrade. Generally, ancient terracottas are rather softer than the contemporary vases, a sign that they were not fired at such a high temperature.

Terracottas were regularly decorated. Two distinct methods were employed. The first is the so-called glaze used on Greek vases from the Mycenaean period onwards. Applied before firing, it fired a shiny black or reddish-brown; the basic colour was sometimes supplemented by touches of white and purplish-red and by incised lines. This system was current in terracottas from the Early Bronze Age down to about 500 B.C.

The second process, by which matt colours were laid over a white slip, first appeared in the seventh century B.C., and became general by the end of the sixth. The figure was covered, before firing, with a slip of white clay; after firing, tempera colours were laid over the slip. A wide range of colours was employed, black, red, yellow, blue and green being regularly found. Unfortunately, these colours, originally much gayer than the glaze decoration, do not survive well, and in many cases have completely disappeared. Consequently, while we can often see a glaze-painted terracotta in its original condition, it is more difficult to visualize the original appearance of the matt-painted variety.

The prehistoric period

Terracottas of the Late Neolithic period and the Early Bronze Age in Greece, about 3,000–2,000 B.C., are hand-made and mostly very crude. An honourable exception is the recently-discovered 'Aphrodite of Lerna' in Argos Museum, an astonishingly mature work for such an early period (about 3,000 B.C.).† In Crete, in the Middle Minoan period (2000-1550 B.C.) figures of men, women, and animals were dedicated in sanctuaries, and were occasionally buried with the dead. The British Museum possesses a few such offerings, mostly fragmentary, from a sanctuary at Petsofa in East Crete.

It is not till the later part of the Mycenaean period (1400-1100 B.C.) that we can speak of anything like a terracotta industry. Mycenaean terracottas are extremely numerous on sites throughout the Aegean and beyond, wherever Mycenaeans settled, and they are remarkably similar wherever found, from South Italy to Syria. Surprisingly, very few have been found in Crete, where figures of an entirely different kind were popular. Like their counterparts of the Classical period, Mycenaean terracottas have been found in houses, in votive deposits and in tombs. Standing female figures, believed to be goddesses, are the most popular subjects. The modelling is stylized in the extreme, details such as the features and the drapery being added in reddish glaze. The goddesses wear long dresses, reaching to the ground, and (frequently) crown-like spreading head-dresses. The commonest varieties are shown on pl. 1; they are known to archaeologists by the letters of the Greek alphabet which each happens somewhat to resemble.

The *phi* (*Φ*) type (pl. 1a) is the oldest. It evolved rather before 1400 B.C. and lasted until shortly after 1300. The goddess stands with her arms across her body; sometimes they are modelled or painted, sometimes (as here) they must be imagined. A variant has a baby at the breast. The *tau* (*T*) type (pl. 1b) has the arms folded rigidly across the breast. It was current from 1400-1200 B.C. in the form illustrated, and from 1200-1100 in a degenerate form. The *psi* (*Ψ*) type (pl. 1c) differs from the *phi* type in having the arms raised, perhaps in a gesture of benediction. It lasted from about 1300 to 1200 B.C. as here illustrated, and in a degenerate form for a further century.

† *See Illustrated London News for 12th Jan. 1957, p. 69.*

Other Mycenaean varieties are known, of which oxen and chariot-groups are represented in the British Museum, while enthroned goddesses, empty thrones, ploughing groups, and other animals can be seen in other collections.

The style of these terracottas is unimaginative in the extreme when compared with the brilliance of contemporary frescoes, ivories and engraved gems. This craft was, however, one of mass-production, and such simple figures were doubtless sold at very low prices.

The Mycenaean world came to an end about 1100 B.C. after a century of turmoil. It was probably now that the Dorians invaded Greece, bringing in their wake poverty and chaos, from which it took the country some four centuries to recover. The period between 1100 and 700 may be considered as one; it covers the Submycenaean, Protogeometric and Geometric pottery-styles.

The three centuries from 1100 to 800 B.C. were too impoverished for luxuries such as terracottas to be at all common. In fact, the total of surviving materal amounts to little more than a few dolls. In the eighth century Greece grew more prosperous, and the output of terracottas increased. Crude hand-made figures of men and animals predominated in tombs and sanctuaries. There were also a few wheel-made animals of a rather higher standard; a horse with a load of wine-jars represents this class in the British Museum.

The seventh & sixth centuries B.C. IV

The seventh century sees the real beginning of the Greek terracotta industry. About 700 B.C., influences from North Syria, Phoenicia and Cyprus, which had started as a trickle about 800 B.C., now came flooding in. This century covers the so-called Orientalizing period of Greek art, when the culture of the more civilized East was being rediscovered and assimilated. In terracottas a new technique and a new style made a simultaneous appearance.

The new technique is the use of the mould. At first only solid-moulding was employed, for relief-plaques and for heads attached to hand-made or wheel-made bodies. This innovation meant that an unskilled worker could mass-produce terracottas of a much higher standard than before.

The new style, which came with the use of the mould, is today called rather fancifully the Dedalic style, after Daedalus, the legendary Cretan artist. The attribution is not entirely inappropriate, since the style does seem to have developed in Crete and to have spread from there to the rest of Greece. It is characterized by a particular way of representing the human head, a fashion ultimately of Egyptian origin, which reached the Greek world at second hand from the Oriental sources mentioned above. Not only terracottas, but also bronzes and stone sculptures were made in this, the first sculptural style since the Mycenaean period. The face is flat, with the hair arranged in a fringe over the forehead and falling down on either side of the face like a modern judge's wig. This sophisticated treatment is completely different from the primitive heads on eighth-century figures. The style changes somewhat during the seventh century, the heads becoming less angular and more lifelike.

A characteristic of this period, and of the following two centuries, is the prevalence of local styles. Every major community evolved its own peculiarities, in marked contrast to the astonishing uniformity of Mycenaean art. The chief centres of production in the seventh century were Rhodes, Crete, Corinth and Sparta. There are examples in the British Museum from all these centres.

Pl. 2 shows a typical Dedalic terracotta from Rhodes of about 670 B.C., with a hand-made body and a moulded head. It was evidently made specially for funerary use, since it depicts a female mourner. Originally she was tearing her hair with both hands in the traditional gesture of mourning; her right arm is now missing. Red-filled scratches on breast and cheeks indicate where she has already drawn blood.

A more complicated seventh-century piece is shown on colour pl. A. Two women are seated side by side. As in the previous pieces, the heads are moulded and the bodies hand-made, but instead of being cylindrical they are flat. The faces are in the developed Dedalic style of about 625 B.C. Although this piece is believed to have been found at Thebes, the clay and the style indicate that it was made in Corinth. The details are indicated in glaze. The women are probably the earth-goddesses Demeter and Persephone, who, although mother and daughter, were sometimes represented identically at this period. They sit on the seat of a country-cart. It was originally equipped with a pole and a body, presumably of wood, and was probably drawn by terracotta beasts. The goddesses wear the peplos and the divine headdress, the polos.

In the sixth century the principal areas of production were an unidentified East Greek centre, Corinth, Argos, Attica and Boeotia. All these areas are represented in the British Museum, Boeotia particularly well. Terracottas followed much the same course as in the seventh century, except for one class, which will be considered shortly. On pl. 3 is a typical Boeotian terracotta, of about 570–550 B.C. The body is still as flat as before, with no attempt at modelling apart from rudimentary arms; but the moulded head follows the increase in naturalism which is to be seen in contemporary sculpture. The details are indicated in a good black glaze, picked out with red. Her high polos suggests that she is a goddess; to judge from the pomegranate-ornament on her necklace, she should be Demeter or Persephone.

Boeotia was particularly rich in terracottas from the sixth century onwards. A popular variety existed side by side with that illustrated on pl. 3; it had a similar body but a crude hand-made head with virtually no indication of the features. Another common type consists of a horse and rider, the horse striped like a zebra and the rider without legs. Both these varieties are represented in the British Museum.

Somewhere in the Eastern Greek world, perhaps in Rhodes or perhaps in Samos, the picture was different. Shortly before 600 B.C. potters started to make, with the aid of moulds, scent-bottles in human and animal form; they decorated them in the usual way, with black glaze, helped out with added red and white and with incision. These scent-bottles soon became extremely popular and were exported throughout the Greek world and beyond, especially into Etruria. It would seem that they were treasured as much for themselves as for the scent which they contained. Favourite subjects are gorgon's heads (after which the class has been christened the Gorgoneion class), female busts, warrior's heads, animal-heads and complete animals. This class is well represented in the British Museum amongst the finds from the cemeteries of Camirus in Rhodes.

About 550 B.C. a new type of scent-bottle evolved. The style was modernized to conform with the advances made in sculpture; the size was increased, complete human figures being introduced; and a new method of decoration was adopted. In place of the black pottery-glaze, brilliant matt colours were laid over a white slip (see p. 11). When new, these figures must have looked much more brilliant than the 'Gorgoneion' class, which is no doubt why the new kind so quickly ousted the old.

Another innovation is associated with this class. In certain examples the spout is entirely omitted, so that the figure is not a scent-bottle but a statuette. Such statuettes are the source from which stemmed all the hollow-moulded terracottas with which the subsequent chapters will be concerned. Both kinds, the scent-bottle and the statuette, are illustrated on pl. 4. Both were made about 540–530 B.C., and were found at Camirus in Rhodes. That on the right is a scent-bottle, that on the left a statuette, but they are otherwise almost identical. They represent the goddess Aphrodite, wearing a chiton and mantle and holding one of her attributes, a dove. Her sleek, well-fed appearance is typical of East Greek art of this period. The backs of these pieces are as well modelled as the fronts and the moulded surfaces have been carefully retouched. Altogether, so well designed and well made are they that they have every right to be considered as minor works of sculpture. The repertoire of this class includes seated women, squatting satyrs, sirens (woman-headed birds), and animals. All these varieties are represented in the British Museum, principally from the cemeteries of Camirus.

A *Corinthian goddesses, about* 620 B.C.

B *Aphrodite and Eros, about* 350 B.C.

The fifth & fourth centuries B.C. V

By 500 B.C. moulded figures, sometimes solid but more usually hollow, were common but were not yet universal. The type illustrated on pl. 5 was made in Athens from about 510 to about 470 B.C. It occurs in many sizes. These figures were made solid, the front moulded and the back flat, and the larger ones were afterwards partly hollowed out underneath. The decoration is in matt paint. A goddess sits stiffly on a throne, her feet on a footstool and her hands resting on her lap. There is practically no modelling on her body but the drapery is indicated in paint, in some examples very elaborately. She wears a chiton, a mantle which goes over her head, and in her curly hair a large diadem. Her jewellery consists of earrings and, in many examples, several necklaces.

We may suppose that the goddess represented is Athena. In some examples her aegis is actually painted on the breast. To judge from the clay, the majority, if not all, of the surviving examples were made in Athens; many have indeed been found there, for the most part buried in trenches on the Acropolis after the Persian sack of 480 B.C. It is possible that these figures are copied from the venerable wooden cult-statue of Athena Polias which was kept in the Erechtheum, but the evidence is not conclusive.

Another type, also found on the Acropolis, consists of a young woman standing, wearing a chiton and transverse mantle. This type, not present in the British Museum, possibly represents a worshipper of Athena rather than the goddess herself.

In the early fifth century a special class of terracotta was very popular in Boeotia, and was copied elsewhere. These pieces were hand-made, but were very carefully modelled, thanks no doubt to the influence of the mould. People are represented in the course of their everyday occupations; a woman makes bread, puts a loaf in the oven, teaches her child to cook; a barber cuts a customer's hair; a carpenter saws a piece of wood. The British Museum is not rich in this class, but it has numbers of animals, some with riders, which we may regard as offshoots of it. One of these terracottas, which were probably intended as toys, is shown on pl. 6a. A bearded man, wearing an Oriental headdress, rides on a goose. The colours are unusually well preserved: the rider's headdress is red and his garment blue; his flesh is pink and his beard and moustache black. Other pieces of this class include a boy on a horse, a boy on a dolphin, a dog, a goat, a ram and a deer.

Good hand-made toys were also popular in Corinth; here they were made right down to about 330 B.C. Satyrs, monkeys, mules and other creatures are portrayed in an amusing manner. Pl. 6b shows a monkey sitting at a mortar, holding a pestle in its left hand and putting a cake into its mouth with the right. This piece was made in Corinth about 420 B.C.

But these pieces are exceptional. The typical figure of the fifth century is hollow-moulded, a process derived from the East Greek scent-bottles and related figures of the later sixth century. They are more plentiful than their predecessors, but technically inferior, being carelessly mass-produced; and stylistically they tend to lag behind the spirit of the times. Backs are no longer moulded, and frequently have large, unsightly vents, and retouching is seldom employed. The principal centres were now Rhodes, Athens, Corinth, and Boeotia. Although Boeotia and the Italian and Sicilian Greeks still retained certain peculiarities, which will be discussed below, there is a feeling of uniformity throughout most of the Greek world, in marked contrast to the pronounced local styles of the seventh and sixth centuries.

In sculpture we rightly draw a distinction between the rich style of the Late Archaic period (500–475 B.C.) and the austerity of the Early Classical (475–440). This distinction has little validity as far as terracottas are concerned, where the early style simply shades off into the later. The maker of terracottas evidently obtained his ideas at second-hand, and any innovations had lost their intitial impact by the time they reached him. On pl. 7a is an Athenian figure of a woman of about 450 B.C., wearing a peplos. The vertical-horizontal emphasis is typical of the sculptures of the middle years of the fifth century, and is seen to perfection in the figures from the Temple of Zeus at Olympia. This style, which has been aptly named the Severe Style, soon fell out of favour in sculpture, but its influence on terracottas was considerably longer-lived.

In Boeotia, hand-made figures and groups ceased to be made about 470 B.C., but Boeotian terracottas continued to pursue a course of their own throughout the fifth century and beyond. They deserve a special mention not only for their highly individual style, but also for the great numbers in which they were produced. Two principle varieties may be noted. The first consists of standing female figures not unlike those made in the rest of Greece, but considerably larger, with larger vents in the back, and higher bases. In the middle of the fifth century the women wear tall headdresses of a peculiarly Boeotian form; towards the end of the century they wear a low polos surmounting a bulky and highly elaborate arrangement of the hair, an arrangement found nowhere else in the Greek world. Pl. 7b shows such a figure of about 430 B.C. It derives from such Severe Style figures as that illustrated on pl. 7a. The hand is raised to the breast in an archaic gesture which had survived into the later fifth century in the conservative craft of terracotta working. The second variety consists of statuettes of youths, naked except for a cloak draped over the back and shoulders, and holding a cock in the crook of the left arm. Towards the end of the fifth century the elaborate hairdressing of the youths comes to resemble that of the contemporary female figures. This type, well represented in the British Museum, was made in vast quantities and in a variety of sizes.

The fourth century sees a revival of standards in the design and craftsmanship of terracottas throughout the Greek world. Side by side with commonplace pieces, comparable with work of the preceding century, we see to an increasing extent terracottas of a higher quality, echoing (however faintly) the great works of sculpture of the fourth century.

Such a piece is illustrated on colour plate B. It was found at Olbia in South Russia, but is too good to have been made at this outpost of Greek culture. To judge from the clay, it may have been made at Corinth, but we cannot be sure. The date is about 350 B.C. Aphrodite and a childish Eros stand together on a semi-circular base. She is performing a stately dance, to which Eros beats time on a tambourine. Her softly voluptuous face echoes the style of Praxiteles. Apart from the charming composition and the careful workmanship, the range of colours is unusually wide: pale blue, dark blue, red, two shades of pink, yellow and black. Instead of the usual chalky surface, the white slip has a high gloss, which gives an enamel-like sheen to the colours laid over it.

In general, the increasing uniformity which was apparent in Greek terracottas in the fifth century is even more noticeable in the fourth. In Boeotia, however, side by side with echoes of sculptural types common to the rest of Greece, we find continuations of the characteristic local figures of the fifth century, with their high bases and their peculiar fashion of hairdressing.

In the fourth century, comic actors, wearing grotesque masks and the traditional padded costume, form a very popular subject. This preference, which seems to have originated in Athens, soon spread to the rest of Greece. In view of the religious nature of most Greek terracottas, such a choice of subject might cause surprise, but it should be remembered that dramatic performances, comic as well as tragic, were in origin religious ceremonies, and never completely lost this function.

These pieces were evidently made (and sold) in sets, each set comprising the complete cast of one play. There are two such sets in the Metropolitan Museum in New York, from a tomb in Athens. The plays which they represent belong to the so-called Middle Comedy of the mid-fourth century B.C.: later than the Old Comedy of Aristophanes but earlier than the New Comedy of Menander. Two examples are illustrated, both Athenian, of about 350 B.C., contemporary with the sets in New York mentioned above. On pl. 8a is an actor playing the part of a young woman; an actor rather than an actress, since all the parts were played by men. On pl. 8b is a stock comic character, a slave who has run away from his master and has taken sanctuary on an altar. He sardonically raises a hand to his ear, indicating that he is deaf to appeals to leave the safety of the altar.

It was noted above that dolls were one of the commonest forms of Greek terracottas. The earliest dolls are bell-shaped figures with movable legs, which were made from the tenth to the eighth century. There is then a gap in the series, which starts again about 500 B.C. The chief centres for the production of dolls in the fifth and fourth centuries were Corinth and Athens. In Corinthian dolls (well represented in the British Museum), the body is moulded solid; arms and legs were made separately and attached by cords or wires. The figures take the form of dancers, and many hold castanets or a tambourine; in the top of the head is a hole, evidently for a peg to which a cord was attached, so that the doll could be made to dance like a modern puppet. Some examples are clothed, whilst others are naked. The latter are probably intended to be dressed by their young owners. Pl. 8c shows a naked Corinthian doll of about 350 B.C., found in Corinth; it originally held castanets in both hands.

Athenian dolls are also well represented in the British Museum. They were made in several forms, the commonest being very like the Corinthian except that the body is hollow.

The Greek colonies of Sicily and South Italy have yet to be considered. They were producing terracottas in vast quantities from about 500 B.C. onwards in a number of distinctive styles. The most important local styles are those of Sicilian Greeks, and of the South Italian Greek colonies of Tarentum, Locri, and Paestum.

The Sicilian colonies produced several varieties which are well represented in the British Museum, mostly from Gela. One variety, illustrated on pl. 9, flourished from about 500 to 450 B.C. A goddess is seated on a wide throne, her feet on a footstool and her hands on her lap. She wears a tall polos, a peplos fastened at the shoulders with large brooches, and three rows of pectoral ornaments consisting of pendants threaded on cords or chains. These ornaments have been connected with certain gold plaques found in seventh century Rhodian tombs; but they have more in common with Argive terracottas of the sixth century. It is not known which goddess is represented.

Another variety, consisting of a standing woman holding a pig, must be connected with the worship of Demeter and Persephone, to whom the pig was sacred. It started about 500 and went on, changing with the current changes in style, till about 330 B.C.

The terracottas from Locri in many ways resemble those from Sicily, but are made of a different clay. The most characteristic products of Locrian workshops were not, however, statuettes but decorative reliefs, which are outside the scope of this booklet.

On pl. 10 is a representative of a type made at the Greek colony of Paestum (near Salerno) and found in large quantities near the temples at Paestum and at the mouth of the river Sele nearby. To judge from the dedications of the temples, the goddess represented is Hera, the consort of Zeus and Queen of the gods. She sits stiffly on a throne with an ornamental back and a footstool, wearning earrings, a chiton, a mantle draped symmetrically over her head and shoulders, and (over the top of the mantle) a polos. Her hands rest on her lap; in the right is a dish for pouring libations, and in the left a bowl of fruit. This piece was probably made about 400 B.C., although the stiffness of the pose recalls an earlier period. Another common Paestan type (of which there are examples in the British Museum) consists of a woman standing, holding a sacred casket on her left shoulder, and pressing a young pig to her breast with her right hand. Like her Sicilian counterpart, she must be connected with the worship of Demeter or Persephone.

The terracottas of Tarentum (the modern Taranto) have many peculiar features. They represent for the most part the god Dionysus reclining on a couch. In some examples a woman sits at his feet, frequently holding a naked male child. The woman is believed to be Persephone, the child Iacchus. These pieces are unusually flat, something between a statuette and a relief; many are supported behind by struts of clay like the supports of modern photograph-frames. Some 30,000 figures, mostly of this kind, were found in a votive deposit at Tarentum, and this is the source of the majority of the Tarentine terracottas in the British Museum.

The reclining Dionysus figures range in date from 500 to 330 B.C. Complete examples are rare, coming as they do from a votive deposit rather than from tombs (see p. 9), but an extremely fine fragment is illustrated on pl. 11. It shows a woman and child from the feet of a reclining Dionysus, of about 350 B.C. There is a monumental quality about it which recalls the sculptures of the great fourth-century masters.

The Hellenistic period

VI

The conquests of Alexander the Great between 333 and 322 B.C. changed the face of the Greek world. Two characteristics of the new age, known as the Hellenistic period, are particularly important to our subject. In the first place, the attitude to established religion became more sceptical, and gods tended to be represented in a less reverent way. Secondly, the processes started in the fifth century were finally completed: regional differences in art were almost completely obliterated, and we find a uniformity throughout the Greek world which had not been seen since Mycenaean days.

About the same time, for causes which are largely unknown to us, Greek terracottas reached a peak of technical perfection not seen since the sixth century, and for the next three and a half centuries they may be regarded as real, if minor, works of sculpture. Before this time, it had been customary to use either one mould, or at most two; henceforth, terracottas were made from any number of elements, made separately (in moulds or freehand) and attached before firing, such as heads, fronts, backs, bases, arms, and minor additions.

The Early Hellenistic period, 330–200 B.C., is characterized by the so-called Tanagra style. This style acquired its name in the seventies of last century when the first, and for long the finest, examples were found in the illicitly-excavated cemeteries of the Boeotian town of Tanagra. As a style it has great charm, but it has been spoilt for many people by forgeries which flooded the market when the supply of genuine 'Tanagras' ran out.

We now know that examples as fine as those from Tanagra were made in Athens, and that is doubtless where the style originated. Outside Athens and Tanagra, the best pieces come from Alexandria in Egypt, where immigrant Athenian craftsmen may well have worked. The style was copied, often in a rather debased form, throughout the Hellenistic world.

The commonest subject is a woman standing in a statuesque but entirely natural pose. The backs are frequently moulded, though seldom with as much detail as the front, and vents are reduced to a minimum. The figures usually stand on a thin rectangular base. The drapery is generally worn tightly stretched in opposing directions, a scheme which allows for many subtle variations.

Other subjects are Aphrodite, standing and seated; women seated; small girls; small boys, sometimes converted into Eros by the addition of wings; and young men. It is highly probable that the 'Tanagra' style originated in works of sculpture. One Athenian tomb-stone of about 320 B.C. shows this style at an early stage, and there are a number of Roman sculptures, copies of Greek originals, which are nothing but enlarged 'Tanagras', The Romans did not restrict themselves to copying these figures direct; ladies would arrange for a portrait-head of themselves to be placed on a Tanagra body.

The repertoire is limited, and there is a certain sameness in the concentration on tightly draped women, but there is enough variety within the self-imposed limits to make these figures probably the most attractive of all Greek terracottas.

The religious element is less apparent then in previous periods, and it has been suggested that we have here contemporary men and women. This is not always so. Gods and goddesses are humanized in accordance with the spirit of the times, but an attribute here and there reveals who they are. Ivy-leaves in the hair denote a Maenad; a mask held in the hand indicates a Muse; wings on a very human little boy make an Eros (or Cupid); and semi-nudity at this date almost certainly indicates Aphrodite. Colour plate C shows a typical Tanagra lady. She stands on a low plinth, holding up her drapery with her right hand and grasping a fan with her left. In her hair are ivy leaves and berries, and we should therefore regard her not as an ordinary mortal, but as a Maenad, one of the female attendants of Dionysus. Such a ladylike Maenad would be inconceivable at an earlier period, but these Tanagra ladies are somewhat impersonal figures, whose identity can be changed by the manipulation of accessories: a mask would have turned her into a Muse, a mirror into Aphrodite.

She wears the costume of the time, a thin chiton and a tightly draped mantle. The colour is here unusually well preserved, and gives an idea of the original appearance of this piece, with the blue chiton and the pink mantle.

On pl. 12 is another figure of this class. Here the lady is dressed for out-of-doors, in a chiton, a mantle going right over the head and on top a shady hat. The hat is like a Chinese coolie hat, and was fastened to the

C *Tanagra figure, about* 300 B.C.

D *Women gossiping, from Myrina* (?), *second century* B.C.

mantle with hat-pins. In her right hand she holds a fillet of wool, of the kind used to decorate a statue or a tomb-stone, and we may imagine her to be setting out on such an errand. The degree of tension in the modelling of the body tells us that it belongs to the late Tanagra period, and suggests a date round 250 B.C. This piece has completely lost the frontality of earlier statuettes, and can be seen with enjoyment from almost any point.

On pl. 13 is an unusually elaborate version of a theme, the knucklebone player, which originated about 360 B.C. and continued into the Early Hellenistic period. This group, which was made about 320 B.C., was found at Capua in South Italy, and was made there or thereabouts. Two women are squatting on a high rectangular plinth, playing the game of knucklebones. Bones from the ankle-joints of cloven-footed animals, or copies of them in stone or bronze, were used as dice, and were also used (as in this group) for a game played by women and known as 'five-stones', a name current today for the same game.† The object is to throw the bones into the air and catch them on the back of the hand. This group recalls a famous painting of the same subject from Herculaneum.

In the Late Hellenistic period, which covers the second and first centuries B.C. and the first few years of the Christian era, we see a change in Greek terracottas. Gone are the limited repertoire and the elegant poses of the Tanagra style. Some of the subjects may have been observed direct from life, but most are direct copies or adaptations of works of sculpture. Terracottas may now, like contemporary sculpture, be appreciated from any angle.

Although, like the Tanagra style, the Late Hellenistic was a universal one, there is one area in which a higher proportion of first-class work was produced than anywhere else in the Greek world. The cemeteries of Myrina, on the coast of Asia Minor near Smyrna, are to Late Hellenistic figures what those of Tanagra are to Early Hellenistic. The terracotta industry of Tanagra appears to have ceased production about 200 B.C., and from this date the real importance of Myrina is felt. Terracottas start here in the third century B.C. but are not in general as

† *Also known as "jacks"*

fine as those of Tanagra at that period.

The cemetery at Myrina was for many years robbed by peasants but was systematically excavated from 1880 to 1882 by French archaeologists. Many terracotta figures were found, the best collections of which are in the National Museum in Athens and in the Louvre, but the British Museum has a few excellent examples, from which those illustrated in pls. 14–16 and colour plate D are taken.

Colour plate D shows two women gossiping on a couch. It was probably made in the second century B.C. To the charm of the Tanagra figures is added a freedom of movement and a choice of subject which denotes a somewhat later period. The one on the right, evidently the elder, bends her head to listen to the other who appears to be telling her a secret. The women's flesh is pink; the couch is red at one end and the hangings are blue. Another second-century piece is illustrated on pl. 14. A naked woman, who must be Aphrodite, leans to her right against a herm of Dionysus, and places a wreath on it. The herm was a square pillar which served as a base for heads of gods. The form, originally restricted to Hermes, was later used for all gods. The exact significance of this theme eludes us, but we can nevertheless appreciate the superb craftsmanship.

Pl. 15 shows a figure of Nike, the goddess of Victory, flying down to earth and holding out in her right hand a wreath with which to crown a victor – whether a victor in a battle or an athletic contest we do not know. The pose is that of the famous Victory from Samothrace in the Louvre. This piece is not very easily dated but it was probably made in the later second or the earlier first century B.C. It is a composite terracotta made up of many pieces. About a dozen separate elements may easily be counted, to include the head, body, limbs, wings and minor attachments.

Pl. 16 shows Aphrodite standing with her arms half-raised; she is evidently putting on a necklace. Her body is elongated and the drapery clings to her body and legs in looped folds. In spite of the unnatural proportions and the equally unnatural treatment of the drapery, this piece has a charm denied to many more lifelike terracottas. This treatment of drapery, which probably originated in the Eastern Mediterranean, was later taken over at Palmyra and even in India.

The date of this Aphrodite is probably the late first century B.C. It is signed on the back with the name of the maker – or perhaps the workshop proprietor – Menophilos. It was the custom at Myrina, and at other centres in Asia Minor, from the late second century B.C. to the early first century A.D. for certain pieces to be signed. These signatures are very useful to students, since pieces bearing the same name were almost certainly made more or less at the same time. The most prolific artisan (or proprietor) at Myrina was Diphilos, but Menophilos did the better work.

Although less complete and less skilfully made, the terracottas from Delos are equally important for this period. Many have been excavated in houses and deposits which date from the early first century B.C. (the island was sacked in 88 and 69 B.C.), and are thus extremely useful for the dating of similar pieces from elsewhere. These terracottas are not represented in the collections of the British Museum, but can be seen in the Museum on Delos.

The production of terracottas did not cease when the Hellenistic period gave way to the Roman Empire. For at least four centuries terracottas continued to be made, especially in the eastern part of the Empire. In some areas, especially in Egypt, standards were still high, but generally speaking there is little to be said for Roman terracottas. One reason for the decline was undoubtedly the increasing cheapness of bronze, which was now within the reach of those who would previously have been content with clay.

The real decline started in the fourth century A.D., when the workmanship became extremely crude. In the fifth century the craft seems virtually to have died out, doubtless because it was too deeply rooted in paganism to survive the triumph of Christianity.

The story of Greek terracottas, in its broadest sense, may be said to cover some 4,000 years of more or less continuous development. In the narrower sense with which this survey has been chiefly concerned, the craft endured in its characteristic form from the seventh to the first century B.C. In this period we have seen how from humble beginnings the Greek terracotta gradually evolved into a real work of art, reaching its culmination in the third and second centuries. B.C., and declining slowly for some centuries thereafter. At its worst the Greek terracotta was the dullest hackwork; at its best, it could take its place amongst the minor arts of antiquity.

Glossary

AEGIS: A special kind of breastplate worn by Athena; it was decorated with a gorgon's head.

CHITON: A linen dress, partially shaped to the figure, and clinging tightly to it.

GLAZE: See p. 11.

MATT PAINT: See p. 11.

PEPLOS: A thick woollen dress, worn draped and falling in heavy folds.

POLOS: A tall cylindrical crown worn by goddesses.

VOTIVE FIGURES: Terracottas when offered to a deity in a temple or a shrine are referred to as votive offerings or votive figures.

Bibliography

GENERAL WORKS

T. B. L. Webster, *Greek Terracottas* (Penguin Books, Harmondsworth, 1950).

SEVENTH CENTURY TERRACOTTAS

R. J. H. Jenkins, *Dedalica* (Cambridge, 1936).

ARCHAIC TERRACOTTAS

P. Knoblauch, *Studien zur archaisch-griechischen Tonbildnerei in Kreta, Rhodos, Athen und Boeotien* (Bleicherode, 1937).

HELLENISTIC TERRACOTTAS

G. Kleiner, *Tanagrafiguren* (Berlin, 1942).

EXCAVATION REPORTS

Athens. *Hesperia*, volumes I ff.
Corinth. *Corinth*, vols. XII and XV.
Delos. *Délos*, vol. XXIII.
Olynthus. *Olynthus*, vols. IV, VII and XIV.
Rhodes. *Clara Rhodos*, vols. III, IV, VI–VII, VIII.
Lindos, vol. I.

RECENT MUSEUM CATALOGUES

British Museum. H. B. Walters, *Catalogue of the Terracottas in the British Museum* (1903). R. A. Higgins, *Catalogue of the Terracottas in the British Museum*, vol. I (1954); vol. II (1959).

Danish National Museum, Copenhagen. N. Breitenstein, *Catalogue of Terracottas* (Copenhagen, 1941).

Louvre. S. Mollard-Besques, *Catalogue raisonné des figurines et reliefs*, vol. I (1954)

List of plates

Numbers prefaced by the letters B, C, and D refer to the *Catalogue of Terracottas* by H. B. Walters (1903). Numbers not prefaced by a letter refer to the *Catalogue of Terracottas*, vol. I by R. A. Higgins (1954). Numbers in the form 1956, 7-19. 1 are the registration numbers of uncatalogued pieces.

COLOURED PLATES

A No. 897. Demeter and Persephone. From Thebes (?). Corinthian. About 620 B.C. Ht. 6½ ins. The strut under the seat is modern.

B No. 970. Aphrodite and Eros. From Olbia, in South Russia. About 350 B.C. Ht. 6½ ins.

C C 295. Maenad (?). From Tanagra. Boeotian. About 300 B.C. Ht. 9¼ ins.

D C 529. Women gossiping. From Myrina (?). Second century B.C. Ht. 8 ins.

BLACK AND WHITE PLATES

1a B12. Mycenaean goddess. From Melos (?). 1400–1300 B.C. Ht. 3¼ ins.

b B7. Mycenaean goddess. From Athens. 1400–1200 B.C. Ht. 3¾ ins.

c B5. Mycenaean goddess. From Athens (?). 1300–1200 B.C. Ht. 4¼ ins.

2 No. 14. Mourning woman. From Camirus. Rhodian. About 670 B.C. Ht. 8¾ ins.

3 No. 779. Goddess. From Tanagra. Boeotian. 575–550 B.C. Ht. 9½ ins.

4 Left: No. 58. Aphrodite. From Camirus. East Greek. About 540 B.C. Ht. 10 ins. Right: No. 57. Aphrodite (scent-bottle). From Camirus. East Greek. About 540 B.C. Ht. 10¼ ins.

5 No. 660. Athena. Unknown provenance. Athenian. About 500 B.C. Ht. 6 ins.

6a No. 806. Man riding a goose. From Tanagra. Boeotian. About 480 B.C. Ht. 4⅝ ins.

b No. 958. Monkey. From Tanagra (?). Corinthian. About 420 B.C. Ht. 3½ ins.

7*a* No. 674. Woman standing. From Lake Copais. Athenian. About 450 B.C. Ht. 9 ins.
b No. 846. Woman standing. From Lake Copais. Boeotian. About 430 B.C. Ht. 15 ins.

8*a* No. 746. Comic actor; young woman. From Athens. Athenian. About 350 B.C. Ht. 5⅝ ins.
b No. 743. Comic actor; slave on altar. From Peiraeus (?). Athenian. About 350 B.C. Ht. 4¾ ins.
c No. 973. Doll. From Corinth. Corinthian. About 350 B.C. Ht. 7 ins.

9 1956. 7–19. 1. Goddess. Unknown provenance. Sicilian Greek. About 500 B.C. Ht. 8½ ins.

10 1956. 7–19. 2. Hera. Unknown provenance. Made at Paestum. About 400 B.C. Ht. 8¾ ins.

11 No. 1354 *bis*. Persephone and Iacchus (?). Unknown provenance. Tarentine. About 350 B.C. Ht. 9½ ins.

12 C 312. Woman in outdoor dress. From Tanagra. Boeotian. About 250 B.C. Ht. 7½ ins.

13 D 161. Women playing knucklebones. From Capua. About 300 B.C. Total ht. 5½ ins.

14 C 528. Aphrodite. From Myrina. Second century B.C. Ht. 8⅞ ins.

15 C 533. Victory. From Myrina. First century B.C. Ht. 9¼ ins.

16 1906. 3–10. 1. Aphrodite. Unknown provenance (Myrina type). Late first century B.C. Ht. 10¾ ins.

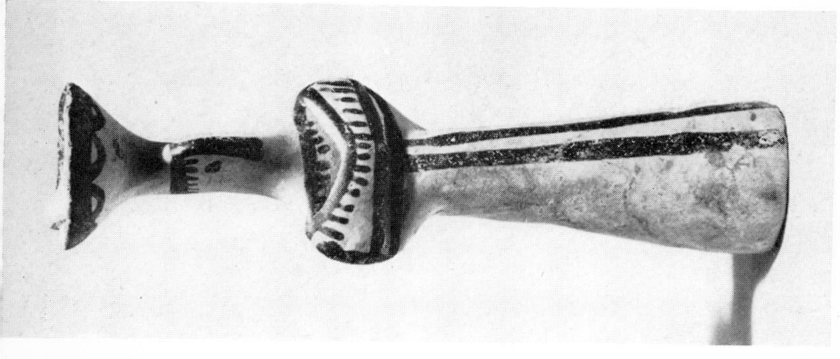

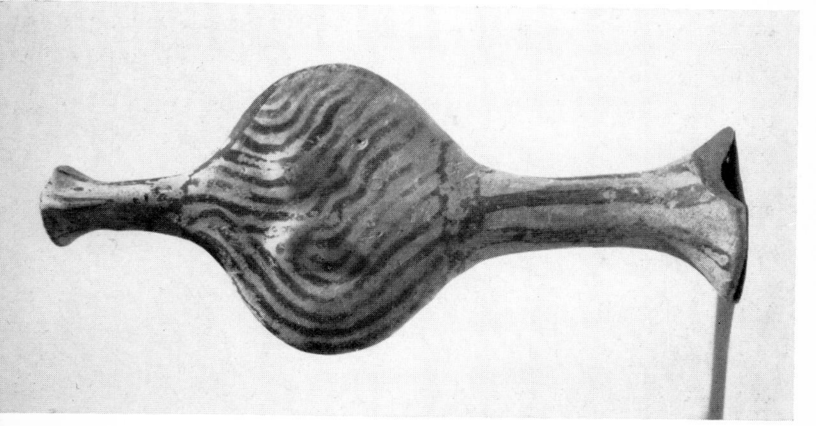

Mycenaean goddesses, 1400-1200 B.C.

2 *Mourner, about* 670 B.C.

Boeotian goddess, 575–550 B.C.

4 *Two statuettes of Aphrodite, about* 540 B.C.

5 *Athena, about* 500 B.C.

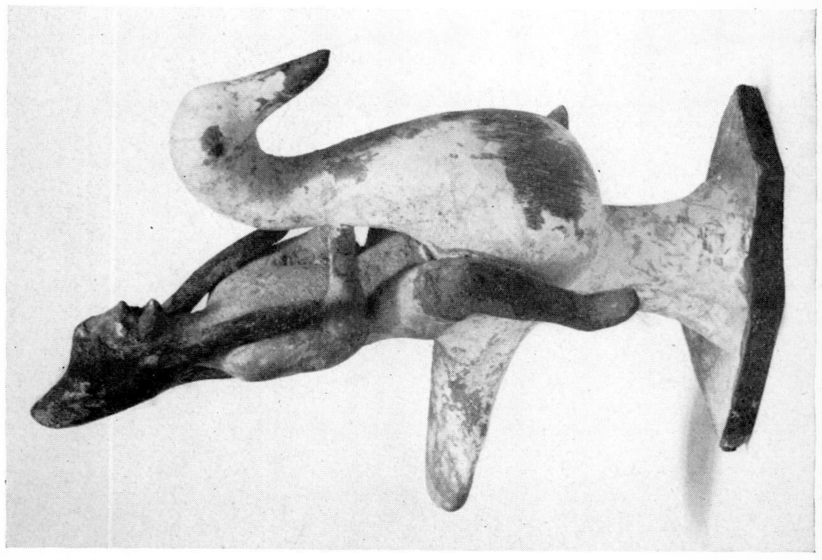

6a *Man on goose, about* 480 B.C. b *Monkey, about* 420 B.C.

Woman, about 450 B.C.

b *Woman, about* 430 B.C.

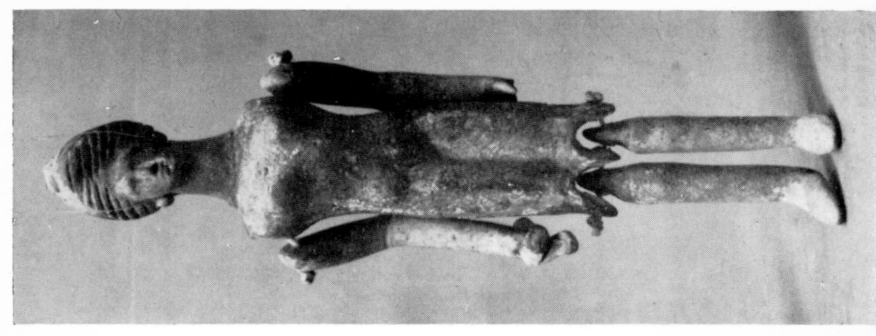

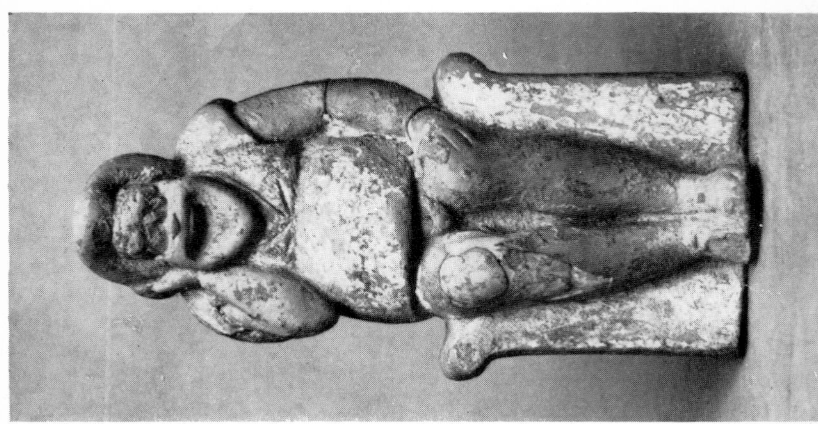

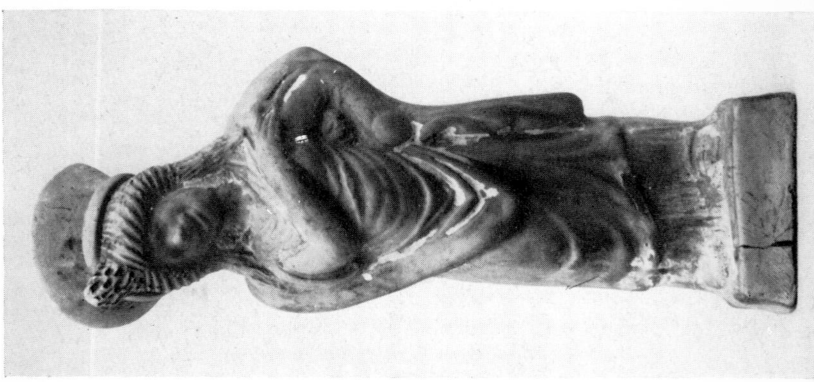

8a & b *Actors, about* 350 B.C. c *Doll, about* 350 B.C.

9 *Sicilian goddess, about* 600 B.C.

10 *Hera, about* 400 B.C.

11 *Tarentine group, about* 350 B.C.

12 *Tanagra figure, about* 250 B.C.

3 *Knucklebone players, about* 300 B.C.

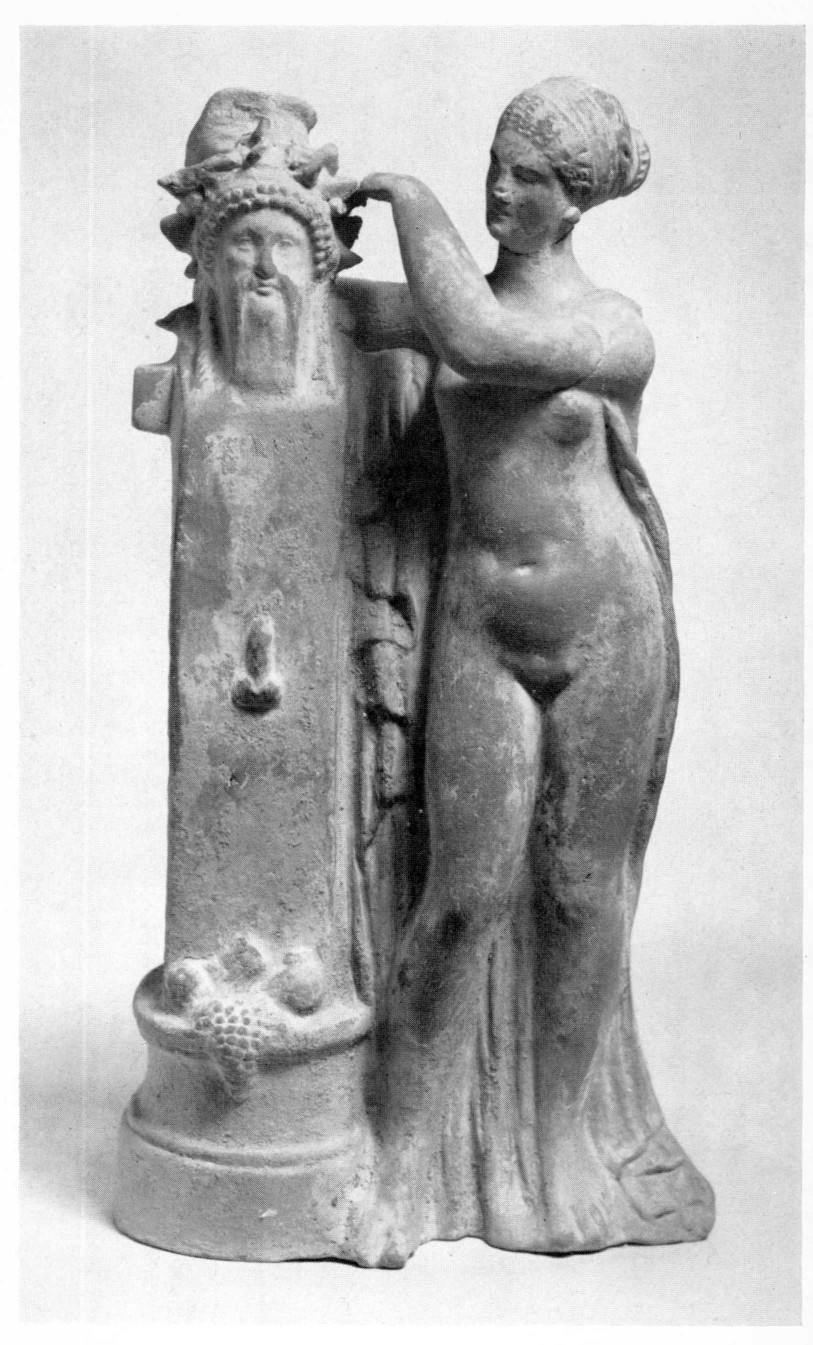

14 *Aphrodite, from Myrina; second century* B.C.

15 *Victory, from Myrina; first century* B.C.

16 *Aphrodite, Myrina type; first century* B.C.

Essays on Full Employment, 1942-1972

by

JOHN H. G. PIERSON

The Scarecrow Press, Inc.
Metuchen, N.J. 1972

For Sherleigh

Library of Congress Cataloging in Publication Data

Pierson, John Herman Groesbeck, 1906-
Essays on full employment, 1942-1972.

1. United States--Full employment policies--Addresses, essays, lectures. I. Title.
HC106.5.P538 331.1'2'0973 72-8135
ISBN 0-8108-0554-5

AUTHOR'S PREFACE

The constant theme of these essays is that a national policy of assured prosperity at full employment has become essential for America's future, and that such a policy is technically and politically possible.

To grasp the first point one must go deeper than many people who deplore involuntary unemployment normally do. What they see is that full employment is a labor goal, and that the unemployment numbers published periodically are more sensitive politically than most of the other numbers in the kaleidoscopic national statistical picture. What they miss is the connection with the viability of our whole socioeconomic system.

Guaranteeing everyone the opportunity to work and earn a living would indeed meet labor's most basic need, but it would also tip the scales toward solving other crucial national problems such as poverty, racial tension, interest-group irresponsibility, conflict over foreign-trade policy. Our national priorities should certainly be reordered in other ways too. This difference remains, however: decisions on life-and-death issues--wars and the environment--aside, no other public policy change could yield so wide a margin of benefit.

As for the point that assured full employment is not merely needed but possible, this naturally is the heart of the matter. Among the propositions in support of that claim that will be found emphasized again and again in the pages to follow (these essays will seem most tediously repetitive, I know, if read consecutively) the main ones are:

1. An insurance approach to economic policy is needed in place of our conventional succession of defensive reactions, tied to fallible forecasts and often delayed unduly by wrangles over both diagnosis and therapy in any case. The guarantees, moreover, would tend to stabilize expectations, which in turn would simplify making good on the guarantees.

2. Social goals are bound to be controversial. Therefore, attainment of the uncontroversially right economic

goal, stability at full employment, has to be assured independently--in particular, it must not be left to stand or fall by the outcome of the perennial struggle over the mix of public and private spending. Taken together with "3" below, this means (novel as the idea may still seem to many people) that not only aggregate employment itself but also aggregate consumer spending requires governmental decision and control.

3. In solving the economic problem, it seems self-evident that we should use and strengthen our traditional system of government, with its division of powers. Good as a President's recommended economic program might turn out to be, the Congress must have the final word. Hence the Employment Act should be amended to assign to Congress an authority--and above all a responsibility--which the original language of the Act fails to give.

4. If conceived and executed in the suggested manner, a full-employment policy would not only _not_ intensify inflationary pressures but, on the contrary, would actually offer the best cure for inflation.

These propositions seemed fundamental to me in 1942 (the year of the first essay included in this book) and indeed earlier. I still believe in them today.

I want to thank the following publications and organizations for permission to reprint essays which are reproduced in Part II: _The Christian Science Monitor_; _The Review of Economics and Statistics_; The American Academy of Political and Social Science; the American Economic Association; _Kyklos_; _The Commercial and Financial Chronicle_; the _Monterey Peninsula Herald_; _The New York Times_; _The Honolulu Advertiser_; _The Washington Post_; the Foundation for Voluntary Service.

Part I is a reprint _in toto_ of the compilation of essays in my 1947 book, _Full Employment and Free Enterprise_, which had a quite limited circulation at that time, partly owing to the bankruptcy of the publisher.

J. H. G. P.

August 9, 1972

CONTENTS

INTRODUCTION

COMPLETING THE EMPLOYMENT ACT*

In the twenty-six years since the Employment Act of 1946 was signed into law, the country has experienced five recessions. Even when business has prospered, the central aim of this Act--useful employment opportunities for all those able, willing, and seeking to work--has seldom been brought within sight, let alone achieved. Only for three years, in the Korea war boom, has the official unemployment estimate averaged below 3.5 percent of the civilian labor force (dropping to 2.9 percent in 1953 and to 2.5 percent, in seasonally adjusted figures, that May and June). In as many as eleven years it has stood above 5 percent (rising to 6.8 percent in 1958 and to 7.5 percent that July). Earlier bench marks, not entirely comparable, were 24.9 percent unemployment in 1933 and 1.2 percent in 1944 under wartime price controls.

In the long absence of recessions after 1961 the unemployment rate finally dropped to 3.5 percent for 1969 (touching 3.3 percent momentarily early that year), but the statistics somewhat overstate the actual improvement since stricter definitions of unemployment were used as from 1965 and 1967. Then in 1970 the jobless percentage jumped to 4.9, and in 1971 it hovered around, and averaged just under, 6 percent.

Six percent unemployment now means more than 5 million persons. Even 4 percent--sometimes treated as though it were an acceptable goal--would still leave some 3 1/2 million persons in this country looking for work and unable to find any. Moreover the published unemployment total understates the real extent of involuntary idleness at virtually all times and especially during recessions. One reason among several is that some persons who want to work full-time can only get part-time jobs. Some others even-

---

*This article appeared in the Congressional Record, March 1, 1972, inserted by Representative Patsy T. Mink of Hawaii.

tually become too discouraged to keep on looking and are then no longer counted as part of the labor force; and so--except for less frequent and less reliable estimating--they slip through the statistical net altogether.

A list of the legislative measures enacted or proposed since 1946 to try to cope better with our national economic problems would be long indeed. Many amendments have been offered to the Employment Act itself, keyed mainly to three objectives: (1) Repeated efforts have been made from the outset to have the Act not only promote employment but also restrain inflationary price increases; (2) Lately, since about 1960, it has often been urged that this law should concern itself with our balance of payments as well; (3) There have also been attempts to go back to the more formal kind of "national full employment budget" planning which was originally suggested in 1945-46 but rejected by Congress at that time.

No amendments other than technical or housekeeping ones have ever been adopted, however, and some of the reasons are easily imagined. Many proposals were addressed to section 2, the Declaration of Policy. --Why load the Act with further policy objectives when its first objective was still not being achieved? Again, the "national full employment budget" concept was originally framed in a way that automatically aroused strong opposition by failing to safeguard the private enterprise interest. And all else aside, tinkering with an Act so broad in scope would have seemed like opening Pandora's box. --Where would the modifications end if once begun?

But are the reasons for standing pat still good enough? The need to have our economy function properly is as great as ever. The quarter-century record of failure of the Employment Act as written is more obvious today than before because of the length and peculiarities of the present slump. Indeed we now have not only the doctrine that full employment and price stability cannot be achieved simultaneously but the experience of the simultaneous nonachievement of both. Meanwhile in engineering, for example, scientifically-minded practical people are every day making progress by simply asking "what would be the conditions under which X" (some desired result) "would be achieved?" and then proceeding to construct those very conditions. Certainly the question must be raised whether the arguments against changing the Act are still convincing.

The answer to this must depend at least partly on whether amendments can be framed that will once and for all complete the Employment Act--make it do what it should, ideally speaking, have done from the start. Can it be strengthened to guarantee jobs to able job-seekers, while at the same time staying clear of irrelevant matters? (To keep full employment from itself causing inflation is of course anything but irrelevant.) Can these things, moreover, be done without prejudging the handling of the touchy public-versus-private-sector issue; or changing the traditional relationship between the President and the Congress (as by expecting Congress to rubber-stamp a Presidential spending program or to give the President unduly wide discretionary powers); or interfering in the legitimate concerns of Congressional committees?

It is here submitted that all this is possible, and textual amendments to the Act are offered below to illustrate how. Much the most important amendment and the key to the others is the addition of a new final section 6 to vest appropriate responsibilities in Congress as a whole. However, for the sake of clarity, this discussion will proceed straight through the Act from the beginning.

* * *

First, however, a word is needed about what is really at stake, because the arguments over the full-employment issue are often pitched on altogether too narrow ground. In briefest summary: (1) Involuntary unemployment is destructive of personality. (2) An assurance of continuous prosperity and full employment would weaken the antisocial (usually inflationary) compulsions of business, labor, farmer, and other interest groups. (3) Racial peace seems impossible in this country without universal job opportunity--the present lack of which is also partly responsible for the alienation of youth, not to speak of the helpless bitterness of many older people. (4) Getting rid of poverty would be greatly simplified as a result of the cash-income effects of continuous full employment (more paid labor; less chance of exploiting labor by paying substandard wages). (5) The extra wealth (GNP) which would be created under those full-activity conditions--the staggering amount now wasted through avoidable non-production--is needed to help finance programs to meet the problems of the cities, backward rural areas, and the environment generally, including again problems of poverty but not limited to them. (6) Internationally, that extra wealth would confirm our ability to extend more generous aid to the world's less developed countries. (7) More (and more fundamental) than that, confidence in our ability to maintain a market adequate for our own full-employment prosperity through domestic policy would substantially deflate our fear of imports and our exaggerated preoccupation with export markets and export surpluses; thus it would enable us to be a "good neighbor" that encourages and helps the less developed countries to shift "from aid to trade" as they become ready for it.

* * *

Section 1 of "AN ACT to declare a national policy on employment, production, and purchasing power, and for other purposes" (60 Stat. 23) (Public Law 304--79th Congress) (approved February 20, 1946) merely states that the short title is "Employment Act of 1946."

Section 2

Section 2 is the "Declaration of Policy." This has received so much attention that it will be quoted here in full, with proposed additions to the text underlined (as also subsequently) and proposed deletions placed within square brackets:

> Sec. 2. The Congress hereby declares that it is the continuing policy and responsibility of the Federal Government to use all practicable means consistent with its needs and obligations and other essential considerations of national policy, with the assistance and cooperation of industry, agriculture, labor, and State and local governments, to coordinate and utilize all its plans, functions, and resources for the purpose of creating and maintaining, in a manner calculated to foster and promote free competitive enterprise and the general welfare, conditions under which there will be [afforded] the assurance of useful employment opportunities, including self-employment, for those able, willing, and seeking to work [, and to promote maximum employment, production, and purchasing power]; and opportunities for training, to improve employability; and healthy growth of production, with full, non-inflationary employment and purchasing power.

COMMENTS: (1) It is necessary to include an assurance of employment opportunity, since that is the heart of the matter. (The rather profuse introductory language of this Declaration might perhaps be pruned a little too without sacrificing vital safeguards, but that is not essential, and the changes suggested here are purposely held to a minimum.)

(2) The concept of "maximum employment..." has been a false lead from the beginning. Maximum purchasing power is inflationary. Maximum employment is either inflationary or simply weak ("let's do the best we can"). And maximum production is now more than ever open to challenge as a national objective, both psychologically and ecologically. Hence there is much to be said for rewording the final clause.

(3) The Employment Act is not the place where training programs should be spelled out. As far as policy is concerned, however, there is or should be a national purpose not only to provide employment opportunities for all those able, willing, and seeking to work but also to fight against so-called unemployability; that is, to help anyone, "willing" and "seeking" but not as yet "able," to overcome his or her inability. Hence the end of this Declaration could well refer to that issue too, as here suggested.

Section 3

Section 3 deals with the "Economic Report of the President." Additional language is proposed for the first subsection in order to give special emphasis to certain recommendations, not now debarred but not explicitly required either, which the Economic Report definitely needs to include:

> Sec. 3. (a) The President shall transmit to the Congress not later than January 20 of each year an economic report (hereinafter called the 'Economic Report') setting forth (1) the levels of employment, production, and purchasing power obtaining in the United States and such levels needed to carry out the policy declared in section 2, including specifically the minimum and maximum levels of employment recommended in the light of that policy, and the minimum and maximum rates of aggregate personal consumption expenditures deemed consistent with that policy in view of the program of Federal Government purchases of goods and services recommended to be undertaken and the anticipated other demands on the national product; (2) current and foreseeable trends in the levels of employment, production,

> and purchasing power; (3) a review of the economic program of the Federal Government and a review of economic conditions affecting employment in the United States or any considerable portion thereof during the preceding year and of their effect upon employment, production, and purchasing power; and (4) a program for carrying out the policy declared in section 2, together with such recommendations for legislation as he may deem necessary or desirable.

COMMENTS: (1) The proposed minimum level of employment (in terms, presumably, of the seasonally adjusted monthly national total reported by the Department of Labor) would reflect the President's view of the correct statistical definition of full employment for the year ahead. This quantity would be derived by estimating the civilian labor force and subtracting the amount of unemployment that seemed to the President reasonable in the light of production shifts, manpower policies, and labor mobility at the time (the allowance for "necessary frictional unemployment"). Apart from labor-force growth due to the changing size and age-composition of the population, an effective full-employment policy would no doubt also bring into the picture at the beginning many persons previously not even on record as wanting to work. No need, however, to attempt the impossible. In the transition period from our present excessive unemployment, the President could if he thought best propose moving up to full employment by stages and reaching it in, for example, the second quarter of the second year.

(2) A maximum limit on employment is needed too, as a safeguard against inflation. (Purely as illustration, if the President in some year proposed a minimum of 86.5 million jobs, he might also state that anything above 87.8 million jobs would represent over-employment--too tight a situation in the labor market, with too much upward pressure on pay scales and on total income payments.)

(3) Key importance attaches to also setting limits to personal consumption expenditures (as compiled quarterly, at seasonally adjusted annual rates, by the Department of Commerce), and to deriving this target in the manner indicated. In the first place, since the President would of course state that any expansion or contraction of his recommended government program would imply an opposite change in needed consumer spending, this approach would eliminate the fear that a government commitment to serve as "employer of last resort" might lead to a degree of expansion

of the public sector that was unacceptable to Congress. Such a government commitment--such underwriting of the job market--would still be essential, of course; and some consequent manipulation of the level of employment on public works and services would result, in compensation for net "error" in estimating other forms of demand and the employment-generating effect of a given demand. But there would be no inherent one-way bias toward government expansion, no greater probability (if the mid-point between the employment floor and ceiling were aimed at to begin with) of a need to accelerate public works and services than of a need to decelerate them. Hence this approach would remove a basic obstacle to the solution of the problem of making continuous full employment possible in practice.

This approach would also greatly help to remove the second basic obstacle, which is the fear of inflation. While that subject can best be viewed in a comprehensive way at a later point in this article, it is evident that a firm ceiling on consumer spending (mentioned here, explained in due course) would act as a powerful brake against inflationary demand spirals, especially when coupled with the proposed ceiling on employment.

To return to the computations envisaged. First of all, all the statistical series needed are continuously available. Second, while all the components of gross national expenditures, or GNP, would be used for deriving the needed consumer spending, there is no proposal here that the GNP itself or any of its components except consumer spending should have lower and upper limits set. The suggested procedures do not imply control over private investment decisions, for instance. (Given the permanently high final-product markets implied by the policy, private domestic investment could be expected to continue reasonably high also, with its cyclical swings damped down considerably. In estimating it for the purposes here in view, there might be advantages in choosing a mid-point figure on the diminished investment cycle rather than an actual forecast figure. This would look toward having fluctuations in private construction offset by opposite _ex post_ fluctuations of public works rather than by opposite _ex ante_ fluctuations of private consumer spending.)

This much having been said, the technical estimating procedure may be clarified, at least in outline. Other things (specifically, the sum of State and local government purchases of goods and services, gross private or business domestic investments, and net exports of goods and services) being equal, the needed total of (a) private consumer spending and (b) Federal Government spending for goods and services would remain constant too. ("Needed" here translates into required for a full-employment level of GNP, at a given level of prices.) In point of fact, other things cannot be expected to be quite equal if the ratio of (a) to (b) changes. In particular, certain common types of government spending yield more employment, dollar for dollar, than does more private consumer spending. A substantial program of public service employment would, moreover, have the great advantage that it would help to ease the disproportionately high unemployment among less-skilled and less-educated workers. But differences such as these can all be roughly estimated, just as can the other components of the GNP. Thus, the President would add his optional items to the relatively fixed or unavoidable ones already there and would state what total volume of purchases of goods and services he wanted the Federal Government itself to undertake. He would then specify the level of private consumer spending that in his view would be required to be associated with that much Federal Government spending in order to have, at the price level which he anticipated, an aggregate market capable of sustaining full employment as he had defined it. And no doubt he would also suggest--without needing to have the law say so--a scale of variations of the consumer component that would be appropriate in case Congress introduced variations of the government component.

Here also appears the third major advantage from pegging consumer spending. An increase of net exports has often been sought in the past as a solution for our unemployment, even though other countries might suffer from the action we took. The proposed approach would turn the problem around, calling for an expansion of the domestic market (via larger consumer spending) when the foreign market (net exports) was projected as declining. Consequently this approach would allay fears of a shortage of markets in the overall sense, and so would help us to maintain a liberal foreign-trade policy based on the widest interpretation of national self-interest.

(4) Part (4) of the subsection asks the President to set forth his program and, if necessary or desirable, recommend new legislation. Although the text here probably needs no formal amplification, the President would clearly be concerned--under this proposal--not only with legislative and administrative measures directly or indirectly affecting the performance of the economy on a continuing basis (welfare reform and anti-trust action, for instance) but also with special compensatory measures. The latter would be for

use only when that might prove necessary to keep total employment, total personal consumption expenditures, or both from straying outside their specified limits. The subject of contingent, compensatory measures, is however, reserved for later discussion.

Not to overlook the regional aspect of the employment problem--the President's program would certainly not limit itself to questions of national averages. Also dealt with in his recommendations would naturally be the continuing special needs of the country's Appalachias, as well as any unusually severe local job shortages of a more temporary nature brought about, say, by technological change or import competition.

No comment is required on the remainder of section 3. Subsection (b) authorizes the President also to transmit supplementary reports to Congress. Subsection (c) states that the Economic Report and any supplements shall be referred by Congress to its Joint Economic Committee.

Section 4

Section 4 of the Act deals at some length, in six subsections, with the "Council of Economic Advisers to the President." The functions of this three-member Council, established in the Executive Office of the President, are essentially those implied by its title.

Section 5

Section 5, the last one as the Act now stands, brings us to the "Joint Economic Committee." Here again the text deals largely with matters outside the scope of the present analysis, such as the Committee's composition (ten Senators and ten Members of the House of Representatives, with the majority party represented by six members in each case), the holding of hearings, the appointment of experts, consultants, and other assistants, the procurement of printing and binding, the authorization of necessary appropriations, and so on. Subsection (b), however, one of the five subsections, is concerned with the vital issue of what happens to the President's Economic Report, and here a brief amendment needs to be incorporated, consequential on what comes later. With the proposed addition, this subsection would read:

> (b) It shall be the function of the joint committee--

(1) to make a continuing study of matters relating to the Economic Report;

(2) to study means of coordinating programs in order to further the policy of this Act; and

(3) as a guide to the several committees of the Congress dealing with legislation relating to the Economic Report, not later than March 1, of each year (beginning with the year 1947) to file a report with the Senate and the House of Representatives containing its findings and recommendations with respect to each of the main recommendations made by the President in the Economic Report, together with a draft Joint Resolution for the consideration of the Congress as provided for in section 6; and from time to time to make such other reports and recommendations to the Senate and House of Representatives as it deems advisable.

COMMENTS: (1) The process which the Act has caused the President and his advisers to initiate each year by preparing the Economic Report should no longer be allowed to disappear in thin air at the end. Rather, if there is to be the practical possibility of assuring continuous full employment, it is essential that Congress as a whole should also assume appropriate responsibilities. Everything hinges on that.

(2) A procedural problem arises at this point because the Joint Economic Committee, in spite of what the law says about its powers to recommend, is not regarded as having the authority to recommend "legislative" action to Congress as a whole. Logically speaking, this Committee, with its detailed understanding of the subject, is clearly the one to prepare the annual draft joint resolution. As an interim measure it might if necessary work with one or more of the other, legislative committees in preparing the resolution for submission to Congress as a whole.

Section 6

We come now to the decisive amendment that would complete the Employment Act by making provision for nearly all the action required to assure continuous full employment from that time on. This proposed new section 6 would presumably be entitled "Congressional Action on the Report of the Joint Economic Committee," and could for brevity be phrased approximately as follows:

Sec. 6. As soon as practicable after the filing of the report of the Joint Economic Committee, the Congress shall by joint resolution of the Senate and the House of Representatives set forth its decisions with respect to--

(a) the minimum and maximum acceptable levels of employment throughout the year in question;

(b) the minimum and maximum acceptable rates of aggregate personal consumption expenditures throughout the year;

(c) the preventive action to be taken by the President if employment should at any time tend to fall below its minimum, or rise above its maximum, acceptable level as defined in (a); and

(d) the preventive action to be taken by the President in case personal consumption expenditures should at any time tend to fall below their minimum, or rise above their maximum, acceptable rates as defined in (b).

COMMENTS: (1) In adopting this amendment Congress would obviously not be committing future Congresses on the substance of their decisions on the four indicated subjects but only on always reaching some definite decisions on them.

(2) Congress would always have the option to agree with or differ from the President on the minimum and maximum acceptable levels of employment, or in other words on what "full employment" should mean for operating purposes. It might take a different view, for example, of the size of the labor force (the Joint Economic Committee has the help of its own staff experts); or of how much frictional unemployment was acceptable (the President might have considered, say, 3 percent unemployment as tantamount to full employment, whereas Congress preferred 3.5 percent, or 2.5 percent); or of how wide a gap should be allowed between minimum and maximum limits.

(3) The decision on acceptable rates of aggregate personal consumption expenditures would above all settle the public-versus-private-sector issue in the way Congress wanted it settled at the time. Suppose that in some year the President's program if adopted would go so far in reordering the country's priorities as to increase not only the overall emphasis on social welfare fields (health, education, low-cost housing, anti-pollution, and so on) but also the percentage of GNP represented by the government's own purchases of goods and services. The majority in Congress might agree--or go even farther. On the other hand, per-

haps the majority would favor maintaining the existing GNP ratios instead. Thus, to illustrate, Congress might some year decide that the acceptable limits to consumer spending would be \$765 billion and \$780 billion, whereas the President, having different GNP proportions (more heavily weighted on the government side) in mind, had recommended a range of only \$745-760 billion.

(4) While decisions under proposed clause 6(b) would thus clearly imply a certain general view of the government's economic role, they would not tie the hands of the Committees on Appropriations, let alone exert any refined degree of control over the elusive question of how much the Federal Government would in fact spend before the year was out. As already noted, the purpose of the pre-announced limits to consumer spending would be quite different: first, to separate the "big government" issue from the full-employment issue; second, to provide, by way of the maximum limit set, a brake against any inflationary upward spending spiral; and third, to make it possible to accept a reduction in our traditional export surplus--since our ability to maintain adequate total markets for domestic output would remain unaffected.

(5) Fundamental to proposed clauses (c) and (d) is that both provide for action that would be made contingent on the showing of the chosen indicators and mandatory in application when one or both of those indicators began to move outside the Congressionally predetermined range. In other words, as far as these compensatory adjustments are concerned (other sorts of economic legislation are dealt with just below), Congress would begin making the rules in advance and would have a more basic policy-making role.

(6) Under clause (c) Congress would be writing the specifications for a government commitment to serve as employer of last resort. Broadly speaking, that commitment would necessarily entail contingent accelerations and decelerations of public works and services. What would be up for decision would be such things as the exact content of that category for the purpose in hand (with reference, for example, to Federally financed State and local government projects and perhaps private non-profit projects); how to secure an adequate, ready reserve shelf of suitable projects; and the best formula for apportioning accelerations and decelerations by States.

(7) Under clause (d) Congress would have a wide range of options. It might, for example, decide that, when and if adjusting aggregate personal consumption expenditures should prove necessary, this would be done by temporarily

reducing or increasing personal income taxes--and (on the "up" side, at least) by taking some other fiscal action that would comparably benefit low-income groups not liable for income tax. Or, if welfare reform had led to adoption of a plan guaranteeing a minimum income to all families and single individuals as a matter of right, and of a negative income tax as the pay-out mechanism for this, then Congress might decide that the income tax itself (positive and negative) should be the vehicle for all the necessary adjustments. The allowances or negative taxes would in that case be raised, and the positive income taxes lowered, when necessary to increase consumer spending, and conversely the positive income taxes would be raised, and the allowances lowered (but never below their base level), when necessary to decrease it. On the other hand, Congressional economists might consider that variations in consumers' saving could still--even in the absence of booms and slumps--partly frustrate any effort to control their spending by merely controlling their disposable income. In that case Congress might decide on a more direct procedure.

(8) For example, Congress could enact a Federal sales tax/sales bonus which would be put on a standby basis to be used only for lowering or raising consumer spending to hold that aggregate within the stipulated limits. As a bonus, when spending was running too low, it would work like a (universal) stamp plan: all buyers of goods and services at retail would during pay-out periods receive stamps convertible (unlike food stamps) into cash at a bank or post-office if promptly presented. As a tax, it would automatically lower the amount of consumer expenditure received net of tax by business, that being then designated the amount required to be held below the established ceiling. Consumer spending could thus beyond any doubt be restrained to any desired extent, any "stubbornness" in spending or saving propensities (and any reluctance to regulate consumer credit) to the contrary withstanding; or alternatively, it could be given a very powerful incentive for expansion. (This fiscal device was first proposed in my communication "On Underwriting Consumption and Employment" published in The American Economic Review in September, 1955.)

(9) To see, finally, how this proposed unified action by Congress as a whole would mesh with the normal functioning of the Congressional committee system, let us suppose, for example, that the House Ways and Means Committee took up again the general subject of tax reform. While such tax changes as Congress ultimately adopted would no doubt alter the distribution of the tax burden and probably

also the level of tax revenue, neither the target-fixing under section 6(b) nor the choosing of a contingent compensatory formula under section 6(d) would be affected. What almost certainly would be affected is the actual (preadjustment) rate of consumer spending and its likelihood of falling within the acceptable range "of its own accord";--and hence also the likelihood that the President would actually have to apply the contingent adjustment measures provided for under 6(d).

(10) Incidentally, there would be some presumption that by a kind of feedback effect any unduly large or frequent need to take either type of compensatory action (to adjust consumer spending or to adjust employment) would lead to the sponsorship and passage of improved legislation relating to distribution of income, enforcement of competition and/or regulation of monopoly, or other factors strategically affecting the self-balancing capacity of the economy.

* * *

The above-described actions required to effectuate this proposal--first, the enactment of certain amendments to the Employment Act; second, the annual sequences of steps by the Council of Economic Advisers, the President, the Joint Economic Committee, and Congress as a whole--would of course need to be supported by operational actions. The proposed approach is broadly describable as Economic Performance Insurance, and the country in taking out that kind of insurance policy could expect to see an "automatic" response to the key signals. But it is important to realize that this "automaticity" could not eliminate the need for decisions at the operating level. On the contrary, judgment would be called for not only in the recurrent formulation of terms and procedures but also in the execution process.

The agencies to be designated by the President to operate under this law need not, it would seem, be specified in the Employment Act. The only two statistical indicators required to serve as primary action signals are currently prepared by the Departments of Labor and Commerce, as already noted. Perhaps the Labor Department would also be given broad responsibility over accelerations and decelerations of public works and services. Meanwhile the Internal Revenue Service would have a major part to play in administering the contingent adjustments in consumer spending or disposable income, but would work, presumably, in close collaboration with the Department of Health, Education, and Welfare and other agencies of the Executive Branch.

Timing would present the big challenge. Postponing

all action until the employment level or the rate of consumer spending was already too high or too low to be "acceptable" would breach the continuity of the system before correction could take hold. Then again, after any correction was made, the question would arise as to just how soon (at what point within the acceptable performance range) the use of the compensatory device should be terminated.

At present the seasonally adjusted monthly employment totals are published some three weeks after the statistical survey--in the early days of the next month; and preliminary quarterly personal consumption expenditures data, at seasonally adjusted annual rates, are published seven weeks or a little less after the end of each quarter. Those time intervals could perhaps be shortened somewhat; in any case, government experts with access to the data can certainly see trends emerging before the results are published. Nevertheless, there must also be considered the further time lag between ordering a compensatory measure instituted and having it put into effect. For example, an immediate acceleration of public works and services is hardly possible on a geographically widespread basis. In signing a $1 billion appropriation bill to create emergency public service jobs President Nixon said on August 9, 1971 that the first group of unemployed should be at the new jobs by Labor Day--nearly a month later. Of course, however, we neither have nor have had anything approaching either an adequate reserve shelf of public works and services or an adequate system of getting ready to use it; to remedy those deficiencies would be a major project to be undertaken concurrently with amending the Employment Act itself.

The best answer to problems of timing would thus probably combine at least the following three elements: (1) Congress might agree that employment and consumer spending could without prejudice be at "unacceptable" levels briefly--say, for a single reporting period. (2) Substantial effort and expense should be undertaken to build up an adequate reserve shelf on a nationwide basis, and also to give local organizations the capacity for swift action in carrying out Washington directives in regard both to "last resort" employment and to the fiscal means chosen for adjusting consumer spending. (3) The Federal agencies in charge should probably issue an "alert" before employment or consumer spending actually went beyond an upper or lower limit, if it seriously threatened to do so. Their staff economists would thus be expected to use a fairly wide range of data and forecasting procedures. Moreover some wrong guesses would inevitably occur, so that some expense would be incurred throughout the country in mobilizing forces to meet contingencies that failed to materialize. Reimbursing such expenses would simply be, then, one of the financial costs of maintaining a full-employment system.

* * *

A concluding word about inflation. If full employment were, as so often alleged, bound to generate inflation, amending the Employment Act to give it real teeth might have little point. But two recent developments have brought that gloomy thesis into the most serious question--first, the ample demonstration that inflation now tends to occur even without full employment, and second, the not unrelated shift of informed public opinion into favoring an incomes policy of some kind to help maintain price stability. Thus full employment need no longer carry such burdens as do not, properly speaking, belong to it.

More than that, however, it is here submitted that a program of guaranteed full employment along the lines suggested would not only not feed inflation but actually be the best cure for inflation. This is asserted for two reasons in combination. First, the ceilings on employment and on consumer spending that would be imposed under this approach would choke off upward demand spirals almost entirely. That is the built-in "mechanical" aspect. It would limit "demand pull" directly, as already emphasized, and indirectly it would also moderate the wage-demand side of the "cost push" by holding down the prices that make up the worker's cost of living. Second, there is the psychological point that cannot be proved but that should appeal to common sense--a point that would arise from the very fact of the government's readiness to commit itself in this unprecedented way. An agreement on the part of the government to assure a total market adequate for business prosperity, and to assure continuous full employment for labor, should be enough to persuade business and labor leaders to agree to abide by some reasonable set of price and wage guidelines.

Those who blame inflation on the incurable wickedness of Big Business or Big Labor or both often seem unaware of how far the behavior of both has been caused by the malfunctioning of our economy--its cyclical instability combined with secular weakness--the inevitability of which is precisely what needs to be denied. Once the government stood ready to assure continuously adequate total demand for products and for workers, (1) all businesses would have more chance to spread their overhead costs and hold prices down; (2) management in areas of administered pricing could logically give up planning for extra profits in boom times to cushion losses in future slumps; and (3) union leaders would feel less pressure to demand extreme hourly wage rates on the one hand, or annual pay guarantees on the other, to fortify their members against the return of unemployment.

To put this in context--as these words are being written, the country is deep in President Nixon's economic Phase II. Whether this experiment with a Wage Board and a Price Commission will be followed soon by selective permanent legal controls or by some other incomes policy is impossible to say. But what the government commitments proposed in this article would in any case contribute, when it comes to resolving the ultimate hard-core part of the "cost push" phenomenon, is to open the door as wide as possible to achieving essential results by voluntary cooperation.

PART I

ESSAYS, 1942-1946*

---

*This part reprints all of the essays originally published in the author's Full Employment and Free Enterprise (Washington, D. C.: Public Affairs Press, 1947).

1

THE NATIONAL INCOME INSURANCE IDEA*

National income insurance means a guarantee ahead of time by the Federal Government of the total number of dollars to be spent in consumer markets in any given year. The purpose of such a guarantee would be to bring about full production and full employment in private industry through the assurance to private industry that the final market as a whole would be of adequate size as specified. The amount guaranteed for any year would be based on the amount of consumer demand deemed to be sufficient to afford a normal rate of profit, on the average, on the total volume of goods to be marketed at the full employment level. An over-all guarantee such as this would, of course, not be designed to eliminate the risks of competition. However, the producer's risks would be held within more reasonable limits than they are at present. This consideration extends to the risks attaching to long-term investment in plant and equipment, which, since they spring from uncertainty about consumer demand in the more distant future, would be reduced by the establishment of national income insurance as a long-run, continuing policy.

The program would operate as follows: The amount spent by each person or family would still depend on the individual money incomes received in the usual ways—namely, on the wages, salaries, dividends, etc., of production, including public works, and on social security benefits, farm benefits, veterans' persions, annuities, and so forth. The only difference would be that there would also be an adjustment by the Government to make the total amount spent in consumer markets agree with the guaranteed total. That is, extra money income would be paid out when necessary to keep the total from falling below the guarantee, and some money income would be held out of action when that was necessary to keep the total from rising above the guarantee and thereby inviting price inflation. Thus whenever it was a question of avoiding a consumer expenditure shortage, the needed extra income would be distributed on some fair and reasonable basis approved in advance by Congress—say as "national income security payments" payable to all heads of families throughout the country. The post-

*A statement in the *Congressional Record,* February 4, 1942, included in the extension of remarks of Rep. Jerry Voorhis of California.

man could deliver these Treasury checks. The finance could reasonably be provided by taxes or loans from the stream of surplus savings, or—to the extent of expansion required by expanding production—by creation of Government credit under authority of Congress. Similarly Congress would specify in advance the tax or borrowing methods to be applied in the opposite case, to prevent the occurrence of an amount of consumer expenditure exceeding the guarantee. The size of the guaranteed total, to which the actual total would thus at all times be kept adjusted, would grow as the armament program tapered off, so that a rising private demand would automatically cushion much of the post-war shock.

This plan would not conflict with any other sound measures to promote employment, such as public programs for conservation, slum clearance, and other useful projects outside the area of private enterprise; encouragement to private initiative, invention, and investment; regulation of monopoly prices; joint management-labor planning to combat shortages in key industries; a tax program laying the burden more on the stream of large savings and less on mass consumption; the raising of substandard wage rates; protection of farmers' incomes; a suitable ceiling on hours of work; and a broad social welfare program, including expanded old-age pensions, adequate public-health provisions, Federal aid to education, and so on. On the contrary, national income insurance would supplement and reinforce all such measures. The special contribution of national income insurance would be the resulting certainty of a large and stable total demand at all times in the nation's final markets for goods and services. This should stimulate business enterprise to produce on a scale securing full employment without the same heavy reliance on public works that might otherwise be needed. Since the individual competitive enterprise would not be burdened with interference but rather would be assured an adequate market for which to compete, the nation's jobs would be more in ordinary enterprise and less on emergency public projects.

2

ELEMENTS OF AN ECONOMIC POLICY*

A plan for winning the peace would help to win the war, for it would foster morale. A nation's fighting power depends on its faith in the future.

Without much doubt the peace aim of most Americans, if it could be articulated, would be to establish guaranteed full employment in the United States, while at the same time strengthening democracy and promoting effective, nonwasteful use of man power and other resources. How can this aim be realized?

Consideration is asked for the following suggestions. The compressed form in which they are set down here is prompted not by dogmatism but rather by a desire to save the reader's time. (Economic analysis on which these suggestions are based was presented by the author in *Full Employment*, Yale University Press, 1941.) The reader in turn is asked, as he proceeds, to bear two things in mind. These proposals are intended as related parts of an over-all economic policy—for piecemeal adjustment here and there is not what the postwar situation will require. Secondly, the proposals assume that the people's elected representatives should lay down the guiding rules, and should change them from time to time to meet changing conditions, but then abstain from constantly usurping administrative functions.

* * *

It should be the policy of the United States Government to establish guaranteed full employment—a state of affairs in which all men and women willing and able to work will always have the opportunity to do so, at prevailing rates of pay and under prevailing hourly specifications and working conditions generally.

Stop there for a moment. What is full employment?

Full employment as referred to herein means employment of all except (a) unemployables and (b) a normal quota temporarily idle because of shifts in demand, technological progress, or any other forms of frictional (i.e., transitional) unemployment. Unemployability should be determined

*Published in the Summer, 1942, issue of *The Antioch Review*, under the title, "An Economic Policy to Insure Permanent Full Employment."

objectively, by medical test, in a manner subject to popular control. This is not to suggest that unemployables, so defined, should not have a perfect right to find work if they can, but rather merely to delimit one of the fields where special assistance is needed and to indicate when involuntary idleness should not affect the unemployment figures. The amount of unemployment designated as the normal quota of frictional unemployment (which may vary seasonally) should be decided democratically; expert opinion should be taken and the final decision should be reached in a manner giving an adequate voice to labor and to all other sections of the population.

These observations in turn point to the need for two further preliminary comments. In the first place, the definition of unemployability herein advocated may create a situation in which the work of some employables is not worth, in terms of value added to product, no matter where they may be employed, as much as minimum wage laws of the United States require that they be paid; in that case, the difference between what they are deemed to be worth when most effectively employed and the minimum legal rates should be a charge on the general economy, to be met out of taxation. In the second place, to assure that prevailing rates of pay, hours, and working conditions shall be decided democratically, collective bargaining and the right to strike should be fully supported by the government.

So much by way of defining full employment. But there are other main objectives as well. The measures taken to support full employment should be such as require the least sacrifice of other desired ends. Not only must democracy be preserved and strengthened, but in addition full employment should not conflict with effective use of resources.

To secure a truly effective use of manpower and other resources, as judged by the success with which these factors are applied to satisfying the wants and needs of the people, planned public enterprise (i.e., production of a socially planned quota of the specified goods and services, whether for sale or for free distribution) is required in some cases. In other cases production is best left to private enterprise producing to order or to meet an anticipated market demand. In still other instances a compromise solution may be most serviceable; for example, joint councils representing management and labor in a given industry may practice some aspects of production planning with approval and collaboration of government, government representatives may sit on boards of directors, and so forth.

In order to promote private enterprise and limit government intervention in economic matters to the necessary minimum, it should in general be the policy of the government to secure full employment by the method of *underwriting the aggregate amount of consumer expenditure and pre-*

venting monopoly price exactions (as hereinafter noted), thus encouraging private employment.

In each specific case where socially planned and organized production may be urged as a substitute for private enterprise, the burden of proof should be on the proponents of public planned production to demonstrate that that procedure would be superior to free or regulated private enterprise.

However, where competition cannot function and regulation of private monopoly or of associated private producers has proved to be unsatisfactory, other methods are obviously required. Wherever the superiority of public planned production—measured against existing practice and against what might be brought about by constructive technical innovations—appears at any time to be established beyond a reasonable doubt, public planned production should be instituted.

In addition, as a second and final line of defense against unemployment (the first line being the guarantee applied to total consumer demand, together with control of monopolies), a planned program of federal, state, and local emergency public projects should be maintained as a regular part of the nation's economic apparatus, and employment thereon should be expanded and contracted as may be required to keep the total number of jobs adjusted to the labor supply.

Insofar as private construction continues to be peculiarly subject to fluctuation in spite of stability in the market for ordinary consumer goods, construction projects (i.e., durable public works) will tend to preponderate in this emergency program. Conservation offers another great field for expansible public employment. However, a sufficiently wide range of projects of all types should be planned in advance so that a selection can always be made that will fit the kinds or skills of labor currently available, whatever they may be and wherever located.

Compensation to labor on emergency public projects should be at rates prevailing in private and nonemergency public work.

Come back now to private enterprise. Contrary to the view formerly held by most economists, prices are not flexible enough to keep the volume of production and employment in the field of private enterprise from contracting when anything happens to check the circulation of money around the production-consumption circuit. Moreover the circulation of money does not maintain itself automatically. It is therefore fundamental to a full-employment program that government take steps to maintain the monetary circulation.

It should be the purpose of the government, by guaranteeing or underwriting total consumer expenditure (thus so to speak organizing a system of national income insurance, to operate as hereinafter indicated), not only actually to maintain an adequate flow of purchasing power, but, by assuring this flow of purchasing power in advance, to let the prospective demand exert its full stimulating force upon all enterprises producing goods or services for market. This suggestion is meant literally: the government should give an unconditional guarantee of aggregate consumer expenditure.

Insofar as the inducement thus offered to private enterprises stimulates economic activity, it will also swell the flow of consumer income and spending by way of the normal channels of income. It is to be expected that a governmental guarantee of total consumer spending will have some *tendency* to secure full employment without the need for emergency public employment, and that regular and emergency employment together will have some *tendency* to fulfill the consumer spending guarantee without the need for special subsidies to consumption by the government. But the consumer spending guarantee given by the government must in any case be accurately fulfilled, whether this requires additions to consumer purchasing power from the Treasury, or whether it requires subtractions from consumer purchasing power to prevent overfulfillment of the guarantee, with consequent possibility of price inflation.

How large a volume of consumer spending shall be stipulated for any given year or other period of time should be determined by experts after due consideration of the factors relevant to the problem, such as prevailing money wage rates, price-level policy (taken in relation to total productivity), the expected extent of the additional market provided by government orders, foreign investment, and consumer credit.

The spending guarantee should within limits of feasibility be presented for a number of years in advance. The purpose of this is to establish a confidently expected trend in total consumer demand, which not only will remove some of the general over-all risk from current investment activity (capital formation), but also, by making price trends more predictable, will lessen the fluctuations in investment activity that arise out of speculative anticipations of price changes.

To bring consumer spending up to the stipulated level when it tends to fall short, orderly and just means must be provided for putting additional purchasing power into the hands of consumers. Congress should therefore determine in advance how the additional income money is to be distributed if and when such distribution proves necessary—whether through established channels of the social insurance system in the form of extra benefits, or by payments to all family units and individuals in the nation, or in some other manner. In deciding upon the formula for distribution of additional income money, so far as that is required, Congress should take into account the desirability of reducing existing income inequalities.

The point need scarcely be labored, today, that it is as essential to prevent an excess of consumer spending as to prevent a deficiency. Monetary measures undertaken without full recognition of this fact carry with them the grave danger of inflation. Congress should therefore legislate in advance the form of taxation or other means whereby consumer spending is to be brought down to the stipulated level in case it tends to exceed that level.

The sources of funds for subsidies to consumption, when needed, are in general the same as the sources of funds for public works or for any other purpose of government. Governments may levy taxes, or borrow, or issue their own noninterest-bearing notes.

In accordance with its objective of a full volume of production and employment, the government should levy any taxes designed to pay for subsidies to consumption or for public works in such a manner that they do not burden production or reduce mass purchasing power, but fall rather on large wealth and large incomes, on inheritances, or on the idle bank balances of individuals and corporations.

The government should also borrow such idle balances as it may require for these purposes, compulsorily if necessary; for clearly it is antisocial to hoard money, refusing either to spend or invest it, and correction of this abuse in no way voids the rights of private *enterprise*, properly construed.

Generally speaking, it is better in maintaining the monetary circulation to tap existing idle pools of money than to create additional money to substitute for what is lying idle. However, if for any reason the program of taxing or borrowing existing money proves inadequate to accomplish the named objectives, the government should be free to issue its own noninterest-bearing notes.

Monetary and fiscal questions are intimately connected with the rate of interest. The government through its central monetary and banking authorities should control the net rates of interest paid on money borrowed at long and short term.

A low basic rate should at first be established, in order to encourage housing and the further development of the nation's physical plant generally, and in order to keep down the cost of any government borrowing incidental to fulfillment of the full-employment policy. Moreover, the future trend of the rate of interest should so far as feasible be determined and announced in advance, both to minimize uncertainties and wastes connected with the construction of houses and other durable equipment and to prevent fluctuations in hoarding such as arise from speculation regarding the future course of the rate of interest.

Ultimately the decision as to what constitutes an adequate rate of return on loaned money should belong with the people; first, because it has an obvious bearing on income distribution, second, because it plays an important part in determining how large a proportion of current economic activity is to be devoted to social saving, or in other words to the production of capital goods rather than goods for immediate consumption. Hence steps should be taken to make the rate of interest a political issue as soon as intelligent debate on the subject is possible, and to settle this issue in a democratic manner.

This in a sense is a digression. The next point, however, is absolutely central.

The government should take the monopoly problem in hand—construing that term broadly so as to include not merely cases in which there is a single seller but also related situations (duopoly, oligopoly, etc.). The concept of control over the volume of production activity exercised by way of control over the volume of consumer spending presupposes the kind of response to buyers' demand associated with (a) competitive producers, or (b) monopolies that, as the result of regulation or for some other reason, act not to maximize their profits but rather to approximate or at least parallel the results given by competition.

Conceivably the beneficial effect of a guarantee of an amount of consumer spending sufficient to assure a normal competitive profit throughout industry as a whole, with industry operating at levels yielding full employment, might be entirely destroyed by the price-raising and output restricting policies of monopolies. Dominating the production and distribution of the necessaries of life, they might levy an increasingly large toll of profit for themselves, without permitting either themselves or others to give the normal competitive response (expansion of production and employment) in the exceptionally profitable lines in question. Meanwhile not enough market demand would be left over for the products of competitive producers in other lines (who incidentally would also have to pay exorbitant prices for any products bought from the monopolies) to justify expansion on their part. Hence total employment would fall short of what could be expected to result from the same total consumer demand in a system of universal competition. These unfavorable tendencies are very much in evidence today, being greatly strengthened by technological progress where patent control is used to increase the dominance of corporations already powerful in their field, and by financial tie-ups, and so on.

In addition to restricting output directly, monopolies by their excessive profits accentuate income inequality, which is undesirable in itself and furthermore tends to depress total consumer spending and increase the volume of hoarded money. Also monopolies can be a grave threat to political democracy.

From all of these considerations it follows that private monopolies must be subject to adequate restraint or regulation to safeguard the general welfare, and consequently it should be the business of the government to see that adequate restraints and regulations are imposed. These may take the form of publicity, price regulation, vigorous action under the antitrust laws, encouragement of cooperatives to enter into competition with monopolies, measures to give small companies access to the loan markets on terms more nearly equal to those enjoyed by the big corporations, public yardstick plants, revision of the patent laws, obligatory output rules based on criteria other than maximum profit—or such other forms as may be held advisable. While so-called monopolistic competition is not necessarily undesirable, and indeed may often be the only kind of competition possible, and while even private monopoly as such is not to be condemned automatically, the crux of the matter is that the restrictive practices of profit-seeking private monopoly cannot be tolerated. The government should therefore prevent these restrictive practices; or, if that is not feasible, then federal, state, or local government should own and operate the economic facilities in question.

Turn finally to the problems of our economic relations with the rest of the world.

Foreign trade and investment must be viewed from the standpoint of the general interest. From that standpoint it is seen that they are desirable insofar as they serve to promote an *effective use of resources* by securing a balance of trade based on regional (international) specialization in accordance with comparative efficiencies, but undesirable where they are used in an attempt to expand the *volume* of domestic production by securing foreign markets not offset by home markets opened to foreign producers, or to exploit foreign labor or foreign natural resources or achieve political domination abroad. The effort to avoid or eliminate domestic unemployment by finding convenient foreign outlets for goods, money, or population leads down the road of economic imperialism to war. In view of the injustice and suffering ultimately involved, it can now be supported only by those who do not understand that a nation like the United States can establish permanent full employment without resorting to external economic expansion or aggression.

What is needed is not an isolationist approach. On the contrary.

While sources for many previously imported strategic materials can be developed at home, the superior foreign sources should still be kept open if it does not take war to keep them open. Existing export trade should be an object of consideration, so as to avoid, where it can be avoided, the dislocation of the particular industries and kinds of farming that rely upon it. When requests are received for funds for development of backward areas, loans should if possible be granted, provided repayment seems assured and the terms are generous and fair, i.e., not such as may drain the wealth, restrict the economic independence or infringe the political sovereignty of the borrowing countries. Every effort should be made to get rid of tariffs and other trade restrictions (on a bilateral or multilateral basis so far as that can be arranged) and thus to move toward a condition of free trade, qualified as required by defense and by considerations of long-run evolution; for in that kind of free-trade world, producing a surplus of those things at which we are most efficient to exchange abroad for those things at which we are least efficient, we can have a higher national standard of living than if we are obliged to be our own jack-of-all-trades. Indeed it is obvious that the more international cooperation in all spheres of peaceful action, the better.

What is essential, however, as the foundation for any kind of sound foreign policy, is recognition that the problem of *quantity* of production and employment—the problem of securing prosperity in the sense of full employment—must be solved by *domestic* economic measures. Only on this foundation can be built a structure of durable peace in which the good will that Americans feel toward other peoples can find adequate practical expression.

While taking steps to avoid needless exchange fluctuations, which discourage trade, and while renouncing the use of currency devaluation as a weapon of economic aggression, the government should vary the exchange value of its currency if and when that proves necessary to correct a deeply rooted tendency for the foreign demand for dollars to fall short of or exceed the domestic demand for foreign currencies at the existing valuation.

If necessary the government should also place limitations on speculative short-term capital movements, and on any other international economic activities, including long-term investment, that may be found to be sacrificing the general welfare to the private advantage of the few.

3

OUR WARTIME GOALS*

This war is not merely a struggle to keep alive. It is also, on our side, a struggle for the right to live—defined as the right of every man and woman to have a real life.

The first elementary requirement, if men and women are to have this right, is that they must be able to participate in the activities of their community by having jobs and thereby earning money with which to support themselves and their families. This fundamental principle of opportunity should apply throughout the world, but in any case we should make absolutely sure that it applies here in America—and that it does not depend on export surpluses. For, if we are honest with ourselves, we must admit that America is likely to be more of a hindrance than a help to the rest of the world if we are unable to avoid an economic and social breakdown here at home.

In laying out the lines on which we want to move to assure jobs at decent rates of pay for all who are willing and able to work, it is important to keep certain landmarks in sight.

There undoubtedly is a large measure of agreement that we want to have our full employment with as little direct government intervention as possible and with as much opportunity for individual competition and initiative as the technical facts of our machine age will allow.

To keep the economic system running at the full-employment level, with as little direct government interference with production as possible, it is necessary that the country be able to count on the continued existence of an ample overall market for the maximum output of goods and services our farms and factories can produce in a reasonable working week and working year. A deflationary gap is just as disastrous as an inflationary gap can be.

Secondly, besides taking steps to give the assurance that the overall final market will be maintained, government must see to it that private monopolies are prevented from destroying the beneficial effects of that consumer

---

*A statement which appeared in the January, 1943, issue of *Life and Labor Bulletin*, published by the National Women's Trade Union League, under the title "The Goals for Which We Fight."

demand by means of restrictive policies that result in needlessly high prices and low levels of production and employment.

Thirdly, to the extent that fiscal measures for keeping up effective demand, and monopoly control measures for assuring low-price and large-volume business policies, do not result in jobs for all those willing and able to work, government must take the responsibility for giving jobs to the remainder at prevailing rates of pay on public work projects.

If we take the full employment objective seriously, as we must, and if at the same time we want to maintain our system of free competitive enterprise, these three conditions must form the foundation underlying anything else we may do.

Of course no one of us believes that full employment plus full opportunity for enterprise is a sufficient goal in itself. A fair deal for every citizen includes a progressive system of taxes (rather than one bearing down heavily on mass consumption) and it includes a wise strengthening of our social insurance system to meet the needs of the aged, the sick, and persons handicapped in various ways. More broadly, every man, woman and child in America has the same fundamental need for food, clothing, shelter and living space, health, opportunity for education.

Food and clothing tend to take care of themselves provided a family has an adequate monetary income to spend. Once we assure full employment at decent rates of pay and make satisfactory provision by way of the social insurance system for the old and for other groups requiring special consideration, the consumer demand for food and clothing will itself bring forth a quantitatively adequate supply by way of the response of private enterprise to that demand.

Experience does not indicate the same for low-cost housing. Perhaps the solution in this field lies in government subsidization of private construction; if not, then the log jam must be broken some other way, and one obvious way is to have slum clearance and housing construction undertaken on a large scale by public authorities.

Similarly with education and health. Where subsidizing the student and the person who requires medical care will itself set in rapid motion the development of adequate educational and medical services, the answer to the problem can be stated in terms of public funds rather than public provision of the services in question. Where this approach reaches its limits, however, either government must organize the services directly, or the promise of a fair deal for every citizen must be admitted to be not intended seriously.

Finally, the resources of the land we live in are a public trust. We cannot any longer permit the soil of this continent to wash into the ocean. We must preserve and develop our forests for other generations. Much of this work of conservation and development of our natural resources can only be done by government. The problem here is to agree on the nature and extent of an adequate long-range program, to be got under way as soon as the war ends.

All of these questions need the best thought that trade unionists and other Americans can give them, and answers must be found before it is too late to apply them.

4

WHAT CHANCE FOR FREE ENTERPRISE?*

It is unthinkable that after this war a situation will again be allowed to exist in America in which men and women will be unable to finds jobs. But is there in fact any possibility that we can prevent the return of unemployment without, in the process, digging the grave of free enterprise? This question may seem indecent to economic prudes, and funny to planners committed to rigid interpretations of planning. On the other hand, all over the country, and in the armed forces, wherever located, there are people who really would like to know the answer.

The answer offered here is in the affirmative. Full employment need not preclude free, competitive enterprise. But that is not to say that free, competitive enterprise will be saved by giving pep talks or invoking "the American way." It won't. Nor will it be saved by merely reapplying, more vigorously than before, the economics of the 1930's. Many economists seem to feel that the political problems involved in securing a full-employment economy after the war present a large question mark, but that the economic problems have all been solved. Surely the latter part of this proposition is not well founded in fact. At least if encouragement to economic individualism is supposed to be part of the picture, the last word has not yet been said.

The question at issue, so far as domestic public policy is concerned, is the proper relation between public investment in the broadest sense, control over aggregate individual purchasing power—or, better, aggregate consumer spending—and antitrust action. The trouble with the usual public investment approach is that it does not show how all the needed jobs can be assured without creation of an environment hostile to traditional forms of enterprise, and does not accurately control purchasing power. Also, on the theoretical side, it needlessly assumes that, when total investment and total saving are out of line, investment is the one that must change. The trouble with much of the consumer-demand theory is that it overlooks or minimizes the power of unregulated monopolies to prevent production and employment from expanding in step with expanding de-

*An article published in the April, 1943, issue of *Free World*, under the title, "What Chance for Free Enterprise After the War?"

mand for commodities and services. The trouble with almost all current formulations is that they pay too little attention to the possibility of applying the underwriting principle in economic affairs on a broad national basis. Or else, if they advocate this principle, they limit economic flexibility by underwriting individual markets one by one rather than the national market as a whole.

If these contentions are correct, then it is still worth while to spend some time on the fundamental or strategic factors in economics. Work must be done on the details of their application in the post-war world, and some of this work as it relates to the ideas contained in the following pages is now going on in Washington. But the present discussion only deals with general alignments among the fundamental elements.

* * *

No one will deny that before the war we had already moved far away from nineteenth-century approximation of laissez faire. It would be somewhat academic to try to measure the further distance we have traveled down that road since Pearl Harbor. As a result of priorities, allocation of men and materials, price controls, and so forth, many small businesses are going to the wall, monopoly threatens to increase, or actually does increase, and the rates of operation of our going production enterprises are being more and more regulated by government. This last is an evident necessity, but it narrows the scope of free enterprise, at least for the duration.

Now the advocates of planned production take the position that, even for peace, the competitive system has reached the end of its usefulness and must tbe superseded. For the sake of the argument, let us make some concessions to that point of view. At some future date it is conceivable that competition, as we have known it, may practically disappear. This is debatable. And in any case, even if it were not, the date could hardly be predicted. However, the advance of modern technology has tended to concentrate production in larger units, and these have very often acquired the characteristics of monopoly or partial monopoly and created a need for regulation in the public interest. The advantage of size — at least, in many cases—is greater efficiency. The penalty is the disappearance of competition as the laissez-faire economists conceived it. It is not a foregone conclusion that technology need always favor bigness, any more than that technology is always the explanation where bigness exists. Moreover, certain services and also certain commodities can never be produced on a large scale. Nevertheless, the possibility arises that at some future date mass-production methods will have driven individualistic competition from practically every corner of our economy. In that case, public regulation of production is likely to become so general that it clears the way for systematic, over-all production planning.

The only reason for tentatively sketching this distant perspective is that it helps by contrast to define the post-war foreground. If we finally do come to over-all production planning—in a country with so deeply ingrained traditions of individual enterprise and competition—the explanation will most likely be technological. This can be ventured because public opinion hardly ever runs ahead of the facts; a lag is more to be expected. On the other hand, the explanation for the current trend toward administrative controls is altogether different. Obviously the war is responsible, not technological change. If this is so, then it reinforces the usual presumption (and the findings of certain public opinion polls) that most or, at any rate, very many Americans will want to go back to a free, competitive economy when the war is over. Barring the possibility of an extremely long war, or an outcome destructive of all the conditions that permit choices to be made, economic individualism will again make a powerful appeal.

How much economic individualism can post-war America stand?

No quantitative guess will be ventured here. Presumably the maximum possibility is somewhat smaller than the maximum possibility was before the war, because of technogical progress in the meantime. But the real issue is whether any approximation of the maximum possibility can be made actual, and if so how. The indispensable condition for stability, democracy, and freedom after the war is sustained full employment. Is there any ground for supposing that we can have full employment in post-war America without accepting a far larger measure of governmental administrative control over our production system than is required by strictly technological considerations?

In certain quarters the tendency is to give up on this question without a struggle. A case in point is supplied in a newsletter put out by a leading firm of management engineers. The authors correctly diagnose our central post-war problem: "Our fundamental problem is how to create an industrial system that will insure a continuous production and exchange of goods and services that people need, so that all who want to work may have the opportunity to do so and the money with which they can buy all the things produced by other workers." But they then propose as a solution a system of planned production, with details unspecified but with the following general characteristics. "Its keystones would be: planning and budgeting industry operation, coordinating it nationally, creating and maintaining cooperation between individual companies and between labor, management, and stockholders, and having necessary governmental support." In other words, what they are suggesting is a further departure from individualistic methods of determining individual business rates of operation. This is probably also the view of many other Americans who are pessimistic about the possibility of getting full employment any other way. The view in question assumes that we cannot hope to secure coordinated control of the over-all volume of production and employment unless we establish some form of coordinated control of individual production quotas.

Without minimizing the difficulty of the problem or saying that competition can revive where the basic conditions for it have gone and cannot be restored, it may be pointed out that we have never had a program capable of combining assured full employment with a technologically given maximum of free competition. The two fundamentals of such a program would be a monetary-fiscal policy able to keep up the effective demand for commodities and services, and a monopoly and competition policy oriented to technological realities.

Both are essential. Neither one is sufficient without the other. Were we to try to sustain full employment through monetary-fiscal instruments alone, the attempt would fail. In a regime of pure competition we could probably control the over-all volume of production and employment rather accurately by controlling the size of the total demand for products, first taking into account any expected changes in costs. But, obviously, this could not be the case if monopolies were able to neutralize an increase in demand by raising their selling prices. On the other side, were we to put our trust entirely in a system of governmental regulation of individual rates of operation, and were we willing to push such a system of administrative controls to its logical conclusion, we could secure full employment, but only by sacrificing free production for market.

* * *

A monopoly and competition policy oriented to technological realities would have the following characteristics.

It would make proper distinctions between areas in which monopolistic situations are "natural" (inevitable for technical reasons) and areas in which monopolistic situations are "artificial" (based on unnecessary unfair restraints of trade).

Then, it would deal adequately with both types of situation. It would support and enforce competition in lines of production where competition has a real chance. For instance, it would help little business to borrow money on fair terms, make the patent system encourage innovation rather than buttress intrenched positions, and vigorously suppress restrictive and collusive practices in general. And at the same time, it would regulate the inevitably monopolistic lines of production as far as regulation was necessary. That does not mean that perfect efficiency in terms of low-cost production would result or be considered attainable or important. Rather it means that the new public utility rules (as they might be called) would be designed to prevent such raising of prices and limitation of output as might defeat the full-employment objective or interfere seriously with a balanced use of the nation's resources.

All this presupposes that it is or might be possible to distinguish areas that are inevitably monopolistic from areas of workable competition. Presumably that can be done with a reasonable degree of success if the available data are assembled and studied, in the light of modern economic theory, with the objective clearly in view. The sources for data include, for example, the case studies made by the Antitrust Division and Federal Trade Commission and the findings of the T.N.E.C. Monopoly Investigation. Out of such materials a practical set of criteria can probably be constructed for identifying workable competition on the one hand and monopoly (monopoly in the public sense rather than the narrow or pure sense) on the other. Our knowledge of the contents of these two major subdivisions of the American economy will then amount to more than a mere enumeration as of a particular date. Our knowledge will include, in addition, an understanding of the main distinguishing characteristics, with the obvious advantage that this will facilitate reclassification whenever reclassification becomes necessary.

A given industry may for a while possess the characteristics of competition and be subject to the rules of the game applying to competition, but later on, as a result of technological progress, that industry may have to come under the different rules applying to monopoly. The criteria will help show when this transition is required. Thus they will facilitate an orderly progression of our economy, based on technological realities. A slight variation of this procedure also might be worth considering. There will doubtless be borderline cases in which the technological picture is not clear. In these cases it might be best to leave the choice between operating under rules of competition and under rules of monopoly to the industry itself. Even in certain intrinsically less puzzling cases the choice might be left to the industry.

For example, an industry might be asked to choose between restricting the activities of its trade association to the point where exemption from scale-of-operations regulations could legitimately be granted and, on the other hand, permitting its trade association to suppress competition and in that case subjecting itself to the regulations in question. Any resulting losses from the standpoint of not securing the technologically possible maximum of free competition might be more than compensated by the gains from the standpoint of retaining more free choice. This could, however, be true only where a choice thus registered represented a fair consensus of the business men affected, and not a vote dictated by a powerful minority in the industry. And of course, it also presupposes, to begin with, a set of monopoly regulations capable of accomplishing what it is necessary to have them accomplish.

* * *

It is now time to turn to the other essential element, a monetary-fiscal policy able to keep up the effective demand for commodities and services. For only through such a monetary-fiscal policy can government give competitive enterprise its maximum support.

The dominant school of thought on this subject is preoccupied with the problem of investment—ordinarily interpreted to mean production of capital goods, including consumers' capital goods such as houses. Much has been said in recent years about the need to make up for deficiencies in private investment by expansion of public investment—which, again, may in part take the form of facilities to provide free services direct to the consuming public. In some quarters it is estimated that we must be prepared to have a public investment program after the war ranging in cost anywhere from zero up to twenty billion dollars a year, or else give up the idea of full employment.

On the whole, this is not, in the opinion of leading spokesmen of the investment school today, a matter of "priming the pump" to get things started. It is a matter of filling up gaps as they occur. Naturally the gaps do not always have to be connected with *investment* activity, or filled with public *investment.* While that is ordinarily supposed to be the case, other possibilities are alto taken into account. More broadly, what is advocated is the filling of any gaps in private *employment* by means of expansion in public *employment.* More broadly still, what is suggested is that government assume *responsibility* for specific employment-giving production activities to the extent that private initiative falls short. It is of course true that public construction expenditures frequently represent payments for work supplied by private concerns on a contract basis, in which case government is not the actual employer. But in any case the essential idea is that government closes up the gaps.

The arguments advanced for this type of policy have rendered two great services. In the first place, they have stressed the fact that governmentally initiated production activity must be used as the final balancing item to maintain full employment. It is hard to see how anyone who supports the objective of full employment can quarrel with that. It is clear that the indicated principle must apply during the stresses and shifts of the immediate demobilization period. Moreover, it must apply at other times as well. For example, some fluctuation would be bound to occur in the level of private employment even if the final markets for the products of private enterprise were stabilized. Because of changes in the rate of introduction of new inventions, fluctuations in the rate of replacement of fixed equipment, and certain other factors, the capital goods industries in particular would tend to be busier at some times than at others even if the sale of consumer commodities and services were proceeding at an uninterrupted and steady pace. The further merit of the gap-filling approach to monetary-fiscal problems in that its advocates, looking around for large chunks of activity with which to fill large gaps, find themselves supporting (more strongly than ever) an extension of public enterprise or responsibility into certain fields in which it is indeed overdue.

There are fields into which government has not yet gone and should in future go, or into which it should go to a greater extent than it has hitherto, simply because certain badly wanted services will otherwise not be supplied. This ought not to startle anybody.

Roads and education, to mention two important historical examples, were once considered to belong in the province of private enterprise. Times change. Looking ahead to the kind of peace we want, it hardly seems open to question that government should lay out very substantial amounts to help clear our slums and bring decent housing to the people, provide some approximation of adequate medical care for everyone, move ahead toward universal educational opportunity, and conserve and develop the natural resources of the land we live in. Moreover, mention of these particularly obvious fields for public activity as well as expenditure is not intended to deny the existence of others, if the need can be fairly shown.

But precisely here is the weakness of the gap-filling approach, which tends to blur the line between need for products and need to create jobs. Normal or non-emergency public activities should in most cases go forward unconditionally. It is not a question of looking to see if there are employment gaps that require filling. It is enough that the end products of these particular public activities are considered by most people to be desirable for their own sake. On the other hand, emergency public works or work projects stand on a different footing. Of course, such work as serves no useful purpose should be barred in any event, and the authorized projects should be carefully selected so that the end products are as valuable as possible. But that does not alter the fact that in these cases employment provides the real justification, not our need for the end products.

Unfortunately, the gap-filling approach, pure and simple, invites confusion of this distinction. Its adherents are tempted to overplay the intrinsic usefulness (usefulness of the end products) of this or that public activity which can, to be sure, fill gaps, but would perhaps not gain general acceptance on that basis. Their argument rings slightly hollow. Under analysis it is found to imply the existence, year after year, of a tremendously broad zone of indifference, a zone millions of jobs and billions of dollars broad, with regard to which it is supposed to be practically impossible to say whether public activity is preferable to private enterprise or vice versa. This may conceivably be so, but, considering the magnitudes involved, it taxes the average man's credulity. Thus in one way it may even hurt a cause for which in other respects the same persons have fought with skill as well as devotion—the cause of the public services that are genuinely needed.

The difficulty arises because the gap-filling school has not devoted enough attention to keeping the gap from opening up in the first place or has not found the right means for the purpose. Many adherents of this school wish to encourage private initiative and make various suggestions as to how it should be done. However, their main concern is to show that gap-filling public investment is itself an encouraging rather than a discouraging factor. To this end they point out that the investment is to be limited to creating products not sold in competition with the products of private enterprise. With varying degrees of emphasis, depending on the extent to which they retain a faith in the pump-priming theory, they add that such public activities stimulate private enterprise indirectly as a result of their demand for raw materials and equipment. Finally, they lay particular stress on the so-called multiplier effect—the consideration that investment (in this case public investment) puts out purchasing power by way of its payrolls, which in turn helps enterprise as a whole find markets for its products.

Much of this, so far as it goes, is perfectly sound. If the pump-priming results anticipated by the more optimistic members of the school could be counted on, it would even mean that public investment could be permitted to taper off after a while because private enterprise would expand as a result of the stimulus received from the original increase in public investment. But that possibility—no stronger word is justified by the record—does not meet the ultimate objection. For it would still be true that, *during* all fill-in periods, the free competitive sector is narrower than it would be if the economic environment supported competitive individual enterprise up to the technologically given maximum. This is the issue that is never met by any program of filling gaps.

Clearly the country needs a policy of positive support for competitive enterprise as a whole, and lip service to that idea is not enough. Furthermore, the policy should be of a fundamental and practical nature. Most of the measures suggested, whether by the public investment school or by the opponents of government intervention, are either good but in themselves inadequate (for example, removal of taxes that deter enterprise) or else of highly doubtful effectiveness and in any case socially undesirable (for example, wage cuts).

By contrast, a fundamental and practical policy would include, with other encouraging measures, a direct and unequivocal support of aggregate consumer demand. It would peg this demand at levels sufficient to provide a market for the output of commodities and services private enterprise can bring to market when it is operating on a scale that leaves no employment gap to be filled. Consumer demand would not in the last analysis be supported indirectly by way of the purchasing power put out by a gap-filling public investment program; the objection to that has just been noted. Rather it would be supported and controlled directly, by having government give and stand back of a guarantee of aggregate consumer spending.

To begin with, government would estimate, on the basis of wage rates and other factors, the amount of consumer spending needed to take next year's full employment output off the market, and would peg the size of the consumer market as a whole by underwriting the total estimated in that way. This would amount to opening up the draft to keep the fires of enterprise burning. Without favoring one enterprise more than another, it would create the environment in which business initiative as a whole would have the opportunity to show what it can do. To describe this still differently, it would provide a full-size framework for private enterprise.

A radio manufacturer, for instance, would not have his own market underwritten, but, since he would know for certain that consumer demand as a whole would not shrink, he would benefit in proportion to his competitive ability to attract customers. An industry like the steel industry, in turn, while it would necessarily still face the competition of aluminum and magnesium, could count on a steadier flow of orders than is possible as long as nothing secures the aggregate sales of consumer goods embodying or produced with the help of steel, aluminum, magnesium, and all other materials.

Whenever full employment was not achieved as a result of the inducement given by this guarantee, government would expand its flexible program of public work projects. Thus it would indeed fill any remaining gaps—but with the distinction that the gap-filling program would here be the final line of defense against unemployment, not the front line. Finally, government would see to it that, by adjustment of the full-employment volume of payments to income thus brought about, a total of consumer spending emerged that was neither in excess of nor less than the amount guaranteed. This it would do by subsidizing or taxing (or lending to or borrowing from) consumption directly, if and as necessary.

Such a policy would not correspond to the view that total saving must always govern total investment. Those who insist on the need for public investment hold that total investment can be allowed to decline when we achieve a more equal distribution of income, since that will weaken the tendency to save, which is of course strongest in the upper income brackets. In the meantime, however, they submit that we have no reasonable choice but to make investment outlays equal to the total of the voluntary savings accumulating at a full-employment level of income. But it is hard to see why that must necessarily be so. We might equally well cut down total saving, inasmuch as that can be done without interfering with the individual's right to save. Suppose, for example, that a tendency toward oversaving required government to subsidize individual consumption, under the consumption-pegging policy, in spite of the existence of full employment and a full-employment volume of money income. In that case, the funds for the subsidies could in whole or in part be borrowed by "tap issues" directed as the savers who had found no investment outlets for their surplus incomes.

So far as expense is concerned, such a program would *raise* the costs of government to the extent that an oversaving problem as such made consumption subsidies necessary for fulfillment of the guarantee. On the other hand, it would *lower* the costs of government, as against what a full-employment program by the straight gap-filling method would involve, to the extent that the incentive provided by the guarantee cut down the size of the employment gaps to be filled. The *net* effect upon costs might well be favorable, provided the program were linked up with advances on other critical fronts in our economy. The monopoly and competition policy already suggested would help translate the inducement of the guarantee into actual private production and employment, and would thus limit the expenditure for public works. A progressive system of taxes and a wise strengthening of our social insurance system to meet the needs of the aged, the sick, and persons handicapped in various ways—the common man's charter to which, as also to adequate labor standards, America already stands morally committed—would favor the spending of individual income and therefore minimize the oversaving tendency.

If the above analysis is correct, then what is needed next on the monetary-fiscal side is a working out in detail of the problems of mechanics involved in the direct adjustment of total consumer spending to guaranteed levels. There are two halves to this. A satisfactory way must be found to support consumer spending when, full employment notwithstanding, it tends to fall short. To date there has not been enough discussion of the problem to indicate the relative merits of tax reductions, tax rebates, special "national income security payments," and other techniques (including timed bond redemptions in the early post-war years) that might be used for this purpose. Further exploration should likewise suggest the most acceptable way of keeping consumer spending from exceeding the guarantee. Whenever that tendency is uppermost rather than the other, the suggested policy requires that the excessive demand be removed from consumer markets. That will avoid a price inflation danger such as we face today.

It will be seen that a monetary-fiscal policy along the indicated lines rests on the following argument. In general, the volume of public investment, including public services to the consumer, should be decided by judging the end products of the various government enterprises on their merits. To be sure, some public investment is needed for another reason—as a final balancing item to offset temporary declines in private investment. Ordinarily a rather small amount should be sufficient under the latter heading, although at times when an abnormally rapid physical transformation of the economy is under way, as will be the case in the demobilization period after the war, the amount may be fairly large.

The volume of private investment over a period of years should be allowed to work itself out as a result of the progress of invention, the rate of interest established, and the demand "derived back" from the demand for consumer commodities and services. Aggregate savings should be cut down to the level of aggregate investment as thus determined by its private and public components. The rest of our potential production energy, up to the level of full employment, should be thrown into producing commodities and services to be bought by individual consumers in the proportions they think best. To make this possible, government should underwrite aggregate consumer spending at appropriate levels, which can be done right away without waiting for income to be distributed differently.

* * *

After this war the first condition for justice, and even for peace itself, is that we make full employment the cornerstone of the American economy. Returning to the opening question—full employment will not necessarily permit us to follow along the trend line of maximum opportunity for free, competitive enterprise. But neither will it make that impossible. We ought to be able to combine full employment with a maximum of free enterprise, if we want to. The requirement appears to be a technologically valid policy for monopoly and competition linked up with a monetary-fiscal program centered on a pegged total of consumer expenditure.

5

POST-WAR JOB PROSPECTS*

No worker needs to be reminded that the worst threat on his post-war horizon is the possible return of mass unemployment such as existed in the thirties. A job is a simple necessity, as a way of earning a living and also as a source of human dignity, yet many are haunted today by the fear that this simple necessity will be denied them.

Besides this direct connection between his job and his chance for happiness, the worker recognizes that an unemployment situation produces a competition for the scarce existing jobs that tends to undermine bargaining power and wage rates. It will be much harder to maintain union standards in the demobilization period if there is no conviction that the shortage of jobs in industry at that time is only temporary.

What are the prospects for jobs when the war is over?

The Prospects for Jobs

When peace finally comes, re-employment will at once overshadow every other issue in American life. We can perhaps expect to have at that moment 11 million men under arms. Even though a much larger armed force may need to be retained than we had in the pre-war period, it is safe to say that at least 8 or 9 million ex-servicemen will shortly be looking for peacetime jobs or going back to school. Meanwhile our war industries are bound to release millions of working men and women, since it takes time to change back to making cars and houses instead of tanks and destroyers. This industrial demobilization may displace 6 million as a net minimum, i.e., not counting many other transfers from plant to plant that will not reduce employment in industry as a whole. We therefore are going to develop very quickly a large volume of unemployment in the United States, unless we can have ready a large-scale program of public works, non-construction as well as construction, to throw into immediate operation.

The brighter side of the picture is that at the same time shrinkage is

---

*This statement, written at the request of the Postwar Planning Committee of the American Federation of Labor, was first published by the Federation as a pamphlet in August, 1943, and was reprinted in the October, 1943, issue of the *American Federationist.* The original title was "Employment After the War."

occurring in munitions manufacture there will be expansion in other lines, some of which is likely to occur automatically and some of which can be encouraged by constructive national policies. However, for the first six to nine months more workers will be laid off than can be hired in regular lines of work, no matter how favorable conditions may be, and it appears improbable that the unemployment problem can be reduced to small dimensions in less than a year and a half.

It is important to realize that this kind of prediction about the immediate demobilization period does not depend on just when the war will end or on just how quickly we can hit our peacetime stride after that. If it takes a year or two more to knock out Japan after we have beaten Germany, some reconversion may take place before hostilities are finished, and this, while perhaps creating some unemployment before the war is over, may shorten the transition period. If industry hesitates and delays the change-back to full scale civilian production, unemployment may run up to 12 million or more in half a year's time, whereas it may not go beyond 7 million—subject to offsets by means of public works—if management, labor, and government tackle our joint problems with real courage and intelligence. But, regardless of events that cannot yet be known, the situation in the first six months is bound to be critical. Discharges from the armed forces and from war production will rapidly outrun new job opportunities in peace production. Millions will be looking for work without being able to find it immediately in private industry and normal peacetime operations. This can be stated flatly now.*

It goes without saying that the impact of demobilization will not be evenly distributed over the country, but will affect some geographic areas, some industries, and some occupations much more severely than others. The war has dislocated most of the familiar patterns, bringing huge aircraft, ordnance, and explosive plants to quiet country towns like Choteau, Oklahoma, and Pine Bluff, Arkansas, expanding key industrial centers beyond anything known there in the past, creating unparalleled demand for certain job skills needed in fashioning the tools of war. The end of the war will reverse much of what has happened since 1940.

---

*This forecast obviously was wide of the mark. The best that can be said for it is that it was made in 1943 rather than two years later. The real point, however, is that it was extraneous, since forecasts, right or wrong, play no essential part in the general method of maintaining full employment proposed in this book. The insurance approach does not rely on predicting what is going to happen at a particular time. It does assume that a general tendency toward too little demand and too little employment predominates in our economy, but it is just the antithesis of the approach that would formulate government programs on the basis of closely calculated "prospective deficiencies" in demand and employment in a particular time period. The importance of this distinction in method is stressed in subsequent papers.

The industrial state of Michigan, for example, will probably find that it has nearly 6 demobilized servicemen and released war workers applying for jobs for every 10 persons employed in the state before the war. In Connecticut, Washington, and Indiana the ratios will probably run at least 4½ to 10. South Dakota will face a real problem too, but here the proportion may well be only 2 to 10. This is about what can be expected also in North Dakota, North and South Carolina, Mississippi, Wyoming, Vermont, Montana, and other states in which very little specialized war production is located. It should, of course, also be emphasized that in any given state the strain will be highly localized in certain communities. In San Diego, California, and Wichita, Kansas, because of war contracts the number of factory wage earners employed late in 1942 was at least 6 times as large as in 1937. In Portland, Oregon, it had risen more than 250 per cent; in Seattle, Washington, and Norfolk, Virginia, more than 200 per cent. It takes little imagination to foresee a critical situation in these production centers when the government stops buyng planes and ships for war.

Just as demobilization will hit some regions harder than others, so it will differ very much in its effects on the different industrial components of our economy. Manufacturing faces the largest total decline. Contrasted with a war peak employment around 18 millions, a peacetime level of 13 million is possible under favorable circumstances. Government employment—swelled to nearly 6½ million in all by the addition of workers in arsenals and Navy yards, other civilian personnel of the War and Navv Departments, and employees of various emergency agencies of the Federal Government—also is slated for a big reduction, a cutback of perhaps 2 million. Transportation and public utilities are likely to decline slightly. On the other hand trade may well expand by 1½ million, construction will expand very substantially, and some increases are to be expected in finance and services and in the proprietors and self-employed group. Agriculture may absorb a million or more workers.

The most spectacular declines in manufacturing will be found in the key war industries. Contrary to the expectations of some workers now engaged in aircraft production, indications are that this branch of industry will toboggan down from its wartime peak until it has released 1½ million or more workers. In shipbuilding the reduction will be almost as drastic, although spread over a somewhat longer period. Another very large contraction will occur in the manufacture of machinery and machine tools. Iron and steel will be cut back severely, as will the production of chemicals and petroleum products. Aluminum and other nonferrous metals too are expected to decline. The converted automobile industry, after employing some 800,000 on war production, is likely to decline to 200,000 during reconversion and then climb back to a level around 600,000. On the other side of the picture, certain manufacturing industries such as those producing refrigerators, sewing machines, and electrical appliances, as well as textiles, leather, lumber, and paper, may show an almost immediate expansion.

As far as occupations are concerned, thousands of welders, riveters, turret lathe operators, machinists, tool and die makers, and other skilled and semi-skilled workers will have to transfer to other kinds of work. Unskilled laborers are likely to face a shortage of jobs in many parts of the country. Generally speaking, any worker who has learned only a single narrow skill, in a war plant for instance, may have a hard period of readjustment ahead. The jobs opening up in construction will offer some employment opportunities requiring skills little different from those acquired in war industry. On the other hand, workers who go into the expanding service fields, in education, health, etc., will usually require a good deal of further training.

The Policy Issues

To prepare to meet this situation, the general outlines of which can already be clearly foreseen, trade unionists along with other Americans need immediately to address their thoughts to at least six major issues.

First and foremost, what can and should be done to assure quick reconversion and create an environment favorable to continued high-level business activity, so that normal enterprise may as quickly as possible provide a real job for every able-bodied American who wants to work? Second, what can and should be done to make it possible to give jobs at fair rates of pay on public work projects to those who otherwise will be jobless in the transition period? Third, what can and should be done to provide temporary financial support for demobilized servicemen and war workers to help tide them over the interval before they secure any job at all? Fourth, what can and should be done to lessen the abruptness of military and industrial demobilization so as to cut down the number of workers appearing in the labor market in the most critical period, the first six months after the end of hostilities? Fifth, what can and should be done to make it easier to provide full employment by reducing the number of men and women who want jobs or by cutting down the hours in the working week? Finally, what can and should be done to promote labor's ability to move not only from job to job but also from place to place and from one type of work to another, and in this way lower the barriers that sometimes keep workers and available jobs apart? Decisions are needed on all these major issues.

(1) Policies should be formulated to bring about speedy reconversion

and encourage high-level industrial and farm production. This goes to the roots of our system of individual initiative and free, competitive enterprise.

One part of this central issue involves those things which business men themselves have done the most to emphasize. What policies should be developed to settle the disposal of government-owned war plants and surplus stocks of war goods, and the release of priorities, on terms that will help rather than hinder private enterprise? What should be done about business taxes during the war, about cash settlements when war contracts are canceled after the war, about loans for reconversion, and about credit and capital facilities for small business, to provide management with the funds it must have in order to operate? What changes should be made in our basic tax policies to give more encouragement to enterprise capital and socially valuable investment?

Another aspect of this issue, and one whose importance could hardly be exaggerated, is that of assuring adequate markets to justify the businessman's decision to hire workers and carry on production. At first there is likely to be too much purchasing power in the market in relation to the goods available, rather than too little, because of the time required to reach full civilian production and the very large volume of savings accumulated by many middle- and upper-income families during the war. This means that the main immediate problem—speaking here not of the individual worker's situation but rather of the sum total of money in the hands of the consuming public—may be one of preventing inflation through continued taxation and sales of government bonds, and continued price controls. But, even at first, expected future markets will play their part along with the current demand in determining the decisions of businessmen about the plant and equipment they can use, and hence will affect the number of workers hired to produce this plant and equipment. This means that policies are needed to assure that the consumer demand will be large enough at all times, but on the other hand not too large, to buy the maximum output of goods and services that the nation is capable of producing. Foreign markets may, of course, provide part of the incentive to production, but assurance is needed that the domestic market will always take up the slack if foreign markets shrink. Nor can we rely entirely upon public works to provide extra purchasing power whenever we are faced with the danger of under-consumption and restriction of markets. We may find ourselves unable to mobilize an adequate volume of useful public works in time; or too large a part of the total income may still go into savings instead of being spent immediately.

The third main aspect of the question of full private production is the necessity for high-output and low-price business policies rather than low-output and high-price business policies. If production and employment are to expand as justified by the demand for goods and services, monopolistic restrictions of all kinds on production must be held in check, except for such restrictions on the use of natural resources as may be required by the long-run interests of the nation as a whole. What policies will be most effective for accomplishing this purpose?

(2) It will be impossible to avoid severe unemployment in the transition period without a public works program. Since it takes a long time to get such a program into the blueprint stage and ready to start, workers have a responsibility to themselves to see that the plans are made now; otherwise it may be too late. A large number of small, widely scattered construction projects will probably be better than a few big ones; very big projects can hardly get to the stage of employing their full quota of workers until many months have passed—when private enterprise may have expanded to the point where jobs on special public works are no longer needed and the projects ought to be shut down. But it must also be remembered that construction, including the conservation of natural resources, cannot shoulder the load alone. For one thing the construction industry cannot be expected, on the basis of its past record, to expand quickly enough to provide jobs for as many as will be looking for work in the early months of peace. In addition, women workers and many others who will be without jobs at that time cannot readily enter the construction industry. Hence the planning of public works should allow for a number of work projects in the fields of public health, research, education, and general public welfare, as well as in construction. And at the same time it must weed out all such projects as do the community no good and offend against the worker's self-respect.

(3) Policies are imperatively needed to assure that proper financial support is given to workers and their families at the time when it is temporarily impossible to provide 100 per cent employment. Returning soldiers and sailors might justly be given a cash bonus—in the form of furlough with pay, mustering-out pay, or some other form—at the time of demobilization, when they are likely to want it most. Aside from this special question, all workers, including ex-servicemen, should have adequate compensation while unemployed. Labor has the right to ask why unemployment compensation should not extend over as long a period as private or public jobs are nowhere to be had.

(4) Policies should be formulated with respect to the rate at which our armed forces are to be demobilized. Anything that slows this process down will gain precious time while the up-swing of peacetime production is just getting under way. On the other hand, unjustified delays will be strongly

resented by the average man in uniform and his family, which means that action along this line has obvious limits. So far as war industry is concerned, most of it will have to be demobilized very rapidly to clear the road for peace production. But this is not so in every case, and policies are needed to decide what war contracts ought to be either continued and gradually tapered off or else transformed into temporary government peace contracts.

(5) Social security and education policies should be formulated to make possible the voluntary withdrawal from the labor market of women who prefer to work in the home, soldiers and other young people who have not yet completed the education they should have, and workers who have reached retirement age. Since emigration and immigration will likewise affect the size of the labor force, policies are needed here too. It will be possible to be generous in deciding the terms on which foreigners shall be admitted to American privileges, but only if full employment itself can be assured.

Policies should be formulated with respect to the length of the work-week. The problem here is to have a reasonable work-week in all industries, but to avoid so limiting the hours of work in the interests of giving more jobs that we have as a result a shortage of goods to enjoy.

(6) In addition to questions of demand for labor and questions of labor supply, already pointed out, measures are needed to assist in bringing demand and supply together. Policies should be formulated to provide American workers with a federalized job placement service equipped to handle quickly and effectively the largest volume of job applications in our history as a nation. Many may also require help in moving considerable distances to take up jobs. Large numbers of wounded soldiers and sailors will need physical rehabilitation before they can resume normal civilian life. All over the country men and women must have new training to fit them for new lines of work. Willingness and ability to make a fresh start will be in greater demand than ever before. Union policies as well as government policies must be shaped to this end.

Fundamental Importance of Job Opportunity

It cannot be repeated too often that the worker's greatest need is the opportunity to work. Moreover, while this is obvious and familiar in a general way, its full force is probably not always apparent, even to workers themselves who as individuals and as union members suffer from the existence or the threat of unemployment. This question therefore deserves further attention here.

One aspect of it, closely related to the maintaining of union standards, is the issue of non-discrimination in job opportunity. Our returning soldiers, sailors, and marines have justly been promised first call on their old jobs as their natural right. But what will happen to the workers who will be dismissed to make room for them? Will jobs open up for these workers elsewhere? What of the women who have taken jobs during the war and who need or want to continue to hold jobs when the war is over? One thing ought to be clearly understood. Whether or not the return of peace is going to usher in a period of discriminations and bitter group feelings—antagonisms and tensions that draw the lines between women and men, Negroes and whites, ex-servicemen and civilians, older workers and younger workers, native born and foreign born—depends almost entirely on whether or not we allow the unemployment situation to get out of hand. The greater the amount of unemployment, the sharper will be the discrimination. Moreover, the greater the amount of unemployment, the harder it will be to reconcile the claims of skilled and unskilled workers. The principles of fair play, fraternity, and equal opportunity, to which trade unionists owe a natural allegiance, are at stake, with the outcome depending to the greatest extent on the existence or absence of universal job opportunity.

A further way in which full employment spells the difference between happiness and hardship for the worker is through its influence on the social security program. In the last analysis social security benefits can come only from production. If our economic system is operating at full production levels, we know that our nation can afford generous payments to the old, the worker in transition from one job to another, the sick, and other persons handicapped through no fault of their own; also it can afford financial assistance to enable every young person to complete his or her education and to enable every family in America to live in a decent home in a decent community. But if we waste our human and material resources through unemployment, it is doubtful how many of these benefits can be afforded.

Finally, we cannot have a sound foreign policy unless our domestic policies are such as to assure jobs to all who are willing and able to work. This needs to be stressed because it is often not fully understood. Unquestionably many Americans will find employment producing food and other supplies for foreign relief in the immediate demobilization period. Thereafter too it is to be hoped that we will continue a large volume of exports, including capital equipment for reconstruction and for the development of so-called backward areas. But these opportunities to help ourselves while we are helping others may become, if misused, an economic boomerang for us and a source of the gravest danger to international relations.

We cannot afford to repeat the mistakes we made at the end of the last war. We want at this peace table to work out a sound policy of two-way trade, fair to us and to foreign countries, to enable imports to come in to match our exports and raise our standard of living. We want to work out lasting solutions to the problem of equal access to sources of raw materials. We want to develop neighborly principles to guide the course of emigration and immigration. But we cannot do any of these things if, through failure to set our own economic house in order, we are forced to treat foreign policy as a technique for accomplishing a different purpose, namely, to provide jobs we are unable to provide through domestic measures. For in that case we must do just the opposite—shut out imports while we push our exports, insist on economic and political domination over foreign backward areas, and deny hospitality to the foreigner at the same time as we encourage settlement of Americans abroad.

Thus the final reason why we must find ways and means for permanently solving our employment problem is that peace as well as employment is at stake. For if, after victory is won, we are so compelled by confusion or weakness at home that we are unable to stand squarely for cooperation with the nations and the peoples of the world, the pressure of events will eventually force us to the brink of another and even more terrible war.

6

UNDERWRITING AGGREGATE CONSUMER SPENDING*

The solid establishment of full employment after the war is a matter of profound importance.[1] Full employment creates its own problems for society.[2] However, if serious unemployment is allowed to develop, the following results may be confidently expected: widespread individual misery and frustration; a tendency for wage rates and working conditions to deteriorate because of excessively keen competition for the scarce existing jobs; bitter conflicts and animosities between Negroes and whites, women and men, ex-servicemen and civilians, older and younger workers, farmers and industrial workers, skilled and unskilled, native and foreign born—tensions from which will come pressure groups endangering democracy itself; a weakening of the production base which constitutes the foundation for the structure of social security and all similar institutions; and the ascendency of aggressive economic foreign policies that violate the spirit of cooperation and undermine the hope of lasting peace.

1. It is frequently asserted (1) that no one knows what full employment means, and (2) that full employment is a "counsel of perfection" and cannot be wholly achieved. The second of these allegations requires some analysis.[3] But the suggestion that full employment cannot be defined or identified carries little weight and may be disposed of in preliminary fashion by answering that full employment means a real job at all times for every able-bodied person who wants to work. That is to say, it means as many real jobs as there are employables wanting to work, *less* a number

*This article appeared in the March, 1944, issue of the *American Economic Review*, under the title, "The Underwriting of Aggregate Consumer Spending as a Pillar of Full-Employment Policy."

[1]I am indebted to Dr. Theodore F. Marburg for assistance in exploring portions of this field, and to Marvin Hoffenberg for statistical assistance; also to Dr. Emile Benoit-Smullyan, M. Elizabeth Fite, Dr. Emory Q. Hawk, Leonora L. Jensen, Edgar E. Poulton, and Betty E. Stern for valuable suggestions made during the preparation of this article.

[2]It tends at first, for example, to create or strengthen inflationary pressures. This will be considered in section 13.

[3]In this article, discussion will be limited to an economy operating on the general philosophy of free enterprise or individualistic production for market, since this condition is usually assumed in these allegations, and since in any case there is little need to debate the possibility of maintaining full employment in a system of planned production such as that of the U.S.S.R.

corresponding to normal frictional unemployment. A job is "real" if it serves a useful purpose and meets currently prevailing standards as to wage rates, hours,[4] and working conditions. Anyone is "employable" who is capable of meeting certain minimum physical and mental requirements. Anyone who "wants" to work can so signify to the Employment Service. "Normal frictional unemployment"—required because the system needs some slack for reasons of turnover, et cetera—is a statistical magnitude representing the amount by which it is agreed that labor force (employables wanting to work) can exceed employment without impairing full employment in the technical sense. The problems of concept and measurement concealed by this explanation are real, but they are not such that practical men cannot know what full employment means and when it exists.

It is, of course, very important to know what full employment means, in the operating sense. Uncertainty on this score would paralyze action with respect to the public work projects that constitute the secondary or final line of defense against unemployment.

The Public Investment Approach

2. The best-known proposal for securing full employment in our peacetime economy encounters such serious difficulties as to raise grave doubt whether it could ever provide a fundamental solution for the problem in hand. This is the proposal, advanced by Hansen[5] and other distinguished economists, that public investment be used to compensate for deficiencies in the private sector of the economy.

This idea has made an indelible impression on the thinking of the past decade. It has an imposing theoretical base—the most famous exposition of which was given by Keynes[6]—in the consideration that, in a modern high-income economy operating at capacity or near-capacity levels, voluntary saving tends to exceed the available (profitable) private investment outlets, so that resources threaten to go unused altogether. Empirically it derives support from the fact that the capital goods industries, whose activity corresponds to real investment, contract and expand more violently in the course of the business cycle than do the consumer goods industries.

But there are serious objections when it comes to drawing from these

---

[4]Prevailing hourly standards may be unsatisfactory, as a result of spread-the-work programs, in the absence of policies that maintain full employment by maintaining effective demand. In discussing policies of this positive type, however, it can be assumed that the prevailing work-week will be about as long as most people want it to be.

[5]A. H. Hansen, *Fiscal Policy and Business Cycles* (New York, Norton, 1941), and other writings.

[6]J. M. Keynes, *The General Theory of Employment, Interest, and Money* (London, Macmillan, 1936).

premises the conclusion that public investment should be used to offset secular as well as temporary deficits in private investment. In the first place, such a policy ultimately risks offending against the canon of efficiency or economy, since it may involve public investment projects yielding smaller benefits than might have been derived from a *different* allocation of labor and other resources. The inference is by no means to be drawn that this is characteristically the case with public investment. Indeed, there are certain kinds of public investment hitherto not developed to any significant extent that are probably at least as badly needed as anything else we could produce. Nevertheless there is clearly no reason to believe that any public investment project undertaken to fill an employment gap must automatically be desirable from the standpoint of relative usefulness, unless we are justified in assuming that alternative employment opportunities and products simply could not be created in other ways. This assumption seems of doubtful validity. There may well be ways of getting just as much employment along alternative lines yielding products that are wanted more than the end results of the public investment projects.[7]

In the second place, public investment applied as a compensatory technique—fill-in investment—does not squarely meet the over-saving problem. It palliates the difficulty by absorbing the excess savings. But it fails to assure a level of consumption adequate to maintain full employment with public investment limited to items regarded by the general public as worth while for their own sake. (Hence, this is really a special aspect of the previously stated objection on grounds of efficiency.) On this point there is little help to be got from the argument that public investment puts out purchasing power and thus indirectly takes care of the consumption level. Public investment does indeed increase consumer income. If pushed to the point of full employment, it will enable us to achieve what may be referred to as a full-employment-*caused* level of national income and of

[7]In the hope of avoiding misunderstanding, the writer wishes to state his preference for public investment projects of almost any kind, as against involuntary unemployment, whenever the choice actually narrows down to that; also his belief that housing, health, education, and conservation of natural resources are so important that the regular program of public investment should be expanded to any extent necessary to secure universally high standards in these fields. He would probably vote to include certain national development programs suggested by Hansen (*e.g.*, rural electrification) on the regular public investment list, and to hold certain others (*e.g.*, some of those related to reorganization and rationalization of transportation) in reserve for slack periods, although this is a tentative judgment, admittedly based on insufficient study of the fields in question.

It is sometimes suggested that expansion of public investment is required because of functional and geographic labor immobility—*i.e.*, so that jobs may be provided in those places and on those types of work to which labor has been drawn in the past. This particular argument may be of some importance temporarily and in certain sections of the country.

consumer income.[8] But it cannot be counted on to give us a full-employment-*causing* level of consumer *spending*—meaning by this a total adequate to induce full employment without public investment fill-in programs. For the independent decisions to save out of income, or to dis-save, have still to be reckoned with. In the immediate demobilization period, *particularly* if public investment can be used to secure full employment, the cashing of war savings may well lift consumer spending above the cost value of the maximum output of consumer goods deliverable at that time. Thereafter, if or when the over-saving tendency reasserts itself, the volume of income payments flowing from full-employment operations will not in itself suffice to assure an adequate return flow of consumer spending in the sense indicated above.

The third objection relates directly to the question of feasibility rather than to economic principle, and must be weighed accordingly. Practically speaking the fundamental consideration, so far as concerns the possibility of maintaining full employment, is that a public investment program, *used as the main weapon against unemployment and expanded to whatever extent might be necessary to prevent unemployment,* would probably seriously discourage private enterprise. Our experience with a limited volume of public works in the thirties, which did not bring about full employment, provides no conclusive test of this statement one way or the other. Many types of public investment are noncompetitive at least in the sense that they do not compete with private enterprise in the market for products. Furthermore, public projects often provide an obvious stimulus to business—notably to contractors and to suppliers of building materials and equipment. Even "noncompetitive" public investment does, however, compete in the labor and capital (and land) markets and, ultimately, in the market where philosophies or systems of production are selected. This is especially obvious if public ownership and operation are involved, but it remains true even if the government merely assumes *responsibility* and the workers are on private payrolls. Systematically applied on a grand and, in principle, indefinitely expansible scale, public investment would probably discourage private enterprise by throwing private enterprise into partial eclipse. Naturally, this is a situation in which business will not readily allow itself to be placed.

The above difficulties with the public investment approach as a solution for the unemployment problem may be reformulated, from the standpoint of its political prospects, along the following lines: (1) The cry of "boondoggling" will be raised to discredit this program; worse than that, ex-

[8]Strictly speaking, consumer income will also depend on the level of business savings, *i.e.*, undistributed profits.

amples of relatively useless public investment projects will be cited to support the allegation that full employment itself necessarily means an inefficient or uneconomical allocation of resources. (2) Incidentally, although this touches on the theoretical premises for the program rather than on the program itself, members of the public investment school will be accused of "selling America short" when they argue that public investment is necessitated by a widening secular gap between saving and private investment opportunity. (3) In the end, these arguments plus straightforward opposition to government competition will to a considerable extent prevail, especially since the concept of investment (as contrasted with the concept of consumption) is somewhat lacking in broad popular appeal. The opposition will not prevent large-scale public investment projects from being undertaken, but almost certainly will prevent full employment from being maintained by this method—which is the question that concerns us here.

At this point it may also be well to emphasize that some of the theoretical apparatus most commonly associated with the case for a public investment solution does not prove that public investment is the answer to the problem. The multiplier principle indicates that an increment of aggregate investment will produce a more than equivalent increase in national income, since it will also raise consumption. It does not tell us that an expansion of *public* investment will yield a corresponding increment (or, for that matter, *any* increment) of *aggregate* investment; this prior question cannot be resolved unless we know the reactions of private enterprise to the public investment program, and these reactions may well depend on the point to which the latter is pushed, as suggested above.

Similarly, the principle of relative constancy of the consumption-income ratio, or consumption function, or propensity to consume does not tell us that a tendency for saving to exceed investment at full-employment levels must be corrected by expanding investment. For it does not settle the question whether public policy might not equally well or better expand consumers' incomes or their disposable cash directly, and in this way increase consumption instead.[9]

---

[9]In real terms, total consumption would be greater and saving less than if the gap were closed by expanding investment; *i.e.*, the whole schedule or curve representing the "propensity" to consume would lie at a higher level, and the whole schedule or curve representing the "propensity" to save would lie at a lower level. But this need not interfere with anyone's personal thriftiness or right to save. Individuals would have more cash and their dollar savings would actually increase somewhat at the same time as their spending increased. This would not necessarily involve anything more than a shift along a given hypothetical schedule or curve relating dollars of consumer savings to dollars of consumer disposable income. (See below, especially section 7 and Table I.)

Elements of an Alternative Program

3. While the "mature economy" or "secular stagnation" thesis—the suggestion that the passing of the frontier and the slowing of population growth are narrowing private investment opportunities—is under fairly heavy fire,[10] the familiar conclusion from this premise seems to be taken at face value. It appears to be pretty generally believed that *if there is* a deficiency of private investment, relative to the tendency to save at full-employment levels of income, the gap must be closed by expanding aggregate investment. The other alternative would be an increase in consumption, which would involve a reduction of aggregate real saving. Before this alternative is examined directly, consideration will be given to the elements that a program would have to contain to meet the objections raised above against the public investment approach.

The objection on the ground that public investment invites an uneconomical allocation of resources would be met if it were possible to have a full employment program in which public investment was limited to permanent priority items and fill-in items according to the following criteria: (1) The permanent prority items would be only those which the majority of persons would prefer as against the alternative of individual consumption out of individual incomes, supposing that existing incomes could be adjusted to the necessary level under a politically feasible program of direct support to individual consumption. (2) The fill-in projects, which would be drawn from a well-planned shelf of public works or work projects, would be operated only when needed to offset short-term deficiencies in employment opportunity that might develop in spite of maintenance of consumption at levels regarded *a priori* as adequate to secure full employ-

---

[10]The "mature economy" thesis is liable to overstatement, as pointed out by Kuznets. (Simon Kuznets, review of Alvin H. Hansen's *Fiscal Policy and Business Cycles*, in *Rev. of Econ. Stat.*, Vol. XXIV, No. 1 [Feb., 1942], pp. 34-35.) Moreover, if the conditions of the problem can be changed by making effective demand correspond more closely to needs, intensive investment will obviously have greater scope than hitherto; this seems to be the one element of value in Moulton's comments on the subject. (See Harold G. Moulton, *The New Philosophy of Public Debt*, Washington, Brookings Inst., 1943, pp. 21-29, and other writings.) Generally speaking, however, after making all due allowances for the probable discovery of important new natural resources within existing frontiers, for a possible rise in the rate of invention, etc., one would hardly expect one factor (technological progress) to be able to provide as much opportunity for private investment in the future as was formerly provided by three factors combined (technological progress, rapid population growth, and territorial expansion). This is particularly the case in view of the qower of monopolistic concerns to hold back the introduction of new processes, and the further fact that many new processes are likely to be capital-saving rather than capital-expanding. Private investment *may* flourish again as in the past, but no disparagement of American initiative need be involved in the suggestion that the chances are against it.

ment.[11] These residual deficiencies would still occur from time to time, particularly as a result of changes in the rate of introduction of new inventions, fluctuations in the rate of replacement of fixed equipment, and, perhaps, fluctuations in inventories. The items on the regular list would be in place of alternative output, but would represent a better allocation of resources so far as it is humanly possible to judge such matters. The only alternative to the fill-in projects, when these were required, would be no output at all. To put it differently, the development of an employment gap in spite of measures taken to provide business with sufficient customers would raise the marginal value of public investment as a whole and require the inauguration of the projects highest on the waiting list. To be sure, there are bound to be sharp differences of opinion about some of the items that might be included on the regular program. But the democratic process resolves these differences into some kind of answer at any given moment and should be able to express the state of public opinion with fair accuracy as time goes by.

The element required to meet the second objection against the public investment approach—that it does not squarely meet the over-saving problem—would be direct control over total consumer spending. If it were possible to exercise such control, consumption could be held at a level adequate to maintain full employment—*i.e.*, full employment with private investment taking its natural course and public investment operating according to the principles enunciated above. Thus, any over-saving or under-spending tendency would be corrected instead of covered up, as under a policy of equating investment to saving.

If it were possible to control total consumer spending, then it should also be possible to underwrite this total. To do so would seem desirable from the standpoint of giving solid encouragement to private enterprise while restraining speculative excesses. In short, consumer spending might be (1) controlled, (2) held at levels permitting public investment to represent on the whole a deliberate social choice of products for their own sake rather than in large part a bowing to the supposed necessity of filling an investment gap, and (3) *underwritten to allow the prospective demand to exert its full stimulating force upon all enterprises producing goods or services for market.* If all this could be done, it would appear that the third objection, the discouragement to private enterprise inherent in an all-out compensatory public investment program, might also be avoided.

4. What has been suggested may be summed up as the principle of

---

[11]In the immediate demobilization period, a program to maintain consumption would aim at levels calculated to buy all the consumer goods that it will be possible for industry, under stress of reconversion, to produce; see section 12.

burden of proof for investment, the principle of underwriting or insuring the economy as a whole, and a combination of these principles through application of the underwriting to aggregate individual consumption.

The principle of burden of proof for investment implies that the criterion for the appropriate volume of private investment should be its natural response (in terms of expansion and replacement) to changes in tastes and techniques, and to levels of and changes in rates of interest; that the volume of public investment should be decided by judging the end products on their merits as against alternatives that might result from higher levels of individual consumer spending; and that the balance of our resources should be employed producing goods and services to be bought by individual consumers in the proportions they think best. In other words, this principle rests on the premise that "over-saving" really means over-saving (under-spending) and not under-investment.

Public investment may from this standpoint be considered as including all public spending for goods and services, and hence extends not only to the purchase of munitions by the army but also to all collective consumption in the sense of community expenditure for general public use (as opposed to consumption represented by individual consumer spending). Thus, it covers public expenditure for free medical service as well as for construction of hospitals and clinics; for teaching and free school lunches and library service as well as for construction of schools and libraries; for the maintenance as well as the laying out of parks and playgrounds. The principle of burden of proof for investment therefore implies that community consumption, like public investment in producer goods, should stand on its own merits—which are often quite sufficient—and should yield to individual consumption wherever the superiority of the former over the latter has not been established. Expansion of community consumption merely to compensate for absence of other demand would fail to satisfy requirements, since the principle in question rests on the assumed desirability of individual consumer sovereignty as well as on the supposition that production should be carried on for the sake of consumption.

The principle of underwriting the economy rests on the inference that underwriting the effort of private enterprise is better than continually meddling with it here and there, so long as private enterprise is supposed to be held in esteem. Of course, it does not preclude government ownership and operation or government regulation where necessary or desirable. Nor does it imply that new rigidities should be introduced through a guaranteeing of markets to individual producers or individual industries. But it does postulate the desirability of assuring an adequate effective demand in the over-all sense—the desirability of seeing that the "game of hazard," as Keynes calls it, played by business men should not be one in which, to continue his phrase, "the players *as a whole* will lose if they have the energy and hope to deal all the cards."[12]

The application of the underwriting to aggregate individual consumption (as well as to employment as a whole) appears desirable if the two underlying principles are valid. A guarantee to fill all employment gaps with public investment, without a simultaneous guarantee of an adequate overall consumer market, would prevent (if it could be made good) a decline in consumer income but would still expose the economy to over-saving—concealed by a corresponding degree of over-investment.[13] A nonspecific guarantee to offset saving one way or the other—either by expanding public investment or by supplementing consumers' spending by way of their incomes—might or might not eliminate over-saving, depending on which of the two courses the government elected to follow. But in any case it would create needless uncertainties and broaden the opportunities for arbitrary government action.

5. We may now formulate a preliminary outline of how a policy of underwriting aggregate consumer spending would operate—always assuming that practical means could be found for executing the steps required. After that the question of ways and means will be explored.

It is clear that the steps to be taken by the government would be three in number. (1) The government would first have to calculate the "right" dollar amount of aggregate individual consumer spending (say for the next year)—this being the amount the confident anticipation of which would be expected to stimulate full employment, with public investment limited to items wanted for their own sake. The government would announce this amount and would guarantee that consumers' incomes would be adjusted if necessary so that the designated amount of spending would actually be forthcoming. (2) It would next have to fill the employment gap, if one occurred in spite of the inducement to private enterprise afforded by the guarantee of consumer spending, by starting or expanding appropriate projects from the public work shelf. (3) Finally, it would have to expand or reduce total consumer spending via consumer cash in-

---

[12]Keynes, *op. cit.*, p. 381; italics in original.

[13]*I.e.*, over-saving in relation to genuine investment opportunity; over-investment by the same criterion, or, in other words, in relation to the amount really needed.

comes,[14] if and as this proved necessary, in spite of the existence of full employment and a full-employment-caused volume of income payments, in order to prevent under- or over-fulfillment of the guarantee.[15]

Consideration shows that numerous combinations or sequences of events would be possible—six altogether. The underwriting of consumer spending might or might not altogether obviate the need for a fill-in program of public work projects. Full employment, whether achieved with or without fill-in employment, might result in aggregate consumer spending equal to the amount guaranteed, might require an addition to consumer incomes to increase their spending in order to realize the guarantee, or might require a deduction from consumer spending to prevent over-fulfillment.

The Underwriting and Control of Aggregate Consumer Spending

6. As a practical matter, how could aggregate consumer spending be guaranteed? How could any guarantee be made good? First and foremost, how could consumer spending be raised when it threatened to fall short?

The general answer to this half of the problem,[16] as already suggested, is that consumer spending would be raised by giving consumers additional spending power. This could be handled in a variety of ways. Congress

---

[14]This article will not discuss the ways in which public work projects and direct payments to consumers might be financed, but it will suggest that on the whole a full-employment program based on the underwriting of aggregate consumer spending might cost the government less than a full-employment program based on public investment. (See sections 7 and 15.) Presumably taxes that increase business costs or reduce consumer buying power would be ruled out as sources of revenue for such government expenditures, since they would operate to defeat the central purpose. On the other hand, savings that are not invested would provide a source from which funds might be secured by borrowing or taxation without detriment to production and with the positive advantage that policies along this line would tend to obviate the need for monetary expansion except as required by increased productivity of the economy. A parenthetical word may be added here about the public debt. The most important consideration with regard to the post-war public debt appears to be that it should not be allowed to occupy the center of the stage in discussions of general economic policy. This can hardly be emphasized too strongly. Proponents of measures to maintain the level of production and employment sometimes permit themselves to be sidetracked on this issue and then placed in a position where they seem to be advocating public deficits and a rising public debt as ends in themselves. It would be more convincing if they would show (1) that full employment, even if it involves expansionist public spending, is cheaper for society than unemployment, (2) that the measures they advocate for support of full employment involve less public spending than alternative measures capable of realizing the same objective, (3) that public borrowing is necessary to finance the necessary spending in so far as taxation and the issuing of paper money are not deemed suitable, and—then only—(4) that the resulting rise in the public debt will not have the injurious effects that many believe to be indicated. (1) and (2) are the crucial arguments, not (4).

[15]The question of the margin to be allowed between minimum and maximum limits of aggregate consumer spending is considered in section 8.

[16]Prevention of *excessive* consumer spending will be discussed in section 8.

would, however, presumably want to consider the following principles in ruling how this should be done. (1) *Adequacy of amount:* the formula selected would have to permit payments to be made to consumers up to a total sufficient to take care of any under-spending likely to arise in a full-employment situation. (2) *Broad and fair distribution:* (a) payments should in general go to the broad ranks of Americans throughout the country, which means in effect that a large part of the total would go to low-income groups. This is necessary for reasons of equity, and it is necessary also in order to keep down the cost to the government, since the low-income groups would spend a larger fraction of these payments and save less. (b) The purpose of maintaining the over-all market should not, however, be subordinated, or normal competitive incentives undermined, by treating the under-writing program as essentially a vehicle for redistribution of income. (c) The distribution should not favor special interest groups. In general, wherever particular groups have a legitimate claim to preferential treatment, such treatment should be accorded by special legislative enactment and not by introducing biases into the program for maintaining the over-all spending level. Any balancing payments required under the latter program should be made available to the general public with a minimum of distinctions between persons. (3) *Flexibility:* the formula would have to contain within itself, as part of the policy laid down by Congress, features enablng the payments to be started, stopped, expanded, or contracted on short notice (say, each quarter) so as to adapt to changes in the ratio of consumers' spending out of their regular incomes. (4) *Operating simplicity:* the program should not be unduly complicated in administration, and as far as possible it should use agencies and mechanisms already in operation.

It is not the purpose of this paper to suggest what formula would best meet these and any other necessary specifications. That is the kind of general policy decision that can only be made by the American people acting through their elected representatives. Some typical alternatives, which by no means exhaust the possibilities, may, however, be mentioned to show that the problem is soluble.

One possibility of considerable interest is that of timing the repayment of war bonds according to the need of the post-war economy for restricted or expanded consumer expenditure. The practical importance of this alternative is no doubt related to the question whether or not the United States shortly adopts a program of forced saving to raise revenue and combat wartime inflation. By the end of 1944 some 50 billion dollars' worth of war savings bonds might be outstanding, of which 20 billion, possibly, might have been subscribed under a forced savings plan involving rebatable income or Victory taxes and rebatable sales taxes. In enacting such legislation, Congress might retain for the government the right to pay back these savings by redeeming the bonds any time within, say, five years after the end of the war. A similar stipulation might be attached, in conjunction with tax exemption privileges, high interest rates, or some other special inducement to future issues of war bonds subscribed voluntarily or exchanged for present holdings of demand bonds. At the right time after the war the government might, furthermore, encourage redemption of bonds not callable at government option by offering full value on accrual bonds if turned in promptly and correspondingly favorable terms on other issues. Conceivably the government might also, by appropriate concessions in the form of higher interest rates, acquire substantial control over the timing of interest payments.

It appears unlikely, however, that any combination of such devices could secure to the government the disposition or timing of payments in excess of, say, 30 billion dollars altogether, on the basis of war bonds subscribed by the end of 1944. Moreover, a large fraction of such payments would undoubtedly be reinvested or held in bank accounts rather than spent; even assuming a large forced savings program heavily weighted to build up the bond holdings of the low-income groups, the increment of consumer spending would hardly exceed 50 per cent of interest and principal payments on the bonds. It therefore appears that the total expansive effect to be gained in this manner is limited—although less limited the longer the war and the period of bond accumulation. It also seems self-evident that bond redemption does not in itself provide an instrument of fine precision for adjusting aggregate consumer spending to guaranteed levels. On the other hand this mechanism, if skillfully handled, could be useful for securing rough first approximations, or at any rate movements in the desired directions, in the early post-war years.

Another possible formula for raising consumer spending in order to achieve guaranteed levels involves the rebating of taxes paid by individuals—*i.e.*, the payment of rebates over and above those which may have been provided for in advance in connection with wartime forced savings programs. Such payments might be made on the principle that it is sound policy to give individuals back their own money to spend when enterprise requires larger markets in order to prosper. The rebates might be applied to the previous year's income taxes and payroll taxes, with provision in the latter case that the government would reimburse the social security accounts for any sums drawn out for this purpose, to prevent impairment of the funds available for benefits. Any spendings taxes or sales taxes enacted could likewise be rebated; as a simpler though cruder alternative to requiring the presentation of sales tax receipts, payments might be made based on standard assumptions regarding the sum of all indirect taxes borne by the average family or individual. The total of the taxes levied on individuals in any one year—which, including payroll taxes, would perhaps have a general order of magnitude around 10 billion dollars—provides a measure of the maximum amount that could be rebated.

Of course, if suspension or forgiveness of current taxes were added to the rebating of taxes for the previous year, the effect would be doubled temporarily, but with the result that in the following year the principle could not be applied except on the pretext that the taxes paid several years before were now being returned. The tax rebate device, therefore, like the timing of bond redemptions, has definite quantitative limits. Nevertheless it might have merit as a control mechanism within a limited range of operation, particularly if applied to taxes levied on low-income groups, such as payroll taxes,[17] the refunding of which would increase consumers' spending considerably more in proportion than would the refunding of even a broadly based income tax with low exemptions.

A third possibility would be a system of "national income security payments" on the basis of residual equity claims assigned to the general public. All families and single persons throughout the country might be treated as though they were the holders of stock in a business enterprise. Assuming 30 million families and 10 million single persons, the payment of $100 (tax free) to each family and $50 to each single person, for example, would increase total disposable income by 3.5 billion dollars. Making the conservative assumption that 80 cents out of every dollar thus distributed would be spent by the recipient for consumers' goods or services (which probably underestimates the marginal ratio of spending to saving in this case), consumer *spending* would thereby rise to the extent of 2.8 billion dollars. A doubling of the dividends would almost double the effect upon spending. The rates actually applied would depend on how much expansion was required, so that this kind of formula, coupled with quarterly distribution, and used either alone or with the other devices when they were insufficient, would permit of complete flexibility over an unlimited range.

7. Because of the relative unfamiliarity of some of the available devices for expanding consumption directly, a discussion of them may have a tendency to obscure two points that it is essential to bear in mind. The first is that the subsidization of consumption here contemplated is merely such subsidization as may be needed (but at other times will not be needed)

---

[17]Or to a spendings tax; *cf.* discussion in section 8.

to prevent under-spending[18] from occurring *in conditions of full employment*—the full employment having been secured either with or without fill-in programs of public works. The second is that the costs and difficulties of this procedure for maintaining full employment must be weighed against the costs and difficulties inherent in other methods.

To make this clear and specific, two parallel columns of figures have been set up in Table I showing a hypothetical post-war total and breakdown of the national product and the uses made of distributed income. The first column depicts a condition of full employment secured by underwriting aggregate consumer spending and subsidizing it to offset over-saving; the second column depicts a condition of full employment secured in the same over-saving situation through compensatory public investment. Interpreted in prices that prevailed in the first half of 1943, the gross national product of 170 billion and the other magnitudes involved might be those of 1946, assuming the war had closed at the end of 1944. The quantities shown are, however, only illustrative and do not represent forecasts.

In the first column it has been assumed that government expenditures for goods and services, including construction, defense, salaries, interest on the public debt, and other expenditures (not forgetting essential public expenditures along these lines in connection with expanded programs of education, health, slum clearance, and conservation), amount to 24 billion altogether.[19] This means, if full employment requires or will yield a gross national product of 170 billion, that the private sector of the economy must utilize 146 billion dollars' worth to achieve full employment. Assuming that private gross capital expenditures, including a large housing program, amount to 22 billion,[20] the full-employment level of consumption output is 124 billion.

A gross national product of 170 billion might involve a national income of 140 billion, with business taxes, depreciation, and other charges making up the difference. If corporate savings amount to 4 billion, this leaves 136 billion to be distributed by business enterprises.

If employer and employee contributions to social security funds, *et cetera*, exceed the transfer payments from government consisting largely of the benefits paid out from such funds—as may occur on a fairly large scale under programs at present contemplated—income payments coming into the hands of consumers at full-employment levels of production may

[18] *I.e.*, under-spending in relation to the underwritten amount, which in turn was originally judged sufficient to be likely to secure full employment without resort to fill-in public investment; see previous discussion.

[19] So-called transfer payments, such as payments from social security funds, are excluded.

[20] No change is assumed in inventories of consumption commodities.

TABLE I.—HYPOTHETICAL NATIONAL OUTPUT, INCOME, SAVINGS, CONSUMPTION, ETC., FOR FULL EMPLOYMENT IN 1946, ASSUMING END OF WAR IN DECEMBER, 1944
(in prices of January-June 1943)

Item		Full Employment via Underwriting Approach, with Consumption Subsidy		Full Employment via Public Investment Approach	
		(in billions)			
1. Gross national product (2+3)		$170		$170	
2. Government expenditures for goods and services:					
a. unadjusted		24		24	
b. adjusted for $8 billion public investment fill-in					*32*
3. Goods and services available for private use (4+5)		146		138	
4. Private gross capital expenditures		22		22	
5. Value of consumption output		124		116	
6. National income		140		140	
7. Business savings (corporate business)		4		4	
8. Distributed income (total shares transferred by business enterprises) (6—7)		136		136	
9. Income payments (8, adjusted for social security and other transfers):					
a. unadjusted for subsidy		134		134	
b. adjusted for $10 billion subsidy to consumers[a]			*144*[a]		
10. Direct personal taxes		8		8	
11. Disposable income (9—10):					
a. unadjusted		126		126	
b. adjusted for $10 billion subsidy to consumers[a]			*136*[a]		
12. Net individual savings:					
a. tendency to save from current income	15				
b. tendency to spend war savings	5				
c. unadjusted savings (a—b)		10		10	
d. savings adjusted for 20% of $10 billion subsidy			*12*		
13. Consumer spending:					
a. unadjusted (11a—12c)		116		116	
b. adjusted for 80% of $10 billion subsidy			*124*		

[a]Subsidization of consumption may or may not increase income payments and disposable income (as these terms are ordinarily used), depending on the method of subsidization followed. For example, repayment of war bonds may be conceived of as raising consumer spending without affecting disposable income or income payments; tax reductions and tax rebates may be regarded as increasing disposable income as well as consumer spending, but not income payments; and special "national income security payments" will evidently expand income payments as well as disposable income and consumer spending.

amount to only, say, 134 billion. If the government takes 8 billion in direct personal taxes, that leaves a disposable income or purchasing power of 126 billion. At this level of current disposable income, consumers may have a "normal" tendeney to save 15 billion. But, quite independent of current income, they will also still have large accumulations of war savings, which they may decide to cash and spend to the extent of 5 billion, thereby lowering net individual savings for consumers in the aggregate to 10 billion, and leaving 116 billion to be spent for goods and services.

Consumer expenditures of 116 billion cannot buy consumption output worth 124 billion without serious losses to the producers of that output. (Of course, this larger output may conceivably be produced and the unsold portion added to inventories—a form of capital formation—but that will discourage production in the ensuing year.) Under a program of underwriting aggregate consumer spending, private enterprise, given a guarantee of a consumer market of 124 billion, would have a reasonable incentive to produce that amount. If it does so, this will secure full employment, *i.e.*, the 170-billion gross national product shown in the table, without the need for fill-in public works,[21] since 46 billion dollars' worth of output is being produced for other buyers—24 billion for government agencies and 22 billion for private purchasers of capital goods. To make good on this guarantee, however, government will have to subsidize consumer spending power, by one of the methods discussed above or some other method, sufficiently to raise actual consumer spending from 116 billion to 124 billion. Assuming a marginal propensity to consume—speaking in terms of dollars available for consumer spending—of 0.8, the subsidy required to expand consumer spending by 8 billion is 10 billion. This balances the picture, enabling business as a whole to sell its product without loss. Incidentally, it also somewhat increases consumers' dollar savings.

At this point, comparison should be made with the figures in column two. According to the public investment approach, the picture is balanced in another way. Instead of lifting consumer spending from 116 to 124 billion, a consumption output of 116 billion is assumed to be the most obtainable, and 8 billion dollars' worth of additional public investment is undertaken to close the gap between 162 billion of private plus normal public production, on the one hand, and the 170 billion required for full employment, on the other.

It will be observed that, with the figures used in this illustration, the compensatory spending required by the public investment approach amounts to only 8 billion dollars, whereas it comes to 10 billion (or at any rate some figure higher than 8 billion, the exact amount depending on the marginal propensity to consume) according to the underwriting approach.

---

[21]Under certain circumstances, a fill-in (which in the illustration will raise government expenditures for goods and services above 24 billion) will still be needed, as is fully explained elsewhere. This qualificatiton does not affect the main contrasts between the underwriting approach and the public investment approach which it is important to establish at this point.

There are, however, certain dynamic considerations, to be noted later, which seem likely to make the underwriting approach an instrument of budget economy if applied over a period of years.[22] Moreover, even in the immediate situation it should be recognized that the 8-billion figure rests on certain assumptions, extremely favorable to the public investment approach, which are by no means certain to be realized in practice.

In the first place, consumption goods are perhaps rather unlikely to be produced in the amount indicated unless the government definitely pledges itself to support income payments (if not consumer spending) by closing all unemployment gaps with public investment. That is, while they might as a result of speculative activity be produced even in *excess* of the volume indicated, the real basis for a consumption output of 116 billion is less solid in this case than is the basis for a consumption output of 124 billion under the alternative program unless the government specifically guarantees full employment—without which consumer spending will not reach 116 billion. In the second place, the production of capital goods as well as the production of consumption goods requires a reasonable amount of encouragement. If 22 billion of private capital formation is the quantity to be expected with consumer spending underwritten at high levels for the current year and for succeeding years as well, a question may be raised whether the same quantity is likely to be forthcoming in the absence of such assurances. Finally, it is not certain that private production—in particular, private capital formation—may not be rendered somewhat cautious and pessimistic as a result of the additional government participation in or responsibility for production represented by the public investment fill-in. If it so happens, for example, that as the result of these various considerations private consumption output amounts to only 114 billion, and private gross capital expenditures to 18 billion, the necessary investment fill-in will cost the government 14 billion instead of only 8.

8. A program of underwriting aggregate consumer spending involves the idea that spending will be held down to the guaranteed level as well as that it will be kept from falling below this level. This two-way operation is one of the advantages of such a program, since it makes it possible to link anti-inflationary measures, when they are needed, with the promise that anti-deflationary steps will be taken later on.

The criteria by which any formula for contracting consumer spending should be judged are essentially the same as the criteria applicable to programs for expanding this spending—namely, adequacy of amount, broad and fair distribution (in this case, distribution of the *deductions* from

---

[22] See section 15.

spending power), flexibility, and operating simplicity. With regard to broad and fair distribution, the plan definitely must restrict the spending of the average man, but, on the other hand, it should be so framed as to avoid regressive features such as are found in the ordinary sales tax.

The spendings tax, which in one form or another seems capable of satisfying these requirements remarkably well, provides an example here. It can restrict spending to any desired extent, both by reducing disposable income and also by causing some people to save more of their disposable income and spend less. It can permit exemptions according to family status, and employ the principle of progression in accordance with ability to pay. It can be collected along with the income tax, thus simplifying the administrative problem. Like the income tax, it can in large part be withheld at the source on a current or short-interval basis, thus allowing the brakes to be applied to consumer spending, and again released, without any loss of time.

A point requiring further analysis, and perhaps some experimentation, is the width of the margin that should be allowed between minimum and maximum levels of aggregate consumer spending. The guarantee should not be so inflexible as to create administrative problems out of all proportion to the gain to be hoped for from elimination of a fractionally small upward pressure on prices. On the other hand, the controlling agency could probably operate quite comfortably with the top limit standing only a very slight percentage above the guaranteed minimum. For example, experience might show that a 2 per cent margin was sufficient. In that case, under the conditions illustrated in Table I, an underwriting of consumer spending at a level of 124 billion dollars would mean that the government would not allow the total to fall below 124 billion or rise above 126.5 billion.

Problems of Administration Connected with an Underwriting Program

9. There would be two main problems of administration involved in carrying out a program of underwriting aggregate consumer spending. First, there would be a problem of *adjusting aggregate employment* to prevent the development of unemployment, which might well necessitate public work projects in spite of the inducement to private production afforded by the guaranteed support of consumer markets, although hardly on anything like the scale required in the absence of this guarantee. Second, there would be a problem of *adjusting aggregate consumer spending* to guaranteed levels, which might well be necessary in spite of full employment, although usually not to the extent that would be required in the absence of full-employment-caused levels of consumer income. Both problems call for flexible administrative control, applied in accordance with policies

established by Congress. The administrative agencies in question should presumably be required to submit reports to Congress at regular intervals.

To maintain full employment, the U. S. Employment Service would require current information on the size of the labor force and the number of persons employed, together with an official definition of the number of persons constituting "normal frictional unemployment." This might be a fixed number (such as 2.25 million) or it might be a number fluctuating seasonally (between 2 and 2.5 million, for example), depending on the rule worked out by experts and approved by Congress. The absolute size of this normal slack in the system would necessarily depend, in part, on the amount of technological development and other change, requiring disemployment and re-employment, going on throughout the country. In part it would depend on decisions previously made as to the amount of effort and money that should be devoted to improving the nation's training and placement services. And, finally, it would depend on how "tight" a labor market was considered workable and desirable. On the last two points the major parties at interest, employers and organized labor, would presumably want to have a voice before action was taken leading to official designation of the number of persons, on record as wanting to work, who could be jobless without creating excess unemployment—*i.e.*, an unemployment situation in the technical or operational sense.

Whenever the Employment Service anticipated the development of unemployment in excess of normal frictional unemployment, it would notify the Federal Works Agency to be ready to start public work projects of some appropriate type in the regions where the unemployment problem was expected to center. This presupposes that an ample shelf of useful public work projects would be in readiness. The shelf should place at least as much emphasis on small as on large projects, to facilitate termination when private employment opportunities again expanded. It should include nonconstruction projects (in the fields of public health, education, research, recreation, conservation, and general public welfare) as well as heavy and light construction items, so as to provide fair opportunities for women and others who cannot or should not be asked to enter the construction industry. It should exclude all such projects as do the community no good and offend the worker's self-respect.

When employment in private production and regular public activities fell short of the total labor force by more than normal frictional unemployment, appropriate public work projects should be started—preferably by state and local units if they were ready to start them. Employment on such projects should be on a par with other local employment so far as concerns wage rates for similar types of work and working conditions. It should also be on a par with other employment in the matter of the number of hours worked per week and per month. An incentive to return to private employment as soon as possible would remain, for many persons, because of the manifest impossibility of using individual skills and meeting individual job preferences on public works even as well as this is ordinarily accomplished elsewhere, and, more generally, because of the uncertainty of job tenure on the fill-in program.

This particular uncertainty should be deliberately fostered, through establishment of the principle of priority for private construction and private work in general. When private employers were ready again to expand employment at locally prevailing rates of pay, *et cetera,* they should be assisted to do so by being assigned prior claims to locally available labor (and equipment and materials), as well as to labor available on a voluntary basis through interregional clearance. In other words, the Employment Service should be kept informed by private employers of their prospective needs for labor, and at the proper time this agency should give notice to the Federal Works Agency to reduce or terminate its fill-in operations as rapidly as possible consistent with preserving the value of the work already done.

10. The other major administrative problem connected with an underwriting program would involve the Treasury Department, Office of Economic Stabilization, or some other agency set up to administer fiscal policy in the interests of full-employment stability. The agency in question would be charged by Congress with the continuing duty of expanding or contracting aggregate consumer spending power, in accordance with the law, to the extent that might prove necessary to make actual consumer spending correspond to the guarantees previously given. In short, power would have to be delegated to this agency to make distributions of money, and to suspend, increase, or even impose certain taxes under conditions prescribed by Congress.[23] Congress would determine what formulas should be used for expansion and for contraction. The agency in the executive branch would exercise discretion as to the rates of subsidy or tax required to effectuate the policy.

As the basis for action, the executive agency would compare the current rate of consumer spending, as shown by the series prepared by the Department of Commerce on "consumer expenditures for goods and services" (if that were designated the official series) with the "right" rate, derived by

---

[23]Congress might levy the taxes in question, but suspend their application subject to the finding by this agency that it was necessary to carry them into effect (at some rate not in excess of the rate designated by Congress) in order to prevent an excess of consumer spending.

applying appropriate seasonal factors to the guaranteed total for the year. The quarter might be the most convenient unit of time for administrative purposes. A guarantee of 124 billion dollars of consumer spending for the year might mean a norm of 29 billion for the comparatively slack first quarter. If, in fact, consumers were spending at a rate of only 27 billion, the agency would proceed to increase consumer spending power, as prescribed by law, by an amount believed to be at least large enough to make up the 2-billion deficit in spending (*i.e.*, by at least 2.5 billion, if the form of subsidization prescribed appeared to involve an 0.8 marginal propensity to consume). If, on the other hand, consumers were spending at a rate of 31 billion, the agency would order the application of a spendings tax formula, or other formula prescribed for contraction, at rates which in its opinion would effect about a 2-billion reduction. Proceeding thus on a quarterly basis and making due allowance for time-lags, the agency should be able to bring the year's total of consumer spending, as indicated by the best statistics available, up to the minimum required to satisfy the guarantee and yet not above the maximum allowed.

The points just discussed emphasize the kinds of delegation of authority by Congress without which it is difficult to conceive of maintaining stabilized conditions of full employment. In some respects these delegations of authority to the executive branch seem large, as compared with present practice. They appear to be necessary and legitimate means, however, for effectuating policy as laid down by Congress, and the actions of the agencies administering these laws would be circumscribed in kind and limited in extent to the mandatory fulfillment of requirements clearly stated in the laws themselves.

11. Determination of the proper amount of consumer spending in connection with an underwriting program would be a technical matter, presumably left to the executive branch but under policy directions from Congress, involving a number of considerations into some of which this paper will briefly digress but cannot enter in any detail. These considerations have to do with choices between alternative price-level policies, with prospective cost levels, with prospective levels of private capital formation, and with prospective levels of demand on the part of foreigners and the government itself.

A large part of the statistical information suitable for preliminary estimates is provided in the various national income series and related series prepared in the Department of Commerce. In general it may be said that the various statistical estimates that would be required in connection with an underwriting program will have to be made in any case, whatever policies are adopted. It also may be said that the statistical tools available to the government are constantly being improved, but that some over-all framework (such as would be provided by the program under discussion) is indispensable to clarify what statistics are really needed and to bring these series into harmony with each other.

As the over-all productivity of the economy rises with the passage of time, output available for individual consumption also is likely to rise, and thus an increase in aggregate consumer spending is required if the consumer-goods price level is to be free from downward pressure. If consumer spending rises more rapidly than consumption output, prices will tend to go up. If consumer spending falls, remains constant or rises less rapidly than consumption output, prices will tend to fall. Thus, selection of the right trend in the guaranteed rate or amount of consumer spending—the particular trend that would be calculated to effectuate the preferred price-level policy—would require appraisals of trends in man-hour productivity, hours of work, size of the labor force as determined by population changes and other factors, and ratio of individual consumption output to gross product. Selection of the best price-level policy is a matter of some importance although probably not, inside reasonable limits, a major consideration. Inasmuch as the gains associated with price competition do not require a falling price level (since they depend on the relationships among prices and not on the way the average trend is moving), and inasmuch as a stable price level makes for justice between debtors and creditors, tends to discourage speculation, obviates the need to change publicly administered or regulated prices repeatedly to keep them in line with other prices, and simplifies reckoning generally, price-level stability is likely to appear on the whole the best policy, at least in principle. It might, however, be decided on grounds of expediency (which will be examined below) to allow a gradual rise in the price level, notwithstanding the fact that this might tend to require some form of compensatory action to preserve normal relations in foreign trade. But in any event, so far as the underwriting of consumer spending is concerned, the relations may be indicated by saying that, if the volume of consumption output purchased by individual consumers were expected to rise, say, 2 per cent each year, and if it were desired to hold the price level steady, the guaranteed aggregate of consumer spending should also rise 2 per cent annually.

Naturally, the costs of doing business affect the amount of employment that can be induced by any given dollar demand for end-products. Hence spontaneous rises in costs (as opposed to rises "imputed" back to the factors of production after a prior advance in business revenues) would, if they could not be prevented, create the practical necessity for a year-by-year increase in the guaranteed amount of consumer spending sufficient to permit prices to rise without restriction of the volume of production and employment. The question of increases in money rates of wages, which would be of particularly obvious and direct importance in this connection, will be taken up shortly. Similar considerations apply to levels of business taxes; also, perhaps in lesser degree, to interest charges and rent payments; also to financial practices with respect to the allowances for depreciation, obsolescence, and insurance of various kinds which are treated as costs before profit is calculated. Finally, great significance attaches to the degree of unregulated monopoly power exercised by producers, since this affects the amount of production and employment that can be expected in association with a given total amount of net profit—or, stated differently, in association with a given combination of aggregate consumer demand and aggregate business cost. For example, if 124 billion dollars of consumer demand were sufficient to induce full employment with the given degree of monopolistic restrictionism in the economy as a whole, this same total of consumer demand would be insufficient for full employment in a situation containing a greater amount of monopolistic restrictionism, and more than sufficient for one characterized by a larger element of free competition.

Turning to the demand side of the picture, it is clear that the size of the aggregate individual consumer spending guarantee requisite to induce full employment at a given price level would be fundamentally affected by the volume of output not sold to individual consumers—*i.e.*, by the volume of output marketed domestically but paid for by business or the government,[24] and by the volume of output paid for by foreigners. In addition, if spending were defined as including only transfers of cash, allowance would have to be made for expansions and contractions of consumer credit, which equally affect the marketing of, and hence the inducement to produce, consumption output, notably in the important industries producing consumer durables. As a practical matter, this last question is taken care of by the technical characteristics of the series on consumer expenditures for goods and services issued by the Department of Commerce, which measures the full value of output purchased on open credit and installment accounts rather than the current payments of cash on account of such items.[25]

Like private domestic capital expenditures, the government's expenditures for goods and services, whether for war or for peace, obviate the need

---

[24] Also any self-subsistence production not otherwise allowed for.

[25] Hence, net increases in consumer credit outstanding are treated as consumer dissaving. (Money paid by consumers to buy residences is regarded as an element of saving, the houses themselves being treated as capital goods.) It should be noted that within a certain range the government could adjust total consumer spending (as defined in practice) toward guaranteed levels by restricting or encouraging the extension of new consumer credit. A progressive expansion of consumer indebtedness on a large scale would, however, hardly be desirable.

for a corresponding volume of individual consumer expenditure. Payments by foreigners for American goods have a similar effect, this effect presumably corresponding rather closely to the magnitude of the item, net export of goods and services (or net change in foreign claims), as included in statistics of private gross capital formation. If experience should show that these quantities were peculiarly hard to estimate in advance, it would be possible to ease the difficulty, without sacrifice of the essential principle involved in the guarantee, by making the amount of the guarantee contingent upon the realization of specified magnitudes of government purchases or net exports or both, the final total of individual consumer spending, however, to be subject to changes that would offset unexpected changes in these specified magnitudes. This safeguard would probably be unnecessary although in the case of government expenditures for goods and services there might be an ulterior advantage in such an arrangement, since it would provide a technical loophole in case the agency charged with adjusting aggregate consumer spending miscalculated the propensity to consume to such an extent that it failed to bring aggregate consumer spending within the prescribed limits by the end of the year.[26]

12. In the immediate demobilization period we face the twin dangers of unemployment on the one hand and price inflation on the other. In this situation the government should do everything possible to expand civilian production, which will raise income payments, and at the same time do everything possible to hold consumer spending down to the level of the available consumption output. An underwriting program would help solve both parts of this problem.

At the production end, the ultimate limits to what can be done all at once will be the limits imposed by stubborn physical facts—the time required to re-tool plants, re-assemble materials and skilled labor, re-schedule production, re-build distributive organizations, and so forth. In spite of voluntary withdrawals from the labor force, the chances are certainly all against our escaping unemployment in the early months after the war, except on the basis of a sizeable program of public work projects. In this particular period, in the face of rapid military and industrial demobilization, fill-in public employment will be needed because of the sheer impossibility of bringing private industry into full-scale operation immediately, even if the effective demand for products appears to be virtually limitless. At the same time, if sound plans are made in advance, this necessity can be converted into a real opportunity to start clearing away our slums and filling accumulated deficits in construction items and services of various kinds.

---

[26]*Cf.* discussion of a closely related point in section 13.

As a matter of fact, however, what is likely to happen, in the absence of definite assurance that a slump in national income and buying power is not going to follow a year or two later, is that private enterprise will look to the storm beyond the horizon and refrain from placing orders with the capital goods department of the economy. Even the current production of consumers' goods may suffer some jolts, if the general public, with its current income reduced[27] and further trouble apparently looming ahead, spends more cautiously than had been expected. If these situations should be permitted to develop, then obviously the attainment of full employment would require a far larger volume of public works than would be called for by the irreducible strains, lags, and frictions connected with transferring the economy from a war to a peace basis. What might be hoped for from an underwriting program would be a limitation of public works to the necessary minimum, as a result of the assurance given to private enterprise and consumers alike that buying power would remain ample and firm indefinitely.

For purposes of illustration, we might assume that the rate of output possible under full employment six months after the war, measured in average prices for the first half of 1943, would be 160 billion (see Table II).[28] Under an underwriting program, this gross national product might be built up as follows: normal government expenditures for goods and services, 31 billion, including armaments not yet fully tapered off and programs of housing, health, education, and conservation not yet fully expanded to their peacetime levels, and including a sizeable lend-lease program of exports for relief and rehabilitation; supplementary public program, 10 billion; private gross capital expenditures, including some replenishing of inventories, 19 billion; and consumption output, 100 billion. If income payments, including any special termination allowances to servicemen and war workers, were running at this time at a rate of 128 billion figured on an annual basis, and ordinary direct personal taxes at a rate of 10 billion,[29] current operations would be making disposable income available at a rate of 118 billion. Assured of future incomes, consumers might cash and spend their war savings at a rate of 10 billion a

[27]For example, factory workers who *keep* their jobs will take home 23 per cent less money when hours of work are cut from 48 (with time-and-a-half for overtime) down to 40, assuming that hourly rates remain unchanged.

[28]*Cf.* Table I. Experience following the last war suggests that a decline in efficiency may be expected at this time, irrespective of the level of employment.

[29]This might include certain back taxes deferred to servicemen during the war, while the net total might take into account a small offset for Victory tax refunds not previously claimed.

TABLE II.—HYPOTHETICAL POST-WAR OUTPUT AND CONSUMER INCOME, SAVING, AND SPENDING TOTALS UNDER CONDITIONS OF FULL EMPLOYMENT VIA UNDERWRITING APPROACH, ASSUMING END OF WAR IN DECEMBER, 1944
(in prices of January-June, 1943)

Item		Mid-1945 (annual rate)	1950
		(in billions)	
Gross national product		$160	$184
public investment fill-in		10	— [a]
Value of consumption output		100	137
Income payments		128	150
Disposable income		118	144
Net individual savings:	unadjusted	4	12
	adjusted	4[b]	13.25[c]
Consumer spending:	unadjusted	114	132
	adjusted	102[b]	137[c]

[a]Assumed not needed; *cf.* discussion in connection with Table 1, column 1.
[b]Assumes a 12-billion supplementary tax on consumers, with savings unaffected.
[c]Assumes a consumption subsidy of 6.25 billion, 4/5 of this being spent and 1/5 saved.

year, which would reduce their net rate of saving to perhaps 4 billion,[30] leaving the unadjusted rate of consumer spending at 114 billion—14 billion in excess of the consumption output made available by the incompletely converted production system. In this situation, a special spendings tax designed to raise 12 billion dollars a year, imposed by the fiscal agency designated by Congress, would immediately bring the actual rate of consumer spending below the established maximum, assuming a 2 per cent margin between minimum and maximum limits.[31]

To illustrate certain other points mentioned in the foregoing discussion, hypothetical figures may be considered for the year 1950, treated as the sixth year after the end of hostilities. At prices prevailing in the first half of 1943, a full-employment gross national product might amount to 184 billion, assuming a 2 per cent increase in over-all productivity (due partly to growth in labor force and partly to greater output per worker) compounded year by year from 1946. Government expenditures for goods and services might be 27 billion. For the sake of the argument we might assume that a negative trade balance had begun to develop, holding private gross capital expenditures down to 20 billion, and that the value of con-

[30]Savings in this period might be reduced by a net expansion of outstanding installment credit, furthered to some extent by "lay-away" plans undertaken during the war; back payments by ex-servicemen on installment purchases and life insurance would have the opposite effect.

[31]Actually, if circumstances were normal, a smaller tax would be sufficient, because such a tax would increase the ratio of saving to spending. Furthermore, in view of the expansion of consumption output expected later in the first post-war year, it might not be considered necessary to reduce current spending enough to secure a mid-year balance.

sumption output, reflecting this shift away from production for foreign markets, would stand at 137 billion. Income payments, assuming a reduced rate of accumulation of undistributed corporate profits and a balance restored between income distributed by production and income received by consumers, might amount to 150 billion. With direct personal taxes at 6 billion and net individual savings—no longer reduced by the cashing of war savings but lowered considerably as the result of elimination of the cyclical pattern which in the past has brought unusually high profit incomes and hence high savings at times of relatively full employment—at 12 billion, unadjusted consumer spending would be 132 billion. In these circumstances, as shown in Table II, direct subsidization of consumption costing the government somewhat in excess of 5 billion would restore the balance between consumer spending and the value of consumption output.

13. The inference that an effective program for limiting as well as supporting aggregate consumer spending would prevent price inflation is subject to this critical comment, that influences from the supply side might send prices up even with demand held at predetermined levels. Indeed, the very fact that under the underwriting program aggregate consumer spending would not be allowed to fall below the guaranteed minimum would in itself tend to support and necessitate rising prices if private production for market were unexpectedly curtailed in the face of the guarantee. This might happen, for example, as the result of business combinations in restraint of trade. It might also happen as the result of strong upward pressure on money wage rates, if the rates rose far enough to reduce profits below prevailing competitive levels.

The underlying problem is, of course, the danger of an upward wage-price spiral, which *would not be caused by the underwriting program* since the same danger is present in *any* situation in which full employment is attained or even approached. If wage rates rise, income payments and consumer spending will also tend to rise if the government has a full-employment policy and absorbs any displaced workers into an expanded public work program. Under close inspection, therefore, it appears that any inflationary pressure associated with the underwriting program would probably be *less* than what would be experienced in the absence of an enforced top limit on aggregate consumer spending, although it would be greater than what would be experienced if the top limit were arbitrarily lowered as private consumption output fell off.

This consideration immediately suggests that the guaranteed amount might be made contingent upon realization of at least the expected volume of consumption output—which reintroduces a question raised above when the possibility of changes in the proportions between government-purchased output and ordinary consumption output was approached from the standpoint of unforeseen spontaneous changes in the government component. At the moment, this modification would hardly seem to the writer to be necessary, or even desirable if it would have to be presented in a way that appeared to weaken the guarantee. A safeguard against such contingencies might perhaps better be sought along the lines of having the government sell some of its own additional output direct to consumers—for example, by charging for various services—or sell them certain surplus stocks accumulated during the war, and thereby restore the supply of goods and services sold to consumers rather than cut down the consumer spending.

The danger of the wage-price or price-wage spiral has to be faced resolutely and realistically in any case, unless full employment itself is deliberately avoided. A program of underwriting consumer spending should prove a positive asset in this connection, since by judicious management it could be made to yield to the upward pressure just enough to enable it to resist and prevent really serious dislocations. The known existence of a top limit on consumer spending would have publicity value in connection with deliberations concerning the advisabilty of increases in particular production costs, including collective bargaining conferences to adjust particular money rates of wages. Where increases in such costs appeared in advance to be desirable or inevitable, this would be taken into account in deciding upon the dollar amount of spending to be guaranteed for the ensuing year. In other words, a slight increase in spending and prices could be allowed.

Advantages of the Underwriting Approach

14. A number of the advantages that government underwriting of aggregate consumer spending might have, as an instrument to help effectuate full-employment policy, may be briefly reviewed at this point.

In the first place, such an approach would emphasize individual consumer choice and sovereignty, which is another way of saying that it would let consumers buy all the goods and services that our economy could produce for them, after taking care of genuine investment needs, and would let them decide by their own preferences what kinds of goods and services ought to be produced in greater quantities. Practically everyone agrees that consumption should be expanded (relatively as well as absolutely) if possible; and although it is definitely arguable that there may be numerous cases in which community consumption paid for out of tax money has social advantages over individualized consumption, at the moment the burden of proof is still on community consumption. It is a noteworthy fact that economists who advocate the public investment approach are themselves for the most part agreed that a greater emphasis on consumption would be desirable if it could only be brought about. But since they do not feel that this could be done, short of fundamental institutional changes over a long period of time, their analysis and recommendations have a somewhat pessimistic tone.

In the second place, the approach by way of guaranteed consumer spending would hold definite advantages for the business man and the farmer. The potential stimulus to the retailer and producer of consumer goods is particularly obvious. But the effect would not end there; the producer of capital goods should also derive some benefit. For example, a manufacturer considering whether or not to buy new equipment would be aware that the market in which the products from that equipment would be sold would not be subject to periodic collapse for reasons of general underspending. Hence he would tend to go ahead, if other circumstances were favorable, and place his order with the maker of the equipment. It may be a debatable question whether in the past the speculative risks introduced by the business cycle have not given us more capital formation in the long run rather than less. On the other hand, elimination of the business cycle on the basis of establishment of continuing full production and employment should stimulate private capital formation, not attributable to this particular form of speculation, up to the level required by the economy. It should render a further benefit by reducing the amplitude of fluctuations in the industries concerned.

A third advantage of the underwriting technique, applied to the over-all consumer market, would be that it would maintain the conditions in which competition would have all the scope possible under modern conditions of mass production. Unlike the proposals sometimes advanced for establishing and underwriting quotas for particular industries or particular producers, it would refrain from guaranteeing anything to any particular industry or producer but instead would assure private enterprise that full-employment levels of production would return a fair profit when averaged over the whole. Thus it would encourage flexibility rather than promote industry-by-industry stratification.

A fourth major consideration is that the underwriting of aggregate consumer spending would, on the one hand, not require unnecessary government actions and, on the other hand, not conflict with other beneficial programs. It seems unwise to count on accumulated war savings to create adequate consumer spending for any protracted period after the war, *but if in fact they do so, then the underwriting would not require any government spending to make it good.* As far as reforms are concerned, no valuable change would be impeded. Selective revision of tax laws to make them more encouraging to enterprise would still be highly desirable; if accomplished, the incidental effect on the underwriting program would be to reduce somewhat the size of the necessary consumption guarantee.[32] Small business would still stand in need of better capital and credit facilities, and sound legislation along these lines might again, to some slight extent, reduce the guarantee requirements. Adequate investment programs in the fields of slum clearance and housing, health, education, and conservation of natural resources, and in any other fields, including areas of community consumption, in which such programs can really stand on their merits, would still have all their original value. If put into effect, they would reduce the volume of ordinary consumption output, and thus again would limit the size of the guarantee necessary and possible for aggregate individual consumption. Adequate social security benefits and elimination of regressive taxes would also still be matters of the greatest importance. As progress was made along these lines, probably raising income payments and certainly reducing net individual savings, subsidization of consumption out of the public treasury to fulfill the guarantee of consumer spending would tend to become less necessary.

Thus, the relation between the underwriting approach and all the progressive programs that command substantial followings is not primarily one of substitution but rather one of mutual assistance. Underwriting would provide immediately such support for consumption as is required to permit the economy to operate at full-employment levels without fundamentally changing its production characteristics. In other words, it would secure immediate adjustability pending fundamental long-run adjustments that, when fiually made, might largely eliminate the need for the underwriting apparatus. The long-run adjustments in question are those increases in personal security and modifications in the distribution of income, and those changes in public and private practice with respect to accumulation of insurance reserves, and in corporate practice with respect to reten-

---

[32]The same kind of effect would be produced if, as is sometimes suggested, primary stress were laid on the reduction of business taxes in general. This would not alter the case with respect to underwriting, but it would substantially reduce business cost, and hence also the appropriate total of consumer spending. Assuming a full-employment national income valued at 140 billion dollars (say, in 1946; *cf.* Table I), gross national product with lowered business taxes would be less than 170 billion, and the value of consumption output less than 124 billion. But the question of how much this would narrow the gap between unadjusted consumer spending and the value of consumption output would depend on how much additional business and individual saving would result from the tax reduction, since this would determine how much less unadjusted consumer spending would be forthcoming at the same (140 billion) level of national income. So far as the budget is concerned, the government would doubtless incur less expense on account of consumer subsidies needed to make good the guarantee, but, on the other hand, it would lose tax revenue.

tion of earnings, that are necessary before a "natural" balance, as between savings and investment at the full-employment level, can be struck.

15. Fifth, an underwriting program might well have advantages over alternative approaches to full employment strictly from the standpoint of fiscal economy. In a previous section it was shown that, if full employment were to be achieved in an over-saving situation by a program of compensatory public investment, the cost to the government could be slightly lower under optimum conditions than the cost of a consumption subsidy associated with an underwriting program, but that in practice it might well be higher rather than lower.[33] To the extent that underwriting eliminated the need for public investment fill-in that would otherwise be required—including what might be required as additional offset to any curtailment of private investment attributable to use of the public investment approach—underwriting would save the government money. To the extent that over-saving out of full-employment levels of income—including any additional saving out of the consumption subsidy itself—required the payment of money to consumers that would not be paid under the public investment program, underwriting would add to the cost of government. A careful weighing of these pros and cons would probably not establish underwriting as likely to be the more expensive approach from the outset.

But the case need not be allowed to rest there. Quite aside from the tendency that continuous full employment would have, by whatever method it might have been achieved, to promote greater equality of incomes and hence smaller total savings, the underwriting approach would appear to have certain characteristics peculiarly likely to reduce the strain on the budget over the course of time. Since it would sharply separate the two halves of the problem—first, the reaction of private-employment levels to an environment judged to be adequate to support full employment; second, the ratio between saving and spending out of full-employment-caused income—it would tend to throw the spotlight of publicity on the causes for government expense with an accuracy not ordinarily obtainable. This should broaden and strengthen the campaigns to eliminate these causes, whether they were monopolistic restrictions on production and incentive-destroying business taxes on the one hand, or regressive consumer taxes and needless institutional saving on the other. Undoubtedly, cost reductions could thereby be brought about. At least equally important is the other consideration that, once the underwriting program was in force, it would thus tend to harness the drive for budgetary economy to the realization of a better general balance—and not merely a better financial balance

[33]See Table I in section 7 and accompanying discussion.

—than our economic system now possesses. In other words, underwriting would not only not conflict with other beneficial changes, and not only effect essential adjustments quickly before it became possible to make these other changes, but would also in an indirect way tend to assist in getting these changes made.

16. A sixth advantage of a full-employment program involving the underwriting of aggregate consumer spending is that it would provide a sound basis for a liberal foreign economic policy. The ability to maintain full employment by domestic adjustments, regardless of the state of the foreign trade balance, is the first prerequisite for securing a continuously ample volume of a country's foreign trade in general and, in particular, the relaxation of trade restrictions, with resulting enhancement of world security and benefit to the domestic standard of living through encouragement to worth-while international specialization. A nation liable to depressions is sooner or later bound to adopt illiberal foreign policies such as high tariffs, export subsidies, harsh immigration laws, exploitation (if the nation is powerful) of low-cost foreign sources of raw materials, and aggressive currency devaluation, since these expedients promise to secure additional markets and additional employment opportunity for the domestic population.

Among various alternative domestic full-employment programs, one utilizing the underwriting technique would evidently have a natural affinity for liberalism in international trade. Perhaps it may be said that it would be as least as favorable as any other domestic program to the kind of international arrangements contemplated in Article VII of the Mutual Aid agreements, since it would have no tendency to strengthen vested interests in any particular industries. As to the matter of mechanics, it would, as previously noted, preserve the over-all size of the market for the products of domestic enterprise by providing for automatic expansion of aggregate domestic consumer spending when the net export balance declined (or the net import balance increased) and for automatic contraction of aggregate domestic consumer spending when the net export balance increased (or the net import balance declined).[34] Thus, it would sensitively adjust to any state of the trade balance, including a negative balance such as would be associated with the repayment of foreign loans. Incidentally, since the consumer spending total would be somewhat smaller when exports exceeded imports than when exports equalled imports, and since it would be at its largest when imports exceeded exports, the public would have a

[34] See section 11.

graphic demonstration of the fact that imports rather than exports are what raise the standard of living.

17. A seventh major advantage of the underwriting technique is its reversibility; as noted, it would guard against inflationary excesses of consumer spending as well as against too little consumer spending. With this is closely linked its special applicability in the immediate demobilization period. The inflationary possibilities inherent in a situation in which current income payments may be supplemented on a large scale by the cashing of savings accumulated during the war, while support for rationing and price controls becomes doubtful and the flow of output has not yet achieved its full dimensions, are generally appreciated. What the underwriting technique would permit is a matching of aggregate consumer spending with the aggregate value of consumption output all along the line—90 billion against 90 billion, 100 against 100, 110 against 110, and so on up.

This introduces a final consideration that might well be of immediate interest today. An advance decision to underwrite consumer spending after the war as a continuing policy would be an indication to the American people that their government not only was interested in eliminating an inflationary gap during the war and for as long after the war as might prove to be necessary, but that it was equally interested in eliminating a deflationary gap thereafter. The term "deflationary gap" deserves a moment's thought. It might refer to a deficiency of consumer spending as against whatever happened to be the current volume of consumption output. The deflationary gap provided against by an underwriting program, however, would be a deficiency of consumer spending measured against the *largest volume of consumption output deliverable at the time, under full-employment conditions.* Emphasis on this central feature of a post-war underwriting program would establish more firmly in the public mind the rational basis of wartime fiscal policies, since it would indicate that the government was concerned at all times with having the public spend up to the limit of whatever goods and services could be made available to it but not any greater amount. This might appeal to the public as a rather sensible idea. In short, it is not altogether improbable that a decision to apply an underwriting program after the war would make it easier to combat inflation during the war.

The Problem as a Whole

18. Lest criticism fasten on minor details and neglect the basic difficulties connected with the program herein discussed, full emphasis should now be placed upon those difficulties. In the first place, the underwriting of aggregate consumer spending would be hard to justify in the absence of an

established policy to give jobs on public work projects to persons who might remain involuntarily idle in spite of the inducement afforded to private enterprise by the guarantee. The underwriting could serve as a pillar of full-employment policy, but in itself it could never take the place of the determination to prevent unemployment. Applied by itself, if such a thing could be imagined, it could involve the government in large expense for consumption subsidies at the very time when men and women were trying in vain to find jobs. This expense would then be challenged as indefensible—with some justice, since it would clearly be better to secure a tangible product in return for the money spent—and the whole policy might under these conditions be condemned as a kind of fiscal sleight of hand.

In the second place, the benefits from underwriting could be rendered rather trivial if restrictions of all kinds on production were allowed to multiply unopposed. A rapid increase in monopolistic restrictions, keeping output down and prices up, could drive the guarantee to great heights and still prevent the attainment of full employment without a heavy fill-in program of public works. Successful application of the underwriting would therefore require an active campaign to enforce competition and control monopoly prices—presumably with stress on the former wherever that alternative was available.

These difficulties should provide sobering food for thought, if such be needed. But it is worth recalling also that the approach to full employment by way of the underwriting of consumer spending would tend to confine government intervention, in the sense of competition, mainly to the capital or money market, where government intervention or competition absolutely cannot be avoided if men and resources are not to be allowed to go out of use. This means that, while it would invite the opposition and other risks that any full-employment program of necessity must encounter, it would escape the further conflicts inherent in programs that raise uncertainty as to who is to be responsible for production. With total consumer spending underwritten at a reasonable level, responsibility for production would be clearly assigned.

7

A PROGRAM TO SUSTAIN OUR ECONOMIC SYSTEM*

The basic employment issue was not created by the war. Nor was lack of security for industry, the farmer, and the worker. Business cycles with their depressions, ruin, and misery have existed since the beginning of the industrial era. The war has, nonetheless, shown us what our economy can do in providing what we once considered incredible expansion, prosperity, and economic security for industry, farmer, and worker—the security and high national income resting upon full employment which in turn rests upon an ample market.

The plan to be outlined was developed with the following goals in mind: (a) full employment, (b) consequent elimination of the business cycle, (c) absence of regimentation, (d) establishment of an ample and expanding market for business to compete for, (e) insured security for industry, farmer, and worker. Briefly, it is suggested that these goals could be reached by underwriting the national consumer income (actually, the total consumer expenditure for goods and services) with much the same results on confidence as are achieved in preventing runs on banks by insuring depositors' accounts.

Thus the proposal looks to having private enterprise itself provide the needed jobs. This probably is the alternative that most Americans would prefer, but it presents difficulties when the stimuli of war or of transient speculative booms are absent. Any attempt to deny these difficulties, or to go further and suggest that laissez faire is what is needed, must be set down as pure politics.

A word about full employment. In the society of the future the right to a job will rank with the right of free speech and other precious rights we consider fundamental to the preservation of human dignity. The right to a job is more than getting an income; it is the right to perform a useful function and to preserve a respected social status. Psychologists, sociologists, and economists agree that long-continued unemployment distorts and destroys human personality.

---

*This paper was awarded one of the $1,000 prizes in an essay contest sponsored by the Pabst Brewing Company in 1944. It was published, under the title "A Program to Underwrite Full Employment," in *The Winning Plans in the Pabst Postwar Employment Awards,* 1944.

The right to a job cannot be assured unless we resolve as a national policy to maintain full employment. This goal does not require that people have jobs who do not want them, or that unemployables be given jobs, or that all others without exception must be employed at a given time. But it does mean that, except for a small, defined quantity of normal frictional or between-jobs unemployment, there are real jobs—jobs that serve a useful purpose and meet prevailing standards as to wage rates, hours, and working conditions—for all persons able and wanting to work.

It is generally recognized that production and employment depend, with us, on the volume of effective demand for output. Strictly speaking, they depend—temporary shortages of equipment and materials aside—on the relation between: effective demand (current and anticipated); production cost (wages, taxes, interest, depreciation, etc.); and the degree of monopolistic restrictionism (or tendency to limit output to increase price and profit). In addition they may be affected by business optimism or pessimism. But chief stress belongs on current and expected demand, because this is the factor that society can most promptly adjust up or down; moreover business expansion and contraction, and new business ventures, seem particularly responsive to the revenue side of the equation.

Savings do not create demand until they are invested. Thus the savings-investment relation is central. Furthermore, there now appears to be a general tendency for the savings that accrue at full employment to exceed the available profitable investment opportunities. Hence total demand—for consumer goods plus capital goods—tends to fall below the level required to secure or maintain full production. The solution frequently proposed is that, pending adjustments toward a better natural balance, we high-pressure private investment and fill the remaining gap with public investment.

However, conceding that we are not yet investment-saturated, neither are we investment-starved. Also, although our capital-goods industries are now expanded, we are not immobilized for all time in particular industries and localities. Most important, we are not likely to create enough jobs through public investment, because of the dilemma of "boondoggling" on the one hand and "government competition" on the other, and because the private-enterprise sector tends to become pessimistic when this policy is pushed to its logical conclusion.

It is therefore suggested here that government instead maintain aggregate consumer spending at the level needed to give jobs in the consumer-goods industries to all who are not employed by "naturally occurring" private investment or "preferred" public investment, and that government *under-*

write this aggregate in advance so as to open the draft on the fires of business enterprise, including capital formation.

Federal, state, and local government would still carry on all public investment considered desirable for its own (rather than employment's) sake. For example, housing, health, education, and conservation of natural resources are so important that public investment should be expanded to any extent required to secure universally high standards in these fields. To the degree that private enterprise cannot be encouraged by low interest rates, incentive taxation, or other legitimate inducements to satisfy requirements, or where it is entirely excluded by the nature of the situation, public investment and, where necessary, public operation should be extended.

Moreover, government would also originate employment projects, drawn from a well-stocked, diversified shelf of useful, planned undertakings, whenever a temporary lag in private construction or some other circumstance (such as incomplete reconversion) made this necessary for full employment in spite of the assurance of customers for private enterprise in general. The underwriting would thus apply to employment as well as to consumer spending. Indeed, the only purpose of underwriting consumer spending at all would be to have a larger share of the full employment in normal enterprise, leaving less to be supplied by fill-in projects.

Then, finally, supposing the consumer money income flowing from full-employment production (from wages and salaries, rents, interest, profits, and also social security benefits, etc.) brought about less than or more than the guaranteed consumer spending, which could happen as the result of either too much or too little saving, government would subsidize or tax consumption directly to prevent spending from falling below the guarantee or rising more than a stipulated amount above it.

This constitutes the core of the proposal for maintenance of effective demand, and the distinguishing feature of the proposal as a whole. Its detailed application is a matter in which there are numerous options. What requires particular emphasis, however, is not the detail but the way the main prinicples—on (a) government underwriting of total consumer spending, (b) private and normal public investment, (c) fill-in public works, (d) financing of public expenditures, and (e) control of monopoly prices—are linked together.

Excessive prices restrict production and employment in spite of the demand, besides limiting progress and fostering concentrations of wealth. Fiscal measures would therefore be greatly aided by an active campaign to enforce competition and control monopoly prices—presumably with stress on the former wherever that alternative was available. In this connection we need prompt settlement of subcontractors' claims, wise war plant and surplus disposal policies, patent reform, better capital and credit facilities for small business, grade labeling, vigorous antitrust action. The further growth of cooperatives would also assist. For monopolies that are here to stay, prices should be fixed by commissions, or controlled indirectly if methods can be devised to give management incentives for expansion.

With respect to the public-works regulator, the first requirement is a decision on normal frictional unemployment—some fixed amount (for example, 2 million) or a seasonally varying figure. Experience with "loose" and "tight" labor markets should suggest the range within which a compromise fair to both workers and employers can be struck. The Employment Service—which must be greatly strengthened against demobilization—can then know when to signal the agency responsible for starting and stopping public work projects.

To avoid inflationary and deflationary gaps, the agency estimating for the consumer spending guarantee would calculate trends in productivity, deduct for private investment and output purchased by government, and adjust for expected changes in wage rates, business taxes, other production costs, and profits. This technique offers an additional instrument, operating through publicity, for combating the wage-price spiral feared in connection with full-employment situations. In calculating, the guarantee would be raised when the export balance was declining and vice versa, so that reliance would not have to be placed on exports to sustain the over-all level of domestic employment.

For ability to adjust total consumer income in either direction, as required by deviations of currently recorded consumer spending rates from guaranteed rates, administrative discretion would be necessary, based on policies established by Congress. The law would perhaps call for application of a spendings tax, for example, against excessive spending; the demobilization period might bring this into play, especially if rationing controls were lifted immediately.

A number of factors including minimum-wage, social security, and progressive tax laws, highly desirable in themselves, can eventually be expected to minimize the underspending tendency. In the near future, however, the underwriting would usually require consumption subsidies. It is suggested that, after exploring the practical limits of timing the redemption of war bonds and rebating selected taxes, the government bridge any remaining gap with outright "national income security payments," distributing these (through the post office or otherwise) on some share-alike basis to all families and single persons. This would be equitable and would result in the spending of a high percentage of the total subsidy. And the subsidization under these circumstances could hardly be impugned as an inferior substitute for payments for useful work, being actually required to neutralize oversaving in a situation with everyone already at work.

The financing of this program—consumption subsidies and work projects as needed—would be self-defeating if it involved taxes that reduced purchasing power, increased business costs, or penalized genuine enterprise. Uninvested (hoarded) savings, however, could be tapped without detriment to production or infringement of legitimate rights, thus using the existing money supply to the full and avoiding needless creation of new money. A penalty tax on "excess" demand deposit balances and currency, but with option to the holder of buying special low- or zero-interest government securities, would stimulate private investment and spending, and to that extent obviate subsidies and projects, as well as bring money into the Treasury. Additional amounts needed to sustain production could perhaps most readily be borrowed at low rates from the banking system.

Any other full-employment program would encounter similar financing problems. The underwriting plan would probably be less expensive than the public investment approach. To begin with, the extra cost of the latter due to larger volume of projects—increased by the discouraging effect on business of the public investment approach itself—might well be greater than the cost of consumption subsidies required to neutralize underspending of full-employment income. Moreover, the underwriting procedure would throw the spotlight on monopolistic restrictionism and over-saving as causes for necessary expense, and should therefore hasten the removal of those causes.

A full-employment program must be essentially "shockproof" in relation to foreign trade. As noted, the underwriting procedure would free our economy of dependence on a "favorable" trade balance. A further requirement is that exchange rates be not held rigid. In addition, the greater the predictability of our foreign trade, the better, so that our industry and agriculture may avoid needless dislocations and frictional unemployment.

For our part, we should take fullest advantage of opportunities to raise the American standard of living and promote world security through beneficial foreign investments and relaxation of trade restrictions. Receding prosperity, however, develops an enormous pressure for tariffs and export subsidies—for all measures that restrict, preempt, and exclude. Only if we are secure in our ability to maintain full employment will we, in fact, avoid the rise of policies that deny the spirit of international cooperation and undermine the hope of lasting peace.

8

CRITICAL NOTES ON CERTAIN PROPOSALS

I am somewhat puzzled as to whether Dr. Morris A. Copeland* thinks the problem of full and stable employment can be solved, inasmuch as his paper includes references to the "certainty of general unemployment," the "likelihood" of as much unemployment as in the interwar decades, etc. Surely by now we can agree that it must be solved, and get on to studying the implications of the alternative solutions. Dr. Copeland submits that we probably cannot afford the waste of unemployment, especially because of competition from the Soviet Union. But the case should be put even more strongly. If any considerable unemployment develops in the United States, the resulting pressures will not only poison our whole relation with the Soviet Union, unsettle Anglo-American intercourse, and give a somewhat sinister tone to our foreign relations generally, but will also dangerously intensify group conflicts here at home.

With much of Dr. Copeland's diagnosis of the problem I am in cordial agreement. Deferred demand cannot provide a full solution. Stabilization of employment is not enough, since the stabilization point might lie below full employment. (Hence, incidentally, we need more than cycle theory in the strict sense to cope with this question.) Certain recent changes have affected the general economic environment in ways that make it more difficult to avoid unemployment; for example, the passing of the frontier, the loss of rural semi-self sufficiency, growing cost inflexibilities, a shift toward more replacement and less innovation in our capital formation. On the other side, as he points out, such developments as the SEC, FDIC, and unemployment compensation now tend at least to keep the bottom from falling out entirely.

Dr. Copeland's estimate of the numerical magnitude of the postwar labor reabsorption problem seems about right. Possibly he is a little on the high side when he speaks of 12 million more than after World War I. At any rate we might in favorable circumstances find that our problem con-

*This discussion of a paper by Dr. Morris A. Copeland entitled "How Achieve Full and Stable Employment" was presented at the annual meeting of the American Economic Association held in Washington in January, 1944, and was published in the *American Economic Review: Papers and Proceedings*, March, 1944.

sisted, in net terms, of 5 million dismissed from manufacturing, 1½ to 2 million from government service, and 9 million from the Army and Navy —or, say, a net total of 16 million before deducting several million who might return to college, the home, etc.

On the other hand, I feel that Dr. Copeland may have underestimated the real difficulty of achieving his initial period of "relatively buoyant business." Of course this is bound to depend in very large degree on whether the war ends abruptly or tapers off in such a way as to permit considerable reconversion to take place before the armistice. The extent to which export markets will be bolstered by foreign lending is another important question to which no answer is as yet available. Recognizing that these unknowns make any statement likely to turn out wrong, and agreeing with Dr. Copeland that boom tendencies will undoubtedly appear as a result of war savings and deferred demand, I am still by no means confident that these boom tendencies in certain markets will be generalized throughout the economy. The parallel with World War I has this important qualification, that this time we had 8 or 9 million unemployed before the war came along. Moreover, although the accumulated savings this time are very much greater, it should be recalled that, when factory hours are cut from 48 to 40 with overtime eliminated, a factory worker will take about 23 per cent less pay home at the end of the week (assuming he keeps his job at constant hourly rates and is not among the 5 million squeezed out by demobilization of war production), which raises some question about the ready spending of any savings that he, at least, may have salted away.

Dr. Copeland's recommendations with respect to selective controls—notably, to dampen fluctuations in durables, construction, and inventories, and to prevent development of unsound financial structures—certainly deserve serious consideration. I shall limit my comments here to three suggestions. First, more stress might well have been laid on the necessity to combat monopolistic price restrictions. Second—and I shall return to this in a moment—it may be that, in spite of the undoubted necessity for certain selective or particularistic controls, the problem of selective controls in general would become somewhat less important if our over-all or general economic controls were adequate. Third, such individualized control as is implied by Dr. Copeland's plea for a "firming up" of businessmen's plans, to the end that we can be sure these plans will be carried out, seems to me something of an anomaly in a program that in other respects envisages minimum interference with private enterprise. Will not the businessman hesitate to sign on the dotted line? Or, if he has to submit his plan, and knows that he must keep it "firm," why should he commit himself to more than a cautious minimum?

The most important issues of all are those connected with the over-all controls, or general system of measures to sustain and stabilize employment. Dr. Copeland proposes that we combine a system of incentives and checks with compensatory public expenditures. Identifying the latter to all intents and purposes with construction and other public employment projects, and pointing out the necessity for an ample shelf of ready projects, central control over timing, and a system of budgeting by short time-periods, he calls attention to the difficulty of finding enough projects—outside of "make-work" categories—even assuming that state and local projects are properly coordinated as to timing and that the common carriers and public utilities are nationalized. This leads him to stress the importance of the checks and stimulants, to minimize the necessity for projects. He would apply these checks and stimulants, however, to the stabilization of specific forms of business fluctuation; for example, to the utilities, or the automobile industry.

I should like to suggest that this problem can be better solved by having the government underwrite aggregate consumer spending, thus leaving the individual industries free to compete for a market sufficient to maintain a normal profit on the average at levels of operation that add up to national full employment. Time is lacking to discuss this proposal at length, but in essence its effect on public expenditures for actual production would be to limit them to investment expenditures considered worth while for their own (rather than employment's) sake, plus expenditures for fill-in projects when and as required in spite of existence of the inducement to private enterprise afforded by the over-all guarantee of effective demand in the private consumer market. This arrangement would avoid the difficulties of a massive (and, in principle, unlimited) public investment program, which would be likely to require uneconomical allocations of labor and other resources and would almost certainly not prove feasible politically. Definition in quantitative terms of normal frictional unemployment would be necessary, as for any full-employment program. Administrative control over subsidies and taxes, for adjustment of total consumer spending up or down, would probably be required, as suggested by Dr. Copeland in another connection. It should be noted, however, that consumption subsidies would be called for only in case of oversaving, and would not be needed if the optimists to whom Dr. Copeland refers are right in supposing that adequate demand will be forthcoming automatically.

Dr. Arthur R. Upgren's very stimulating paper on "Objectives and Guides to Policy"* has a range and depth entitling it to much more extensive review than can be given here. In the main I shall confine myself to certain issues posed by the way in which he states his objectives.

Many differences of opinion about policy proposals evidently depend upon the fact that one school of thought conceives of the objective as a large output while another thinks in terms of assured full employment. Obviously for many practical purposes the two schools find themselves in agreement. But this does not make the distinction academic. Attainment of some objective other than full employment (*e.g.*, a specified volume of gross national product) is likely to leave a substantially larger number unemployed than normal turnover requires; furthermore, objectives defined in dollars, physical output, etc., may be more readily compromised whenever they become difficult to attain. But if universal employment opportunity is not maintained, then a personal right with profound intrinsic significance will have been denied, and society moreover may expect mounting social tensions connected with job discrimination, and strain in our international relations connected with our effort to export and not import. Certainly all this might happen while unemployment still stood below the 10 per cent level (say, 6 million persons) at which Dr. Upgren would have the government apply decisive measures to prevent further deterioration.

Dr. Upgren is right, I believe, in stressing the difficulty of achieving a satisfactory solution, as well as the importance of attacking unemployment through "*general* measures" and avoiding "planning either in fulsome detail or 'at any price.' " He rightly emphasizes the necessity of keeping in mind a whole series of major objectives—involving gross national product, prices, productivity, and wage policy as well as employment—and the desirability of setting quantitative goals in each case. Two questions arise, however: (1) must it be inferred that a real full employment program requires excessively detailed planning and the sacrifice of other, comparably important values? and (2) are the several quantitative indicators mentioned by Dr. Upgren all of equal significance for operating purposes, as would almost appear to be implied in his discussion? I believe that the right answer is "no" in each case.

There is good hope that full employment can be maintained without an excess of detailed planning and intervention by the government, because properly constructed fiscal policies, aimed at maintaining demand and coordinated with advance guarantees, can minimize the necessity for direct

*Dr. Upgren's paper and the following discussion of it, as well as the paper by Paul G. Hoffman which is discussed herein, were prepared for the fifty-seventh annual meeting of the American Economic Association. The meeting was canceled because of the war, but the papers in question were published in the *American Economic Review: Papers and Proceedings,* May, 1945.

interferences with business. While in recent years many writers in advocating fiscal measures have paid too little attention to the individual rigidities and restrictions that constitute the other great problem area, nevertheless continued assurance of a high level of demand could well make all the difference between possible success and inevitable failure in tempering these rigidities and restrictions without extravagant doses of compulsion. Why should a deflationary decline in demand (or an inflationary increase in demand) be permitted to take place at all? Of course care needs to be exercised that a sufficiently large part of the total demand occurs in regular private markets, since otherwise full employment will not be maintained without unduly large amounts of direct job provision by the government.

Hence presumably government should underwrite total consumer spending as well as total employment, thus supporting the production of consumer goods and, indirectly, sustaining private investment. Remaining variations in private investment could then be offset by opposite variations in public investment, thereby creating approximate stability in the construction industry. The number of supplementary jobs the government would have to give would be lessened because of the adequate market demand for private output. (Dr. Upgren, incidentally, refers to job underwriting as though it were synonymous with job provision, which surely it is not, even in the absence of consumption underwriting.) The amount of direct support the government would have to give to individual consumer demand, through tax offsets or through distributions of extra purchasing power, would be no greater than required to cancel the effects of oversaving, since there would already be a volume of disposable income derived from full employment.

With such a policy in force, no undue burden need be placed on gross national product (expenditure) statistics —which sometimes seem about to be saddled by advocates of full employment with almost overwhelming responsibilities. An advance estimate of gross national expenditures at full employment would be used for deriving the size or range of total consumer spending to be underwritten, but any final adjustments required to maintain full employment as administratively defined would be made directly in jobs, not in dollars. Thus there would be two main indexes actually used for operating purposes: (1) employment (or unemployment), and (2) consumer spending. Other elements would tend to fall into place.

Special interest attaches, for this reviewer, to Dr. Upgren's "anti-monopoly - anti-inflation tax"; the promised fuller elucidation will be awaited with keen anticipation. It needs to be decided soon whether it is necessary and feasible to define and identify "monopolies" for tax purposes and lay on them, in return for immunity from antitrust prosecution, a form of tax calculated to promote low prices and expansion of output, or whether a formula such as Dr. Upgren's, applying to all corporations, can be adopted instead without unduly penalizing the temporarily high profits of successful competitive risk taking.

Mr. Paul G. Hoffman's interesting discussion of "Business Plans for Postwar Expansion," outlining the program and philosophy of the Committee for Economic Development, bears further witness to the constructive work being carried on by that organization. Any criticism of this statement would seem to be gratuitous. I should like, however, to offer two suggestions for future consideration by the C.E.D.

Mr. Hoffman repeats the standard C.E.D. estimate "that if fifty-three to fifty-six million civilian jobs were available in the immediate postwar period the situation would be highly satisfactory." Admittedly it is difficult to be exact, especially when it is impossible to specify the year under consideration, the size of the postwar armed forces, and other relevant factors. Furthermore, in general discussion there is even a danger that excessive preoccupation with a purely numerical target of so-and-so-many jobs, conceived of as capable of specification in advance, may tend to obscure the ultimate goal of jobs for all who are able to work and desire to work, whatever their number may turn out to be. (Of course, some kind of numerical target is essential for administrative purposes if "full employment" is to be defined and maintained. But the real goal behind the administrative definition should be unrestricted employment opportunity for men and women.) Finally, having once adopted the 53 to 56 million approximation as the target for businessmen to keep in mind, the C.E.D. will naturally not wish to change its position without good cause. Nevertheless, it now appears that this target probably is too low, except at its upper margin.

Statistical computations being used by federal agencies, as well as by such private organizations as the National Planning Association, indicate that the so-called "normal" labor force, derived by projecting prewar trends, will be about 59 million by 1947, 59.5 million by 1948, and 60.5 million by 1950. An allowance of 1 million additional workers, net of war casualties, as the permanent legacy of the "abnormal increment" occasioned by the war, would appear to be conservatively low. Hence if 1948, for example, is assumed to be the postwar year under discussion, it is probable that the number of employable persons looking for work or working will not be smaller than 60.5 million, and may as a result of fewer voluntary withdrawals from the labor force be somewhat larger. If, then, we assume a postwar military force of 2.5 million, the provision of 56 million civilian jobs in, say, 1948 would probably leave a minimum of 2 million workers unemployed, and might thus approximately meet requirements since 2 million might perhaps be considered not far from the necessary amount of frictional or turnover unemployment consistent with "full employment" in the operating sense. On the other hand, the provision of only 53 million civilian jobs would probably leave 5 million or more workers unemployed in 1948. (Even in 1947 or 1946 the unemployed remainder would probably be at least 5 million, since it would seem unrealistic to assume that the "abnormal increment" could reduce itself to 1 million by such an early date.) It is hard to see, in short, how 53 million civilian jobs could be regarded as "highly satisfactory." It is therefore suggested that, if the C.E.D. finds itself in agreement with the labor force computations currently in use in Washington, it may wish at this point to revise its quantitative formulation of the employment target at which business should shoot.

My second suggestion relates to the manner in which the C.E.D. might utilize all available quantitative data bearing on the relationship between aggregate dollar volume of demand for products, aggregate employment, and price and wage levels. The "economic climate favorable to expansion" obviously has its quantitative as well as its qualitative aspects. In particular, the total volume of demand expected to eventuate for goods and services—demand by consumers, by federal, state, and local government, and by businessmen themselves—should have a great deal of strategic significance. Businessmen usually base their expectations on recent experience and trends within their own industry rather than on what may happen to national expenditure as a whole. In most cases, however, the market for the individual company's product will in point of fact be somewhat affected by the number of dollars being spent in the aggregate. If the postwar employment estimates made by C.E.D. community committees fail to yield a satisfactory picture in the individual community and for the economy as a whole, that need not settle the matter. It may be that new estimates yielding a much more favorable picture could be obtained if this relationship between total demand and demand for a given product were given full attention and if a definite expectation could be created that total demand would be maintained at a high level.

On this hypothesis, it would seem desirable for the C.E.D.'s Research Division to concern itself with calculating, and discovering means of obtaining, the volume of consumer demand necessary to justify the desired business expansion, taking into account (a) the probable concurrent amounts of private domestic investment expenditure, the expected net exports, and the government expenditures within those areas—referred to by Mr. Hoffman—"where public enterprise should prevail because it best serves the public interest," and (b) the expected levels of wages and prices. The Field Development Division might then shoulder the task of getting individual businessmen to add to their existing postwar estimates, which are linked up with a variety of implict assumptions about demand conditions, a new set of estimates—even though these would be only tentative and theoretical at first—based upon the explicit assumption that the specified "necessary" volume of demand would actually materialize. The results might contribute significantly to the understanding of the ways and means by which involuntary unemployment may be prevented from recurring.

9

EXPORTS, IMPORTS, AND JOBS*

How many American jobs will be in fields connected with the great business of exporting and importing if we can succeed in expanding our postwar foreign trade as we hope to do? That is a good question. Another good question is this: aside from what full employment will contribute to expansion of foreign trade, how much can we expect foreign trade to contribute to the maintenance of domestic full employment?

The trouble is, these two questions about actual jobs *in* foreign trade and the net number of jobs *dependent* on foreign trade keep getting mixed up, and arguments run in circles. Perhaps it is presumptuous to assume that these questions can be untangled. Nevertheless I want to raise my voice on behalf of those who think it is most important to try to keep these two questions separate, judging each one on its own merits.

Of course they really are separate, because we might have the same total number of jobs at two quite different levels of foreign trade; the jobs would simply be distributed somewhat differently. Let me take an analogy from another field. At the present time nearly 1,700,000 men and women are at work in the manufacturing of aircraft and parts. Two years after the war the number may be in the neighborhood of 200,000. Does anyone think that total national employment must be a million and a half smaller after the war on that account? I hope not, because we are going to need a number of million *more* civilian jobs after the war than we have right now, and yet aircraft production certainly is going to decline, not to mention the ordnance industry, shipbuilding, and others.

* * *

Now, question number one—how many jobs will be in fields connected with exporting and importing if we can succeed in expanding our foreign trade?—is obviously of the greatest interest to a large number of people. For instance, it is of the greatest interest to businessmen's associations where the importing or exporting of primary products or manufactures

---

*An address presented at a meeting of the Institute of World Economics on March 29, 1945, and subsequently printed in the October-December, 1945, issue of *World Economics.* The original title was "Exports, Imports, and Full Employment Policy."

bulks large so far as the industry in question is concerned. That point does not need any special elaboration.

I do not have much to contribute toward answering this question. So far as past experience is concerned, the Department of Commerce has made an estimate of the number of persons engaged in the production and distribution of goods for export in 1929, 1933, 1935, and 1937. Preliminary estimates made by a unit in the Bureau of Labor Statistics of the non-agricultural employment attributable to exports in the year 1939 seem to tie in pretty well with the 1937 Commerce figures. Of course, whenever such estimates are constructed, certain simplifying assumptions necessarily have to be made, and it may not be possible to keep these assumptions 100 per cent realistic. I would suggest that the B.L.S. inter-industry relations method of estimating—sometimes referred to as the "input-output" method—may be capable of yielding the most refined results, relatively speaking, because this method makes it possible to trace the indirect effects and also makes it possible to state with a good deal of precision exactly what is being estimated.

All such computations as these essentially rest on ratios of dollar value of exports to dollar value of an industry's total output. It is assumed that employment ratios will be about the same as dollar value ratios, except where we have definite evidence to the contrary. Hence you can take your pick of the various guesses now in circulation as to the probable or possible dollar value of our total postwar trade, the size of our gross national product, and the total number who will be employed, and make your own rough estimate of jobs connected with foreign trade. The trade volume estimates vary rather widely at the present time. Take a guess near the upper end of the range—say $14 billions of exports and $8 billions of imports. If 60 million were employed altogether, and the total gross national product stood at $200 billion, we might say that 7 per cent (14 divided by 200) of our jobs, or about 4.2 million jobs, could be considered to be tied up in some manner with exporting, with a substantial number of other workers engaged in the handling and processing of imports.

This is only for purposes of illustration. As to what the actual size of our exports and imports may prove to be, I can only say I trust that this will be determined on the basis of mutual advantage to ourselves and other nations, and that the role of our national policy in helping to determine the outcome will be based on the broadest conceptions of our common welfare, in the light of all the relevant economic and political considerations.

* * *

This brings us back to question number two—how much can we expect our foreign trade to contribute to the maintenance of full employment in this country? If trade expands, it certainly should make for greater world security and higher standards of living—in other words, increasingly *productive* jobs. But what about the *number* of jobs?

We are now no longer trying to count up the jobs in particular industries in which we may personally happen to be especially interested, but rather we are thinking of the national situation as a whole and trying to assess the net difference, if any, between the total number of American jobs if foreign trade is restricted and the total number of American jobs if foreign trade is suitably expanded. This is not simply a question of adding or subtracting certain specific jobs, because—as in the case I mentioned of wartime aircraft production—the possibility of substitution, or different proportions, comes in. The fact that at a given time 5 million, say, are holding jobs connected with exports or imports is no indication that, if we had no foreign trade, these five million persons would necessarily be unemployed.

I don't know how many people will be shocked by this, but my own view of the net contribution of foreign trade to U. S. jobs is that foreign trade will significantly raise U. S. employment only as long as we have an export surplus, resting on foreign investment, and that it will have practically no effect as soon as imports come to equal exports, *no matter how large they both become.* I am going to qualify this a little in a moment, but not very much.

Let me first say a word about the situation in which the dollar volume of imports—I mean services or "invisibles" paid for, as well as commodities—equals the dollar volume of exports—merchandise plus services. (Incidentally I am inclined to suspect that some persons who find it hard to see why, with large imports and large exports, the net gain in our employment should be zero, just because these two magnitudes happen to be equal, are not really thinking in terms of imports equal to exports. They may believe in the abstract that trade is a two-way affair in which the two movements of goods and services must balance out in the long run; but, when they turn to employment, what they actually have in mind is a particular export industry, or perhaps a so-called favorable balance of trade in which exports are larger than imports.)

Why should the net effect of foreign trade on our employment be practically nil if our exports and imports balance? The shortest answer to this is, I think, that the money we spend on imports subtracts from our markets, our production, and our employment just about as much as the money foreigners spend for our exports adds to our markets, our production, and our employment.

A slightly more elaborate answer would run somewhat as follows: First, the *marginal* employment per dollar of exports is probably somewhat smaller than the *average* employment per dollar of output in the export industries as a whole. I mean by this, for example, that a typical industry that exported 10 per cent of its product would probably not fire 10 per cent of its workers if its output fell off 10 per cent as a result of losing its foreign market. In manufacturing that might happen. But certainly it seems doubtful that agricultural employment—in cotton, for instance—has fallen off proportionately, if at all, when farm exports have declined in the past. In other words, if all our exports were to disappear completely, it is questionable whether the number of people who soon afterwards would have to change their jobs would be as large as the number who appear to be dependent on exporting if you merely use average ratios of workers to dollars' worth of output. In the second place, the aforementioned factor of *substitution* comes into play. If we lost an equal dollar volume of exports and imports—keeping, say, our really critical or strategic imports but giving up the rest—the reduced payments to foreigners would leave us with additional purchasing power to expend at home, and this would create about as many new jobs as were lost through elimination of exports. Some of these added jobs probably would be in the same industries as before, although most of them no doubt would be new jobs in different lines of activity.

Now certain qualifications are necessary, as I said before. For instance, as long as we continue to be subject to business cycles, with their alternating periods of boom and depression, a severe shock to a series of important industries could easily start or intensify a down-spin. This seems to me to be the reason why the free trade doctrine of the Classical School of economists looked so unrealistic to so many practical people. The theory said that substitution of one use of labor and capital for another—for instance, when protective tariffs were removed—would take place *automatically*. Skeptics replied that a bird in hand was worth two in the bush. In other words, we should hold on to the *particular* industries we already had, and not count too heavily on developing others if we lost those. And this argument never could be settled in the absence of a fundamental policy to eliminate business cycles by insuring continuous full employment.

Moreover, quite aside from the phenomena of the cycle as such, no one would claim that we could calmly face the loss of major exports and imports all of a sudden and expect a quick and painless reshuffling of workers into new jobs. Men and women are not like statistical tables—subject to immediate revision. Their geographic and functional mobility, as economists would say, is not perfect. In short, they get attached to a particular job in a particular community. So does capital. Neither labor nor capital can be uprooted and transplanted without hardship.

But I think it can fairly be said, without seeming thereby to belittle the seriousness of such shifts for the individuals affected, that difficulties of the kinds just mentioned are not the central issue. They do not destroy the presumption that the additional purchasing power made available domestically by a decline in payments for imports is likely after a while to stimulate new production and employment to an extent capable of offsetting the effects of a comparably large decline in exports. Still less do they suggest that a balanced *increase* in both exports and imports will be likely to add materially to the total volume of demand for domestic products.

A more fundamental argument is sometimes made, however. It is sometimes said that imports, far from subtractitng jobs, actually are neutral or even add jobs to the total. It is pointed out by those who take this position that some of our imports consist of luxuries and specialties not produced in the United States, together with "invisible" imports in the form of expenditures for travel abroad and remittances to relatives abroad. Why should these things adversely affect employment in this country? Moreover, American jobs are created in the shipping, unloading, processing, transporting, and distributing of our merchandise imports, so that a substantial fraction of the consumer's dollar paid out for imported articles or articles using imported raw materials never goes abroad at all but stays in this country to help furnish jobs to Americans.

This kind of argument has a practical sound, but I am reasonably sure that it is not practical at all, because it concentrates so closely on the factors in the foreground that it completely overlooks the offsetting factors in the background. If American consumers spend money on foreign travel, foreign remittances, or imported specialty articles, that *does* detract from domestic industry because it uses up dollars that would otherwise have been available to purchase the products of American industry. You cannot have your cake and eat it too. Moreover, the jobs created in the shipping, unloading, processing, transporting, and distributing of imported commodities would equally well have been created in handling alternative goods produced at home to meet additional domestic demand.

It all comes back in the end to the question of the *motivation* for productive activity. What *causes* production to take place? The answer to this question cannot be disregarded without losing touch with reality. Hence the answer is worth giving here, obvious though it may seem. In the Soviet Union, production takes place almost entirely as the result of the forming of a national production plan. On the other hand, in the United States production takes place for the most part in response to the pull of the market: no market, no production. Hence, if imports use up the same number of dollars that exports bring in, employment tends to remain unaffected.

At this point certain further qualifications will be conceded, these being true qualifications in the long-run sense and not merely temporary or cyclical factors, like those previously mentioned. (1) First and perhaps most important is the fact that an expansion of both exports and imports, if this is brought about by reduction of trade barriers, will probably cause some net addition to production even without any increase in the dollar demand for products, because it will lower prices and increase competition. This is the same effect that would follow elimination of monopolistic restrictions of a purely domestic character. (2) Production may be stimulated, without any net increase in total demand, if we ourselves have something of a monopoly position in acquiring our imported raw materials. By getting these raw materials for less than they would bring in a truly competitive market, we may cut our costs of production and sell more at a lower price. (3) If we are importing luxury goods, spending money on foreign travel, and so forth, this may come in part out of money that would otherwise have been saved but not invested, instead of entirely out of money that would otherwise have been spent for domestic products.

In addition, the amount of labor used in export industries may be higher per dollar of output than it would be in other lines that might take the place of the exports achievable by an expanded foreign trade program. This of course depends on circumstances. The fact that our exports so largely come from mechanized, mass-production industries, and from agriculture in which employment is relatively insensitive to markets, suggests that it might well work the other way round.

These seem to be the main considerations, although there are doubtless others. The essential point about them, however, is that they appear to be only relatively minor qualifications to the proposition that employment is *not* increased by expanded exports and imports if the additional exports and imports are equal in volume. The exceptions should not be confused with the general rule. The desirability of a balanced expansion of exports and imports does not rest on increased domestic employment, but rather on the likelihood of improved standards of living and greater world security. If we want to talk about how foreign trade can expand U. S. jobs, we must talk about an export surplus.

* * *

The same line of reasoning, by which it can be seen that jobs are not markedly increased by foreign trade if imports equal exports, shows that

U. S. jobs probably *will* be increased if our exports exceed our imports. Our exports will exceed our imports if we put the necessary additional dollars into the hands of foreigners who want to buy our products. We can do this, if we like, by lending them the money. In other words, we can develop an export surplus and increase our employment by means of a foreign investment program. Is that, perhaps, the answer to our employment problem? I get the impression that many people think it is.

I should like to emphasize as strongly as I possibly can my own belief that the idea that foreign investment can for any considerable length of time solve our employment problem for us is a dangerous illusion.

It can be readily conceded that various foreign countries—Latin American countries, Russia, China, parts of Africa, India, and others—will need help in the form of long-term investment for development purposes, quite apart from relief and rehabilitation needs resulting from the war, and that the United States will be uniquely qualified to lend a helping hand. I believe we should be generous in extending such assistance to other countries to enable them to raise their standards of living, even if this results in some temporary abstention from the maximum of consumption we might be enjoying here at home. From a long-run point of view it can be seen that this will be in our own interest, since it will promote world security. The Bretton Woods proposals show how some of this might be accomplished. Our liberality, incidentally, should not only appear in the amounts we are willing to lend abroad, but should also extend to the terms on which we make these funds available. Interest rates should be as low as possible.

Not only will such capital exports be desirable from the standpoint of international relations, but they will also provide a considerable number of jobs here in the United States. What is particularly important is that they will provide jobs in our heavy goods industries, the very industries that have expanded most phenomenally during the war and face the greatest cut-backs when the war is over. In order to industrialize, foreign countries will need to place orders with our metal products industries in particular, especially orders for industrial machinery and transportation equipment. This dovetails nicely with our own capacity to produce, and can therefore materially assist us in reducing the severity of industrial dislocations and frictional unemployment in the early postwar years.

These are the obvious advantages of foreign investment. But to say that foreign investment can solve our employment problem is quite another matter. Let me briefly mention three reasons why I have called that conception a dangerous illusion.

First may be considered the sheer magnitude of the employment problem to be solved. No one can tell at this moment how wide the so-called deflationary gap is likely to be when the sustaining effects of deferred demands by domestic consumers and producers begin to wear off. There are still too many unpredictables. But suffice it to say that many careful estimators think they discern a very wide gap indeed, so much so that an appraisal could reasonably be defended in which the export *surplus* might have to be in the neighborhood of $15 billion a year to keep this gap closed. Foreign investment on such a scale as this, year after year, looks quite impossible. Cultures widely different from our own would probably not be willing and able to adopt our machine technology over night even as a free gift, but in any case the practical question narrows down to the considerably smaller amounts they will take at the lowest rates of interest and on the most favorable terms of repayment we are willing to accept.

In the second place, if we exert too much pressure to expand our foreign investment, the favorable international effects obtainable from a more moderate policy are likely to turn into just the opposite. Any sense of *compulsion* on our part to have a big export surplus year after year certainly could lead to actions at variance with our desire to maintain the best of political and economic relations both with the borrowing countries and with, let us say, Great Britain, whose need to expand her exports is more obvious than our own. I need not labor this point. Surely anyone familiar with the history of foreign investments to date will recognize that, in spite of their advantages, and in spite of the improved chances for avoiding frictions which the new international approach to foreign investment appears to offer, there are limits to this whole process which can be transcended only at the risk of dangerously straining the friendly relations among nations and among peoples.

The third and perhaps most serious objection of all to trying to solve our employment problem through exports supported by foreign investment is the risk that this policy might stand in the way of the development of a fundamental full-employment program in this country. Thus, after stimulating our production temporarily, it might actually contribute to economic collapse when the export surplus tapers off. Our experience growing out of our foreign loans in the twenties should warn us that to place heavy emphasis on an export surplus as a basis for domestic prosperity is a short-sighted policy. Yet by relieving for a few years the symptoms of a deep-seated lack of economic balance, a big export boom would in all likelihood make it more difficult to face up to the necessity for a genuine cure. Then would come the relapse—at a time when, both psychologically and in terms of the size of adjustments needed, a cure would be much harder to bring about than immediately after the war.

* * *

It is clear enough that the real reason why so much effort is devoted to trying to prove that expanded foreign trade is good for domestic employment is the fact that many people do not think full employment can be achieved at all without tremendous export markets. Any attempted solution—even on a piecemeal and highly precarious basis—seems better than nothing. On all sides we hear it said that the United States has become so productive that it cannot possibly consume its whole product, but must export a part of it to other lands. Where is foreign purchasing power coming from to pay for this? Well, never mind, we'll loan them the money. When it comes to building up purchasing power, distance apparently lends enchantment.

In the more specialized language used by economists, it is said that we need a volume of investment, and other non-consumption offsets to saving, equal in magnitude to the volume of savings forthcoming at a full-employment level of national income; that we are not likely to come anywhere near attaining such a volume of investment, etc., through the unaided operation of natural forces; and that foreign investment is a peculiarly strategic kind of investment for purposes of closing the gap.

This poses two basic questions—aside from the precise relative advantages of foreign investment as against domestic investment. The first is the question whether we really are faced with a big savings-investment gap (or deflationary gap, or under-spending problem—call it what you will) assuming that matters are simply allowed to take their natural course. To this question I personally am ready to answer "yes," reserving judgment only on the subordinate question "how soon?" which is particularly difficult to judge since deferred demand backed up by accumulated savings, and other special factors including a possible export boom, may obscure the real structure of the problem for a few years. As a matter of fact, the issue of "how soon?" does not really matter so far as my own views on solving the problem are concerned, since my proposals are based on the insurance principle, as will be made clear in a moment. The only thing that is essential for my point—and here I don't see how there could be any controversy at all, for could anyone be found to deny it?—is the proposition that we have absolutely no assurance that a wide gap will *not* develop.

The second basic question is whether the gap, if and when it develops, must be filled by additional investment and other non-consumption offsets to saving. And here I personally will answer "no." In fact, it seems to me to be necessary to go farther than that and say that only a policy that expressly assures that *consumption* will be expanded so that additional investment can be held to a minimum will have the character of a practical full-employment policy for the United States.

As I see it, the basic factors in employment policy in this country are these:

(1) For the unparalleled benefits this will confer both domestically and internationally, employment opportunity must be assured in this country after the war. This involves setting up an administrative definition of full employment in terms of existing labor market statistics and having the Government underwrite full employment as thus defined.

(2) In achieving full employment, maximum stress must be placed on incentives to private business to expand its volume of production and employment. The key to this—and the suggestion I am making is comparatively a new idea—is the underwriting of total consumer spending at a level high enough to provide a market for a full-employment volume of output minus the output to be covered by normal business capital expenditures and normal government expenditures. For example, if $185 billion appeared to be required to buy a full-employment output in a particular year, and if expected private capital formation including foreign investment, plus government expenditures excluding any that might be made for the sake of employment, added up to an estimated $50 billion, consumer spending would be underwritten at $135 billion. Among the companion measures should be an active antitrust policy to foster competition, and effective forms of regulation to prevent price profiteering and output restriction where monopoly is unavoidable.

(3) Public investment and public services should be planned first of all on their own merits without reference to current employment considerations. The confidence generated in business by the assurance of continuously high private consumption—a confidence affecting private investment as well as the production of consumer goods—will very much reduce the need for supplementary public works. In spite of this, however, an ample reserve shelf of construction and non-construction projects should always be kept in readiness, and, when full employment requires it, supplementary public jobs should be provided by accelerating regularly budgeted programs or taking new programs off the reserve shelf.

(4) The condition of full employment thus brought about (either with or without supplementary public works) will produce a full flow of income, and consequently as high a rate of consumer spending as existing taxes and existing savings habits will permit. Where consumer spending is still below the level underwritten, however, government must provide additional purchasing power in some manner—for example, by suspending, refunding, or offsetting direct and indirect taxes in whole or in part while the tendency toward deficiency persists. Of course, great emphasis should be placed on getting rid of the root causes for this tendency toward deficiency

—notably the following causes: excessive inequality in the distribution of income, caused by low wages and other factors; exercise of monopolistic powers to restrict production; needlessly large institutional saving; and financial insecurity in the face of the various contingencies confronting individuals and families. Any supplementary tax adjustment or similar measures to bring consumer spending up to the guaranteed level is to be regarded merely as a balancing device at the margin which is necessitated because we have not yet dealt saisfactorily with the underlying maladjustments. Incidentally, since we want to guard against the possibility of inflation as well as against the more generally prevalent likelihood of deflation, it will also be necessary to provide for reducing total consumer spending by taxation or otherwise in the event that it threatens to rise spontaneously above the guaranteed level by more than a reasonable margin, this margin to be specified in advance.

That is a very brief outline of a subject that might be elaborated at almost any length. Actually the principles involved in this combination of factors are simple. The heart of this approach to full employment lies in its use of the insurance principle for the broad national purpose of establishing a sustained feeling of security and confidence on the part of employers, as well as on the part of the general buying public. Useful public investment is not in any sense restricted. My own personal feeling is that we ought to devote far larger public expenditures than ever before to facilities and services that will assist in attaining high standards for the whole population in fields basic to the general welfare, such as education, health, housing, social security, and the conservation and development of our natural resources. But—be the duly accepted public functions large or moderate—the suggested procedure should prevent those paralyzing situations from arising wherein legislators feel forced to choose between their interest in maintaining full employment and their interest in avoiding government expenditures that appear to them to be either wasteful or unduly competitive with business.

In terms of savings and investment, the proposal runs directly counter to the often repeated dictum that investment must be expanded to equal savings. What is suggested instead is that, except as investment is judged to be intrinsically necessary by business or by the voters and their representatives, the expansion should take place in consumption and in free consumer choice. This involves a reduction of real saving down to the level of investment, but need not in any way interfere with the individual right to save. Savers may do as before, or as they would do under conditions of expanded investment.

Government fiscal action to maintain employment is by this procedure limited to offsetting deficiencies as they actually materialize, whether in private consumer spending (as indicated by comparison of current spending rates with the rates found necessary and underwritten) or in total employment (as indicated by comparison of current employment figures with full employment as administratively defined). Employment on public works is expanded only when that is clearly necessary as a device to back up all other measures. When consumers' incomes are increased directly, by tax offsets or otherwise, that is in no sense a substitute for wages that might have been earned by doing useful work, but only an additional measure necessitated by a tendency for too little money to be spent for goods and services even when everyone willing and able to work already has a job. In short, subsidies to consumption that may be called for under this policy are not given for nothing, but rather are given to maintain the level of demand that business requires—which might be put slightly differently by saying that they are given to avoid having to have public enterprise instead of private enterprise in places where there is no evidence that public enterprise is preferred.

How does expanded foreign trade fit into this picture I have tried to sketch? To that question I would give a threefold answer.

In the first place, expanded foreign trade does not need to be justified as a means of increasing domestic employment. It is fully justified and required on other grounds. Assuming it is brought about in a situation in which trade barriers and discriminations are at a reasonable minimum, so that advantage can be taken of regional specialization in accordance with comparative efficiencies of production, expanded foreign trade should make a striking contribution to international harmony and security and to higher standards of living here and abroad.

In the second place, expanded foreign trade may make some slight net addition to our employment even with exports and imports in balance. This is particularly likely if trade barriers are low, because competition will then tend to be keen and prices reasonable. Moreover, trade will definitely make a net addition to our employment as long as we have an export surplus, such as can be created with the help of a foreign investment program. Practically speaking, however, the employment-creating effects of foreign investment are not sufficiently great or sufficiently permanent to constitute anything like a solution to our employment problem. Pursued in a liberal spirit, foreign investment can be another agent making for a better world of tomorrow, but any attempt to treat foreign investment as a domestic full-employment program would create serious dangers on both the domestic and the international fronts.

Turning the relationship around, a sound domestic program for full employment is the best guarantor of expanded foreign trade. The high national income and production associated with full employment in the United States will tend to contribute more than anything else we could do to the expansion of our imports and of our purchase of other world-trade commodities upon which the prosperity of other nations depends. This in turn will expand the markets for our exports, and will minimize the reluctance of other nations to abandon practices that restrict trade—a reluctance that is quite understandable in the absence of a reasonably assured market for their products in this country. Finally, a sound domestic program for full employment, founded on internal measures and not dependent on export surpluses, will create among American business men, workers, and farmers the conditions and the psychology on which broad American support for liberal trading practice must ultimately rest.

10

THE ROLE OF FISCAL POLICY*

Fiscal policy sounds technical and remote to the man at the bench and the man behind the plow. Translated as the government's policy on raising and spending money, it clearly is anything but remote. The way the government raises and spends money—the way it taxes, borrows savings, creates new money, sells, buys goods and services, retires debt, lends, transfers payments from social insurance funds, and subsidizes—directly affects the welfare of every man, woman, and child and every business in the country.

There is no disagreement over the fact that the government must raise in one way or another whatever sums of money it must spend to carry out its functions. The government's programming of its fiscal operations begins therefore with a careful review of the need for various types of services and of the amounts that it is necessary to spend to secure these services. In developing the necessary revenue measures, thought must always be given to equity, adequacy of revenue, and the other traditional tax objectives. In any discussion of fiscal policy it must be assumed that considerations of this sort, both with reference to the need for expenditures and with regard to preferable methods of raising funds, will continue to receive the full attention of fiscal authorities.

But the financial operations of the Federal Government, even on their prewar scale, necessarily influence the distribution of income among individuals, the proportion of the national income that is spent for current consumption or is saved, the vitality of private investment, and in general the ways in which individual initiative expresses itself. Because of its bearing on all of these things, the fiscal policy of the Federal Government will inevitably affect the volume of employment either favorably or unfavorably. There are also of course direct effects on employment through expenditures for public works and public services.

---

*This paper was prepared for, and in cooperation with, the Labor Committee on National Policy of the National Planning Association. Sponsored by the Committee as a technical report, it was published by the Association in May, 1945, as Planning Pamphlets No. 45, under the title *Fiscal Policy for Full Employment*. The section on Summary and Recommendations was reprinted in the *Congressional Record* of June 11, 1945, in the extension of remarks of Senator James M. Tunnell of Delaware.

Major Objectives

Under these conditions it is a mistake to think of fiscal measures exclusively or even primarily in conventional or financial terms. Fiscal measures should be designed to implement the major aims of national policy. With these considerations in mind, we state our own position as clearly as possible at the outset. Our objectives, to which we direct our proposals with reference to fiscal measures, are as follows:

(1) *Maintenance of full employment.* Fiscal policy is a powerful instrument for sustaining the level of production and employment. In the past, fiscal policy has developed without enough regard for the paramount interest of our people in the opportunity to work, and in this respect among others it has not served society as well as it might. This must be changed. After the war, fiscal policy must make its maximum contribution to the permanent maintenance of a condition of full and productive employment. No other objective must be placed ahead of this. Our country must face the fact that the problems involved in attaining this objective are extremely grave. Nevertheless, they can be solved—without regimenting the American people.

(2) *Promotion of private business and promotion of maximum initiative and enterprise in private business.* The government's revenue and expenditure programs should be designed to encourage investment, research, innovation, and the taking of risks from which society can hope to derive benefit.

(3) *Provision of adequate standards of education, health, housing, social security, conservation and development of resources.* For the protection of society and the establishment of real equality of opportunity, including equal freedom in the choice of jobs, we support whatever public expenditures and whatever public enterprise may be necessary to secure high standards of education, health, housing, and general social security for the whole population. Cultural and recreational facilities should be expanded. In justice to future generations, we support adequate conservation of natural resources, and a generous measure of development of these resources.

(4) *Achievement of equity, adequate revenue, economy, certainty, and convenience in taxation.* Equity implies, in our opinion, a tax system based on ability to pay—a progressive system emphasizing increased rates with increased income, not one that is regressive. As to adequacy of revenue, we favor balancing the budget to the fullest extent consistent with maintaining full employment, and we would actively seek removal of grounds for conflict between these two objectives. We do not regard deficits as

essentially desirable, or view them with indifference. On the other hand we are unalterably opposed to any policy based on the idea that currently balancing the government's financial budget is more important than guaranteeing the opportunity to work and earn a living wage.

The Role of Fiscal Policy

There probably exist few if any other instruments available to government, and hence to the people of this country who control their government, as fateful at the present moment as fiscal policy, either for improvement or for impairment of the general welfare. This follows from the fact that fiscal policy can be used, within fairly wide limits (less wide, of course, in peace than in war), to expand or contract the opportunities for employment by modifying the volume of market demand for, and the cost of producing, goods and services.

On the other hand, no mere instrument of government, no matter how powerful and how well directed by popular representatives in the public interest, can take the place of the individual citizen's energy, responsibility, and vigilance in defense of his liberty and in prosecution of his interests. Nor can it replace concerted private action, as in cooperatives, union-management cooperation, and collective bargaining.

Collective bargaining and high wages are cornerstones of our democracy, and are equally fundamental to the economic solution we seek. There is no conflict between these essentials and a sound fiscal policy. Rather, the relation is one of harmonious mutual dependence. Experience shows that, in the absence of intelligent fiscal measures, the national income can decline to the point where the effectiveness and even the practice of collective bargaining are endangered. On the other hand, common sense tells us that low wages, against which collective bargaining must remain the chief bulwark, would create a fatal shortage of purchasing power, Unless wages, the main component of purchasing power, are sustained, the effort to bolster consumer demand through measures within the scope of fiscal action—through social security benefits, supplements to farm incomes, and consumer tax reductions or offsets, for example—must sooner or later prove inadequate. If excessive reliance is not to be placed on fiscal policy, wages should rise in relation to prices to the full extent made possible by rising productivity.

Some other limitations of fiscal policy should be emphasized. Fiscal policy will not obviate the need for price controls and other direct controls in the postwar transition period. It is no substitute at any time for a strong, nationally coordinated employment service, which is a prime requirement to help bring workers and available jobs together. It cannot eliminate excessive seasonal fluctuations in employment and income, for which the remedy must be provided by other measures including, where practicable, the payment of wages on an annual basis. Moreover, it does not of itself induce price or cost flexibility, or speed the adjustment to changing relationships of demand and supply. In particular it cannot, generally speaking, take care of the restrictionism frequently practiced by monopolies. Policies to support competition and control monopoly prices are needed in addition to fiscal policies. Otherwise production and employment may, in the interest of monopoly profits, be held below the levels it would be reasonable to expect in view of the existing relation between demand and cost. In that case it will be possible to achieve full employment only on the basis of excessive government expenditures and excessive deficits, which could have been avoided through proper measures of antitrust enforcement and monopoly control.

Our conclusions with regard to fiscal policy are therefore based on the idea that fiscal measures directed at full employment should be part of a larger framework of public policy committed and consistently shaped to that same end.

I. WHY A POSITIVE FISCAL POLICY IS NEEDED IN ASSURING FULL EMPLOYMENT

Why is there any need for a positive fiscal policy?

The answer is that full employment will not be maintained unless the effective market demand is sufficient to buy the goods and services produced at full employment; and that this balance between supply and demand at full employment cannot be counted on to occur automatically but can be promoted by means of a properly planned and organized, positive fiscal policy.

Automatic forces may in some circumstances bring about an adequate volume of effective demand without the aid of conscious fiscal action. The demand may occasionally even be too large. But there is absolutely no *assurance* that the right volume of demand will be forthcoming automatically year in and year out. This has been repeatedly and amply demonstrated by experience.

Of course, through its revenue and expenditure measures government has always exercised an influence over both demand and cost of production, whether this was done purposely or accidentally. The needed change, therefore, amounts only to this: the process should become one hundred per cent purposeful and should have as its guide the necessity for assuring a total demand that will buy a full-employment output.

On the basis of prewar experience, there is every reason to anticipate that the effective demand in the postwar period usually will be too small, unless a satisfactory fiscal policy is adopted. There is a prevailing tendency toward over-saving or underspending in our economy. The amounts saved by individuals, corporations, and private and public insurance institutions in years of high national income tend to be larger in total than private enterprise wants to invest in capital goods. Thus we are apt not to achieve a high national income at all, because business does not see the prospect of successfully selling an expanded output; or if, for the time being, we do achieve a high national income, we then slump because a part of current income fails to be re-spent for either consumer or capital goods.

Even if unforeseen changes should create a situation in which overspending tendencies were about as strong as under-spending tendencies, this would not eliminate the cycle or rule out random disturbances. Conditions would still vary from year to year, and hence stability would still require a flexible fiscal policy to offset the dominant pressures of the moment. The likely return of the familiar, persistent difficulty in maintaining large enough markets is, therefore, not the only reason why a positive fiscal program needs to be developed. But this danger of persistent underspending does emphasize the great urgency of the need for such a program, and it suggests where much of the stress in such a program belongs.

The Over-all Magnitudes[1]

Let us take a concrete example. The quantities discussed are not predictions, because we doubt the possibility of making close predictions and in any case are not concerned to attempt it. Nevertheless, these quantities are as realistic as possible, under the stated assumptions, which are purposely chosen to present a favorable set of possibilities and therefore err if anything on the side of optimism.

In 1948, assuming victory over Germany and Japan by the winter of 1945-46 and physical reconversion substantially completed in 1946 or early 1947, the value of a full-employment output, as measured by the Commerce Department's "gross national product," would probably be about $185 bil-

[1]See Appendix, tables 1-4, for method of deriving quantities presented in this section. The reader is cautioned against interpreting these estimates as forecasts. They are in general based upon prewar relationships, and therefore serve to indicate roughly what may be expected to occur if these past relationships are restored essentially unaltered. It should be noted that in this report we advocate a number of federal policies that would have the effect of changing these relationships in a direction tending to improve the general economic balance and hence tending to render compensatory fiscal action and budget deficits less necessary.

lion,[2] or a little higher, at present prices.[3] This visualizes a slight decline from present levels of gross national product, since the shorter work-week and somewhat smaller labor force here assumed outweigh our conservative allowance for continued increase in output per man-hour. Of course $185 billion is in no sense a final goal. Increases in productivity and in the size of the labor force should operate to raise the value of a full-employment output by something like $6 billion a year in the early post-readjustment period.

For gross national product to reach $185 billion in 1948, somebody must spend $185 billion for goods and services. True, some goods may be produced and not sold, in which case business will be adding to its own capital expenditures (net increases in inventories are classed as capital expenditures) by piling up stocks of unsold goods. But any large-scale unplanned accumulation of unsold goods obviously can not continue for long without depressing production. In general, therefore, a gross national product of $185 billion requires an actual demand of that same size in the form of: (a) private gross capital expenditures by business, including planned but not accidental inventory expansion; plus (b) government expenditures for goods and services; plus (c) consumer expenditures. These three types of expenditure exhaust the possibilities.

If matters are allowed to take their natural course, can we reasonably expect $185 billion of expenditures under these three headings?

Private Capital Expenditures. In the light of past performance, private business might make capital expenditures for replacement and expansion amounting to $25 billion, and might continuously maintain some such rate as that without overbuilding and thereby inviting a later slump. Included in this figure might be $15 billion for plant and equipment, $6 billion for residential construction (usually classified here rather than under con-

---

[2]This rough estimate corresponds, when allowance is made for difference in year and difference in price level, to estimates previously published by the National Planning Association. See: *National Budgets for Full Employment,* Planning Pamphlets Nos. 43-44, April 1945.

[3]While we do not favor a decline in the general price level, our price assumption here is mainly a matter of convenience. Our discussion is concerned with the problem of *proportions,* which would be about the same under any other price assumption (barring the effects of wide or violent price changes). Our choice of the third year after assumed victory is likewise dictated by convenience. Any other post-reconversion year might have been selected without changing the main outlines of the picture, although naturally certain components are likely to vary (*e.g.,* inventory accumulation, expenditures for defense) and it may be more difficult to reach full private production by the third year than slightly later. The assumption of victory by the winter of 1945-46 is of course purely a working hypothesis and in no respect a prediction.

sumer expenditures), and $2 billion each for inventory expansion and net exports.[4]

Such a sum as $25 billion has never been spent for private capital formation in any year up till now, the closest approach being $19 billion at slightly lower prices in 1941, when we were tooling up to become the arsenal of democracy. The suggested amount is more than half again as large as the total of publicly financed war facilities in this war; some 15 times the value of the net tangible assets of all automobile manufacturing plants in the United States in 1938 (here adjusted for price change), not including parts, accessory, body, and tire manufacturers; one-third as great as the present estimated value of all tangible farm property in the United States, including land and livestock along with buildings and machinery. It is obvious that sums in the order of $25 billion will hardly be spent for private capital formation year after year in the absence of steady expansion and high continuing prosperity.

On the other hand, this amount might well be exceeded temporarily if a strong boom materialized. Past relationships between capital formation and total output must be used with great caution, for among other things it is likely that, as we become more and more thoroughly industrialized, a growing proportion of our new inventions and improvements will be of the type requiring less capital per unit of product rather than more. For what the comparison is worth, however, it may be noted that, while $25 billion represents a higher percentage of $185 billion than the percentages of gross national product achieved by private gross capital expenditures in 1931-39, it falls short, percentagewise, of what we experienced in the boom of the twenties, before the crash.

In other words, it is not a ceiling figure. We select it because it appears to represent a moderately high estimate, providing for replacement and a substantial rate of growth, and because we do not find any evidence that these expenditures could of their own momentum long continue at a still higher level without running ahead of the consumer market and precipitating a collapse. If in fact a runaway boom should develop in the post-reconversion period, this would make our private capital formation estimate for 1948 too pessimistic, but such a boom, in all probability, would only store up additional trouble for 1950 or perhaps 1953. In concen-

[4]The amount here assigned to plant and equipment is somewhat generous by comparison with other current estimates, and the figure for inventory expansion could presumably not be maintained much beyond the third postwar year without a subsequent reaction. On the other hand, under favoring policies net exports might exceed the figure here presented and might remain at a higher level for a period of years. See, for example: *America's New Opportunities in World Trade,* Planning Pamphlets Nos. 37-38, November 1944.

trating on a less spectacular alternative, we are not predicting that in the natural course of events no runaway boom will occur. Rather, we hold that a sober investigation of the basis for a permanent solution for unemployment must not be sidetracked by the possibility of a short joy-ride ending in disaster.

Government Expenditures. Expenditures for goods and services by Federal, State, and local government represent the second element of demand. These also might amount to $25 billion in 1948 (as against $93 billion in 1943, $16 billion in 1939), if expenditures which are more or less inevitable are made, no ambitious welfare programs are undertaken, and no work relief is required. The Federal share might be $15.5 billion, including $7 billion for the defense establishment, $5 billion for interest on the national debt, and substantial amounts for various services that raise the real income of citizens generally.

These figures do not include government transfer payments to individuals—veterans, social security beneficiaries, etc.—which are equally government expenditures but do not constitute demand for goods and services until they come into the market as part of consumer demand. We may, however, take them into account by noting that Federal, State, and local taxes will have to amount to over $33 billion (not $25 billion) if receipts and expenditures on general and special accounts are to be kept in balance. This estimate includes social security taxes, devoted in part to payment of unemployment and old-age and survivors' insurance benefits, but also, to a considerably greater extent, to increasing the reserves in social insurance trust funds. The total Federal budget would be around $22 billion.

Consumer Expenditures. We come, finally, to consumer expenditures, the major element of demand and the main barometer of our material welfare as a nation. If total expenditure for goods and services is to amount to $185 billion, and if business and government spend $25 billion each, individual consumers must spend $135 billion.

There is little likelihood, however, in the absence of positive fiscal action, that this will occur. In all probability, too large a part of income will be absorbed in savings and the payment of taxes.

With taxes at levels needed to balance the budget, and with savings at levels consistent with past experience, *even the income produced by full employment itself, if we had that income,* would probably not result in more than about $127 billion or $128 billion of consumer demand. This may be seen by considering the way consumer demand is related to gross national product.

If we had a gross national product of $185 billion, the net national income might be expected to be about $159 billion; this allows for business taxes and business reserves which, along with certain other items of lesser importance, must be subtracted from gross product to obtain net income. Actual income payments to consumers, however, would be a little smaller—perhaps $155 billion—chiefly because corporate undivided profits (business net savings), which form a part of the national income, do not enter into the stream of money payments going into the hands of consumers. (Transfer payments from government, referred to previously, do not enter in, but these would be more than offset by a deduction for payroll taxes.) After paying personal taxes, including as the main item say $9 billion of Federal income taxes, consumers would have left a "disposable" income of about $143 billion. Out of this amount they would normally save nearly $19 billion, if their behavior in the past may be taken as a guide.[5] On the other hand, the fact that many persons will have accumulated nest-eggs of savings during the war introduces the probability that for some years after the war consumers will react to this added element of security, assuming their current incomes are successfully maintained, by spending somewhat more and saving somewhat less than they otherwise would.[6] If we allow $3 billion for this factor in 1948, we conclude that consumer expenditure would amount to only about $127.4 billion, instead of the necessary $135 billion, *even if we assume a gross national product of $185 billion to begin with.*

From this it follows that, if income were *not* flowing into their hands at a full-employment rate to begin with, consumers could be expected to spend some amount *smaller* than $127.4 billion. Thus, even if we started the year 1948 with full employment, the drag on the system resulting from insufficient consumer demand would depress prices and reduce business volume and would soon bring gross national product down from an annual rate of $185 billion to an annual rate of $177.4 billion, assuming government expenditures and private gross capital expenditures unchanged; *this in turn would further reduce the rate of consumer spending and employment; and so on, in downward circles,* until the reduced saving at lower income levels eliminated the savings-investment "gap."

Actually, of course, it is unrealistic to assume that government and business would maintain their rates of expenditure unchanged under these

---

[5]That is, the relationship between consumer spending and consumer disposable income that was maintained with remarkable consistency over the whole period from 1923 to 1940 gives us $124.4 billion of consumer spending when disposable income is $143 billion. For this relationship see Appendix, table 4, footnote f.

[6]It is probable that the most significant share of the wartime savings is not in the hands of low-income wage earner groups. The postwar effect of wartime savings and deferred demand will no doubt be primarily felt in durable goods and luxury goods industries.

conditions. Private gross capital expenditures would probably *decrease* as consumer markets weakened. Government—especially Federal—expenditures, on the other hand, would be likely to *increase,* both in the form of expenditures for goods and services and in the form of transfers to consumers, because of the necessity of providing relief for unemployment. Just how far the gross national product and employment would decline is a matter for conjecture, because of the complicated way in which the various controlling influences, including the government's policy decisions, would interact.

Conclusions

We began by asking why a positive fiscal policy is needed to assure full employment. We rephrased this question by asking whether, if matters are simply allowed to take their natural course, it is reasonable to expect to see a full-employment volume of expenditures—that is, the level of effective demand necessary to buy a full-employment output of goods and services. We conclude, after reviewing the strategic elements in the problem, that it is not reasonable to have this expectation, and that, on the contrary, the probabilities are for too little demand and hence for too little employment, unless fiscal policy intervenes.

It must be emphasized that this conclusion does not depend on the figure for gross national product we have used in the foregoing calculations. If the gross national product corresponding to full employment should be smaller or larger than $185 billion, either because of a change in the general price level or because of error in our estimate of America's real productive capacity when operating at full employment, the results for all practical purposes would still be the same.[7] For example, a smaller gross national product might seem to simplify the problem because it would not require such a large total of expenditures. But actually it would make no great difference, because income going to consumers, and hence expenditures by consumers, would be correspondingly reduced at the same time, in addition to which the level of private gross capital expenditures would probably be somewhat lower also. In short, the total demand would still be too small.[8]

---

[7]This is not intended to deny that, if violent price fluctuations occurred, they would be likely to distort the relationships under consideration.

[8]Similarly, a more rapid rise in productivity would necessitate a larger total of expenditures to buy a full-employment output, but in this case a full-employment stream of consumer income, if initially achieved, would also be larger. Hence, so far as inherent lack of economic balance is concerned, this situation would differ from the one discussed above mainly in that the additional income payments would probably not all be spent by consumers but would also in part go to increase total savings.

This does not mean, it should be repeated, that we offer the above calculations as a forecast. We recognized, above, the possibility that larger private gross capital expenditures may occur for a period of years as a result of unusually high levels of foreign investment, heavy inventory accumulation, or some other factor—although we regard this possibility as one that holds real danger of a violent collapse later on. We recognize also that the backlog of war savings and deferred demand might temporarily lead to an even higher consumer spending-saving ratio than we have suggested—although, as noted, there is little evidence that these war savings are distributed in such a way as to affect very substantially the spending of low-income groups.

On the other side, we point out that private capital expenditures and consumer expenditures might at least equally well be smaller, and savings larger, than we have estimated. Up till now, consumer spending has never quite reached an annual rate of $100 billion. A return to former peacetime proportions of spending to saving, while we retain approximately our wartime levels of income, may at first be a difficult matter, since this adjustment will involve spending at rates far beyond any ever experienced. In particular, the tendency for savings to run ahead of investment will be dangerously accentuated if wage rates are not maintained as we go from war to peace, for experience shows that the ratio of saving to consumer spending rises when wages go down in relation to profits. It will therefore be especially important to safeguard wage income and secure wage advances, through all means available including the improvement of minimum wage standards. Finally, our calculations throughout have assumed general optimism and prosperity to begin with. Aside from the very great problems of readjustment, even assuming no policy mistakes or loss of forward momentum, the development of needlessly heavy unemployment in the reconversion period would obviously add to the difficulty of realizing our estimates by the third year after victory.

Summing up—the details are bound to be shrouded in uncertainty, but the general conclusion is unmistakable. Unless our whole conception of the problem of cost and demand and of savings and investment, as we have set it forth in this section, is entirely wrong, it is clear that a positive fiscal policy is essential. We do not think that any conscientious person who grasps the nature of these relationships, and who is concerned to assure full employment, will want to gamble on having enough effective demand develop automatically. Nor do we think, on the other hand, that many people will continue to be satisfied with governmental fiscal expedients that are merely improvised as we go along. We think rather that the natural reaction, as the problem itself becomes clear, is to ask: what can be done to make sure that the demand *will* be as large as is needed for full employment?

The answer to this question, as we hope to show in the following sections, is partly one of allowing certain expenditures that ought to be made for their own sake to help us, in addition, to solve the unemployment problem. Partly it is a matter of progress with tax reform. And finally it is a matter of setting up a balancing mechanism, utilizing the underwriting principle, to assure us the volume of demand we need without waiting for our basic expenditure policies and our basic tax policies to strike an ideal balance.

II. BASIC EXPENDITURE POLICIES

In this section we call attention to certain programs of housing, health, education, conservation and development of natural resources, and social security that we believe our country needs and can well afford under full employment. The attainment of adequate standards in these fields would make an enormous contribution to opportunity, welfare, and happiness, and undoubtedly forms a part of our national war aims as millions of our people would like to see these aims defined. Vigorous action is essential if adequate standards are to be attained within reasonable time limits. We support such action for its own sake, as a matter of basic social policy, quite aside from the incidental effect it will have upon employment. In some of these fields the only way to achieve significant results is through community—or public—expenditures. Centralization of control or administration is not necessary, but Federal sponsorship and Federal financial assistance will usually be required to assure that real progress is made.

Because advances in the realm of public welfare are in the first instance a matter of social policy, it is sometimes argued that the whole subject lies outside the scope of fiscal policy as such. This distinction cannot be granted, however, if we are concerned with the amount as well as the type of taxes, and in particular with finding a basis on which full employment can be permanently sustained without continual budget deficits due to purely compensatory fiscal action—that is, government expenditures or tax reductions to offset deficiencies in private expenditures.

It is not to be expected that a full-employment level of demand can be assured in time of peace simply as a by-product of pursuing other national goals that are quite separate and distinct. That would be to place too much faith in coincidence. Nor is it sensible to spend money for goods and services through public channels, or through private business channels kept open by special public assistance, merely to get the money spent.[9] That would be to confess that as a nation we are bankrupt of ways and means of raising the purchasing power of individual consumers, or that we doubt the capacity of individual consumers to find objects on which they would like to spend their purchasing power. But, to the extent that socially planned welfare programs call for expenditures that *can* stand solidly on their own merits—because they are at least as worthwhile as equal additional expenditures that might have been made by consumers—they clearly deserve support. And, to the extent that they will *also* contribute to elimination of under-spending, these programs, worth undertaking for their own sake, will incidentally acquire the further character of instruments of fiscal policy and full employment.

How far that is likely to be the case depends on two things. First, it depends on the magnitudes of effective demand directly generated by the programs under consideration—the government expenditures for goods and services, the additional private capital expenditures that become possible as a result of the over-all plans, and the consumer expenditures based on government transfer payments under certain of the programs. In the second place, it also depends on how the money is raised to finance the public share of the welfare expenditures. The situation will not be improved from the standpoint of the relation between demand and cost of production if taxes are so laid that consumer expenditures are reduced one dollar, or so that business costs are increased one dollar, for every dollar added to government expenditures. There may be a net social gain under these circumstances, but the under-spending difficulty will remain as great as ever.

Needed Welfare Expenditures

The question of where the money is coming from is discussed in the next section, in which we deal with basic tax policies. This section considers housing, health, education, conservation and development of natural resources, and social security, from the expenditure side.[10]

---

[9]This of course is not meant to deny the desirability of having government exercise its lending function in the interests of creating a more perfect loan market—one in which all business borrowers, including small businesses, will have fair and equal access to capital and credit. The Reconstruction Finance Corporation or other instrumentalities of the Federal Government should make or facilitate the making of loans to credit-worthy borrowers who would otherwise be unable to secure financing on reasonable terms. This would tend to assure that, in the presence of adequate potential markets, artificial financial restrictions would not block the natural and appropriate expansion of enterprise and investment.

[10]See Appendix, table 5, for additional detail relating to this section. It should be pointed out that the estimates and appraisals here presented do not represent a commitment with respect to the programs in question. The Committee expects to examine many of them more thoroughly at a later date and work out specific recommendations.

Housing. The world that Americans are fighting to achieve has in it a decent home and ample living space for everyone. The men who come back will not willingly bring up their children in cramped, insanitary, noisy slums. Our urban and rural slums must go, and in their place we must put attractive and convenient modern houses, taking care to provide our future city homes with sunlight and air and to allow enough space for community parks and playgrounds. Today, in urban centers alone, more than 30 million people live in houses that, structurally or because of their location in slums or blighted areas, are below reasonable minimum standards of health, safety, decency, or convenience. In the rural South, only 9 per cent of all farmhouses are even equipped with inside running water.

More than half a million new nonfarm dwelling units a year are required merely to provide for increase in the number of families and to maintain existing standards. A general consensus of expert opinion indicates that we need to build a million and a half new farm and nonfarm units a year for from 10 to 15 years, to put our housing in order. The annual capital cost for housing construction and urban redevelopment in accordance with these conceptions, including erection of these new homes plus the necessary rehabilitation of existing units and an allowance for parks and playgrounds in residential neighborhoods, would be about $9.5 billion at present prices, or slightly over $8 billion exclusive of the cost of acquiring land.

In the preceding section we estimated that $6 billion might be spent for residential construction in 1948 without any special national housing program, assuming a high level of general economic activity and market demand. If so, then additional construction expenditures of $2 billion would still be needed. A program combining a reduction of interest rates and Federal guarantees to private capital along Federal Housing Administration lines might possibly accomplish half of this increase. Under these highly favorable circumstances, the necessary public expenditures would be only $1 billion for construction plus $1.5 billion for site acquisition. These public expenditures presumably would be financed through Federal and local public housing authority borrowing in the private market and would be self-liquidating except for the equivalent of a relatively small annual rental subsidy (possibly $100 million in 1948) for public housing occupied by the lowest income groups.

Health. America can become the healthiest land on earth for all groups regardless of income. Yet thousands of people suffer needlessly because proper medical or surgical care is not available to them, and diseases that we have the technical knowledge to wipe from our land continue to take heavy toll year after year. The working days lost through preventable illness represent, furthermore, a waste of human resources reflected in lower national income.

A comprehensive health program for the nation should make available to everyone in the population all health and medical services necessary for the preservation and promotion of health, the prevention of disease, and the treatment of illness. It must also emphasize the personal responsibility of every individual for making good use of these facilities.

This program would have many aspects. It would assure all communities a sanitary environment through provision of pure public water supplies, sewage disposal systems, and milk pasteurization plants. This among other things would prevent typhoid fever, cholera, and dysentery, and would check the outbreaks of milk-borne disease of which 30 to 50 are reported each year. It would also provide hospitals and health centers where the need is demonstrated. (There is an estimated immediate need of more than 400,000 hospital beds in the United States for civilian use.) It would expand public health measures for the prevention of disease, and develop new public health activities in such fields as dental service and public health nursing. It would give additional support to private research on dental caries, the upper respiratory diseases, mental disease, cancer, diseases of the heart, tropical diseases, etc. (Every five years we spend $1 billion for such care as we give to those suffering from mental and nervous diseases, but less than $5 million for research in this field.) It would secure the training of a competent and numerically adequate health personnel. And finally, it would find ways and means of bringing adequate medical care within reach of all.

Our health service personnel—physicians, dentists, nurses, other hospital personnel, etc.—probably should be increased after the war by 50 per cent, or an increase of around 600,000 persons in all. It is reliably estimated that the public expenditures for an adequate 10-year national health program would be nearly $24 billion, or an average of $2.4 billion a year[11]—roughly double what may be expected to be spent if we merely maintain our prewar standards and add the veterans' hospitals for which legislative provision has already been made. Nearly one-third of the total

---

[11]This estimate does not include allowance for expenditures under a possible national system of medical care and hospitalization through social insurance. It has been estimated that, under the Wagner-Murray-Dingell Bill, the payroll taxes collected by the Federal Government would include approximately $3 billion a year to be expended through the United States Public Health Service in purchase of health services for contributors and their families. Other things being equal, and disregarding certain additional sums to be raised through general taxation, this would increase total government expenditures for goods and services by $3 billion above the estimate presented in this report, and would reduce total disposable income of consumers by a corresponding amount.

would be capital expense for sanitation facilities and for hospitals and about 2400 well equipped health centers, while the remainder would cover current health and hospital services. In addition, preliminary estimates of the Bureau of Agricultural Economics indicate the need for a food stamp plan, food discount plan, or some other nutrition program, costing not much less than $900 million a year, to improve health by supplementing the diet of families with incomes of less than $1500. Related to this we believe there should be established a broad school lunch program assuring nutrition education for all and providing free or partly free meals to children who cannot afford to pay. According to preliminary estimates of the United States Office of Education, the public cost in connection with a suitable program would be at least $150 million annually.

Education. Without universally adequate educational opportunity, democracy cannot be complete. But the system of free public education for all the people in which we take so much pride is in practice largely a system of educational opportunity according to financial ability of the local school district, and also according to economic ability of the family to take advantage of the education available. In 1940, for example, the per-pupil current expenditure for public school education in Mississippi was less than one-fifth the expenditure in New York, and variations between individual school districts are greater than between state averages. More than 2 million boys and girls are even now being taught in one-room, one-teacher schools, of which over 100,000 are still in operation. Moreover, as late as 1940 an estimated three-quarters of a million children of elementary-school age and more than 2 million of high-school age were not in school at all, commonly because of low family incomes, while those enrolled in educational institutions above the high-school level probably represented only a small fraction of the number with the ability to do acceptable college work.

The cost of completely revamping our system of elementary and secondary public education, including allowance for optional attendance at nursery schools, kindergartens, and junior colleges, was recently estimated by the Research Division of the National Education Association. This program would provide for an expansion of over 5 million in student enrollment, and an increase of nearly 50 per cent (or about 400,000) in the teaching staff. Assuming adjustment for present living costs, it would roughly double the average yearly salary of about $1500 that was paid to teachers, supervisors, and principals in 1942 (eleven states paid less than $1000 on the average, and the average in all rural communities throughout the nation was less than $1000). It would lengthen the school term where that is desirable. It would reorganize school districts and provide the necessary increase in transportation facilities, etc. On a 20-year construction basis, the annual capital cost for new schools and better equipment under this program would be nearly $1 billion at today's prices. The current operating cost would rise to $5.7 billion; this would mean a per-pupil expenditure nearly double the prewar average for the country as a whole—a standard comparing favorably with standards already attained in such cities as Hartford and San Francisco, and not far below New York City and most of the other cities of various sizes that lead in making financial provision for their public schools. Adding appropriate allowances for private schools, higher and professional education, part-time adult education, and libraries and museums, the total annual capital expense for education in this country would be about $1.4 billion, and the total annual operating expense about $8.6 billion. Because of time required to expand enrollment, raise teacher qualifications, etc., the maximum operating expense for 1948 would probably be about $2 billion lower under the program contemplated, but perhaps one-third of this difference would be offset by special training programs provided for veterans under existing legislation.

The figures cited contrast with capital and operating expenditures of perhaps $400 million and $4 billion respectively (including $300 million and $3.5 billion of taxpayers' money) implied in the over-all estimates of expenditures in the previous section, which assumed no material rise in our educational standards. Undoubtedly the needed increase must be financed very largely with Federal funds. The Federal Government should keep its hands off the curriculum, however, its role being to provide funds, under suitable safeguards, according to a formula designed to hasten the equalizing of educational opportunities among the states, which in turn should equalize as far as possible among their local school districts. A student aid program should also be inaugurated to make it financially possible for all young persons to attend high school to completion. At the higher educational levels, the Federal Government should provide student aid in the form of scholarships for capable students who need such assistanc and do not receive it from other sources.

Conservation and Development. The natural resources of America are a trust. Our people cannot afford from any point of view to continue our present wasteful practices. Nearly twice as much saw timber is being cut and destroyed as is replaced through new growth. Erosion has blighted 300 million farm acres; as a result 100 million acres have already been, or may soon be, abandoned, and on another 100 million more than half of the topsoil has been lost. With every heavy rain, with every week in which we continue to mine or liquidate our forest reserves, the beauty and wealth of the American land suffer further deterioration. Government must help to educate, must find means to help prevent the wasteful private practices that do irreparable damage to the nation as a whole, and must embark as a regular part of its own work on a many-sided program of conservation and development, so that the ultimate physical assets of the nation may grow greater rather than less as the years go by.

Preliminary estimates of the Department of Agriculture's Soil Conservation Service and Forest Service give an indication of the most vital requirements in the conservation field. A 20-year soil conservation program, involving the application of such practices as terracing, contour tillage, banding with strip crops, fertilizing, draining, irrigating, and seeding for range or pasture, could rehabilitate our farm land to the point where maintenance of a satisfactory balance thereafter would be merely a matter of normal farming operations. Such a program would cost, at present prices, nearly $19 billion, or an average of slightly more than $900 million a year. Experience at the grass-roots in more than a thousand soil conservation districts, organized under State laws, indicates that farmers would meet at least half this total cost once government took the lead. In the case of forest conservation a considerably longer period of reconstruction is required. Under a suitable program the Federal Government would establish standards for the regulation of cutting and related practices on private forest lands; would provide better protection from fire, insects, and disease; would broaden and strengthen a series of public aids to facilitate good private forest management; and would acquire forest lands where watershed or recreational values are so important or growth conditions so adverse that private owners cannot be expected to give the management required by public interest. The average annual cost of such a program during the first 10-year period would be about $500 million for capital and operating expense combined (including the purchase of land for national forests), with perhaps two-thirds of this cost being borne by the Federal Government and the remainder divided about equally between other government jurisdictions and private owners. The total suggested annual expenditure, public and private, under both programs—$1.4 billion—represents something like a 600 per cent increase over what can be expected in the ordinary course of events.

Beyond conservation, we look to the creative development of new resources, especially through programs of river valley development. To regions caught in stagnation or wasted by flood or by drought such programs will bring opportunity, activity, and an American standard of living. Examples such as Boulder Dam and the Tennessee Valley Authority have shown the way. Economic and engineering knowledge gained to date should now be applied to transform the face of nature and instill new life in many other areas. This will be accomplished by checking the destructive force of floods and the silting of rivers, making prosperous farms for thousands of families through irrigation of fertile land, generating electric power, promoting a diversified industrial growth, increasing cheap water transportation, expanding purchasing power and markets.

From 1935 to 1942 we spent on the average $275 million annually for the development of irrigation, power, navigation, and flood control. The War and Interior Departments together have several billion dollars' worth of projects for the Missouri River basin and numerous other waterways already authorized by Congress, and additional plans under study and review. How large an annual program should be recommended depends in the main on judgment, since standards are not as readily set as in conservation, housing, education, or health. However, in view of the enormous potentialities of river valley development, we believe it would be uneconomic to spend less than $700 million annually on this work. Incidentally it is probable that half or more of this outlay would eventually come back to the government as income from irrigation and power.

Social Security. With respect to this matter a joint statement was recently issued with the Agriculture and Business Committees,[12] containing certain estimates to which we refer for the purpose of the present discussion. This statement reviewed the need to extend coverage under existing programs to uncovered groups in agriculture, domestic service, government, non-profit institutions, the self-employed, etc.; to liberalize benefit provisions and other terms under old-age and survivors insurance and unemployment compensation; to inaugurate a national system of sickness and disability insurance; to strengthen public assistance programs, providing for Federal grants-in-aid to be distributed according to a formula that would give relatively greater financial assistance to the poorer states; and to provide through national insurance or in some other manner a satisfactory basis for meeting the costs of medical care and hospitalization. Here we wish to emphasize the fiscal effects that would flow from a broad expansion of the income maintenance features of social security. In a year of minimum unemployment, such a system of benefits as was there recommended would probably add more than $2 billion to consumers' incomes, over and above the benefits to be expected under the terms of present legislation, and a nearly equivalent amount to their expenditures for goods and services.

---

[12]See *Joint Statement on Social Security*, by the Agriculture, Business and Labor Committees on National Policy of the National Planning Association, Planning Pamphlets No. 33, April 1944.

Summary

We have briefly outlined a series of programs, in housing, health, education, conservation and development, and social security, for which we see an urgent need. The high level of national income and purchasing power associated with full employment would not automatically solve these particular problems. While the figures we have cited are approximations, calculated from the best data available, we believe they present a reasonable minimum estimate of our national postwar needs in these fields—in the light of our productive capacity, potential national income, and ability to raise public revenue through progressive but not oppressive taxation. It seems evident to us that careful national and local planning should immediately be undertaken in these basic fields, looking to early action.

There may be additional major collective needs that should be met, not merely when conditions call for compensatory public works but even in preference to adopting measures for assuring a higher level of individual consumer income and expenditure. We are prepared to extend our support whenever we become convinced that such a need exists.[13]

To indicate the net effect of the recommended welfare programs upon employment by way of their effect upon demand, we now turn to the revenue side of the budget. After considering the subject of taxes in the light of the public expenditures required if the recommended programs are to be carried through, we shall be in a position to deal with the practical necessity of compensatory fiscal mechanisms for assuring a balance between demand and cost at the full-employment level.

III. BASIC TAX POLICIES

Public revenue systems are ways of raising the money that governments find it necessary or desirable to spend. A good tax system is one that is effective in promoting full employment, fair as between persons and as between different types of business, and generally simple and convenient. It will also be stiff enough to balance the budget unless balancing the budget conflicts with full employment—in which case, it will restore a budgetary balance as soon as the underlying reasons for that conflict have been removed.

As we have shown, the American economy after the war will as a general rule be threatened with under-spending or over-saving. This means that,

[13]Increased public expenditures are imperatively needed for the public employment service and should also be secured in such fields as labor law administration and social services generally. We also look to future extension of public support for cultural programs—music, drama, etc. We favor an acceleration of the rural electrification program. Such considerations are here omitted from discussion not because they lack importance but merely because of the lower order of magnitude of their fiscal effects.

if taxes are to be helpful in promoting full employment, they must perform their function of financing *public* expenditures in a manner that will as far as possible avoid canceling out *private* expenditures that would otherwise have been made. To a large extent such cancellation is inevitable: government through taxation reduces the expenditures of consumers, for example, and substitutes its own expenditures. Insofar, however, as taxes can be levied on income that would not be spent for consumer goods or invested in capital goods, the process of taxing and spending makes a net contribution to effective demand and hence—as long as the under-spending tendency is present—to the maintenance of employment. If, temporarily, the situation is reversed and over-spending threatens, the immediate fiscal goal will be to reduce private spending without correspondingly increasing public spending. But the other is our main problem.

The primary conclusion from this is one that strongly reinforces the case for taxation in accordance with ability to pay. Fairness requires that the poor man should not be asked to bear a disproportionate share of the burden. The fundamental economic consideration of markets underscores this principle. Savings, which create a market only when channeled into capital expenditures, naturally concentrate where incomes are well above the subsistence level. In 1935-36, for example, it is estimated that the upper income third of the nation's 39 million families and single individuals (incomes of $1450 and over) had aggregate savings of $7.4 billion, while the middle third (incomes of $780 to $1450) had negative savings—due to excess of total borrowings over such savings as life insurance, etc.—of $250 million, and the lower third (incomes under $780) had negative savings of $1.2 billion. Data on family spending and saving obtained in more recent studies are not cited here because the relationships are somewhat distorted by wartime conditions, but in all studies of this type the same striking contrasts in ability to save as between income groups are evident. The best way to support effective demand is, therefore, to base government spending upon taxes levied chiefly on those with substantial incomes.

Most property taxes, as well as sales taxes and the other excises so prominent in our State and local revenue systems, bear with undue severity upon the lower income groups. Thus it becomes all the more important that the Federal Government should combat the tendency toward a failure of purchasing power by reducing or eliminating regressive taxes and concentrating instead on taxes that are progressive.

Along with supporting the profitability of production by supporting purchasing power, our Federal tax system should have every other reasonable regard for the incentive to undertake production in hope of personal profit. This does not mean that we favor abandonment or near-abandonment of the corporate income tax, or a sharp reduction of wartime personal income tax rates in the upper brackets. We do, however, favor ending present discriminations against equity financing, which burden the stockholder and put a premium on unsound capital structures, and we advocate finding new means of encouraging genuine enterprise. If the man with an idea, or exceptional energy, or willingness to take a business risk with his money feels that it is a case of "heads you win, tails I lose", the fiscal system will have failed in one of its major purposes and will be obliged to pump needlessly large streams of money through government channels to keep production going.

In order to cover expenditures, assuming inauguration of the welfare programs recommended in the preceding section, the Federal Government would have to raise the large sum of about $28 billion in 1948 through taxes, inclusive of social security taxes and miscellaneous receipts.[14] The recommended expansion of welfare programs accounts for over 20 per cent of the total revenue requirements.[15] This total is about three-fifths of the amount paid in Federal taxes in 1944. What program for raising these sums will be most equitable and at the same time most effective in promoting full employment?

Excises (Yield Around $3 Billion) and Customs (Yield Around $700 Million)

Excise taxes restrict production, since the added cost is in general passed aong to the consumer in the form of higher prices. They are in most instances strikingly regressive, since families and individuals with small means spend a higher proportion of their incomes on articles subject to tax than the well-to-do. We recommend the elimination of all Federal

[14]It would be desirable to adopt a budgeting system in which capital expenditures were segregated from current expenditures and only the annual amortization on capital items appeared in the current budget. If that were done, the Federal tax revenue required in 1948 to cover the proposed expansion of welfare programs alone would be reduced by perhaps $4 billion. In the absence of indication that this budgetary reform is contemplated, we have assumed that in a balanced budget situation even federal loans for public housing purposes, for example, would be covered in full out of current revenues. We have also assumed that miscellaneous receipts, insofar as derived from sale of surplus war materials and plant, will be applied to reduce the national debt, leaving only an estimated $400 million (derived from miscellaneous fees, seigniorage, etc.) to be used for meeting current expenses.

[15]This is the net change as compared with estimates in section I. We have assumed reduced social security taxes because of elimination of reserve accumulation (see below), and we have also assumed that $1 billion could appropriately be cut from other expenditures, mainly routine public works, if we undertook a full-scale program to overcome deficiencies in our housing, schools, hospitals, social security benefits, etc. See Appendix, tables 2 and 3.

excises after the war, with the exception of moderate taxes on liquor, tobacco, and gasoline. We are opposed to all sales taxes because of their retrogressive nature and their definite tendency to reduce consuming power. We urge, moreover, that local and State taxes be re-examined to reduce the share of these taxes carried by low-income groups.

If our foreign trade expands, a development that is to be expected under full employment and that would be further stimulated by the lowering of tariffs and other trade barriers, customs revenue should rise somewhat above prewar levels.

Individual Income Tax (Yield Around $12 Billion)

The great majority of competent students of taxation agree that the graduated individual income tax should be the backbone of any tax system designed to distribute its load in accordance with ability to pay. We should count on obtaining roughly half of Federal tax revenue, exclusive of pay-roll taxes, from this source after the war, and at the same time we should exempt incomes at or below the subsistence level. This creates a difficult but not insoluble problem.

The 3 per cent normal tax—formerly the Victory tax—should be promptly abolished because of its unreasonably low $500 exemption irrespective of size of family. In addition, we consider that personal exemptions and allowances for dependents should be raised to the level where, together with deductions, they exclude from Federal income taxation altogether the minimum requirements for an American standard of living as described by the Heller Committee for Research in Social Economics, University of California—at present prices, about $2750 for a family of four if not required to pay an income tax. It is obviously bad policy to reduce still further by taxation such incomes as are known to be already below the minimum acceptable standard. If these changes are made, the collection of, say, $12 billion of personal income taxes will permit only modest reductions of present burdens (other than elimination of the 3 per cent normal rate) on income brackets subject to tax. It may be possible under the specified revenue requirements to reduce the basic rate by 1 or 2 per cent. Application of the top rates might also be limited to incomes over $500,000 or $1,000,000, levels above which relatively small amounts of potential investment capital exist, instead of starting at $200,000, as at present.

Estate and Gift Taxes (Yield Around $2 Billion)

These taxes are capable of yielding substantial revenues for a number of years, without any restrictive effect on production, but their possibilities have never been seriously exploited. They should now be completely overhauled. We recommend that exemptions on estates be substantially lowered, perhaps with a differentiation according to relationship of the heir; that excessive deductions permitted at present be disallowed; and that rates be increased all along the line. The estate and gift taxes should be integrated to close the loophole whereby nine-tenths of the tax on a $100,000 estate can be avoided by prior distribution of gifts. Provision should also be made to eliminate the avoidance of taxation on capital gains which occurs when capital assets are held until death.

Corporate Income Tax (Yield Around $7 Billion)

If the Federal revenue structure is not to be weakened, substantial reliance must be placed upon corporate income taxation. Rates calculated to produce around $7 billion, or roughly half the peak wartime yield and more than three times the yield in 1941, may represent the fairest compromise between revenue and incentive considerations. Such rates would assume: (1) that there are better ways of building up purchasing power than through virtual elimination of the corporate income tax; (2) that continued business growth does not require rates of corporate saving such as were necessary in an earlier period, since the country's total savings tend in any case to be excessive rather than deficient; (3) that present discriminations against equity capital should be removed; and (4) that this can be accomplished while still retaining a tax of the dimensions indicated.

The present excess profits tax is an essential war measure, but not suited to peacetime conditions because it does not distinguish between the profits of monopolies and the profits that represent a reward for taking a real production risk. We therefore recommend its repeal after final termination of hostilities, along with the capital stock and declared-value excess-profits tax combination, which is complicated, capricious in action, and not worth the small amount of revenue returned. The former change should not take effect, however, as long as other war controls have not been lifted, reconversion is still in process, and inflationary tendencies still exist. This is particularly important inasmuch as immediate repeal would give an unwarranted advantage to those companies most favorably situated from the standpoint of reconverting and tapping the deferred demand, and could therefore produce serious dislocations in our economy. Moreover, we advocate the framing of an excess profits tax that will get at monopoly profit specifically. (No allowance is made for this in our present revenue estimate; with such a tax in effect, we could expect some increase in the corporate income tax yield and would recommend a corresponding reduction of the levy on personal incomes.)

The total rate of taxation on corporate income can hardly be reduced below 40 per cent if the yield is to reach $7 billion. It is, however, necessary to encourage risk-taking by ending the present discrimination in favor of income on bonds and against income earned on stock. One method might be to give small corporations the option to be taxed as partnerships, while applying to others a tax in two parts consisting of (a) a levy on net profit plus interest on future bond issues, and (b) an incentive or unusued earnings tax in the form of a levy on earnings ahead of depreciation, with an escape for distributed dividends and for real investment, including replacement, in plant and equipment, as averaged over an appropriate period of years. If some other method is generally preferred, we would be inclined to support it provided it does not unduly sacrifice revenue and provided it stimulates corporations to distribute or use their earnings so that spending by consumers and by business will be promoted and idle savings curtailed.

In addition, we consider it important to bring in new blood in business, and as one way of assisting that process we recommend that present tax provisions be modified to give more encouragement to new businesses. This kind of stimulus, together with Federal action that we urge be taken to help overcome present handicaps of small businesses in obtaining capital and credit, should do much to promote enterprise and competition.

Social Security Taxes (Yield Around $3 Billion)

We recommend that action be taken to introduce the principle of government contribution to social insurance, and also that of pay-as-you-go financing, whereby reserve accumulation would be halted. Both principles have been widely discussed and increasingly advocated. The former would limit the direct burden on employers and employees by supplementing the proceeds of payroll taxes out of general tax revenues, thereby giving fuller application to the advantages of progressive taxation. The latter would for the next several decades reduce the tax revenue required in connection with a given level of social security benefits, and hence would very considerably assist in maintaining purchasing power. The total effect in combating over-saving would be especially pronounced if these two principles were linked with the expansion of social security benefits proposed in the preceding section.

Under continuously assured full employment, even unemployment reserves would be unnecessary. For the amount of unemployment benefits required to provide income in the intervals between jobs—periods of temporary idleness accounting for the small volume of frictional unemployment necessary for the economy as a whole—would be as predictable on a national basis as the amount of benefits required under old-age and survivors insurance and under the recommended system of sickness and disability insurance.

Modified Rates, Assuming a Smaller Budget

Our suggestions on the amounts of revenue to be yielded by the various taxes are based upon an assumed total Federal tax yield around $28 billion. In the event that Congress does not provide funds for various public welfare programs in amounts such as we recommend herein, or in the event that capital expenditures are budgeted separately in a manner that reduces current revenue requirements, the total tax load should be correspondingly reduced. In that case we believe that the individual income tax should be lightened by $1-$2 billion in favor of the lower brackets before reductions are applied to the corporate income tax and the remaining excises.

Incentives Through Taxation

Without much doubt the best incentive taxation is a well proportioned system of taxes integrated and balanced with fiscal expenditures in such a way as to maintain at all times a full-employment level of demand for products. Removal of discriminations against equity capital, and granting of tax concessions to new businesses, will also be beneficial in reinforcing initiative. It seems to us, however, that the need for special incentives to investment and enterprise should not be as great as is sometimes claimed. If the time comes when enterprising money is felt to require an exaggerated positive incentive, we would wish to see introduced at the same time some real penalty on unenterprising money. At present we incline to the view that the measures already mentioned, together with elimination of the anomalous tax-exemption privilege on State and local securities, and a policy of low interest rates consistently maintained by the Treasury and Federal Reserve Board, may well prove sufficient.

Further Considerations

Every effort should be made to avoid wasteful expenditure; we advocate financial economy in government administration, to relieve the taxpayer, wherever this does not sacrifice efficiency or depress the wages and salaries of government employees. For reasons of equity, and to reduce burdens on the average taxpayer, we advocate strong and comprehensive enforcement, as well as the closing of all loopholes which serve as avenues of escape from the essential intent of our tax laws. Finally, we favor continuation of efforts to simplify taxation.

In addition to simplifications that can be introduced in Federal taxation, it should be possible to do a good deal toward eliminating conflicts and overlap between Federal, State, and local taxation. It is of great importance that studies of this question be pushed through to practical conclusions, so that action may be taken which will assist in making Federal fiscal policy effective, minimize tax inequities, and secure proper distribution of Federal aid to State and local jurisdictions where required in connection with essential programs of public welfare.

We have dealt herein with basic tax policies—policies that we believe should shape the main outlines of our Federal revenue system. The element still missing is a flexible balancing mechanism. We next bring our recommendations on basic expenditure policies and basic tax policies together, and propose a flexible system of compensatory tax offsets or other adjustments, and a reserve shelf of public works, to round out the picture by making sure that a full-employment level of demand will actually materialize.

IV. ASSURING A BALANCED ECONOMY AT FULL EMPLOYMENT

In the two preceding sections we have recommended certain basic expenditure and taxation measures that would, if adopted, in themselves provide a major corrective for over-saving and under-spending. Thus, in proposing policies that would vastly improve the material well-being of the average citizen, we have at the same time proposed a program that would much reduce the need for compensatory measures involving deficit financing.

If our program as set forth above were adopted in its entirety, and other conditions fundamentally affecting consumer income and spending patterns remained as previously assumed, it is possible that under-spending would be almost wholly neutralized, so that for a considerable period of years full employment would come close to maintaining itself.

This can be seen from calculations similar to those, in section I, which indicated a substantial deficiency of demand in the absence of such a program. If we keep our underlying assumptions as they were before, but change our tax and expenditure totals to take account of the recommended housing, health, education, conservation and development, and social security measures, and assume also that the added taxes are of a sufficiently progressive character so that a substantial portion of the additional revenue would come out of saving instead of curtailing spending, we reduce the spending shortage from $7.6 billion to $1.4 billion.

The additional $6.2 billion of effective demand here indicated is accounted for by the following changes implied by introduction of the recommended measures: Government expenditures for goods and services would rise by $5.4 billion. Private gross capital expenditures would rise by $600 million net—assuming part of the increase resulting from the expanded public welfare programs to be counteracted by the effects of heavier taxation. Consumer expenditures would rise by $200 million—since (a) the effect of higher business and personal taxes, partly compensated by lower payroll taxes, would be to reduce consumer purchasing power by $6.5 billion, but (b) transfer payments to individuals would increase their incomes by $3.3 billion and private saving would decline by $3.4 billion.[16]

Caution is in order, however, in interpreting the results of such computations for purposes of policy. They certainly make it clear, regardless of the wide margin of error in all present estimates of postwar national income magnitudes, that adoption of the recommended welfare programs would materially reduce the need for purely compensatory fiscal measures to sustain demand and employment. But they do not suggest that these programs would eliminate that need altogether. This is especially significant in view of the purposely optimistic nature, as previously noted, of the assumptions underlying our original estimates.

Moreover, for practical purposes the crucial consideration is that it may not be possible to advance the public welfare programs so rapidly on such a broad front immediately after the war. There seems to be no reason to doubt that the construction industry could expand by 1948 to enable the indicated building of homes, schools, and hospitals to go forward, even though this would set a new total construction record. On the other hand, we know that there are many obstacles not necessarily of an engineering kind to be overcome in carrying through such a vast improvement of our standards of education, health, and living generally, for the benefit of the whole population. It would be reckless to assume that these construction and other programs will all go ahead without delay at the end of the war, merely because such a development would be desirable.

We therefore cannot escape the conclusion that a sound compensatory fiscal policy is essential—a policy providing advance assurances that the right amount of spending will occur, and then providing flexible balancing mechanisms that come into action if and to the extent they prove to be needed to supplement the results of all the other motivations at work in our economy. At best, it will have only minor maladjustments to correct. If no action at all is taken to develop basic policies that work to rectify the inherent tendency of our economy toward over-saving and under-spending, the compensatory program will in most years have to make a substantial net contribution to the spending stream. How, then, should this program operate?

[16]For detail, see Appendix, table 4; also tables 2 and 3.

The right kind of compensatory fiscal program will include two major elements:

(1) It will contain a mechanism for adjusting the total volume of purchasing power so that a condition of full employment will provide for its own continuation through adequate consumer demand. This is a matter of avoiding over-saving—or, in special circumstances, over-spending. For example, if full employment yields income payments to consumers at a rate of about $155 billion, and if consumer spending of $135 billion is needed to bring total demand for goods and services to $185 billion (as in the situation considered in section I), the function of this mechanism is to see that consumer spending, out of about $155 billion of income payments, actually does reach $135 billion, rather than, say, only $127.4 billion.

(2) The right compensatory fiscal program must also contain a mechanism for filling in gaps in employment if these occur in spite of the maintenance of purchasing power. This is the role of compensatory public works and work projects. To continue with the same example—production of $135 billion of consumer goods will be sufficient when $185 billion is the total output needed, *if* business and government between them spend $50 billion for goods and services. But if business only buys $22 billion of capital goods, instead of $25 billion as expected, then unemployment will occur unless government institutes a compensatory public works program to provide additional jobs, and this action will raise government's own expenditure for goods and services from $25 billion to $28 billion or thereabouts.

Not only are both elements necessary to make compensatory fiscal policy complete, but also, if they are properly dovetailed, each will lighten the task of the other. The assurance of ample consuming power year after year in the hands of the public at large should exercise a major influence in sustaining private capital investment, as well as the production of consumer goods. It should therefore reduce to a minimum the necessity for falling back on the final line of defense, compensatory public works. The existence of a policy that automatically leads to the starting of compensatory public works, if normal employment does fall below the level defined as full employment, would create a consumer demand as large as current saving habits will permit, because it would continuously maximize consumer *income.* It would therefore reduce to a minimum the necessity for using the mechanism for adjusting total purchasing power.

Thus the two stabilizers working together would assure jobs, emphasize consumption and individual consumer choice, give business a real opportunity—which is usually has not had—to provide all the jobs needed other than those normally in government, and keep budget deficits as low as possible consistent with maintaining full employment in an economy in which the over-saving tendency still exists. *Moreover, they would have the advantage, peculiar to insurance mechanisms, of removing insecurity while limiting the remedy to the need as it actually develops.*

Public Works For Stabilizing Jobs

To meet the requirement for supplementary jobs in the demobilization period, as well as requirements that may develop after reconversion if private enterprise at any time fails to provide the jobs expected, it is necessary to prepare an ample, diversified, and geographically distributed reserve shelf of public works and work projects. Federal, State, and local programs are all needed, and all should so far as possible be operated when private employment is insufficient rather than at other times. The Federal Government, however, necessarily has final responsibility for supporting employment when other government jurisdictions fail to act. We urge that advance preparations to make the reserve shelf ready be pushed with the utmost speed. Since it takes a long time to get projects into the blueprint stage and ready to start, it is essential that plans be made now. A grave danger exists that it may already be too late to provide a program adequate in quantity and quality for the immediate demobilization period.

The reserve shelf should contain service as well as construction projects, since otherwise it often will not be possible to utilize the skills of those who may be temporarily without jobs in private industry, or to derive the maximum public benefit from the compensatory program. All projects included should be clearly useful to the community. Some examples are: work on streets, roads, airports, and terminal facilities; land reclamation, drainage, erosion control, irrigation; construction of libraries and museums; improvement of public forests and parks, including development of fish and game resources; construction of theatres, stadiums, auditoriums; music, theatre, art, and recreation programs; river and harbor work; rural electrification; modernization of public buildings; health and safety inspection and promotion; laboratory research; compilation of municipal and other governmental records and statistics; preparation of maps, catalogues, guides, histories, yearbooks, and directories. Exactly what might be included on the reserve shelf would depend, of course, on what items were scheduled as non-deferable and placed on the regular budget. Thus if the housing, health, education, and conservation and development programs we are proposing herein were to be scaled down for purposes of the regular budget in the early postwar years—a line of action which we would definitely consider unwise—the construction and other work necessary to speed up these programs would logically have top priority whenever additional jobs were needed.

We recommend that construction projects be operated through private contractors. On all compensatory projects, whether construction or nonconstruction, we emphasize the importance of paying standard union rates and making the hours and other terms of employment correspond to those prevailing locally for similar types of work. Full employment means jobs for all at fair pay and under regular working conditions. Hence a compensatory public works program which, as we visualize it, would be in no sense a relief program but on the contrary would be a mechanism to back up other programs here recommended to maintain full employment, would have to provide jobs conforming to standard specifications. The incentive to return to regular private employment as soon as possible would be introduced, not by substandard pay on public jobs, but rather by establishment of the principle of priority for private construction and private work generally. This principle would operate by having private employers keep the Employment Service informed of their prospective needs for labor, and by requiring that at the proper time the Employment Service call upon the agency responsible for public works to reduce or terminate its compensatory projects as rapidly as possible consistent with preserving the value of the work already done.

National Income Insurance[17] *for Sustaining and Stabilizing Consumption and Promoting Private Jobs*

To prevent a deficiency of consumption, which might well occur as a result of over-saving even when production (supplemented if necessary by expanded public works) was paying out income at a full-employment rate, we recommend adoption of the following procedures: first, the underwriting of total consumer spending at an adequate level by the Federal Government, to set the target for business; and second, the provision of additional purchasing power to consumers, as far as practicable through adjustment of taxes, when that proves necessary in order to realize the level of spending underwritten. This would amount to establishing a system of national income insurance,[17] which would guarantee the over-all market for the final products of private enterprise.

The amount of consumer spending to be underwritten would be calculated by subtracting the sum of (a) expected private gross capital expenditures, estimated as accurately as available data permit, and (b) pro-

[17]Actually, total consumer *expenditure* insurance. Expenditure is the key, since expenditure has decisive significance for producers, whereas income may be divided between spending and saving in proportions that fail to maintain sufficient demand.

posed government expenditures for goods and services, excluding any compensatory public works, from (c) the total of gross national product or expenditures regarded as sufficient to maintain production at the full-employment level. For example, if the conditions were those pictured in section I, with $185 billion representing the value of gross national product at the expected general price level, with regularly scheduled government expenditures at $25 billion, and with private gross capital expenditures also expected to reach $25 billion, the guaranteed amount of consumer spending would be $135 billion. A failure of private capital expenditures to reach $25 billion would, as noted, require the inauguration of compensatory public works, to prevent unemployment. On the other hand, a failure of consumer spending to reach $135 billion would require compensatory action directly at the point of consumer income and expenditure.

We have emphasized throughout this report the desirability of taking steps to create a fundamental balance in our economy—a balance under which full employment would tend to maintain itself, by way of high consumption, without the need for supplementary and, as it were, artificial measures in support of consumption. We have advocated more progressive taxation, tax incentives to corporations to distribute their earnings or invest them in plant and equipment, expansion of social security benefits, elimination of social security reserve accumulation, expansion of community consumption expenditures for education, health, etc., and higher wages. All these measures would help create the needed balance by reducing the over-saving danger. Measures to eliminate substandard incomes in agriculture would have a powerful effect in the same direction; here national full employment itself, by enhancing the demand for farm products while also providing opportunities for surplus farm labor and farmers on submarginal land to find better-paid employment, can be expected to make great improvements. Nevertheless, realism requires that we do not assume the over-saving problem away before it actually is eliminated. In our illustration, a failure of consumer spending to reach $135 billion would indicate the continued presence of over-saving. Compensatory action at the point of consumer income and expenditure would therefore be required.

This action might take various different forms, as further consideration and experimentation might indicate to be most desirable. The suggestion that follows will serve to illustrate the principles involved, but is not assumed to be the only, or necessarily the best, method of accomplishing the objective.

When the current rate of consumer spending fell below the required rate (both calculated, perhaps, on a quarterly basis), tax payments might be returned to consumers in a volume sufficient to eliminate this deficiency. In general the principle might well be followed of rebating or offsetting indirect taxes ahead of the income tax, since the indirect taxes have the larger relative effect on consumption. It would, however, be desirable to have every family or individual consumer file an income tax statement with the Treasury as a condition of eligibility for tax rebates. Those who pay income taxes, on a withholding basis or otherwise, could then receive any refunds of indirect or of direct taxes in the form of a reduction of their current income tax liabilities. Those with incomes below the exemption level, who would file income tax statements without paying an income tax, would receive any offsets against indirect taxes directly in cash upon proper identification. In calculating indirect taxes paid, it could be assumed for purposes of administration that every person in the country pays hidden taxes up to at least a substantial minimum sum, and an amount believed to represent a reasonable approximation of the per capita minimum could be designated as the amount to be refunded in whole or in part if and when necessary to sustain consumer spending.

How this might work can be illustrated by again referring to the calculations presented in section I. The total tax bill of $33.4 billion for the year would include perhaps $5.6 billion of Federal taxes properly classifiable as indirect taxes for purposes of consumer tax adjustment (counting excises, customs, and, say, half of the corporate income tax), along with $8 billion of State and local business taxes that also indirectly fall on the consumer. The total, $13.6 billion, represents a per capita burden of about $100. In computing allowable tax offsets, it might reasonably be assumed that no one pays less than one-third the average per capita amount, other than those at poverty levels whose incomes should in any case be increased if possible.[18] Each individual taxpayer might therefore be rated as entitled to indirect tax offsets up to $33 during the year, if required for the satisfactory operation of the economy; the head of a family with a wife and two children would be rated as entitled to $133 under the same conditions; and so on.[19]

Assuming a tendency for total consumer spending to run to only $127.4

---

[18]According to estimates presented by Helen Tarasov in "Who Does Pay the Taxes?" (Supplement IV, Social Research, 1942, p. 6), consumer units—families and single individuals—with incomes under $1,000 in 1938-39 paid taxes equal on the average to 18 per cent of their income, although not subject to income tax. Thus, for example, a family with an income of $500 would have been likely to pay about $90 under tax laws in effect at that time, and one with just under $1,000, nearly $180; similarly, consumer units with incomes of $1,500 are estimated to have paid about $263 (17.5 per cent of income).

[19]In computing net income for income tax purposes, deductions for other taxes paid would properly be reduced, under this proposal, by the amount of any offsets to indirect taxes.

billion, with $135 billion required and guaranteed, the offsetting of $4.5 billion (one-third of $13.6 billion) of indirect taxes would still leave a gap of more than $3 billion. This gap, however, could be closed by reduction of personal income taxes, the allowance here being perhaps computed as equal to a fixed percentage of the taxpayer's current income tax obligation but not to exceed some reasonable ceiling figure. Thus, if a taxpayer with a wife and one child with a net taxable income (after exemptions) of $1600 would otherwise be paying an annual income tax of $240, he might be entitled to reduce this by $100 for indirect taxes and a further $120 for a 50 per cent cancellation of his income tax obligation, and hence might pay only $20 in all, instead of $240. Just what would be the right percentage of income tax refund to close the gap would have to be calculated by tax authorities on the basis of the schedule of rates and other relevant factors, including the extent to which the tax refunds would be likely to increase savings instead of being spent on consumer goods and services. Because of the need for more spending money in the lower and middle income brackets, this factor would undoubtedly be a minor one as long as the tax refunds were broadly distributed throughout the whole population. However, it would be necessary to allow for some additional savings. The closing of the indicated $7.6 billion gap in consumer spending would therefore require a rise in consumer income, and hence an aggregate amount of tax refunds somewhat in excess of $7.6 billion.

It should be noted that tax refunds or any similar payments to sustain consumption would be conditional upon the development of actual deficiency of consumer spending, measured against an over-all national quota established in advance, would be no greater than necessary to eliminate the measured deficiency, and would cease as soon as the deficiency disappeared. The object would be simply to make sure of maintaining effective consumer demand at gradually rising levels, high enough to justify full employment through expansion of private enterprise, but not so high as to create or permit price inflation. Our proposal therefore has nothing whatever in common with inflationary schemes to create new purchasing power on the theory that the more money the better. Such schemes, of course, hold the gravest dangers.

During the reconversion period it would be necessary under our proposal to limit the guaranteed amount of consumer spending to the maximum of consumers goods and services likely to come on the market. According to our belief, the best safeguard against excessive spending and price inflation in this period will be a continuation of price and rationing controls, coupled if necessary with new safeguards against speculation, until deficiencies of supply disappear. On the other hand, direct regulation, during this transition period of shortages of goods, should as a matter of precaution be supported by fiscal controls, so that we may be sure to avoid a flash flood of demand in the nation's markets, leading to a rise in the cost of living. Moreover, any sound program for supporting total consumer spending must in any case specify maximum as well as minimum limits, so that it may become an instrument for stabilizing as well as sustaining consumption.

Our proposal here is that a reasonable margin—perhaps $3 billion—be allowed over the guaranteed minimum, and that any rise in total consumer spending above the limit provided by that reasonable margin be prevented by imposition of restraints on excessive spending. One way of accomplishing this would be through adoption of a graduated spendings tax, enacted in advance but suspended until actually required.

One important advantage of this particular tax would lie in the fact that unlike the sales tax, it would exempt all subsistence spending. For the purpose of our proposal there probably would be no need to have the tax apply to any family whose spending was not at least equal to the average per capita share of the maximum national spending quota, multiplied by the number of persons in the family. For example, with $135 billion as the guaranteed minimum of consumer spending, the allowable national maximum might be $138 billion, and the spendings tax, coming into action only when necessary to prevent a rise above $138 billion, might exempt all spending below $1000 per person per year. A second major advantage of this approach is that the spendings tax would be at least as much a device for persuading people to save their money for later as it would be a measure to collect revenue. It would therefore be well adapted to a situation in which under-spending is the characteristic problem, and over-spending only an occasional phenomenon. Finally, the income-tax form could be used in administering the spendings tax.

Financing Compensatory Public Works and Consumer Tax Refunds

If compensatory government outlays are required, either to finance public works not included in the regular budget or to sustain consumer expenditures, through refunding of tax payments or otherwise, a budget deficit will presumably be created. A deficit could perhaps be avoided by means of a heavy tax levied directly and exclusively on uninvested savings. This is a possibility to be borne in mind in weighing the relative disadvantages of other measures.

The chief difficulty with financing deficits through ordinary forms of borrowing arises in connection with the burden of annual charges, which will amount to at least $5 billion a year on our national debt by the end of the war. While it is true of an internally held public debt that citizens owe it to each other, so that for citizens as a whole there is no net liability, it also appears that a large and continually rising debt tends to redistribute income in an undesirable way. The bond holdings on which interest must be paid come to be concentrated in the hands of wealthy individuals, banks, and insurance companies, while the taxes to finance these service charges are laid on the public at large.

One answer to this is to finance deficits by issuing interest-free money—for example, by having the government borrow without interest from the Federal Reserve system. In this way the total cost of servicing the debt would be held down. We do not share the view that this procedure would be more inflationary than the customary borrowing procedures involving the banks. The crucial question is whether expenditures are kept in proper quantitative relation to the productivity of the economic system at full employment, not whether interest is or is not paid on funds required to finance the expenditures. If desired to hold the creation of new money to a minimum, that could be accomplished by a program that required uninvested savings to be loaned to the government at nominal rates of interest, under penalty of a tax on idle bank balances and currency.

Since there are difficulties with all the methods that can be suggested, we are not disposed to lay disproportionate stress on the desirability of adopting one approach rather than another. We suggest simply that public expenditures not financed by taxation be financed by public borrowing, at minimum rates of interest, from individual and business holders of uninvested savings and from the banks. The important thing, however, is to remove the underlying reasons why deficits tend to be necessary.

The Relation of Foreign Trade and Investment to Domestic Full-Employment Stability

Without the assurance of being able to sustain full employment through domestic policy at any level of exports and imports, the United States will not be likely to pursue continuously the liberal economic foreign policies so essential for world prosperity and security. The expansion of foreign trade required for the promotion of world security and peace, and for the enhancement of standards of living here and abroad, is a two-way trade, freed from elaborate encumbrances and discriminations. If depression threatens, however, enormous pressures will inevitably develop to raise tariffs, subsidize exports, exclude immigrants, secure exclusive or preferential export markets and sources of cheap raw materials, and, perhaps, without consultation with other nations, devalue the dollar. This is merely a sober picture of reality. We emphasize it in order to underscore again the necessity for making fiscal measures and other domestic measures produce the assurance of full employment—first, because economic policies whose success must be at the expense of other countries are inherently undesirable, and second, because such policies are in any case more likely to produce retaliation from other countries than to produce full employment.

On the other side, it is clear that the task of domestic measures to secure full employment and rising standards of living will be facilitated by international cooperation and the negotiation of international agreements, looking to reduction of trade barriers and discriminations, establishment of concerted monetary action, ending of cartel restrictions, and creation of a greater degree of stability and predictability with respect to specific exports and imports. Foreign loans and investments, with which we can make a contribution toward the raising of living standards in other countries, will also assist us to maintain employment in our export industries. Such loans and investments will therefore be very desirable, provided they go to meet genuine needs in the borrowing country, can be repaid and payment accepted, specify minimum labor standards, are not permitted to lead to imperialist exploitation, and are not conceived of as a substitute for a fundamental domestic policy for full employment.

A potentially important consideration in connection with international economic arrangements, as these affect full-employment stability here at home, is the management of the foreign-exchange market. It would clearly be most unfortunate if our domestic price and wage levels and interest rates would by reason of rigid rates of exchange have to be determined by the exigencies of our international balance of payments rather than on the basis of the needs of our own economy. The enormous accumulations of gold in this country, with which net balances against us could be settled abroad, make it actually most unlikely that international dealings would subject us to pressure to lower our prices and wages or raise our interest rates under any circumstances. Nevertheless, we call attention to the necessity of tempering day-to-day stability in exchange with adequate provisions for ultimate flexibility, for the successful operation of any future international monetary arrangements. We also point out that exchange controls might in special circumstances come to be needed to prevent an excessive flow of capital abroad.

The most critical question, however, relates to the direct effect of exports and imports upon employment in this country. If we are to be sure of maintaining full employment, it is essential that we provide a mechanism to offset changes in the size of our foreign market by opposite changes in our domestic market. If the loss of export markets or the acceptance of additional imports not only threatens the profitability of particular types of farming or particular manufacturing industries but also lowers the level of demand for the products of the economy as a whole, it is obvious that any such development will tend to generate unemployment. Public policy will therefore tend to become enlisted in support of measures calculated to increase exports and reduce imports, even if these measures are in conflict with liberal trade principles and even if, as a result of foreign retaliation, they ultimately fail to have the effect intended. Our experience in the late twenties and at the turn of the decade, when we raised our tariffs to new heights and refused to accept the imports on which repayment of our earlier foreign loans depended, provides a good case in point.

Vital as international agreements are from the standpoint of achieving world security and the highest practicable standards of living both here and abroad, the solution for our difficulty in continuously maintaining a large enough market to justify full production and full employment does not depend on obtaining international agreements. The solution for this difficulty lies within our own control and largely consists in the use of fiscal policy to regulate the over-all level of domestic demand, as we have recommended. The excess of exports over imports, or net export balance, which appears in national income calculations as a component part of private gross capital expenditures, is one of the elements determining the amount of consumer demand plus government demand needed to hold production at the full-employment level. Under our proposal, therefore, the volume of consumer spending underwritten will be reduced when exports grow or imports decline, and will be increased in the opposite circumstances.

By this kind of arrangement, therefore, in addition to the other advantages of such a policy, the United States can render its economy reasonably shockproof with respect to changes in foreign trade. Repayment of loans can then be accepted without fear of depression, and no particular relation between exports and imports will be inherently more stimulating to production than any other. The United States can thus without hesitation pursue its best long-run interests in international economic affairs by proceeding along the road of cooperation.

V. SUMMARY AND RECOMMENDATIONS

This report has analyzed the reasons why a positive fiscal policy is essential for assuring full employment, and has drawn conclusions as to the kind of fiscal policy needed.

A review of the strategic factors governing the flow of income in our economy indicates that automatic forces cannot be counted upon to bring about a sufficient volume of effective demand after reconversion without the aid of conscious fiscal action. As a general rule, saving will tend to be too large and spending too small to make an automatic balance possible. It will therefore be necessary to raise consumption or match the surplus savings with additional investment.

We believe it is desirable to raise consumption as long as this does not deprive society of genuinely needed investment. We also believe that the individual is ordinarily the best judge of his own consumption requirements, and therefore we especially favor an expansion of purchasing power in the hands of individual consumers. Some public capital expenditures and some community consumption expenditures, however, are so important for the general welfare that they should be given priority even over a rise in individual consumption. We have listed substantially increased public expenditures for health, education, housing, and conservation and development of resources as clearly belonging in this preferred category, and we urge the initiation of these programs immediately after the war.

To raise individual consumer demand to levels that will re-establish a full-employment balance in our economy, it is necessary to increase the incomes of the lower income groups in our society. Sooner or later this reform must be put on a permanent basis, through adoption of fundamental improvements such as a more progressive system of taxes, expansion of social security benefits, higher wages wherever possible, and elimination of unnecessary amounts of governmental or corporate saving. In this report we have recommended changes with respect to both the collection and the disbursement of social security funds. We have also dealt at some length with taxation in general, paying particular attention to the question of securing enough tax revenue to cover desirable regular expenditures of government, and to the question of distributing the burden in accordance with ability to pay and the need to maintain mass markets for goods and services.

If our program with respect to basic expenditure policies and basic tax policies were adopted in its entirety, over-saving would be strikingly reduced. Of course it would still be necessary to have additional fiscal measures ready in reserve, so that they could be applied in a flexible manner whenever required to compensate for either an under-spending or an over-spending tendency. Meanwhile, until these long-run measures actually are adopted, the role of purely compensatory fiscal policy will be even more important.

To provide in a practical way for compensatory fiscal action capable of supplementing the results of all other private and public policies by holding total effective demand at the level required to sustain full employment, we have proposed an over-all insurance mechanism consisting of two parts. One part would be a system of national income insurance whereby the Federal Government would underwrite total consumer spending at a level calculated to buy all the consumer goods and services a normal labor force working normal hours can produce, after allowing for the expected volume of private capital formation and the regularly budgeted programs of all levels of government. This would make for a maximum of consumption by individual consumers, and would consequently assure private business as a whole against a shortage of markets and thereby give private business a real opportunity to provide the jobs required for full employment. Because it would take the size of our foreign market into account in the determination of the necessary size of our domestic consumer market, it would also weaken the pressure to obtain export surpluses larger than justified by the real needs of borrowing countries for foreign investment—pressure which may otherwise prove a barrier to liberal international economic relations on a two-way trading basis. The other part would be a reserve shelf of useful public works and work projects which would be drawn upon for additional jobs at regular rates of pay during such times as sufficient private jobs were not available in spite of the favorable conditions provided by national income insurance. This would serve as the final line of defense against unemployment, and would therefore also underpin consumers' income and hold consumer spending at the underwritten level except insofar as over-saving, or, in exceptional circumstances, overspending, would still need to be corrected.

The final adjustment of consumers' incomes, required to make good the total consumer spending guarantee, could be handled, according to our proposal, through consumer tax adjustments. As long as consumer spending tended to fall short of the national quota, we have considered the possibility of compensating this through offsets to indirect taxes and reduction of income taxes. If, on the other hand, consumer spending tended to exceed the quota by more than a reasonable margin, to be specified in advance, this tendency would perhaps best be counteracted through application of a graduated spendings tax, with generous exemptions for subsistence spending. Thus compensatory fiscal policy would guard against deflation and at the same time would provide a necessary safeguard against inflation.

Recommendations

On the basis of our analysis in this report, we make the following specific recommendations on and relating to fiscal policy:

Recommendation 1. That Congress and the President declare it to be national policy to maintain full employment.

Recommendation 2. That all necessary steps be taken to make the meaning of this commitment practical and definite; in particular, that steps be taken to (a) provide a suitable definition of full employment based on the number of men and women wanting to work; (b) provide current statistics of labor force, employment, and unemployment adequate for application of the definition of full employment; and (c) assign to the appropriate agency the responsibility for giving notice (1) when supplementary public works or work projects are needed in order to avoid falling short of full employment, and (2) when public projects should be curtailed because additional private employment opportunities are in sight.

Recommendation 3. That all necessary legislative and administrative action be taken to develop and carry out a compensatory fiscal program capable of maintaining a full-employment volume of demand for goods and services; that, in particular:

(a) With a view to minimizing reliance on compensatory public works, Congress designate an official series of total private consumer expenditure; approve a general method for calculating the volume of consumer expenditure necessary to provide a reasonable market basis for full employment through expanded private production, having regard for foreign markets and all other relevant factors; through the Joint Committee on Internal Revenue Taxation or other joint budget committee calculate, or authorize the appropriate agency to calculate and report periodically, the volume of consumer expenditure necessary for the ensuing fiscal period; underwrite the volume of consumer expenditure as thus determined; define policies in accordance with which taxes would be refunded to consumers, or other distributions of income made, if necessary to keep total consumer expenditure from falling below the underwritten level; define policies in accordance with which additional taxes, or other restraints on spending, would be imposed if necessary to keep total consumer expenditure from rising more than a specified amount above the underwritten level; and provide for flexible application of these policies as necessary to realize the guarantees given.

(b) Congress provide for the planning and preparation of an ample, diversified, and geographically distributed reserve shelf of useful Federal public works and work projects, nonconstruction as well as construction; assist in the creation of a non-Federal shelf by developing a clear policy with respect to the terms and conditions on which Federal aid will be extended to State and local jurisdictions for both the planning and execution of projects; establish project initiation and termination procedures, and authorize expenditure of funds for projects, in a manner consistent with giving priority to private employment whenever available, maintaining wage rates and other labor standards, utilizing Federal action so far as practicable only when other government jurisdictions fail to act, and maintaining full employment as defined.

Recommendation 4. That, in order to promote equality of opportunity and provide for raising the general standard of living, while at the same time minimizing the necessity for compensatory fiscal action under paragraphs 3(a) and 3(b), Congress establish a joint Welfare Standards Committee, charged with (a) estimating and reporting on the character and financial costs of adequate programs of housing, health, education, conservation and development, and social security, and (b) recommending a suitable over-all program, with a suitable division of cost and operating responsibility as between the various private and public jurisdictions concerned. Associated with this Congressional committee should be a Welfare Standards Advisory Committee, consisting of representatives of business, agriculture, labor, and the professions, and having access to all relevant data available in any of the Executive agencies. Labor should also be represented, along with other groups, in the administration of these programs when adopted.

Recommendation 5. That, in order to provide for an equitable sharing of tax burdens, sustain purchasing power, stimulate enterprise, and minimize the necessity for compensatory fiscal action under paragraphs 3(a) and 3(b), Congress develop a postwar Federal tax program that will: (a) provide sufficient revenue to cover regular expenditures, including desirable welfare expenditures as may be recommended pursuant to the provisions of paragraph 4; (b) distribute the burden in accordance with ability to pay; (c) place main emphasis on the individual income tax, with suitably graduated rates, elimination of tax-exemption for State and local government securities, closing of other loopholes, and allowance of adequate exemptions for subsistence incomes; (d) provide for proper integration and strengthening of estate and gift taxes, so that they will yield substantially increased revenues; (e) eliminate excise taxes, except for excises at moderate rates on liquor, tobacco, and gasoline; (f) modify corporate income taxation to end discrimination against equity capital, and allow suitable tax exemptions for new enterprises, but retain rates on established corporations sufficient to avoid undue impairment of revenue, enact provisions to stimulate distribution or use of corporate earnings, and develop as a substitute for wartime excess profits taxation a selective tax on the excess profits of businesses that are substantially monopolistic; (g) meet a part of the cost of social insurance benefits from general tax revenues; and (h) include adequate provision for enforcement. In addition the Federal tax program should (i) provide for the flexible application of anti-deflationary tax refunds and anti-inflationary supplementary taxation as necessary to effectuate the provisions of paragraph 3(a); and (j) be developed with a view to eliminating unnecessary conflicts and overlaps with State and local taxation.

Recommendation 6. That the Federal Government also (a) assist in securing provision of capital and credit to small businesses on reasonable terms; (b) assist in maintaining suitably low interest rates on borrowed capital generally; (c) in any international monetary agreements, cooperate fully in avoiding unilateral action that would be disruptive to foreign economies but at the same time adequately safeguard the integrity of domestic fiscal policy, especially through avoiding excessive rigidity of exchange rates; and (d) adopt all other practicable measures that are consistent with those herein specified and will further promote enterprise, investment, and competition.

TABLE 1. DERIVATION OF 1948 FULL-EMPLOYMENT GROSS NATIONAL PRODUCT AT PRESENT PRICES[a]

A. Derivation from present gross national product

	1944	*estimated 1948 assuming full employment*
labor force	64.0 million	60.5 million
unemployed	1.0	1.5
total employment	63.0	59.0
armed forces	11.5	2.5
civilian employment	51.5	56.5

		(in billions of dollars)
estimated gross national product in 1944		196.0
withdraw: 9 million from armed forces, at $1200 GNP each	—10.8	
withdraw: 4.5 million from war plants (final munitions ouput) at $4680 GNP each	—21.1	
deduct 10 percent of remaining civilian GNP ($161.1 billion) for return to prewar workweek	—16.1	
add 9.5 million civilian workers, including 2 million for growth of labor force in 1944-48, at $3450 (estimated non-agricultural average) GNP each	+32.8	
add 4 percent for increase in output per man-hour, 1944-48 ($180.8 billion × .04)[b]	+ 7.2	
estimated 1948 gross national product at full employment		188.0

B. Alternative method

National Planning Association estimate for full-employment GNP in 1950, at 1941 prices[c]		170.0
deduct 6 percent for smaller labor force and lower output per worker, 1948 as against 1950	—10.2	
1948 full-employment GNP on National Planning Association basis, at 1941 prices		159.8
at 1943 prices, adjusted with Commerce deflators ($159.8 billion × 113.2÷100)		180.9
at 1943 prices, adjusted with B.L.S. cost of living index ($159.8 billion × 117.5÷100)		187.8
at 1944 prices (Jan.-Oct. average), adjusted with B.L.S. cost of living index ($159.8 billion × 119÷100)		190.2

[a] gross national product as measured by the Department of Commerce, assuming present price level for civilian output; (prices of items not being sold at present are assumed to have advanced from prewar levels comparably with other civilian items).

[b] ordinarily assumed to be about 8 percent for 4 years; here conservatively estimated at 4 percent to allow for lag due to demobilization readjustments.

[c] National Planning Association, *National Budgets for Full Employment*, Planning Pamphlets Nos. 43-44, April 1945.

TABLE 2. HYPOTHETICAL POSTWAR GOVERNMENT EXPENDITURES, YEAR 1948 (A) NOT ASSUMING AND (B) ASSUMING EXPANDED WELFARE PROGRAMS[a]

Classified (I) by Usual Expenditure Categories and (II) by Categories Related to Income Circulation

(in billions of dollars)

I

	A	B
Federal		
interest	5.0	5.0
defense	7.0	7.0
veterans	2.0	2.0
social security	(4.1)	(3.5)
additions to trust funds	3.1	[c]
benefits	1.0	3.5
other	4.0	10.6[d]
total Federal[b]	22.1	28.1
State and local	11.3	11.8
total[b]	33.4	39.9

II

	A	B
goods and services	25.0	30.4[d]
transfers to individuals	(4.4)	(7.7)[d]
social security benefits[e]	1.6	3.8
other	2.8	3.9[d]
additions to social security funds[e]	4.0	[c]
acquisition of land	..	1.8
	33.4	39.9

[a] see discussion of programs in section II of text.

[b] excludes any compensatory expenditures for maintenance of full employment.

[c] pay-as-you-go basis assumed; cf. section III of text.

[d] increase for housing, health, education, and conservation and development (cf. Table 5) is partly offset by assumed reduction of .8 other normal public works and .2 other transfer payments rendered impractical or unnecessary by the expanded welfare programs.

[e] difference from social security items under I accounted for by inclusion of State and local components.

TABLE 3. HYPOTHETICAL POSTWAR TAXES, YEAR 1948

(A) NOT ASSUMING AND (B) ASSUMING EXPANDED WELFARE PROGRAM EXPENDITURES[a]

Classified (I) by Usual Tax Categories and (II) by Categories Related to Income Circulation

(in billions of dollars)

I

	A	B
Federal		
individual income	9.0	12.0
estate and gift	1.0	2.0
corporate income	4.0	7.0
excises	2.9	3.0
customs	.7	.7
miscellaneous receipts[b]	.4	.4
social security	4.1[c]	3.0[e]
total Federal[d]	22.1	28.1
State and local	11.3	11.8
total[d]	33.4	39.9

II

	A	B
personal	11.8	16.0
business	16.0	20.6
social security	5.6	3.3
total	33.4	39.9

[a] cf. Table 2.

[b] excludes proceeds from sale of surplus war materials and plant, assumed used for debt retirement.

[c] assumes that employers and employees pay 2.5 percent each under old-age and survivors insurance, as contemplated under the present law.

[d] makes no allowance for compensatory tax reductions or tax refunds, as discussed in section IV.

[e] assumes no medical care and hospitalization insurance, a 3 percent total contribution rate under the general social insurance system (for old-age and survivors, unemployment, and temporary and permanent disability insurance), and a $500 million contribution to social security benefits from general taxation; cf. Table 2.

[f] difference from social security item under I accounted for by inclusion of State and local component.

TABLE 4. HYPOTHETICAL COMPOSITION OF POSTWAR GROSS NATIONAL PRODUCT AND EXPENDITURES, YEAR 1948 (A) NOT ASSUMING AND (B) ASSUMING EXPANDED WELFARE PROGRAMS[a]

(in billions of dollars)

	A		B	
gross national product, assuming full employment[b]		185.0		185.0
(a) private gross capital expenditures		25.0[c]		25.6[d]
(b) government expenditures for goods and services		25.0[c]		30.4
(c) consumer expenditures				
1. assumed gross national product		185.0		185.0
2. deduct: business taxes	16.0		20.6	
3. deduct: depreciation and other business reserves	10.0		10.0	
4. equals: net national income		159.0		154.4
5. deduct: corporate undivided profit	3.0		2.0[e]	
6. deduct: social security taxes	5.6		3.3	
7. add: transfer payments, including social security benefits	4.4		7.7	
8. equals: income payments		154.8		156.8
9. deduct: personal taxes	11.8		16.0	
10. equals: disposable income		143.0		140.8
11. deduct: normal individual saving[f]	18.6		16.2[e]	
12. add: reduction in saving due to accumulated war savings	3.0		3.0	
13. equals: consumer expenditures		127.4		127.6
* * * * * *				
(check for internal consistency)				
total expenditures (a) + (b) + (c)		177.4		183.6
deficiency as against $185 billion gross national product		7.6		1.4
savings: private (3 + 5 + 11 — 12)	28.6		25.2	
government: additions to social security trust funds	4.0			
purchase of land			1.8	
total savings		32.6		27.0
private investment (item (a))		25.0		25.6
deficiency of investment as against savings		7.6		1.4

[a] for effect of programs on taxes and government expenditures cf. tables 2 and 3.

[b] cf. Table 1.

[c] see section I of text.

[d] increase of $1.6 billion in private capital expenditures directly due to expanded welfare programs (cf. Table 5) assumed partly offset by reduction of $1 billion due to higher tax rates.

[e] $3 billion of added taxes assumed to come out of savings ($1 billion corporate, $2 billion individual).

[f] based on correlation by L. Paradiso as presented in Appendix C of National Planning Association, *National Budgets for Full Employment, op. cit.* The formula is: Y = 5.50 + 0.04 (year [e.g., 1948]—1935) + 0.828 X, where Y is consumer expenditure and X is disposable income.

TABLE 5. ESTIMATED POSTWAR EXPENDITURES FOR HOUSING, HEALTH, EDUCATION, AND CONSERVATION AND DEVELOPMENT, YEAR 1948 (A) NOT ASSUMING AND (B) ASSUMING EXPANDED PROGRAMS TO RAISE STANDARDS TO LEVEL OF NEEDS[a]

(in billions of dollars, at present prices[b])

	Housing (including slum clearance)		*Health (including nutrition programs)*		*Education*		*Conservation and Development (soil, forests, river valleys)*		*total of previous columns*		*difference: total B minus total A*
	A	*B*	*A*	*B*	*A*	*B*	*A*	*B*	*A*	*B*	
Capital expenditures[c]											
total	6.0	9.6	.4	.9	.4	1.4	.5	2.0	7.3	13.9	6.6
private	6.0	7.0	.1	.2	.1	.2	.1	.5[g]	6.3	7.9[g]	1.6[g]
government ..	..	2.6	.3	.7	.3	1.2	.4	1.5	1.0	6.0	5.0
Government expenditures											
total[c]	*	2.7	1.2	3.1	3.8	7.3	.4	1.6	5.4	14.7	9.3[h]
capital[c]	..	2.6	.3	.7	.3	1.2	.4	1.5	1.0	6.0	5.0
operating ...	*	.1[f]	.9	2.4[f]	3.5	6.1[f]	*	.1	4.4	8.7[f]	4.3[f]
transfer payments[d] ...	..	..	..	.8	.5	1.0	..	..	.5	1.8	1.3
goods and services[e] ..	*	1.2	1.2	2.2	3.3	6.2	.4	1.5	4.9	11.1	6.2

* less than $50 million.

[a] needs as defined in selected estimates quoted (see under Sources, below); 1948 expenditures assumed equal to annual average in first postwar decade, except as otherwise noted below.

[b] estimates of needs when originally given in prewar (generally 1940) prices were raised 25 percent for purposes of rough adjustment to 1943-44 levels.

[c] includes purchase of sites.

[d] cash payments (or food stamp allotments) to individuals other than for services currently rendered.

[e] excludes purchase of sites; this explains why lines 7 and 8 do not add to totals in line 4 (e. g., figure in final column, 6.2, excludes 1.8 for sites).

[f] average annual expenditures slightly higher; appfoximate annual totals at end of first postwar decade; housing (rental subsidy) .4, health 3.2, education 7.2.

[g] makes no allowance for effect of river valley development in stimulating private investment; total by end of decade probably substantially higher on this account.

[h] Federal share, including Federal aid to States and localities, assumed to be 7.6 (housing 2.1, health 1.4, education 3.0, conservation and development 1.1); balance State and local.

Sources for table 5

"A" columns: based on figures for recent prewar years, with slight adjustment for higher prices and with allowance for assumed high level of housing construction, and for veterans' legislation (hospitals, education) now in force.

"B" columns:

Housing. Based on consensus of selected estimates. Includes urban redevelopment with allowance for neighborhood parks, playgrounds, and recreation buildings (annual total for all non-residential facilities about $250 million). Assumes annual construction of 1.5 million new housing units (including farm units) and rehabilitation of about 370,000 units, continuing for from 10 to 15 years. Includes $1.5 billion a year for site acquisition.

Health. (1) Public health needs (10-year hospitals and sanitation facilities construction program, $670 million a year including veterans' hospitals and including sites; current services, average of $1.7 billion a year) from published reports of U. S. Public Health Service and additional unpublished estimates; payment for medical care through social insurance not assumed. (2) Private hospital construction, etc., from preliminary, unpublished estimates. (3) Food stamp or food discount plan for low-income families (about $800 million a year classed as transfer payments, plus administrative costs) from preliminary estimates of Bureau of Agricultural Economics. (4) School lunch program (public share of cost, $150 million a year) from preliminary estimates of U. S. Office of Education.

Education. (1) Elementary and secondary public education through junior college (capital expenditures, including sites, $1.0 billion a year on 20-year construction basis; annual operating expense rising to $5.7 billion) based on Research Division of National Education Association, *N.E.A. Research Bulletin*, April 1944; $80 million a year added for student aid at high-school and junior-college levels, based on preliminary estimates of U. S. Office of Education. (2) Elementary and secondary private education, higher education, adult education, and libraries and museums, roughly estimated from miscellaneous sources. (3) Training programs for veterans (total cost $2.8 billion, including $2.0 billion of transfer payments for maintenance) from Research Division of N.E.A., *ibid.;* about one quarter of total is here assumed spent in year 1948.

Conservation and Development. (1) Soil and water conservation (on assumed 20-year basis, annual capital expenditures of $940 million, half public and half private) from preliminary estimates of Soil Conservation Service, U. S. Department of Agriculture. (2) Forest conservation (average annual public capital plus operating expense in first 10-year period of long-term program, $410 million, including $80 million for land; private capital expenditures, $70 million a year) from preliminary estimates of Forest Service, U. S. Department of Agriculture. (3) River valley development ($700 million annual public capital expense) roughly estimated on basis of programs proposed by Bureau of Reclamation in Department of the Interior, and Flood Control and Rivers and Harbors divisions of Corps of Engineers in War Department.

11

GUARANTEEING EMPLOYMENT OPPORTUNITY*

On all sides we hear talk of the desirability of postwar full employment, but the real issue that is shaping up is whether or not employment opportunity should be *guaranteed.* If it is to be guaranteed, it must be done by the Federal Government. Obviously, no one else can do it—no one business, no one community, no one trade union. Well, then, shall the Federal Government guarantee to maintain conditions in which everybody will have—and nobody will be denied—the chance to work?

Personally, I think the answer should be yes. If we do not guarantee full employment—which, of course, by definition allows of a small, agreed-upon amount of frictional or turnover unemployment—but merely agree to *try* for as much employment as possible, then that is nothing at all new, costs nothing, and may be entirely inadequate.

I don't want in the least to belittle the efforts of business men and groups like the C.E.D. It must be true that hard work, hard thinking, enthusiasm and a sense of public responsibility are resulting in plans for business ventures—and hence for employment—that might otherwise be overlooked. But as much employment as is possible without invoking the powers of the Federal Government is not enough. Nor is there any reason to believe that it is easier to maintain a level of employment three or four million less than full employment than it is to maintain full employment.

If you have no arrangements for holding a flag at the masthead, is it any easier to hold it at some point lower down on the staff?

Some people are sincerely distrustful of specific employment goals and commitments. They view the idea of setting such goals with alarm. If told that specific goals were necessary, they would regard them as a necessary evil. I think that their view of the matter is entitled to respect. But I also think it can be said to such people that, however good the reasons for their point of view may be, they at least overlook one tremendously important fact—the fact that the right kind of goals and guarantees can in

*In slightly different form this paper was originally given as an address on "Postwar Employment Policy" at a University of Michigan Extension Service meeting in Detroit on June 22, 1945, and was printed in the *Congressional Record* of July 27, 1945, in the extension of remarks of Senator Lister Hill of Alabama. The revised version here presented was published in the August, 1945 issue of the *American Federationist,* under the title, "A Full Employment Program."

themselves have a great lifting power and make the solution of the employment problem much easier.

To get down to cases, here, in brief, is my suggestion. I hope that my sketchiness will be forgiven—it is a huge subject and my space is limited. Also let the reader be warned against thinking that my suggestion or any other could prevent reconversion unemployment during the transition. I don't want to leave the impression that there may be some formula by which our economy can swing back to peacetime production overnight or without causing a large number of people to go through short periods of unemployment. Undoubtedly we are going to have to lean heavily on our unemployment compensation systems at this stage of affairs, and undoubtedly also, as the President has said, these systems will have to be strengthened.

Now let me come back to full employment program in the broader sense, as distinguished from demobilization program. Three things seem to me to be needed. First, an insurance approach to the problem. Second, a number of basic national policies, including but certainly not limited to government expenditure and tax policies. And third, a balancing mechanism to make sure that we actually deliver on the employment commitment even before we have succeeded through our basic policies in bringing our economy into a natural balance. Let me take these three points up one at a time.

First is the insurance approach. This means the giving of commitments in advance. In other words, it involves government underwriting. There are, I think, two essential things involved—first, a guarantee of full employment itself, and, second, a guarantee of the total national consumer market at a high level. I want to emphasize that this refers to *aggregate* employment opportunity and *aggregate* consumer demand, and is not a proposal to guarantee any individual jobs or the market for any individual products.

A guarantee of full employment itself would obviously assure us of a high national income. This would provide security to the worker, would stimulate confidence, and would prevent the kind of hoarding of money that grows out of fear of future depression. To carry it out, a national budgeting approach is needed, as recommended by the sponsors of the full employment bill, with additional public jobs available as a last resort if other employment falls short.

But it surely is not a good idea to put exclusive or even primary emphasis on government jobs. We want all jobs—public and private—to result in worthwhile products and we don't want to have business exposed to the risk that an unlimited number of jobs may have to be artificially created. Therefore, in addition to a guarantee of full employment as such, I think we need a further guarantee that total consumer spending will not fall below a specified high level. This would in particular provide confidence for private business because the consumer spending target would show that business itself could profitably provide the bulk of the number of jobs guaranteed, so that public works would not have to be expanded unduly.

This kind of guarantee would meet the over-saving problem head-on. The income paid out by full employment production does not necessarily yield an ample market for business because too much of this income may be saved and too little may be spent. The consumer market guarantee, on the other hand, would give to business the assurance that this unfortunate thing would not happen.

I want to stop for a moment to give additional emphasis to the importance of this insurance approach, as I see it, because it is a rather new idea and seems to have tremendous possibilities for cutting the Gordian knot in which our economy was tied for a number of years before the war. Its possibilities are such, for both labor and management, that the exploration of these possibilities would seem to offer a very promising new field for cooperative action. Of course, without the support of management and labor, no approach to these problems is likely to get very far.

The first advantage of the insurance approach is that it provides security and confidence. Let me give an analogy. Now that bank deposits are insured, people are not very likely to start runs on banks. Similarly, if employment and markets were insured, business men would not be so likely to take their money and energies out of the economic game.

But this is not the only advantage. Besides promoting confidence, the insurance approach would greatly reduce the government's need to rely upon forecasts for the determination of what it should do. It would therefore very much reduce the disputes about the necessity for government action—disputes that are bound to arise when people disagree about the accuracy of the forecasts the government is making.

Let me clarify this point. If employment and expenditure goals are set for the economy and then, because of deferred demand, accumulated war savings or any other factor, these goals are met automatically by the unaided operation of the system, then in that case the government, which is acting as underwriter, need not and should not take any additional action in behalf of expenditure and employment. But if, on the other hand, the goals as finally determined by Congress are not being met out of the unaided operation of the system, then clearly government action will be called for, and it is hard to see how any dispute could arise over that.

Parenthetically, most of the calculations made by the economists who have thoroughly studied this subject show that there is every likelihood that shortages of expenditures and employment will tend to develop after the war—at least when temporary demands have been satisfied—if nothing is done to prevent it.

There is, therefore, a strong probability that the government, acting as underwriter, would have some gaps to fill.

But the point is that, if we adopt the insurance approach, we don't need to waste an undue amount of time wrangling over just what we see in the future as each of us looks into his favorite crystal ball.

Notice further than a guaranteed total consumer market, by taking pressure off the public works device, would make guaranteed full employment entirely favorable from the standpoint of business, instead of partly favorable and partly a threat of competition from bigger and bigger government operations. Also it would be a sure way of promoting high consumption—and nothing could be better than that for standards of living throughout the country. Hence, it would relieve us of the necessity of expanding investment, for the sake of employment, more than was really needed by any other test. In fact, it would really free us from the piece-by-piece approach to full employment. If the various other pieces failed to add up to full employment, this would simply mean that general purchasing power would be expanded instead.

Thus, in the last analysis, this approach would relieve the haunting fear that we have become too productive in this country—that we are unable to consume as much as we are able to produce—a haunting fear that tends to drive us into a search for larger and larger export markets even if this finally goes beyond the bounds of common sense and of mutual advantage to ourselves and other nations.

So much for insurance. Let us turn now to the next idea. The second thing we need is a series of basic governmental and private policies designed to make our economy balance as well as possible, so that the guarantees would be as nearly self-enforcing as possible without further government action. Of course, these basic policies deserve the fullest discussion. But this is out of question here, and therefore, in the limited space at my command, I shall merely try to review a few of the main ones for the reader's further consideration. I hope this will not be interpreted as an underestimation of their importance.

First of all, there is the desirability from the economic point of view of having wages as high as productivity will allow. This is important, and hence collective bargaining is important, if for no other reason than that the wage stream largely goes into spending and adds very little to the over-saving problem.

Next, there is the need for a low-price, high-output policy on the part of business. Such a policy should also be enforced through government anti-trust action when necessary, and through sound patent legislation, regulation of cartels and monopolies, aids to new and small businesses, etc.—all such measures being aimed at promoting competition and checking the restrictive practices of monopoly. This line needs to be taken in order to encourage new investment, dampen down over-saving and make sure that an adequate market for goods and services really gets translated back into full production and full employment.

Thirdly, it seems essential that we do everything possible to eliminate substandard incomes in agriculture and in whole regions, such as the South. Quite aside from other considerations, this will help greatly to maintain the markets we need.

Fourthly, we need a permanently strong, efficient and properly recognized nationally coordinated employment service, to help bring available workers and available jobs together.

Coming to those basic policies which are financial or fiscal in character, we have the whole question of taxes and government expenditures. As to government expenditures, the Labor Committee on National Policy of the National Planning Association recently sponsored a report which, in a preliminary way, goes into our national needs in the fields of housing, health, education, conservation and development of natural resources.

In these fields alone, and without including other important matters, such as recreation, cultural programs, social services, research, rural electrification, etc., where the sums involved are much smaller, it was estimated that additional amounts of nearly ten billion dollars a year would need to be spent by Federal, State and local governments to attain adequate minimum standards of living and opportunity for the whole population. This amount does not allow for the possibility of national medical care insurance. Of course, there is little doubt that our social security system should be broadened in various ways and the benefits expanded. I believe it would also be helpful to the solution of our employment problem were these benefits financed in a less deflationary manner than at present by adoption of the pay-as-you-go method and by contribution to the funds from general taxation.

Turning to taxation as a whole, the important thing here is to give fullest application to the principle of ability to pay while at the same time not discouraging genuine initiative and investment. Taxes should fall more heavily on those with large incomes than on those with small incomes because this is fair and because it will help to sustain mass buying power. This means that excises ought to be largely eliminated, gift and estate taxes strengthened, and heavy reliance placed on the individual income tax—but with higher exemptions to take the burden off subsistence incomes.

In the complicated matter of corporate income taxation, my personal opinion is that the best solution might be to set the rates where they will strike a level about halfway between wartime and prewar corporate tax revenues. In this connection, everything that will help to remove discrimination against risk capital, as compared with passive loan capital, certainly ought to be done.

Now I want to get to my third main point—the need for a balancing mechanism. Let me repeat that the basic policies I have so lightly touched on are of the utmost importance. If they are given the attention they deserve, this will very much reduce the necessity for running a Federal budget deficit in connection with maintaining full employment. It will also mean that we are going after fundamental problems, like monopolistic restrictions and the distribution of income. Nevertheless, we also need a balancing mechanism operating by means of fiscal policy, because it is totally unrealistic to act as though we had solved all the basic problems and got rid of over-saving any time before these things actually have been accomplished.

Following the lines of the guarantees mentioned earlier, there are two parts to a well-rounded and practical balancing mechanism. The first is a public works reserve—an ample, diversified and geographically distributed reserve shelf of construction and service projects. Construction should be carried out through private contractors unless for special reasons that proves impossible in a given case. I think it is important that jobs on the public works reserve should pay prevailing rates of wages. The reserve, after all, would not in this setting be a relief proposition, but rather a part of the provision made to assure everyone the opportunity to have a real job. These supplementary public employment projects, unlike the regularly budgeted items for schools, hospitals and so forth, which cannot afford to be postponed, would be shut down when private employers again had more jobs available. But the readiness of government to shut them down as private employment opportunities expanded—this, and not substandard rates of pay—should be the safeguard against anyone's staying on the public payroll too long.

The one thing that is always emphasized in connection with the public works reserve may as well be said here again, because it cannot be stressed too much or too often. This is the need for *advance planning*. I wish it were possible to feel that the Federal Government and the States and local communities were ready at this time to meet the demands for extra public works that they are likely to encounter in the transition period.

The second part of the needed balancing mechanism lies at the point in our economy where money is spent for consumer goods and services. The government keeps current records of the total rate of consumer spending.

Having guaranteed a certain minimum rate, it would have to match the actual rate against this commitment. If the actual rate was falling short, the government would have to promote additional consumer spending by some device that left or put more money in consumers' hands. One way of doing this would be to refund, suspend or offset certain taxes that affect consumption. But it would be important, for the sake of avoiding a leakage into further excess savings, to offset the hidden or indirect taxes that affect the poor man and not merely reduce the withholding rate on the income tax which is paid by those who are better off.

A crucial point to note is that any such offset to taxes would be allowed only if and as long as current consumer spending tended to remain below the guaranteed rate. Hence, the proposal is not in the least inflationary. In fact, on the contrary, I am sure that the commitment ought to set a ceiling over consumer spending as well as a floor underneath it. Many people with real justification are afraid that full employment may lead to price inflation. One of the best ways of ruling that out is to set a maximum as well as a minimum limit to total consumer spending. If, then, in some period—for instance, in the immediate transition period—consumer spending should threaten to go through this ceiling, a special tax or some other restraint would be brought into play temporarily. Possibly the best device for this particular contingency would be a graduated spendings tax. This could have generous exemptions at the bottom and would avoid the unjust and undesirable features of the sales tax, which has little to be said in its favor.

To sum up in as few words as possible the things that I think might be accomplished by the kind of full employment program I have tried to present in this brief sketch, here are some of the main possibilities:

First, insurance of our economy against depression. *Second,* a contribution to the safeguards we need against inflation. *Third,* a spotlight on the importance of getting ahead rapidly with our basic policies, while at the same time we do not postpone full employment until all the basic policy issues have been settled. *Fourth,* development of a sound relation between domestic and foreign markets, meaning by this the promotion of beneficial foreign trade and investment without the pressure to go to dangerous extremes in our dependence upon them. *Fifth,* creation of confidence based on job security and high markets—a state of confidence free of those conflicting emotions which might develop in the business community if it seemed that full employment could only be maintained through a forced expansion of the government's own operations. And, *finally,* conditions in which opportunity in the broadest sense of the word could become real for everybody, regardless of race, sex or any other consideration.

12

THE NATIONAL BUDGET*

Formerly, the dominant opinion was that serious and prolonged unemployment must be due to wage and price rigidities, creating structural maladjustments in the economy; or to artificially easy credit policies, generating boom and inflation inevitably followed by recession and deflation--in short, to interferences with the free and normal working of competition. In recent years the proponents of fiscal policy have gained in prominence, paying scant attention to such doctrines and gravitating toward the position that the only way to avoid unemployment is to have the Government so regulate its expenditures and revenues as to maintain an adequate volume of demand for current output. Many adherents of the earlier school remain unconvinced; in their view the new policies, not content with moderation of the admitted instability of the system, unbalance the budget continuously and evade the fundamental issues.

In view of the shortness of time, it is important that common ground be found, if possible, between these two views, so as to advance the practical work in behalf of a postwar America free from unemployment and also free from major price distortions and other dis-equilibrating factors (such as excessive income inequality) which interfere with a balanced use of resources and necessitate large, continuing deficits in the Federal budget. It is believed that such cooperation is possible if there is agreement that full employment should be definitely assured. The suggested meeting ground is the national budget—more specifically the full-employment national budget.[1]

The policies required for a general program to assure full employment may be divided into (a) basic policies to minimize long-run deflationary

---

*An article published in the August, 1945, issue of the *Monthly Labor Review,* under the title, "The National Budget as an Aid in Reducing Deficits Under Assured Full Employment."

[1]The "national budget," as the term is here used, is a statement summarizing for a given year the various types of expenditure for the goods and services currently produced by the economy—expenditures by business, by Federal, State, and local government, and by consumers. A full-employment national budget is one in which this total of expenditures is large enough to buy the volume of output produced when there are employment opportunities available to all persons able and wanting to work. The magnitude of this total depends, of course, on price and cost levels. It should not be so large as to induce price inflation.

tendencies and hence the need for deficit-creating compensatory fiscal measures to maintain employment opportunity, and (b) policies to "close gaps," i. e., to compensate remaining deflationary tendencies or, on the other hand, inflationary tendencies when and if these appear. In this discussion, it has been assumed that adequate compensatory fiscal policies will be adopted.[2] They are, of course, essential. It is clear, however, that everything possible should be done to reduce our reliance upon them. This requires placing emphasis on basic policies. The urgency of the need furthermore suggests the advisability of a systematic approach such, for example, as modern industrial research has learned to employ.

Organizing Effort and Pooling Information Toward Identifying Desirable Basic Policies

Drawing upon experience, especially prewar experience, it is possible to prepare, as a working tool, a picture of how the national budget might normally look in a postwar year, assuming levels of business capital expenditures, regular government expenditures, and consumer expenditures consistent with the observed historical data, and assuming that compensatory fiscal policies are applied to close any remaining gap so as to maintain full employment. A good deal of work along these lines has already been done both in and out of government. This projected normal budget will, of course, vary in accordance with assumptions as to year and price level, and also in accordance with the way in which the data on trends are interpreted and applied to the imagined postwar situation. The margin of uncertainty thus introduced is not, however, of importance for present purposes. Certainty would be needed only if it were a question of trying to fill exactly a gap whose size was accurately known in advance. That, of course, is not the situation. It is impossible to foresee the size of the gap precisely, and the necessary instrument for final adjustment when a measurable gap actually opens up is compensatory fiscal action and not policies of the basic type. A so-called "normal" estimate is therefore supposed to supply only a scaffolding of reasonably adequate dimensions to which a variety of anticipated "abnormal" developments and possible policy measures can be attached experimentally, in the mind's eye, for purposes of a rather systematic appraisal of their potential effects.

It is immediately apparent that any normal economic picture will be modified in a favorable way, during the early postwar period, by several

---

[2]Policies of this type are discussed in section IV of the author's *Fiscal Policy for Full Employment* (National Planning Association, Planning Pamphlets No. 45, Washington, May 1945); see also his "The Underwriting of Aggregate Consumer Spending as a Pillar of Full-Employment Policy," in *American Economic Review*, March 1944.

unusual factors arising out of the war situation, notably accumulated war savings and deferred demands both at home and abroad. These effects will follow more or less automatically, assuming that general confidence and prosperity are maintained. On the other hand, other and more permanent favorable effects will wait on the adoption of new policies with respect to taxation, competition and monopoly, wages, social security, foreign investment, etc. Assurances that employment, national income, and the total market for the output of industry and agriculture will be sustained should also be mentioned among these policies, since such commitments could in themselves have a powerful effect in increasing private expenditures and reducing the necessity for deficit financing. Thus, consideration needs to be given to the following subjects, among others:

- War savings and deferred demand:
  - Abnormal consumer demand.
  - War-caused deficiencies in plant, equipment, and inventories.
  - Foreign demand for relief and reconstruction.
  - Deferred public improvements.

- Taxation.
- Banking and currency.
- Competition and monopoly:
  - Antitrust action.
  - Patents.
  - Monopoly regulation.
  - Cartels.
  - Special aids to new and small business (finance, research, etc.).
- Wages:
  - Higher wage-price ratios.
  - Minimum wage.
  - Annual wage.
- Agriculture:
  - Commodity-support programs.
  - Miscellaneous aids.
- Social security:
  - Broader provisions.
  - Pay-as-you-go financing.
- Foreign policy:
  - Foreign investment.
  - Commercial policy, etc.
- Housing and urban redevelopment.
- Health program.
- Education program.
- Conservation and regional development.
- Employment service, etc.
- General assurances:
  - Insured full employment.
  - Insured full employment plus insured consumer market.
- Capital budget.

This list is, of course, merely illustrative and also incomplete in other respects. The broad categories shown simply indicate certain convenient points of departure. Clearly, before the effects of a policy not yet adopted can even be guessed at, the content of the policy must be specified in some detail.

Once specification is supplied, the main questions are: (1) Just how—i. e., at what point—would each of these various developments or policies be likely to affect the national budget as previously described, and about how large an effect would it be reasonable to expect from each? (2) As far as any given change in policy is concerned, would it require new legislation, an Executive order under existing legislation, or merely a campaign of education and publicity?

Illustration of Analytical Procedure

How the first of these questions may be attacked is illustrated in the accompanying table, which presents a hypothetical example of how the national budget might react to the adoption of new policies designed to promote competition and limit the restrictive effects of monopoly. It must be emphasized that this illustration is purely hypothetical, in that the indicated quantitative effects of the assumed new policies A, B, C, etc.,[3] have been arbitrarily chosen and do not represent an attempt at actual evaluation of probabilities. The so-called estimated situation under present policies (column 1) represents a rough blocking in of magnitudes that might be reasonable under certain assumptions but are here intended as illustrative only.

Other examples might equally well have been chosen. For instance, it is evident that certain types of tax policy would increase the relative share of disposable income in the hands of families and individuals with small incomes, thereby increasing consumer expenditure and reducing the tendency to save. Other forms of taxation might especially encourage private capital expenditures; still others might reduce undistributed corporate profit, etc. Anything that increased the percentage of income going to wages would also tend to increase consumer expenditure in relation to consumer saving and would therefore reduce the need for deficits to sustain total demand unless the measures in question cut into profit to the point where private production was curtailed as a result. Pay-as-you-go financing applied to the social-security system would expand total income payments, and hence consumer spending, by reducing social-security taxes without changing the established scale of benefits. A public hospital-construction program would tend to narrow the deflationary gap somewhat if financed through tax increases that chiefly affected savings, unless private investment reacted adversely to the higher taxes, and it would clearly increase disposable income

[3]Content not specified; as is well known, we are still a long way from agreement on any such policies.

HYPOTHETICAL EFFECT OF HYPOTHETICAL COMPETITION AND MONOPOLY POLICIES ON "FULL-EMPLOYMENT NATIONAL BUDGET" [1]

[Amounts in Billions of Dollars]

Item	Estimated Situation Under Present Policies	Situation Under Assumed New Policies
Gross national product assuming full employment	185.0	183.0
(a) Private gross capital expenditures [2]	25.0	26.5
(b) Government expend. for goods and services	25.0	24.5
(c) Consumer expenditures:		
1. assumed gross national product	185.0	183.0
2. deduct: business taxes	16.0	15.7
3. deduct: depreciation etc.	10.0	10.0
4. equals: net national income	159.0	157.3
5. deduct: corp. undiv. profit	3.0	3.0
6. deduct: social security taxes	5.6	5.6
7a. add: social security benefits	1.6	1.6
7b. add: other transfer payments	2.8	2.8
8. equals: income payments	154.8	153.1
9. deduct: personal taxes	11.8	11.6
10. equals: disposable income	143.0	141.5
11. deduct: individual saving [3]	15.6	14.5
12. equals: consumer expenditures	127.4	127.0
Total expenditures, (a) + (b) + (c) 12	177.4	178.0
Deflationary gap (cf. line 1)	7.6	5.0
Government deficit required to close gap	[4]7.6+	[4]5.0+
Savings and investment:		
Savings:		
Private (3 + 5 + 11)	28.6	27.5
Government (6 - 7a)	4.0	4.0
Total	32.6	31.5
Private investment (item (a))	25.0	26.5
Savings-investment gap	7.6	5.0
Government revenues and expenditures:		
Taxes (2 + 6 + 9) {excluding deficit operations to close gap}	33.4	32.9
Government expend. ((b) + 7a + 7b + (6 - 7a)) [5] {excluding deficit operations to close gap}	33.4	32.9

Shows effect [6] of policies A and B, which stimulate new investment by facilitating freedom of entry, use of patents, etc.

Shows effect [6] of policies C, D, and E, which reduce the prices of "monopoly" products, hence also the volume of expenditure needed to buy a full-employment output, and the amount of tax revenue needed to cover regular expenditures of government (as well as, incidentally, the tax base in so far as dependent on profit). [7].

Shows effect [6] of policies A-E, which reduce monopoly profit, increase the relative share of total income going to low-income groups, and thus reduce saving by increasing the "aggregate propensity to consume." [7]

[1] The year might be 1948, assuming 1944 prices except that "monopoly" prices are by hypothesis reduced in column 2; see footnotes 2 and 3 for assumed deviations from "normal" tendencies.

[2] Includes 15 billion dollars in plant and equipment and 2 billion dollars in inventory accumulation on account of deferred demand, and 2 billion dollars in net exports which assumes moderate Government encouragement.

[3] Assumes 3 billion dollars' less saving than "normal" on account of accumulated war savings.

[4] Will exceed size of gap (see previous line of table) by amount of (a) reduction in private capital expenditures if gap is closed through supplementary public investment, or (b) additions to saving if gap is closed through tax reductions or transfer payments that increase consumer incomes.

[5] Additions to social-insurance reserves (6-7a) are included with Government expenditures to indicate the level of total taxes required to balance the budget under present accounting methods.

[6] Amount of effect is arbitrarily assumed; no actual evaluation intended.

[7] Part of the reduction of individual saving might by attributed to smaller disposable income resulting from policies C, D, and E (i.e., the same formula applied to disposable income yields slightly smaller saving in column 2 than in column 1); for simplicity this effect is not shown separately but is combined with the effect by way of relative reduction of the income share going to profit.

and consumer expenditure if a capital budget were set up so that only interest and amortization were treated as current costs to be covered by taxation. Similar or related considerations apply to any other item on the list.

Naturally, in studying the problems in this field, it is not always necessary to begin by taking a given policy and trying to determine its several main effects (if there are several) upon the national budget. There may sometimes be advantages in taking a given section of the budget—such as, for example, the gap between national income and income payments—and reviewing the several policies by which this particular relationship might be improved.

Implications for Action

The purpose of the table here given, with its purely illustrative quantities, is to show that it ought to be possible to narrow down arguments over policies that are thought to have an effect on employment, by indicating *how* or *where* these effects are supposed to appear in the national budget. *How much* then becomes the next question. Many exact answers should not be expected, and some persons will be tempted to assert that even the roughest approximations are out of the question. This need not be granted offhand, however, especially in view of the practical importance of achieving a better understanding than now exists of the relative quantitative significance of some of the measures most widely advocated as means of promoting expansion of private enterprise and limiting the tasks of government.

In summary, the full-employment national budget, because of its stability, provides the nearest thing to laboratory conditions the appraiser of economic stimuli is likely to see. Doubtless it may be impossible to show, in terms of this budget, that the assured or minimum effect of the basic policies proposed and certain to be adopted exceeds the maximum deficiency of expenditure and, finally, of employment, to be expected without them. This will not detract from the necessity of framing and securing enactment of basic measures that will at least greatly improve the self-activating power of our economy. On the other hand, it will also demonstrate that those who object to providing for the use of compensatory fiscal measures in a supporting role are satisfied to let full employment take its chances.

13

FULL EMPLOYMENT IN PRACTICE*

In discussing "Full Employment in Practice," I propose to observe two limitations. First, I am not going to speak about how full employment might be practiced in any country other than the United States. It may be that the practice of full employment in Great Britain, for example, or in Australia, would be largely like our practice here; or, on the other hand, perhaps it would be quite different. That is an interesting question and an important question, but it is also a question on which I do not care to speculate here. If what I have to say can contribute to the understanding of the ways and means that are open to us in the United States, I shall be fully satisfied.

The second limitation that seems essential is this: the phrase, *full employment in practice,* does not, I take it, refer to how things might look at that happy but possibly rare moment between painful recovery and tragic collapse—that moment when the man of affairs and the business cycle theorist can clasp hands and say: "Boy! This is it!" On the contrary, when we speak of full employment in practice, we undoubtedly mean the way of operating our economy whereby full employment would be *permanent, continuing, and assured.* That, at any rate, is how I interpret my assignment, and I ask you to bear this carefully in mind as we go from step to step.

The point where innumerable discussions of full employment go off the track is the point where one party begins to talk about things to do to moderate our depressions. This brings scientific exchange of ideas on how to maintain full employment to an abrupt close. The practice of full employment is not the practice of moderating our depressions and our unemployment; it is the practice of not having any depressions, or any unemployment beyond the inevitable amount consistent with full employment.

What is full employment? Although I mean to come back to that again

*This paper was presented on December 19, 1945, as an address before a special seminar on "Full Employment in a Free Economy" conducted by the Institute on Postwar Reconstruction at New York University. It was subsequently published by the Institute in pamphlet form.

later, certainly something should be said at once to make it clear that this distinction between maintaining full employment and moderating unemployment is not just a play on words.

Of course full employment allows some slack in the system—some between-jobs or frictional unemployment—no one has ever denied it so far as I am aware. But please take note of these two points about genuine full employment. In the first place, employment does not fall below, or unemployment does not rise above, some quantity agreed upon in advance. In other words, performance is checked against and governed by a standard. In the second place, the standard adopted is intended to produce a situation in which there will really be work opportunity for all who are able to work and desire to do so, and, from time to time, the operation of this administrative standard is reviewed to see if this standard needs revision to make it correspond to the essential idea of universal employment opportunity.

There in a nutshell is why maintaining full employment is not the same thing as seeking to moderate unemployment or, as some propose, seeking to avoid mass unemployment. Whether or not it is the same thing as maintaining *high* employment would seem to depend on how high a level of employment is meant.

If full employment in practice means a state of affairs in which employment is not allowed to fall below a certain mark set ahead of time (or one in which unemployment is not allowed to rise above a certain mark set ahead of time), how in practice is full employment to be maintained?

Surely there can be no doubt about one part of the answer. There cannot be the assurance that continuing full employment will be maintained unless in the last analysis the Federal Government stands ready to hire extra workers if necessary, directly or through private contractors or agents. Let us call this rather obvious conclusion point number one.

Point number one is enough to give a great many people the shudders. Certainly a point number two is badly needed to take the weight off point number one by showing that the necessity to rely on extra government jobs can be minimized. We are not prepared in this country to look with any pleasure at the possibility of an unlimited expansion of public works or public employment in general. There are limits to public construction in the ordinary sense, and if other public jobs are expanded too far the twin dangers arise of useless "leaf-raking" projects and unfair competition that will discourage business.

Fortunately, analysis shows that there is a point number two ready at hand in the form of certain measures that should minimize reliance on public works, etc., our measure of last resort.

When production falls below the level required to provide full employment, this means that, in relation to existing costs and existing profit requirements—neither of which can be forgotten in this connection—the total volume of demand for goods and services is too small. The total volume of demand for goods and services consists, let us say for convenience, of three components: consumer demand, business demand or capital formation (including here any surplus of exports over imports), and the demand of Federal, State, and local government.

Theoretically, when these three components add up to a total that is too small, the Federal Government can provide the needed extra jobs by sufficiently increasing its own expenditures for goods and services. That is the method described under point number one. Unfortunately we have no assurance that business demand plus consumer demand will automatically be large enough to keep the need for this extra government employment within manageable limits, *even if our economy is running at full employment initially.* The income earned and for the most part paid out at full-employment levels of operation of our economy may not return in the form of consumption and investment sufficiently completely to prevent a wide gap from opening up. It would, of course, be rash to assert that such a deflationary tendency must always be present. But it would be equally rash to trust that such a tendency will *not* appear when the special wartime factors of accumulated savings and deferred demands at home and abroad have spent their main force. In fact, the analysis of habits and trends in consumption, saving, and investing as exhibited over a lengthy period before the war indicates that, once the special factors no longer dominate the situation, the emergence of a strong tendency of this kind is the likeliest thing in the world.

I ask you to join with the average business man in considering again the impracticality of trusting to public employment to meet this situation—the impracticality of closing this gap (which might be a very wide gap, year after year) solely or primarily with extra public employment, over and above the employment already being provided on regularly budgeted public works and public services. As I have said, I find it impossible to believe that this method would yield continuing full employment in practice.

Let me therefore suggest the answer that seems to grow out of the logic of the case. If it is not feasible for government to maintain full employment by expanding *its own* demand in the market whenever private demand tends to fall short, the government can instead so regulate its revenues and expenditures that, by and large, *private* demand is prevented from falling short. In the main, this involves expansion when necessary—and also contraction when and if necessary—of *consumer* demand, brought about through government action affecting *directly* the level of purchasing power.

Thus the government does not go into competition with business but instead supports the general market for the normal products of business.

This is, I believe, the way continuing full employment will be practiced if we are going to practice it in the United States. One other main element needs to be added, however. Since business is a forward-looking process, and investment in particular is based on calculations of probable consumer demand for years ahead, the effectiveness of a policy that continuously maintains a high but not too-high level of consumer demand will be strengthened by having the government adopt the practice of underwriting from year to year the volume of consumer demand considered to be adequate.

* * *

Before I proceed to particulars I want to spend a few minutes calling attention to some of the general implications of this approach to the employment problem. I shall here mention, in turn: (1) how it would affect the proportions among private consumption, private investment, and government expenditures for goods and services; (2) its relation to balancing the Federal budget; (3) the way it would integrate our compensatory policies with what may be called our basic policies; (4) its relation to forecasting; and (5) its significance for policy on foreign trade and investment.

1. In the matter of proportions, the main point about this approach is that it emphasizes expanded consumption. It does this by making the production and sale of consumer goods and services take up most of the slack that is likely to occur in the system. No obstacle whatever is put in the way of private investment or worth-while government expenditures for goods and services. I believe that everyone wants to encourage private investment, and parenthetically I may say that personally I am a believer also in very substantially expanded public expenditures for health, education, slum clearance and low-cost housing, conservation, and development. Suppose, however, that businessmen are already making all the private investments that they will naturally make under conditions of continuing prosperity. The voters' representatives will meanwhile have brought public works and services to the level that they regard as necessary and proper. The approach I am proposing assumes that it is more logical to have the rest of our labor force producing for consumption than to be forced to make additional expansions of public works and services merely to create jobs. At the same time this approach does recognize that expansion of public investment and public services is the proper way to adjust for a contraction of private investment where the latter is not the manifestation of a long-run trend but rather occurs temporarily in spite of steady support given to consumption.

2. One of the most controversial questions in the debate over full employment is this: Will not a full employment program involve a continuous and disastrous series of deficits in the Federal budget? Some opponents of full employment not only say that it will and must involve continuing deficits, but also say that we cannot stand these unbalanced budgets and therefore cannot afford full employment. Some advocates of full employment, not satisfied with pointing out that deficits are inevitable if we run into unemployment and depression, go on to argue further that full employment will bring a balanced budget because it will create a large taxable income.

The approach we are considering here takes neither of these extreme positions. Rather it assumes two things: first, that, if the objective of full employment and the objective of a balanced budget come into conflict, it is the balanced budget that must for the time give way; and second, that firm and intelligent action must be taken to rectify more and more those things that so unbalance our economy as to make full employment and a balanced budget likely to be incompatible. As you can see, this second point presupposes the view that full employment will not, in the first instance, normally bring a balanced budget—that it will not tend to do so until we, ourselves, do something about such things as excessive inequality of income, monopolistic restrictions, and several other very troublesome problems. I may say that, in my opinion, we would overlook this obligation at our peril.

3. This question may be clarified further by emphasizing a distinction between basic policies on the one hand and compensatory fiscal policies on the other. The role of basic policies, in the approach under discussion, is to minimize reliance on compensatory policies that will usually occasion budget deficits to prevent deflation and unemployment or else may involve last-minute, emergency action against a threatened inflation. The role of compensatory fiscal policies is to provide further support and flexibility as needed, to the end that assurance can be given that full employment will be maintained without inflation, irrespective of how sufficient or insufficient the basic policies currently in operation may be for that purpose.

A commitment is therefore given that compensatory policies will be used if necessary to prevent over-all deflation, or to prevent over-all inflation. But at the same time basic policies are pressed vigorously—i.e. policies, of whatever kind, that will minimize long-run deflationary tendencies—not forgetting measures to prevent speculation and localized inflation from getting started and thus setting the stage for a violent tendency toward deflationary reaction at a later period. In this context, obviously, the question asked about any basic measure that may be proposed is not "How much additional employment, if any, will result if basic policy X is adopted?"

but rather, "Will the deficit or other difficulty associated with maintenance of full employment become smaller if basic policy X is adopted?"

4. I have mentioned that the insurance idea is an essential part of the approach under consideration. The first advantage of insurance is that it provides security and confidence—in this case, both to consumers, who will be able to look ahead to steady jobs and steady incomes, and to business. Business under this approach will be assured not only that the total national market will be maintained, but also that the final market for normal products of business will be maintained at a high enough level to preclude a threat of competition from bigger and bigger government operations.

This, however, is not the only point to be noticed about the insurance approach. Another feature of equal importance is its relation to forecasting. One way of trying to maintain full employment is to have the government estimate in advance what deficiencies in expenditure and employment are likely to result in the absence of government action to create additional expenditure and employment, and then set forth policies and programs designed to keep these prospective deficiencies from materializing. Unquestionably it is difficult for the government to make such estimates with a high degree of precision a considerable period ahead. It is also doubly difficult for the government to secure general acceptance among private experts of the accuracy of the forecasts made.

The approach we are considering here is therefore based on a different principle. The thing to be settled by the government is not the prospective deficiency, if any, but rather the levels of expenditure and employment regarded as necessary and the means to be employed *if* (but only if and so long as) those levels do in fact fail to be maintained automatically. Thus the speculative factor disappears. The need for compensatory government action, if there is a need, is proved by events.

At this point it may be well to recapitulate what has been said thus far about the nature of the government policy visualized in this discussion. The main elements may be set forth briefly in four general "rules."

A. *Federal budget rule:* Incur deficits if necessary for full employment, but develop basic policies to make deficits unnecessary.

B. *Public works rule:* Be ready to increase expenditures for public works and services as a last resort to maintain full employment, but, in general, use revenue and outlay measures that will maintain private expenditures for goods and services in preference to increasing such public expenditures beyond the recognized need for the works and services themselves.

C. *Insurance rule:* Underwrite total employment at the level regarded as corresponding to full employment, and underwrite total consumer expenditure at the level likely to maintain full employment in a manner consistent with rule B; *i.e.*, without excessive reliance on extra public works and services.

D. *Anti-inflation rule:* Avoid basic policies likely to create undue inflationary pressure; in underwriting total employment and total consumer expenditure, set ceilings as well as floors; and be ready to hold these ceilings should that prove necessary.

5. The final point before I go on to questions of Executive recommendation, Congressional policy determination, administration, and statistics has to do with policy on foreign trade and investment. We are all aware, I take it, of the great advantages in the form of strengthened international security and higher living standards to be gained from an expansion of world trade along liberal lines permitting countries to specialize and exchange in accordance with comparative efficiencies of production. We are also aware of the economic and political advantages of expanded foreign investment that will help to repair the ravages of war and also help to develop and raise up those countries and areas where methods of production are primitive and standards of living low. Finally, we know that the market outlets created by such foreign investment on the part of the United States will be a boon in the immediate future to our own heavy-goods industries which so greatly developed their productive capacity during the war.

All this, however, does not alter the fact that any compulsion to find additional foreign markets as the only way of preserving full employment in this country could lead in time to the most unfortunate consequences both abroad and at home. Instead of being in the position to make foreign trade serve us by promoting the cause of welfare and peace, we would then become slaves to the dangerous necessity of an export surplus.

Such a predicament, it should be noted, need not arise under the methods contemplated here. If total consumer spending is underwritten, the level at which it is underwritten will take account not only of normal government expenditure for goods and services but also of total private capital formation *including* the export surplus, if any. In other words, domestic consumption will be held at a slightly lower level if exports exceed imports than if imports equal or exceed exports, but no question of a failure of demand as a whole is admitted regardless of how the foreign trade balance may happen to stand.

* * *

We come now to operating problems. Please keep in mind the general principles already discussed. If these are applied, I think you will find that the problems of recommendation, legislation, administration, and statistical information present no insuperable difficulties.

1. *Executive recommendations.* It is clear that, in making recommendations to Congress in connection with the maintenance of full employment, the President and his advisers—I assume that he will have the benefit of the advice of various nongovernmental groups as well as of his Executive Office and Cabinet—will need to deal with the basic economic policies on which the ability of the economy to operate at high levels without compensatory adjustments largely depends. He will also have to deal with the compensatory adjustments to be made if the current performance of the economy actually proves not satisfactory. Moreover, some kind of quantitative evaluation of the problem in the form of a full-employment national budget will be indispensable.

Great importance attaches to the first requirement—the basic policies required to set our economy on a course where excessive dependence on compensatory action and Federal deficits will not be needed. These in general are long-run policies, not dependent on the situation of the moment or the situation believed to be immediately ahead but rather dedicated to the continually valid propositions that private enterprise and competition need to be encouraged through removal of deterrents and restrictions, that purchasing power needs to be broadly distributed and sustained, and that welfare needs to be promoted by direct government action in areas where it cannot be otherwise made secure.

A full-length exploration of these basic policy fields is neither possible nor necessary here. Obviously one very crucial field is that of taxation, where we face the twin problems of eliminating regressive influences in our tax system in order to protect mass-purchasing power, and of finding ways, over and above the maintenance of mass markets, of preserving and improving the incentives for venture capital. Another field is that of competition and monopoly, involving such considerations as special aids to new and small business, antitrust policy, patents, international cartels, and regulations to prevent the raising of prices and the restricting of output and employment by those economic units that in the nature of the case must inevitably be in a position to exercise a substantial degree of monopolistic control. A third field is that of wage policy, where the general frame of reference is given by the desirability of achieving the highest feasible wage-price ratios. Another relates to the special problems of agriculture. Still another, the field of social insurance, involves not only such questions as adequacy of benefits and coverage, but also pay-as-you-go financing versus reserve accumulation, and, again, the problem of the best distribution of the taxes to support the benefits.

A fifth broad field, or series of fields, covers policy with respect to government's own direct contributions toward welfare through its expenditures for health, education, housing, conservation of natural resources, regional development, social services, scientific research, etc. The substantial capital investment connected with some of these welfare programs, not to mention other standard forms of public works, creates a further question of possible recommendations for budgeting capital items separately and carrying only the interest and amortization on the current budget. The basic policies of importance also include those affecting the ability of our system of public employment exchanges to do a good, nation-wide job of helping to bring available workers and available jobs together.

So much for this part of the President's recommendations. No one could tell, in most cases, exactly how much compensatory action could be spared if a given policy change of the basic type were proposed and adopted by Congress. Nevertheless, it seems clear that substantial results of this kind can be expected from appropriate action in some of the areas mentioned. The problem is, therefore, one of moving with as little delay as possible in all sectors where the potential gains seem large, and then reviewing at least once a year the scope and effectiveness of the existing basic legislation to see what further modifications or additions should be proposed.

The President's compensatory recommendations are quite another matter. Here quantitative guides will be necessary. Following out the line of thought developed earlier in this discussion, I think that the really essential quantities are these three:

A. The estimated volume of employment (including the self-employed in industry and agriculture) corresponding to full employment in the year ahead, taking into account the estimated size of the labor force and allowing for necessary frictional unemployment.

B. The estimated aggregate volume of expenditure for goods and services by private enterprises, consumers, State and local governments, and the Federal Government, required to purchase, at the expected level of prices, a gross national product of such volume as would be created at full employment.

C. The estimated aggregate volume of expenditure by *consumers* required to purchase, at the expected level of prices, such portion of a full-employment gross national product *as will not be purchased* by private enterprises, State and local governments, and the Federal Government under what may be considered as optimum conditions—these conditions being: (1) a level of capital expenditures by private enterprises based on the confident anticipation of continuing full employment and continuing high-level consumer demand, and (2) no extra government expenditures for goods and services required in order to combat unemployment. (The private capital expenditures item, of course, as previously noted, includes the export balance.)

For example—to use some purely illustrative figures that are not intended as a prediction—in a given year full employment (item A) might be estimated as equivalent to an average of 56.5 million civilian jobs, with 2.5 million others in the armed forces; at the expected level of prices aggregate expenditures for goods and services amounting to about $185 billion might be estimated (item B) as needed for full employment; and it might be estimated that private gross capital expenditures and government expenditures for goods and services would each, under the stated conditions, be likely to reach about $25 billion. In that case, the necessary volume of consumer expenditure (item C) would be $185 billion minus $50 billion, *i.e.*, $135 billion.

Having had this kind of computation made, the President will be in a position to add to his basic recommendations the compensatory recommendations needed to round out his report. Essentially the latter recommendations fall into two categories, those relating to maintenance of consumer demand and those relating to public works.

Under maintenance of consumer demand will be a recommendation that total consumer spending be underwritten at a certain level (say $135 billion); recommendations in regard to preferred policies for raising consumers' incomes if observation shows that their spending is falling below the rate underwritten; and recommendations in regard to preferred policies for preventing, if necessary, a rate of consumer spending yielding more than a slightly larger amount such as, for example, $138 billion.

Under public works what will be presented is a diversified and geographically distributed reserves shelf, including also nonconstruction or service projects and including feasible expansions or accelerations of regularly budgeted items, with a request for authority to initiate or expand operations based on this shelf if necessary, *i.e.*, if support of consumer demand at the specified high level, together with all other measures taken, proves insufficient to maintain full employment at an average level of, say, 56.5 million civilian jobs. Authority will also be asked to close down the operation of projects from the reserve shelf if employment rises appreciably—perhaps half a million or so—above the level designated as full employment. Further authority will be asked to slow down certain items included in the *normal* budget if employment threatens to rise too high, as it may do if the original estimate of private capital expenditures proves too low.

A question arises regarding the ways that might be recommended for raising consumer spending to the underwritten level if—as will normally be likely to happen until real progress has been made with our basic policies—it tends to remain too low even when income payments are running at a full-employment rate. No attempt will be made here to catalogue the various methods available, but two possibilities will be mentioned by way of illustration. The President might recommend, contingent on a demonstrated need for more consumer spending, a reduced rate on the personal income tax, coupled with cash offsets or refunds, on a reasonable basis, applied to Federal, State, and local indirect taxes which largely burden those too poor to pay an income tax. Or, alternatively, he might wish to recommend, along with a reduced rate on the income tax, the distribution to low-income families of stamps enabling them to improve their nutrition and living standards by buying food and, possibly, other necessities such as clothing in the market at reduced expense. For the opposite contingency of a tendency toward an inflationary excess of total consumer spending, he might recommend, for example, a graduated spendings tax with generous exemptions at the bottom.

Before leaving the subject of Executive recommendations, it should be made clear that the recommendation on underwriting consumer spending can be kept as flexible as desired. For example, the President might consider that, in the light of experience, $25 billion was the probable aggregate of regularly budgeted Federal, State, and local government expenditures for goods and services, but at the same time he might feel that Federal expenditures for such things as education, health, conservation, etc., should be substantially increased, bringing the total to $28 billion. A good method of handling this situation would be for the President to recommend that Congress underwrite consumer spending at $132 billion if it went along fully with his new programs on education, health, conservation, etc., that it underwrite consumer spending at $135 billion if it rejected these new programs, and that it set an intermediate figure for consumer spending if it accepted these programs in part.

2. *Legislation.* Under our Constitution our national policies are established by Congress. If the first operational step in maintaining full employment is the preparation of Presidential recommendations, the decisive step is the enactment of legislation. Let us therefore try to visualize the general nature of Congressional action under conditions corresponding to those established as the subject for this discussion—namely, full employment in practice.

Speaking broadly, the type of action required of Congress in these circumstances involves the final establishment of goals and the commitment to attain them; the enactment of basic legislation tending to promote the spontaneous occurrence of high-level production and employment; the approval of tax reductions to be made or contingent funds to be expended if and when these goals are not being reached spontaneously; and the determination of rules, governing such tax reductions or supplementary expenditures, to guide the President in maintaining the operating levels called for by Congress.

In the light of what has been said already, much of this requires no further comment. The first point that concerns us here is this: unless Congress will decide what it means by full employment by setting a floor below which it will not allow employment to fall, there can be no assurance, and probably no likelihood, of continuing full employment.

Congress, of course, need not accept the President's recommended definition. It may set the goal somewhat lower. But if it sets the employment goal so low that operation at the indicated level would not in fact provide everyone with the opportunity to work, then "full employment" becomes a misnomer. Presumably the pressure of public opinion on Congress can prevent this from happening, once it is recognized that, with private consumer spending underwritten at a suitable level, full employment will not require the expansion of government operations at the expense of private enterprise.

To be sure, the question of the proper relation between the level of consumer spending and the level of employment will require careful consideration. If Congress sets too low a level of consumer spending—or if, perhaps, it underwrites employment without making any separate decision about consumer spending—what can normally be expected to happen is that the spending and saving habits of the public will make it necessary in maintaining total employment to expand government employment unduly. To take the opposite extreme, in theory at least, Congress might underwrite consumer spending at a high level, and employment at a low level or not at all. This, however, would be likely to create an undesirable situation in which the government was subsidizing consumers while many job seekers were out of work. In short, the problem confronting Congress, as well as the President, is partly one of absolute levels and partly one of balance.

For this and other reasons it seems clear that, in an economy that provides continuing full employment, Congress will have some kind of joint committee of both houses to which the President's report with its national-budget estimates will be referred for study. This committee will then make its own report to Congress as a whole, and Congress, finally, will decide what it wants to accomplish and how it wants to accomplish it.

According to the analysis set forth herein, this means, as noted, that Congress will: (1) set minimum and maximum limits for employment and for consumer spending during the ensuing year; (2) designate specific methods to be used by the President if necessary to keep employment and consumer spending from falling below the minimum limits or exeeding the maximum limits; and (3) appropriate as contingent appropriations such sums for supplementary public works and for supplements to consumer incomes as may possibly have to be used, according to the methods prescribed, to achieve the results demanded. In addition, Congress can be expected (4) to legislate on general measures tending to reduce the relative importance of the program of compensatory adjustments.

3. *Administration.* Without embarking on a lengthy discussion of problems of administration connected with full employment—a field in which, in any case, our knowledge will largely have to be developed as we go along—I should like to call attention to the general nature of the administrative apparatus required if the foregoing conclusions on policy are valid.

Consistent with the distinction between maintaining employment as such and maintaining consumer spending as a means of supporting private employment, the problem divides itself into two main parts. One agency or set of agencies must watch employment, set in motion the expansion of public employment when that is needed, and bring about the contraction of public employment when that in turn is the action indicated. Another agency or set of agencies must watch the flow of consumer expenditure, provide for expansion of consumer disposable income, under the rules established by Congress, when consumer expenditure would otherwise be too small, and if necessary also provide for the application of temporary restraints on consumer expenditure.

Each of the two administrative centers, incidentally, has its own indexes to watch, irrespective of the operations of the other. This follows from the fact that, while employment naturally tends to create consumer spending and consumer spending naturally tends to create employment, neither one when maintained at the level at which it is underwritten can be counted on to maintain the other at *its* underwritten level.

As far as employment aggregates are concerned, there is obviously needed a Federal agency in the labor field which will keep an up-to-date count of the labor force, employment, and unemployment, together with the distribution and composition of each and such information as can be obtained on trends and outlook. When total employment is about to dip below its established floor, this agency must be in a position to advise the agency responsible for Federal action on public works concerning the type and location of reserve-shelf projects that need to be called into action or are likely to tbe required soon.

Similarly, when private employers are increasing their demands for labor to an extent calculated to raise total employment above its ceiling, the agency keeping track of employment must advise the public works agency to stand by to terminate certain of its operations. Finally, appropriate standards must be applied in the field to make sure that placement, vocational guidance, retraining, and relocation operations are coordinated with each other and with unemployment compensation in an efficient and equitable manner.

On the side of consumer spending, much depends on the specific legislation enacted. In any case, however, what is required first of all is an agency such as the Department of Commerce to keep track of the actual rate at which consumer expenditures are flowing. The facts can presumably be reported at any given time with a lag of no more than a month or six weeks, and if, after due allowance for normal seasonal variation, consumer spending proves to be too low or too high, the proper agency or agencies can be notified and can act in accordance with Congressional instructions to rectify the situation.

For example, if it proves too low, and if Congress has decided that such deficiencies should be handled exclusively through specified tax adjustments at quarterly intervals, fiscal experts must calculate the additional consumer spending likely to result per dollar of tax relief or rebate granted, and consequently the size of the adjustments needed to restore consumer spending to within the acceptable range. It should, however, be recognized that the subsidization of purchasing power, whether handled through tax adjustments or otherwise, will in all probability require the maintenance of files showing the income status of all families and single individuals, rather than merely the records now kept by the Bureau of Internal Revenue for income-tax payers.

4. *Necessary statistical information.* It is sometimes thought that an enormous mass of statistical information is required for the practice of full employment. Yet perhaps this view of the matter exaggerates somewhat the difficulty of the operating problem.

The first thing needed—primarily because it sets the main goal and secondarily because it is one of the elements upon which our estimates of the requisite aggregate of expenditures for current output must be based—is information about the prospective size of the labor force in the coming year. From this the President and Congress can determine, after making allowance for the fact that a small volume of turnover unemployment is necessitated by dynamic growth and movement in our economy, what they consider the volume of employment to be that best expresses for administrative purposes the true meaning of the concept of full opportunity to work.

Current series of this kind are now compiled by the Bureau of Labor Statistics, the Bureau of the Census, and the Bureau of Agricultural Economics. While by no means perfect, they are certainly usable for the purpose of setting a goal and checking performance. A decision must, of course, be made regarding the best method of handling seasonal variation, but this raises no very serious problems. During the present transition period a considerable degree of caution is required in predicting the size of the labor force, swelled as it has been during the war by millions of abnormal entrants into the labor market, some of whom will leave while others elect to stay. In this period caution is needed also in determining the volume of frictional unemployment required by industrial and geographical shifts. Ordinarily, however, trends are steady enough to make the probable range of miscalculation of the over-all labor magnitudes rather small.

According to the procedures described in a previous section, the expenditure estimates required in drawing up a national budget are not very numerous or hard to obtain. Essentially what is called for is, first, an approximate magnitude for a full-employment aggregate of gross national expenditures for the next year, and second, a magnitude representing the probable sum of (a) normal government expenditures for goods and services and (b) business expenditures under continuing full employment and full consumption. From this and the aggregate expenditures magnitude is derived by subtraction the magnitude actually used for operating purposes —namely, the volume of consumer expenditure to be underwritten.

Inasmuch as offsetting errors in calculating the total and the other components tend to cancel out in arriving at this consumer expenditure goal, and inasmuch as the purpose of the consumer expenditure commitment itself is only to keep ordinary private markets large enough to make extra public works more or less unnecessary, a high degree of precision is hardly essential. It is not the case, under this formula, that everything hinges on the accuracy of the estimates. When the volume of private capital formation fluctuates, or if cost and price levels move a little out of the expected line, some adjustment in the volume of publicly created employment will be necessary in any case to make the final adjustment. The estimates of dollar magnitudes therefore serve in the last analysis as a scaffolding with the help of which a frame of policy can be erected to maintain full employment and yet minimize reliance on those public works that are not valuable enough to be approved on their own merits. A scaffolding need not be set up as carefully as the house it helps to build.

This is not to say, of course, that the wealth of detail on various subcomponents of business, government, and consumer expenditures now being accumulated is not extremely valuable. Undoubtedly it is valuable, and undoubtedly it also needs to be improved—especially, perhaps, in the field of prospective business capital expenditures. For immediate purposes, however, the essential point is that the work already done by fiscal experts in the Bureau of the Budget and elsewhere appears to be sufficiently advanced to permit the preparation of usable national budgets along lines here described.

Two further kinds of statistical requirement remain to be mentioned—the compilation of current figures on consumer spending, to see whether or not adjustments are necessary to keep consumer spending from falling below or rising above the limits established by Congress, and the more or less detailed continuing analysis of employment and unemployment, to see among other things whether the administrative definition of full employment under which the economy is operating is a satisfactory definition.

Since the former requirement has been mentioned already in connection with administration, no special comment is necessary here. The Department of Commerce, along with its other national income series, keeps records of consumer spending which will readily develop into the official guide for the purposes of this part of full-employment administration.

As far as the labor-force data are concerned, however, stress should be placed on the need for both quantitative and qualitative research with the aim of steadily improving our ability to register through our administrative definitions and devices the essential meaning of the concept of jobs for all. Unemployment should be analyzed by type, by location, by duration, and by group affected. Part-time employment should be studied to see where it is involuntary and where it is preferred. If concealed unemployment exists in agriculture or elsewhere, because of absence of other opportunities, this should be made known. The number of unfilled vacancies offering reasonable wages should be compared with the number of employable job applicants. Out of such investigations as these can be expected to come valuable suggestions for improvement in the services rendered by our employment offices and allied agencies, as well as knowledge that may lad to significant changes in the level at which, or possibly the terms or form in which, full employment will be administratively defined. In short, such studies can promote the growth of human opportunity.

* * *

In conclusion, let me point out that this attempt to picture how I believe that full employment in practice is likely to operate in the United States neither depends on any special theory of how unemployment originates, nor implies that we can forecast the future accurately, nor seeks to define how far the government should go in expanding its own works and services.

This approach does not imply acceptance of the stagnation hypothesis or of any particular brand of business-cycle theory. It does assert that few if any know the measure of the over-all inflationary pressure in coming months, or exactly when deflationary strain will develop, or how great this strain will be, and it challenges the contention that we can be sure of maintaining full employment without taking out some form of insurance on our economy.

Regarding the form of this insurance, some may feel confident that needed and ready programs of public works and services will always be able to offset any tendency toward deflation and unemployment. I imagine, however, that not very many who have fully considered the technical and the legislative problems have confidence in this special solution.

The procedure whereby the assurance of continuing full employment is facilitated by the underwriting of aggregate consumer expenditure presents, by contrast, a general and not a special solution. It does not attempt to prejudge or predict the things that cannot be prejudged or predicted. Essentially all that it requires is that, as a nation, we decide how much employment we consider desirable, and about how much public employment, and agree to see that we get what we want, in the proportions we have chosen.

14

FACTS, ISSUES, AND POLICIES

The keynote of Dr. Albert G. Hart's remarks on the problem of full employment* is that economists should recognize the uncertainty of future developments and the consequent need for flexibility in our stabilization policy. In this I heartily concur. Forecasts are a precarious basis for stabilization programs. I also concur in a majority of the other detailed opinions expressed in Hart's paper.

But has Hart carried his reasoning through to its logical conclusion? His recommendations would have us meet uncertainty by a "feeling-out process." I do not think that this is sufficient. I believe we should meet uncertainty by a form of over-all economic insurance. Insurance eliminates guesswork, promotes confidence, and guarantees results. A feeling-out process is too tentative to yield these benefits.

While I say "insurance" advisedly and am not indulging in a figure of speech, I admit to using the word in a loose sense. I do not have actuarial soundness in mind. Existing governmental insurance systems may or may not be thought to operate on actuarial principles; no such claim is advanced in this case. Nevertheless I hope that my usage may be condoned, because I am looking for a strong word that rejects the idea of "doing the best we can" in the matter of employment and instead conveys the idea of a definite commitment.

I do literally suggest the establishment of a form of *underwriting* whereby the Federal Government *assures* whom it may concern that unemployment will not exceed the amount decided upon as consistent with full employment in the operating sense. This seems a reasonable proposition if full employment is attainable in practice and is what we want. If we want it, we want to be sure of it—especially since confidence actually simplifies attainment. To be sure of it we need to insure it. This applies to the period of launching stabilization as well as to any other period.

Hart's recommendations are not, I take it, necessarily in conflict with this,

*Dr. Hart's paper, entitled "Facts, Issues, and Policies," and this discussion of it, were presented at a Round Table on the Problem of Full Employment held at the fifty-eighth annual meeting of the American Economic Association, in Cleveland, January, 1946, and were printed in the *American Economic Review: Papers and Proceedings*, May, 1946.

providing it can be done. His argument does move back and forth a bit between maintaining full employment and combating serious unemployment. But I notice that, when all hell finally breaks loose in his manuscript, with his "gong" sounding the rise of unemployment above a stated moderate figure at the same moment that his "whistle" warns of an upward cost-price spiral, he is all for heeding the "gong" as well as the "whistle."

For insurance of full employment to be workable, two things are clearly necessary: (1) Uncertainty must be removed as to what full employment is, in order to avoid dispute as to when the government should expand or curtail its own employment-giving operations. (2) The body of full-employment policy as a whole must be such that the government action available to back up a solid and meaningful guarantee of full employment can be seen to be in harmony with the other traditional values of our economy. This has two main corollaries: (a) reliance on compensatory fiscal action of any kind must, as time goes by, be kept within reasonable limits; (b) reliance on extra public works and services to provide employment must be kept within limits that are definitely narrow.

Can uncertainty be removed as to what full employment is? Hart has given us his conceptual definition (a situation where unemployment is exclusively "frictional") and he has also pointed out the need to set specific standards and to formalize machinery for keeping track of current events, so that we may know when to act. Being in agreement with these suggestions, I should like to try to clinch the matter with some further observations about procedure. Concretely, a satisfactory working definition of full employment would appear to be attainable through a continuous process operating roughly as follows:

(1) *Recommendation:* The President in an annual economic message to Congress proposes, let us imagine, a numerical employment or unemployment standard for the coming year—one that his economic advisers believe will create a situation in which all those wanting and able to work will have a chance to do so. This standard may be in the form of an annual average—for example, in a particular year it might be an averge of 59 million jobs, including self-employed and armed forces—or the allowances deemed necessary for seasonal variation may be mentioned specifically. Probably, in addition to a floor, there will also be suggested a ceiling at which curtailment of public works, etc., should be brought into play to prevent a further rise in total employment.

(2) *Legislation:* After analysis of the President's recommendation by a suitable Congressional committee, Congress makes its own determination and underwrites the minimum level agreed upon, presumably also setting a top limit. This action establishes the official, administrative definition for

the ensuing year. At the same time Congress instructs the President to use specified means—including, as last resort, variations in the volume of public works and services—to effectuate its stated purpose with respect to the level of employment, and provides contingent appropriations for use in the specified ways if necessary.

(3) *Administration:* A designated agency keeps track of current employment and unemployment and notifies the agency responsible for public works, etc., when expansion or contraction is required to keep total employment within the limits set by Congress. The resulting action by the public works agency serves as the final guarantee that full employment, as defined, is maintained.

(4) *Re-evaluation:* The appropriate agencies continue their quantitative and qualitative studies of the labor force data. For example, they analyze: unemployment by type, by location, by duration, by group affected; part-time employment; the relation of vacancies to applications; the existence or absence of concealed unemployment in such sectors as agriculture. These studies show how well the current numerical definition of full employment accords with the underlying aim of universal job opportunity. Allowing also for secular growth of the labor force, changes can if necessary be suggested in the level at which, or possibly the terms or form in which, full employment should be defined thereafter. The President is thus prepared for his next year's recommendation to Congress. This completes the circle.

The reason I have discussed the question of definition at such length is that there appear to be many who believe that full employment must always remain indeterminate. We are told that full employment is a goal so high and so vague that, while we should strive in the direction of it, we cannot hope to achieve it and therefore cannot assure that it will be achieved. My discussion, however, has aimed to show that, on the contrary, full employment is perfectly determinate for working purposes. This surely is all that matters.

Of course the chief problem remains — the development of a policy approach consistent with the other fundamentals of our economy and hence acceptable in practice. This problem is difficult enough so that failure to get at the issues could easily be fatal to full employment. Here I feel that Hart's treatment is deficient. Although his individual propositions seem reasonable, the principle needed to serve as a "binder" is missing. This principle I believe to be that *total consumer expenditure should be underwritten* at a high level, as well as employment itself.

The reason for underwriting consumer spending separately is that the maintenance of an aggregate of gross national expenditures sufficiently high to sustain full employment might otherwise entail more reliance on public works and services than was physically possible, or more reliance than the system of private enterprise could stand.

Forecasts of time and amount are treacherous and, in any case, unnecessary. It is enough to take warning from past saving and spending habits that a situation can easily arise, once wartime savings and the backlog of deferred demand no longer control the situation, where even the disposable income resulting from full-employment conditions would tend to leave effective demand considerably short of what is required to have the full-employment conditions continue. May I introduce for Hart's consideration a new sound—the "squawk"? The "squawk" will occur, with both "gong" and "whistle" silent, when employment is full momentarily but markets start dwindling because of insufficient re-spending of full-employment income. In short, the "squawk" registers the pure, initial strain of deflation. Seriously, with this deflationary virus latent in the system and no remedy visualized except expansion of government expenditures for goods and services—chiefly for public works—it seems to me quite unrealistic to suppose that the government would guarantee full employment.

Assume, however, a floor and ceiling for consumer expenditure as well as a floor and ceiling for employment as a whole, and assume the consumer expenditure quota to be calculated from probable business plus government demand subtracted from a roughly computed full-employment volume of gross national expenditures. This creates a very different perspective, not dominated by public works. I presuppose that private investment will here be estimated as optimistically as warranted by prevailing incentives to business expansion—including the encouragement provided by continuously assured full employment not based on expansion of government programs—while government demand will be accounted for on the basis of programs approved for their own sake irrespective of labor-market conditions.

This policy approach, unlike the other, gives tangible assurance that the main emphasis in the full-employment program is on expanded private employment, and that supplementary public works can therefore be held within suitably narrow limits. Hence I believe that it meets the crucial difficulty noted above.

Naturally the added support for consumer spending that may often be required under this policy will involve a reduction of tax revenues or an increase in transfer payments, either of which will tend to unbalance the Federal budget. Since the practical possibility of insuring full employment might be endangered by the prospect of continuing heavy deficits, even without the aforementioned threat of vast public works, the other main requirement is action to keep the need for compensatory measures as a whole within reasonable limits.

Success in this endeavor depends in substantial degree on wage-price policy. Parenthetically, the existence of the complex and difficult wage-price problem cannot be laid at the door of full employment. Indeed, psychologically this problem should be easier to work on cooperatively once a convincing full-employment policy is adopted, bringing income security to the worker and making higher break-even points clearly practicable. Furthermore, a ceiling on consumer spending provided by an underwriting formula will help prevent an inflationary spiral.

In the fiscal-monetary field, it is necessary to distinguish between compensatory measures as such and basic measures of permanent value in reducing the need for compensatory action—such as taxation that is progressive but encourages risk-taking, expanded public welfare expenditures, preferably with suitable use of a capital budget, and an overhauling of social-security financing methods. A third type of action mentioned by Hart, which overlaps the foregoing in the realm of credit control, involves heading off speculative, inflationary movements that would lead to collapse and deflation later on. A fourth great field involves promotion of competition and control of inevitable monopoly.

I need not extend this list. Hart has referred to the necessity for disagreements among economists. One of the areas in which disagreements are bound to continue and are bound to prove fruitful is the area of detailed blocking-in of these basic policies for promoting a better natural balance in our economy and thus reducing the need for artificial compensations. A second area for disagreement involves the best form of compensatory adjustment of consumer purchasing power and expenditure, under a policy based on the underwriting principle.

Hart has urged maximum use of "built-in flexibility" of policy—which is to be secured, under given tax and benefit rates, through heavy reliance on income taxes and social security. I think that a warning should be sounded against exaggerated reliance on built-in flexibility in just this particular sense. What is implied is large variations in income and employment levels. The argument therefore relates essentially to an economy that is expanding and contracting, rather than to a full-employment economy.

I agree, however, with Hart's emphasis on the need for deliberate short-term changes in tax rates or exemptions and in monetary policy, as well as in public works. Money and debt management should have considerable leverage on consumer spending if the government will create new money with which to retire its debt. The personal income tax should be readily adjustable, and perhaps social-security levies also. Persons not affected by reduction of such taxes might possibly be compensated in cash by rebate of imputed indirect taxes paid to any tax jurisdiction, or in kind through a stamp plan or other arrangement allowing purchase of basic necessities at reduced prices. If necessary to prevent an inflationary rise in consumer spending above the established ceiling, a graduated spendings tax with high exemptions might be brought into play, other methods failing.

These, as already conceded, are issues on which there is much to be gained from present disagreements. What I hope will *not* be a subject for disagreement indefinitely, among political economists concerned with the esttablishment of continuing full employment, is the need for an advance commitment underwriting total employment, this commitment in turn made workable by the underwriting of consumer spending. It seems to me that a policy to assure an ample market for the normal products of business, and keep government out of unpremeditated competition with business, should commend itself to common sense.

PART II

ESSAYS, 1949-1972

15. EMPLOYMENT THE KEY*

Current events are stirring up the dormant interest in full employment. More and more people are beginning to say that something had better be done. What is not as commonly recognized even today is that the need to do something has been there all along. The premonitory fear of a future depression in the United States--a fear which has at no time been absent--is a potent factor for ill in both our domestic and our international relations, quite aside from the damage that results if depression actually occurs.

For instance: Large American business corporations insist on operating at low break-even points, with prices and profits high in boom times in relation to wages, because they expect to need the extra profits as a cushion against losses that will occur if markets and production later shrink--as no one at present can be sure they will not.

American labor, in turn, is always worried, and justifiably worried, about that most fundamental security problem, the job: will it last and, if it does not, will other job opportunities be available?

In this situation unions, like industry, are prone to insist on getting every possible concession for themselves here and now, and labor-management relations, in particular, suffer.

Again, other countries with which we do business--including major powers like England--have conclusively shown in recent international conferences that they will not and cannot give anything like hard-and-fast undertakings to abolish import quotas and discriminations against our trade in the absence of reasonable assurance that we on our part will maintain full employment and thus maintain the necessary high level of demand for their products. Meanwhile, the Russians say that recurring depression is inherent in the very fabric and "laws of motion" of our capitalist econ-

---

*Reprinted by permission from The Christian Science Monitor, July 23, 1949;

omy. We know how this assertion is used for propaganda purposes. We also know that it is part of the longstanding, basic Marxist text. We perhaps do not know how firmly the Kremlin now holds this belief but, above all, what we are not yet in a position to assert conclusively is that the belief is wrong. This is unfortunate because, all other difficulties aside, it is evidently a massive barrier against coming to a satisfactory understanding with Russia and laying the basis for genuine and lasting peace.

Considering such facts as these, it would seem that the answer lies in not merely taking steps to combat depression when it arrives, but in developing ways and means of assuring that prosperity and full employment will actually be maintained indefinitely.

It is often said that we can't afford the unbalanced budgets. But this puts the blame for deficits in the wrong place. The real villain of the piece, if deficit financing is required, is the too-little spending or oversaving tendency, not the full-employment policy. For, in the absence of a full-employment policy, the budget will be unbalanced anyway by shrinking tax revenues and growing relief handouts. Of course, we should develop basic long-run policies (to maintain mass markets, encourage venture capital, prevent monopoly restrictions, etc.), so that the too-little-spending tendency will be less likely to appear.

Another objection--of which a good deal has been heard lately, for obvious reasons--is that full employment means inflation. Undoubtedly too much spending must be avoided along with too little spending.

The problem of holding prices within bounds should then prove soluble on a case-by-case basis, by action against groups in intrenched positions trying to "get away with murder." Moreover, the alternative seems to be to keep always so "safely" below full employment that there is no risk at all of any prices rising--surely a counsel of despair.

The third big argument, that we cannot assure full employment unless we are prepared to have the government take over the economy, deserves careful attention. For one who may feel himself personally endangered by unbalanced budgets, a hundred will rise to the defense of individualism and the American enterprise system.

Just how the case is put depends on who is talking. Some see bureaucrats telling people how to run their business. Some visualize the government deciding where workers shall work, and on what terms. Probably the main fear, however, is of a big governmental apparatus forced by its promise of jobs to expand and expand to make up for shortages of private jobs, until private enterprise, tied right and left by miscellaneous regulations, is finally in competition with the government on such a vast scale that the traditional American system is virtually eclipsed.

Such fears have no doubt been played on and magnified for selfish ends. Some critics also have a confirmed narrow view of the fields in which public enterprise is legitimate and necessary. Nevertheless, I think it would be a grave error not to recognize that our prewar efforts to combat unemployment failed to indicate how the issue could be met squarely and the difficulty overcome. Nor have we yet an officially sponsored program that seeks to cut the Gordian knot.

If the government assures full employment, this means in the last analysis that it must be prepared to give jobs to all who cannot find them in private industry.

If there is danger that the too-little-spending tendency will become severe, and if the government has no effective way of bolstering private spending in the face of that tendency, it must either stand ready to put an enormous number of extra persons on the public payroll (or on contract work for the government) or--not assure full employment.

There are definite physical limits to the amount and rate of expansion of normal public works. Beyond those limits, the government would ultimately have to buy output for stockpiling or free distribution, organize projects of no intrinsic value, or find areas in which to take managerial decisions out of private hands. Here is the basic dilemma.

It will not arise in poor countries with small savings, in underdeveloped or war-devastated countries with a crying need for every type of capital equipment, in countries that do not dislike public competition with private enterprise. In the United States it does arise.

The Employment Act of 1946 made it the continuing policy and responsibility of the Federal Government to try to maintain "conditions under which there will be afforded useful employment opportunities, including self-employment, for those able, willing, and seeking to work."

The President, assisted by his Council of Economic Advisers, transmits to Congress at least once every year an Economic Report containing, among other things, an estimate of "the levels of employment, production, and purchasing power ... needed to carry out the policy," together with an action program. In Congress a Joint Committee on the Economic Report studies these messages and reports its findings and recommendations to the Senate and House.

I suggest that the essential amendments to the Employment Act to achieve the goal of assured full employment, in a way that avoids the aforementioned dilemma, are as follows:

1. A provision that Congress, after receiving the report of its Joint Committee on the Economic Report, should by joint resolution or otherwise specify (a) the number of jobs deemed to be required to carry out the policy declared in the act, and (b) the dollar total of consumer spending deemed sufficient to secure that level of employment without undue resort to direct creation of jobs by the government.

For example, in some year "(a)" might be 60,000,000 jobs and "(b)" might be $175,000,000,000. "(b)" would be calculated by subtracting normal private investment, regular public works and services, and the expected export surplus (if any) from the total volume of demand needed to buy a full-employment output. Hence it would be the amount that ought, if realized, to rule out oversaving and give business adequate markets for which to compete. Naturally, both the job total and the consumer spending total would tend to grow larger from year to year in line with the expansion possibilities and tendencies of our economy.

2. A provision that Congress should underwrite and agree to support the levels of employment and total consumer spending which it had thus determined to be the minimum necessary, and should also agree on a maximum level of consumer spending, as well as probably a maximum level of employment, which should not be exceeded.

Having reached its own decision on what needs to be achieved, Congress would here go on record as standing back of the carrying out of that decision.

3. A provision that Congress should lay down rules, involving contingent expenditures and contingent tax changes, and should direct the President to make periodic adjustments under those rules to raise or lower total consumer spending or total employment if, as, and when these magnitudes would otherwise tend to fall short of the minimum or exceed the maximum thus prescribed.

Under this provision, Congress would presumably direct the President to expand or contract public works and services, etc., if the designated official employment series threatened to move outside the range established by Congress. That would, of course, still happen from time to time, in spite of the steady support given to the consumer market, since moderate swings in private investment would still occur.

As for ways and means of boosting consumer spending, when necessary, Congress might (for example) prescribe as follows: that the President should--only if, as, and when the official consumer expenditure series dipped too low by comparison with the specified minimum--(a) lower the standard or basic income-tax rate, and either (b) have the Treasury transmit to nonpayers of income tax, or to all families, some uniform cash sum to be considered as a partial rebate or offset to indirect taxes paid by them to various tax jurisdictions, or (c) allow nonpayers of income tax to buy from the government at a discount a limited quantity of multipurpose "stamps" or coupons which retailers would be asked to accept at face value for all ordinary purchases (the Treasury then reimbursing retailers for the amount of the discount).

For keeping total consumer spending from going above the ceiling, Congress might (for example) enact a spendings tax or some kind of obligatory savings program, suspend its application, and direct the President to bring it into play if needed.

The approach here suggested avoids regimentation and industrial rigidity. It avoids excessive reliance on forecasts. It is fully consistent with basic policies to encourage private investment. Also with basic wage policies, social security policies, farm income measures, etc., calculated to make the distribution of income more favorable to what might be called an "automatic" maintenance of adequate consumer demand--only it would not let everything depend on those controversial policies.

Also, with the carrying out of all desirable government programs--but it would remove the major hazard that a commitment to maintain full employment might prove a commitment to expand government jobs or government controls beyond practicable or acceptable limits.

Finally, by taking the export-import balance into account as a factor in determining the needed level of domestic consumer spending, this approach would free us from any supposed necessity to send a net surplus of goods abroad in order to escape "overproduction." Our economic foreign policies would thus not reflect domestic economic worries, and could always be decided on their merits.

Events have carried the world to a point where it appears that certain conditions must soon be fulfilled if history is not to be rudely interrupted. Among those conditions--not to bring in the millennium, but to assure survival and lay the basis for further gains--would seem to be the following: new institutions, preferably through amendment of the United Nations Charter, to make resort to war virtually impossible as a matter of practical mechanics; full employment--above all, the assurance of continuing full employment in the United

States; growth of a new kind of tolerance--the psychological "maturity" for which Dr. G. Brock Chisholm, now Director-General of the World Health Organization, has issued an inspiring call; economic development, particularly programs to raise living standards in the poorer countries of the world, as contemplated under "Point Four" of the President's inaugural message.

To some extent these conditions interlock. Full employment, if assured in the United States, would be a major factor in promoting development programs to advance productivity and living conditions all over the world, because it would allay doubts that we can afford to lend generous and continuous aid. Full employment would make some contribution to psychological maturity. It offers no substitute for the international law and political machinery necessary to prevent war.

It would, however, both directly and by helping to narrow present extreme international differentials in living standards, reduce pressures that lead to political movements and events capable of breaking down the finest international peace machinery.

Assured full employment does appear to be possible--here, in the country where it matters most. We need not risk national bankruptcy or inflation in order to get it. We need not overturn our individualistic habits and institutions. We can solve this particular problem any time we like, without international negotiations. We would derive from assured full employment new freedom and power to deal with our other problems in a confident, firm, and generous manner.

16. THE UNDERWRITING APPROACH TO FULL EMPLOYMENT: A FURTHER EXPLANATION*

Benjamin Higgins' review of my Full Employment and Free Enterprise[1] in the May 1948 issue of this Review shows that the proposals I have made for assuring continuous full employment in the United States are not always understood. This has also been demonstrated from time to time by the remarks of other critics--for example, Professors Hansen[2] and Alan R. Sweezy.[3] I am frankly mystified by some of the interpretations, and welcome this opportunity to try to clear up the main misunderstandings involved. These misunderstandings, as the following discussion should show, are fundamental. Confusion is multiplied when the reader is given to understand that my thesis--which offers, I believe, a distinctively new combination of elements--is quite familiar; e.g., Higgins says that "many [economists] are ready to accept it"[4] and that these are now "old ideas,"[5] while Hansen calls the view in favor of underwriting private consumption "widely held."[6]

May I emphasize that my purpose in this article is not to argue my position but to clarify it by removing misapprehensions about it, so that future arguments about it may be more fruitful.

First, some ideas that, with all due respect to my critics, my proposals do not contain: They do not contain the idea that full employment can be assured by underwriting or by maintaining private consumption alone. They do not assume that private consumption can be maintained by the mere act of underwriting it. They do not involve the notion that the maintenance of the "right" level of private consumption will (a) render private investment perfectly stable, or (b) raise private investment to the point where, averaging high and low years together, all tendency for savings to exceed investment is removed. They are not hostile to public

---

*Reprinted by permission from The Review of Economics and Statistics, Vol. XXXI, No. 3, August, 1949.

works and services. These points, along with certain related issues, will be examined below in some detail.

Underwriting Private Consumption Alone Not Sufficient

Hansen's critique of underwriting private consumer expenditures is based on his thought that the proponents of this technique regard it as sufficient of itself to maintain full employment. "The view is widely held," he tells us, "that underwriting private consumption would ensure full employment... this misconception widely prevails...."[7] "But underwriting consumption will not provide full employment. The belief that it will is based on an inadequate conception of the factors on which full employment, in all modern societies, is based."[8]

I am not sure who the numerous persons are to whom Professor Hansen attributes this view which he criticizes; they remain unidentified. I hesitate to assume, just because the footnote in which he comments on my proposals is placed in this context, that he would consign me to this abysmal ideological niche. Yet I am disturbed by what is conveyed when he says that "His [Pierson's] proposal to underwrite private consumption is... inadequate (as I believe he would himself admit)...."[9]

Of course, I have never suggested that full employment could be assured by maintaining, let alone by merely underwriting, only consumption. In the pamphlet that Hansen cites by title I strongly emphasized (pp. 158, 160, 162, 166, 168, and 169)[10] that it would also be essential to underwrite total employment as such, and that the effectuation of this further guarantee would bring into play a second balance wheel--namely, expansions and contractions of public works and services.[11] I have repeatedly stressed this point in other writings as well (pp. 19-20, 40-41, 43-44, 76, 78, 123-25, 135-36, etc., and in my earlier book, Full Employment).

I have gone further and warned of the consequences of any attempt to underwrite consumption alone. I will quote this warning (pp. 67-68)[12] at length: "In the first place, the underwriting of aggregate consumer spending would be hard to justify in the absence of an established policy to give jobs on public work projects to persons who might remain involuntarily idle in spite of the inducement afforded to private enterprise by the guarantee.... Applied by itself, if such a thing could be imagined, it could involve the government in large expense for consumption subsidies at the very time when men and women were trying in vain to find jobs. This expense would then be challenged as indefensible--with some justice, since it would clearly be better to secure a tangible product in return for the money spent--and the whole policy might under these conditions be condemned as a kind of fiscal sleight of hand." Surely, this ought to be clear.

Reason for Underwriting Private Consumption

But, if full employment cannot be guaranteed by underwriting and maintaining private consumption alone, just what is the point of that particular proposal? My answer is: (1) The continuously assured maintenance of a suitably high level of consumer spending would certify that the total market (gross national expenditures) would be large enough to preserve full employment with resort to supplementary public works and services kept within practicable limits; it would thus make the guaranteeing of full employment itself politically possible. On the other hand, in the absence of such a program with respect to consumption, the volume of public works and services likely at times to be required to preserve full employment would exceed practicable limits--so clearly so that, in our economy, it would not be politically possible, under those conditions, to guarantee full employment (pp. 14, 36-39, 70, 91-93, 145-46, 158-60, 173, 176-77). (2) Underwriting consumption and employment--assuring their maintenance at stated levels in advance--would have a double advantage: (a) it would provide security and confidence to, and thus tend to sustain the expenditures of, producers and consumers alike (pp. 6, 22, 63, 70-71, 92, 123, 124, 146, 150, 162); and (b) it would obviate undue reliance on, and disputes over, forecasting, by placing the government's compensatory action on an if, as, and when basis dependent on current events as reflected in current operating statistics (pp. 63, 92-93, 124, 146, 162).

Could not the maintenance of consumer spending be assured by the very act of assuring the maintenance of employment itself, so that a separate underwriting of consumer spending would be superfluous? My answer to this is as follows: The guaranteeing of full employment alone would indeed (assuming it were politically possible) give the prospect that income would remain at levels associated with, and in a meaningful sense derived from, full employment. But personal consumption expenditures would not be assured of remaining at levels favorable to the continuation of full employment. The larger the aggregate of business, governmental, and personal savings, the smaller, of course, the total of personal consumption expenditures. The great danger of over-saving, as I see it, would here be precisely the danger that personal consumption expenditures would be too small, even when income was initially at the full-employment level, to keep such a full-employment guarantee from breaking down by reason of the impossibility, under normal peacetime conditions, of boosting government offsets to saving in the form of government expenditures for goods and services sufficiently to maintain that guarantee. If, however, consumer spending were underwritten and sustained independently, at levels held high enough to substantially prevent or offset over-saving when it would otherwise occur, the strain leading to breakdown should be absent.

Level of Private Consumption Selected for Underwriting

I have referred above to underwriting (and maintaining) a "high enough" or "suitably high" level of consumer spending. What level is "suitably high"? Although my position on this had seemed to me to be a consistent one, Professor Higgins has found this part of my thesis particularly unclear.[13] Let me therefore restate.

The objective, as I visualize it, is to underwrite the dollar volume of consumer spending at the level[14] that is expected to buy the portion of full-employment output (gross national product) that is not absorbed by (a) expected regular government expenditures for goods and services, plus (b) an estimate (explained further below) of private gross capital expenditures, plus (c) expected net foreign investment (if this is not already included in b or, it might be, in a and b). This is the substance of what I have said on numerous occasions (pp. 57-58, 70, 72, 91, 125-26, 134, 165-66, 177). The underwritten level of consumer spending would then be maintained irrespective of events. To the extent that (A) realized government expenditures for goods and services, computed before adjustment for any compensatory supplements or reductions, (B) realized private gross capital expenditures, and (if separate) (C) realized net foreign investment differed from (a), (b), and (c) respectively, or unforeseen price-level changes increased or reduced the purchasing power of the dollar--or, more precisely, to the extent that these various "errors" did not cancel out--unemployment or over-employment would tend to appear but would be avoided by adjusting (A) up or down, i.e., generally speaking, by supplementing or reducing public works. Next year this process would be repeated. Other things being equal, the underwritten level of consumer spending would be lifted year by year as our national productivity rose.

The only possible ambiguity I am aware of in this formulation has to do with the preferred method of estimating private gross capital expenditures; and here, although this is to some extent a subordinate point, and one on which my views are more or less implied by my whole argument, I feel that Higgins has reason to complain that I have not made very explicit statements. The issue is this: If the estimate used were to correspond simply to the best guess as to what would happen in the year immediately ahead, cyclical fluctuations in private investment would have to be offset by inducing a cyclical counter-fluctuation into the underwritten level of consumption. (This is Higgins' interpretation of my proposal when he says that occasionally I suggest that consumption "might be varied in a counter-cyclical manner, increasing when investment falls off and vice versa."[15]) On the other hand, if the estimate represented an unadjusted average of the annual amounts expected to materialize over the private cycle, and if the latter cycle continued to be rather extreme, considerable strain might be placed on the secondary employment regulator, expansions and contractions of public works.

The problem thus posed appears, however, to be quite soluble. Fluctuations in private investment would no doubt be much reduced in amplitude once over-all economic cycles (fluctuations in employment and economic activity as a whole) were suppressed. Moreover, when labor and other production factors were temporarily released from private construction and other lines of private capital formation, they could as a rule transfer more easily to the stepping-up of the rate of activity on regular public works, or to the initiation of emergency projects taken from the reserve shelf, than to the production of additional goods for consumption. I am, therefore, inclined to think that the expected cyclical-average private investment figure might come to be a perfectly satisfactory basis for the determination in question. This is, indeed, a logical implication of the role reserved, in my proposals, for public works variations. Nevertheless, I should not want to preclude the possibility that, especially in the beginning, it might prove desirable to raise (lower) the underwritten consumption level slightly in years of maximum deviation of expected private gross capital expenditures below (above) their estimated cyclical average.

By way of arithmetical example, assume that, for the next year, a full-employment level of gross national expenditures was expected to be \$250 billion; that regular government expenditures for goods and services were expected to come to \$35 billion; and that private gross capital expenditures (I am here including net foreign investment), estimated as an average over an anticipated private investment cycle, also amounted to \$35 billion. The difference between \$70 billion and \$250 billion--or \$180 billion--would then be the first approximation of the amount of consumer spending to be underwritten. At this level of consumer spending the market would in fact be cleared of a full-employment output, without any adjustment of public works, if private capital expenditures hit their estimated average level in the year in question and if everything else, including the price level, worked out as expected. If private capital expenditures seemed likely to fluctuate between annual totals of \$32 billion and \$38 billion, then, even if they were expected to be at the bottom of their cycle in the year just ahead, it might still seem best to underwrite consumption at \$180 billion, taking up all slack by expanding public works and thus raising the government component from \$35 billion to \$38 billion or thereabouts. (\$38 billion would be the advance estimate, but unforeseen developments including price-level changes could make the dollar value of the adjustment of government programs required to maintain full employment be somewhat larger or smaller.) But if the anticipated private investment cycle ranged between annual values of \$27 billion and \$43 billion, with only \$27 billion foreseen for the coming year, the best solution might be to underwrite consumption at, say \$183 billion, instead of \$180 billion, and look forward to government expenditures for goods and services aggregating in the neighborhood of \$40 billion. Again, consumption might be underwritten at, say, \$175 billion, and the government total trimmed to around \$32 billion, if the peak load of \$43 billion of private investment appeared to be due.

Turning now to Higgins' other, alternative interpretations[16] of my "objective as to consumption policy," I do not suggest that consumption should be "equal to (estimated disposable income at full employment) x (the average propensity to consume over some previous period)." That would be the very opposite of what I have in mind, since it would accept any over-saving as final, and hence as capable of rectification only through expansion of government expenditures for goods and services. I do not suggest that the aim should be the realization of a stable price level instead of the realization of a predetermined dollar volume of consumer spending. Of course, an estimate of what the price-level trend will be is necessarily involved in the computation of the right dollar volume of consumer spending for underwriting purposes. My point is simply that the government can itself exercise considerable control over this trend, and that a stable or slowly rising price level may prove to be the best assumption for computation purposes and, then, the best objective in following through (pp. 56, 62).[17] I do not mean, in proposing to maintain an amount of consumption "the confident anticipation of which would be expected to stimulate full employment, with public investment limited to items wanted for their own sake" (p. 43), that year-by-year stability in private investment could be expected and that, consequently, no variation in public works would be needed. While the main "lift" would be supplied by keeping up consumption--this part of the program eliminating any average or secular deficiency in total private spending--the public-works balance wheel would still be needed for stabilization. Finally, I do not precisely propose to "stabilize the propensity to consume," in what I take to be the most meaningful sense of that term. This last question, however, will be discussed more fully at a later point.

Maintaining Private Consumption at the Underwritten Level

According to Professor Alan Sweezy's review of my earlier book, Full Employment, I have been guilty of assuming that a guarantee of consumer spending would automatically fulfill itself without requiring the government to take action (and, frequently, incur deficits) in boosting consumers' disposable income. "If it would work," he writes, "the consumption guarantee policy would obviously have great advantages. It would not only keep the government from stepping on the toes of business, but would also avoid the increase in public debt...."[18] "If the government went beyond a mere guarantee and took steps to see that income actually was maintained at the desired level, the outcome would, of course, be different. But the government could maintain income only [?] by...the very New Deal measures Dr. Pierson was hoping to escape through his consumption guarantee plan."[19] "But there would be nothing in a mere guarantee of increased consumption to bring [increased consumption] about. It would be necessary for the government to step in and...[adopt] the very measures the Pierson plan is designed to avoid."[20]

This line of interpretation is quite at variance with what I have actually said.[21] On page 25 of Full Employment, for example, I stated that "Whenever...the requisite consumer money income fails to materialize through the usual channels, so that government must make a net contribution,"

Congress must specify how this is to be done. A great many other passages could be cited[22] in which I have clearly indicated that the government would have to stand ready (on a contingent basis) to supply a compensatory boost to disposable income in order to have the underwriting made good--as well as to reduce disposable income, or its use, when the opposite danger of too much consumer spending threatened.

To be sure, the act of underwriting should in itself help somewhat to bring about higher levels of private spending--although certain speculative types of investment would tend to be discouraged (p. 63). I have also suggested that the budget deficits incurred in supporting consumer spending at its underwritten level might well be less than those required to close all employment gaps--if that were possible--by additional public works and services (pp. 23, 51, 65-66, 73). Finally, various factors should help reduce the need for compensatory action to sustain full employment once a condition of full employment had lasted for a good many years. For example, the rate of saving (*ex ante*) would tend to be reduced when people commonly became able to spend their accumulated savings (dis-save) for the purposes originally intended, instead of losing them in a depression, or during inflation, as has so often occurred up to now. But these are subordinate questions.

I stress the main issue, elementary as it is, because Hansen, too, has missed my point. After stating that I am "extraordinarily vague about how in practice this established level of consumption is, in fact, to be rigorously maintained,"[23] he concludes: "The only way in which I can make his 'insurance' really mean anything would be for Congress to undertake a rigorous commitment to issue money outright to consumers in sufficient volume to maintain consumption expenditures at the desired figure. But in fact he stops short of this extreme proposal and has not, so far as I know, advocated it. The nearest he comes to that procedure is his advocacy of remission of taxes. There is in his work, I feel, a vague reliance on the belief that if the 'insurance idea' were *proclaimed* by Congress, business and consumer expenditures would automatically prove adequate. It is, I feel, never explained just how the insurance commitment is to be rigorously fulfilled. Perhaps I have failed to understand the proposal."[24]

This is, to me, astonishing. I clearly *do* advocate having Congress undertake a rigorous commitment to maintain consumption expenditures at the desired figure (or, to be exact, between desired "floor" and "ceiling" levels). I stop short of the "extreme proposal," that money be issued outright to consumers, only to the extent that I do not insist that this particular method must be preferred in boosting consumers' disposable income. I have suggested several procedures besides remission of taxes, I do not rely on the belief that, given the act of underwriting, business and consumer expenditures would automatically prove adequate.

In my first book and numerous subsequent papers, available to Hansen at the time he offered the foregoing critical comments, appear many statements that should have made these comments gratuitous. Page references to some of these statements have been given above. In my pamphlet, "Full Employment in Practice," which he specifically cites, I said (pp. 166-67): "A question arises regarding the ways that might be recommended for raising consumer spending to the underwritten level if--as will normally be likely to happen until real progress has been made with our basic policies--it tends to remain too low even when income payments are running at a full-employment rate. No attempt will be made here to catalogue the various methods available, but two possibilities will be mentioned by way of illustration. The President might recommend, contingent on a demonstrated need for more consumer spending, a reduced rate on the personal income tax, coupled with cash offsets or refunds, on a reasonable basis, applied to Federal, State, and local indirect taxes which largely burden those too poor to pay an income tax. Or, alternatively, he might wish to recommend, along with a reduced rate on the income tax, the distribution to low-income families of stamps enabling them to improve their nutrition and living standards by buying food and, possibly, other necessities such as clothing in the market at reduced expense. For the opposite contingency of a tendency toward an inflationary excess of total consumer spending, he might recommend, for example, a graduated spendings tax with generous exemptions at the bottom."[25] I should have thought that some attention would be paid to such statements.

The basis for Professor Hansen's feeling that I have been vague about this aspect of my proposal is, I believe, this: In order not to divert attention from the general principle that consumers' disposable income should be subsidized if, as, and when required in order to realize a previously guaranteed level of consumer spending--a principle which is an integral part of the policy I have suggested--I have deliberately avoided emphasizing, to the exclusion of other alternatives, any one particular method whereby this principle should be applied. I have, however, indicated various methods that might be used: the suspension, lowering, rebating, or offsetting of specified taxes affecting consumption (pp. 24,

46-47, 49, 72, 78, 91, 92, 93, 126-28, 134, 135, 150, 166-67, 170, 178-79); the supplementing of existing social security benefits through the general distribution of "national income security payments" (a better term might be "consumption stabilization payments") or other cash benefits to consumers (pp. 1-2, 6, 24, 47, 49, 54, 72); a "stamp plan" for low-income groups to match tax reductions for others (pp. 167, 179).[26] I have, moreover, discussed some of these methods at sufficient length to show that they should be feasible (pp. 45-47, 126-28). I am sure that ingenuity will disclose still other variant possibilities--conforming to the generally desirable criteria of adequacy of amount, broad and fair distribution, flexibility, and operating simplicity (p. 45)--and that fuller investigation of this problem can improve and refine the detail to the desired point if once the rationale underlying these measures is clearly grasped and is approved. But I have wanted to avoid side-tracking the debate. This is a case where the discussion of finished blueprints seems highly premature and unprofitable.

I do, of course, have some tentative views about specific methods. At present I am inclined to think that the best plan for raising consumer spending (when necessary to fulfill the guarantee) might involve one of the two following procedures, either of which holds some advantages over the other: (1) As mentioned first in the passage quoted above, the standard or basic income-tax rate might for the time being be lowered (an idea also favored by Hansen, and facilitated in application, as he points out, by current withholding); and meanwhile non-payers of income taxes might receive their _quid pro quo_ through the payment by the Treasury to them of some uniform cash sum, allowed as a partial (though not strictly proportional) rebate or offset of other (indirect) taxes paid by them to various tax jurisdictions. (2) Income-tax payers might be treated as above, while non-payers might be enabled to make a portion of practically any of their ordinary purchases at reduced expense by buying from the government at a discount a limited quantity of multi-purpose "stamps" or coupons which retailers would be asked to accept at face value, the Treasury then reimbursing retailers for the amount of the discount.[27] I think that either of these procedures would work. However, to repeat once more, while I consider the general approach here indicated as fundamental to my proposal, I regard the precise methods of carrying it out as optional.

Compensatory Measures; Propensity to Consume; Distribution of Income

It must now be obvious that I am not, as Hansen supposes, one who "minimizes the importance of a vigorous compensatory offsetting program."[28] On the contrary, I attach very great strategic importance to a two-sided compensatory program consisting of (a) adjustments of consumers' disposable income[28a] when necessary to fulfill a prior guarantee of consumer spending, and (b) adjustments of the volume of public works and services at times when, in spite of the direct support given to consumption, total employment still tended to fall short of (or too much exceed) its established mark. Incidentally, I have made a particular point (pp. 121-22, 126, 133, 149, 151-52, 161-62, 164-67, 178) of stressing the distinction between compensatory and basic measures--meaning by the latter all those measures that are adopted essentially on their own continuing merits rather than to adjust the level of income, production, or employment. This distinction appears to me to have great methodological and practical importance.

In Higgins' comment on my proposals reference is made several times to the propensity to consume. Higgins suggests, for example, that my criticisms of the public-investment approach to full employment might have been tempered had I taken more note of what Keynes and others have said about the need to control the propensity to consume, and he infers that what I, myself, am trying to do is stabilize the propensity to consume at some proper level.[29]

I do not think, from the context, that Higgins merely means to refer to control over the real proportions between consumption and investment[30]--a concept that, in its broadest sense, corresponds to what Hansen distinguishes as the "national consumption function."[31] In any case, on the particular questions here at issue, such a use of terms would not be very illuminating. It would seem more to the point to concentrate here on the propensity to consume viewed as a schedule of relationships between total disposable income of consumers and what they spend at various levels of disposable income--what Hansen means when he speaks of "the willingness of consumers to spend (consumption function)."[32] So interpreted, the propensity to consume can be controlled only be controlling the proportion between spending and saving out of a given disposable income, not by controlling disposable income itself. On the other hand, the compensatory adjustments of consumption visualized in connection with my underwriting proposal would commonly achieve their effect, not by changing the spending-saving ratio at a given level of disposable income, but rather by raising (or lowering) total disposable income itself.[33] The suggestion that disposable income be thus adjusted whenever and to the extent required to reach target levels of consumer spending has not, to my knowledge, been made by Keynes or in the White Papers or other proposals cited by Higgins. Yet this approach seems required, in the United States, in order to free full-employment policy from precarious reliance on such things as control over the propensity to consume.

A further word about this. In my proposals, the need for basic policy measures that will improve the "self-sustaining" qualities of our economy, and thus reduce the degree of reliance on deficit-creating compensatory measures, is strongly emphasized (pp. 23, 64, 72, 91-92, 106-22, 126, 133, 147-49, 151-56, 161-62, 164-65, 178). (I think it would be desirable to be able to balance the budget "over the cycle," even though I would never favor a policy of trying to balance the budget by letting full employment go. That policy would be self-defeating in any case, since, as long as over-saving was present, reduced tax revenues and enlarged relief expenditures would still bring budget deficits.) Among the basic adaptations referred to are those long-term measures favorable to consumption--measures dealing with taxes, wages, social security, etc.--which will raise the propensity to consume by making the distribution of income less unequal. Satisfactory rules for promoting competition and regulating monopoly will also have this desirable effect, not to speak of their effects in promoting investment and holding down prices.

On the other hand, when it comes to <u>compensatory</u> measures to boost the amount of disposable income in order to fulfill the suggested guarantee of consumer spending, I consider that the devices used should preferably aim at a more or less "horizontal" lifting of all incomes (pp. 45, 126-28, 167, 178-79). To introduce any strong redistributionist bias into these final-adjustment measures would be to lose sight of their true character as scientific devices for protecting everyone's common interest in the existence of an adequate over-all market. Moreover, since such an approach would invite the charge that social changes not admitted through the front door (i.e., by considered enactment of basic legislation) were now being smuggled in by the back door under the pretext of combatting depression, it would risk rejection of the whole compensatory policy. While families with low incomes undoubtedly have the highest individual propensities to consume, so that the subsidization of their incomes would tend to exercise the greatest leverage on consumer spending, per dollar of cost to the government, this consideration is not decisive. For it seems clear that any reasonable, broad plan for subsidizing consumers straight across the board would in fact place most of the extra buying power in the hands of those who are far from rich, and would therefore not cause any damagingly large "leakage" into additional savings.

These comments have a bearing on Hansen's view that "to underwrite private consumption fully...would divorce reward too far from production...would remove financial incentives to effort and efficiency."[34] That might, of course, be true if consumption subsidies were made inversely proportional to the wages, or to the total incomes, received by different persons (just as a scheme that made them directly proportional to wages would tend to distort the labor supply to the extent that it caused relative rewards to exaggerate differences in the marginal productivity of different kinds of work). To a compensatory program that raised incomes "horizontally," however, when consumer spending would otherwise be insufficient, these objections would not apply.

Cyclical vs. Secular Deficiencies of Private Investment

Both Sweezy[35] and Hansen[36] have argued that, inasmuch as private investment is partly of an autonomous character, it is a mistake to suppose that private investment can be stabilized by controlling consumption. Since I have never for a moment entertained this supposition, their arguments on this score do not, as the writers appear to think, apply to my proposals. What I do maintain is that the amplitude of fluctuations in private investment would be substantially reduced once the continuous maintenance of prosperity and full employment was an accomplished fact. Hansen makes the same point.[37] There is therefore no disagreement here.

Cyclical instability of investment, however, is not the whole of the matter. According to Sweezy, I have tried to show in *Full Employment* that the underwriting of consumer spending would stimulate private investment to the point where a tendency for savings (at full employment) to exceed investment would no longer be present. I take it that he has reference not merely or primarily to temporary deviations of private investment below a satisfactory average level, i.e., to instability proper, but also to a secular problem connected with a tendency for the average itself to be "too low."

Sweezy's misunderstanding of my position on the savings-investment issue is reflected throughout his review. "The central...thesis, as I understand it," he writes, recapitulating his interpretation, "is that a proper rate of increase in aggregate consumption will call forth the amount of net investment necessary to offset the saving done by the community at a high level of income and hence will keep the economy operating at a full employment rate."[38] "Now the Pierson scheme is to keep these workers employed in producing capital goods, and at the same time to provide an outlet for the profitable investment of saving...and the government will be freed from the necessity of spending any money itself."[39]

In thus supposing that my proposals involve the maintenance of some particular, high level of private investment, Sweezy is quite mistaken. My whole discussion of the need for the government to stand ready to take compensatory action to raise consumer spending[40] bore precisely upon the likelihood that private investment would often be too small to absorb a full-employment volume of savings; nor do I think, in addition, that there is any warrant for construing my remarks in that book as pre-judging whether the need would be purely cyclical or predominant and possibly more or less continuous.[41]

Certainly it would seem to me over-optimistic to assume that the compensatory measures needed to maintain full employment will henceforth be only contra-cyclical in the literal sense, i.e., that the amount of governmental support required in some years will be balanced by the amount of governmental restraint required in others, so that surpluses will offset deficits. Indeed I think--and I infer that Sweezy, Hansen, and Higgins do also--that there is in the United States, budget deficits aside, an inherent, average tendency toward over-saving or under-spending at full-employment levels of income. (I am not here concerned, of course, with speculations about possible aftermath conditions in the event of another war.) After we have progressed some distance with our basic policies, this tendency should become less of a problem, and may disappear entirely. Pending that outcome, the compensatory measures required will more largely take the form of deficit-creating measures to support the demand for goods and services (not that they will necessarily be thought of in those terms where defense programs are involved) than of surplus-creating measures to hold this demand in check. Finally, while policies to encourage private investment certainly should, in my opinion, form part of the basic program, I see no point in trying to force private investment above the range in which it would naturally move in a generally satisfactory economic environment (pp. 24, 42, 70, 92, 96, 160). Should such an effort succeed, moreover, it would only intensify the problem of avoiding a glut of consumption output at a later date.[42]

Attitudes Toward Public Works and Services

The reader of Dr. Higgins' review is likely to get the further erroneous impression that my proposals are hostile to public investment and government programs generally. The aim of fiscal policy which Higgins attributes to me "is tantamount to 'full employment without inflation, achieved with a minimum amount of government intervention other than paying subsidies and collecting taxes.' Not everyone," he adds, "considers the minimization of government activity an end in itself."[43]

I do not see how a careful reading of either of my books could possibly sustain this interpretation of what I have said. In the passage quoted by Higgins as evidence,[44] what I am alluding to is the undesirability of having to close all savings-investment gaps, whatever their tendency to persist, through emergency public activities that have not been regularly approved by the community for their own sake. I do believe that, in the United States, government programs still have to bear the burden of proof (pp. 5, 24, 42, 62, 92, 106-7, 114). On the page to which he refers, however, and on the page preceding (pp. 20-21), I have made it perfectly clear that I am personally in favor of substantial, permanent expansions of public works and services in various directions. I have time and again (pp. 12-13, 37, 71, 92, 96, 106-14, 124, 136, 142-43, 148, 164-65) advocated expanded public programs in such fields as slum clearance and housing, health and nutrition, education, conservation and development of natural resources, not to speak of an expanded social security system. (Some of these programs come under the head of public investment; some are services--as a rule, community services that enlarge real consumption.) I am perfectly open to persuasion on the merits of additional public programs that Higgins may have in mind.

At the same time, I do not think that my personal predilections, or Higgins', have much to do with the question. We are dealing with majority rule and the democratic process. As this process works out in the United States, the laws, of course, are made by Congress. The President might at some point urge a vastly expanded program of government expenditures for goods and services which, if enacted, might (though it also easily might not) suffice to maintain full employment without any additional, direct support for consumption. What I am advocating, however, is a line of policy that, if accepted in principle by Congress, would definitely maintain full employment whether or not the President put forward an all-embracing public program and whether or not, if put forward, his program was accepted in whole or in part by Congress. The President's uncertainty as to the action Congress would take with respect to his recommendations for various public program items need not, be it noted, create any difficulty, since he could submit his proposals in a form that indicated the need to *raise* the level at which consumption was underwritten if Congress decided to *cut down* his recommended public programs (p. 167).

One sometimes hears the argument that the United States should make sure of full employment by expanding foreign investment. Actually, the case bears a striking similarity, in one respect, to the case for expansion of public works and services. An export surplus and an associated positive value for net foreign investment may sometimes be highly desirable. Situations may arise in which net foreign investment is large enough to play a major part in sustaining domestic full employment. But that is not to say that full employment can safely be made contingent on shipping goods abroad (pp. 9-10, 33-34, 66-67, 73, 87-90, 130-32, 147, 163), any more than it can safely be made to hinge on approval of some particular set of plans for hospitals, schools, roads, river valley development, etc., etc. The trend in net foreign investment and the trend in government programs both follow rather complicated laws of their own. In my proposals, therefore, I have dealt with the means of maintaining full employment, not as a by-product of attaining other objectives with respect to, e.g., public programs or foreign investment, but independently of the size of these other items. In other words, I have tried to set forth the *general* case and avoid dependence on special combinations of other variables.

* * *

In conclusion, I want to plead guilty of preoccupation with finding a practical approach to *assured* full employment in a country with the particular characteristics of the *present-day United States*. This is the reader's clue. Proposals that make sense in this context may fail to do so if applied to other countries or to other times or if considered in connection with a lesser or a different objective. Conversely, proposals that are sensible if, for example, just moderating the business cycle is taken as the objective may be utterly incapable of being "stretched" into a program to assure full employment.

Hansen is opposed to too rigorous a full-employment commitment and quotes the adage that "the reed that does not bend breaks."[45] I am perfectly willing to waive certain rigorous, abstract considerations and settle for a definition of full employment in terms of a number of jobs annually fixed by Congress after studying the recommendations in the President's Economic Report (pp. 167-69, 175-76). This would provide reasonable leeway; I should say that the desirable amount of "bend" or "give" would be taken into account in the definition. But bending like a reed is no great virtue in itself. I think that we need the solid assurance that full employment, thus defined, will always be maintained.

Notes

1. Washington, Public Affairs Press, 1947.
2. Alvin H. Hansen, Economic Policy and Full Employment (New York, 1947).
3. Review of my earlier book, Full Employment (New Haven, 1941) in American Economic Review, March 1944, pp. 134-37; also his Reply to Emile Benoit-Smullyan's Communication, same journal, December 1944, pp. 875-78.
4. Higgins, op. cit., p. 145.
5. Ibid., p. 146.
6. Hansen, op. cit., p. 197. Hansen adds, however, with specific reference to my writings, "Perhaps I have failed to understand the proposal"; ibid., p. 197, footnote.
7. Ibid., p. 197.
8. Ibid., p. 198.
9. Ibid., p. 197, footnote.
10. All page numbers given in the text and in the footnotes (unless otherwise indicated) will refer to pages in my Full Employment and Free Enterprise, rather than in the original publications there collected. Citations will ordinarily be illustrative, not exhaustive.
11. The inclusive category is government expenditures for goods and services. A stabilizing effect will, of course, equally be achieved by variations in govern-

ment purchases of items not associated with public works and services in the usual sense--e.g., military equipment, raw materials for stockpile, commodities for free distribution to consumers. (Theoretically the government might also influence certain private output decisions toward temporary expansion or contraction without varying its own expenditures.) This having been said, it will generally be convenient and sufficiently clear, in what follows, to refer simply to variations in public works or in public works and services.

12. Originally in American Economic Review, March 1944.
13. Higgins, op. cit., p. 145.
14. I use the word "level" for the sake of simplicity; actually, some "play" is necessary, and what I advocate is a range between reasonably narrow lower and upper limits (pp. 52, 129, 166), the upper limit to serve as a brake on price spirals.
15. Higgins, op. cit., p. 145. Incidentally, I fail to find in my book the passage that Higgins cites in justifying this interpretation. On page 44, to which he refers, I speak of inducing expansions or contractions in consumer incomes and spending, not in order to offset investment fluctuations, but rather in order to realize the consumption guarantee, which is quite a different matter.
16. Ibid., pp. 145-46.
17. Also Full Employment, Ch. VII (see esp. p. 176).
18. Sweezy, op. cit., p. 135. It is only proper to call attention to the fact that Sweezy's comments, as quoted and discussed in this article, appeared in 1944, and may not represent his present appraisal of my views.
19. Ibid., pp. 136-37.
20. Ibid., (Reply), p. 877.
21. I infer from certain of Sweezy's comments (esp. p. 135 and footnote) that part of his difficulty stemmed from my use of terms in criticizing the "public spending" approach to full employment. What I had in mind--the more exact terminology now current was not then in general use--was government expenditures for goods and services, i.e., public works and services, etc., not including transfer payments to consumers. I should have thought that the whole context made my meaning clear. Actually, of course, such compensatory governmental measures as will boost the disposable income and spending of consumers directly (i.e., not via public works, etc.) may involve either

(a) government spending in the form of expenditures not for goods and services, or (b) reduced taxes, or (c) a combination of both.

22. Full Employment, pp. 137, 169, 170, 217, 222, 228-33, 247, 258, 271, etc. (In Full Employment and Free Enterprise, this point is made clear on pp. 1-2, 6-7, 23, 24, 43-47, 51-52, 54, 71, 72, 76, 78, 91-92, 93, 126-29, 134, 135, 150, 166-67, 170, 177, 178-79.)
23. Hansen, op. cit., p. 197, footnote.
24. Ibid.
25. Presidential recommendations like these would, of course, require for their effectuation both Congressional decisions and subsequent administrative action. I followed up the above remarks by discussing these aspects of the question (pp. 167-70).
26. Also, timed war-bond redemptions in the early post-war years (pp. 24, 45-46, 49, 72). These various methods, and other possibilities, are also touched on in the more theoretical discussion in Full Employment, esp. pp. 228-30. For reducing consumer spending (when necessary), I have mainly suggested a spendings tax (pp. 52, 55, 60, 72, 129, 134, 150, 167, 179). Other methods of taxation could be used--e.g., a special sales tax (with realized consumer spending then computed as net of the amount thus taxed), although sales taxation is ordinarily objectionable because of its regressive features (p. 52). Or the government might borrow from consumers (pp. 2, 23); this, to be really effective, would involve a forced saving program of some kind.
27. Either method assumes that families or individuals not subject to income tax would nevertheless, as a condition of eligibility, file income statements on a short form with the federal government.
28. Hansen, op. cit., p. 197, footnote.
28a. See footnote 33, below, for a necessary qualification.
29. Higgins, op. cit., p. 145.
30. See his previously quoted reference to "(estimated disposable income at full employment) x (the average propensity to consume over some previous period)"; italics supplied.
31. Hansen, op. cit., p. 44, footnote, and p. 161.
32. Ibid., p. 40.
33. This at least is true of most of the compensatory procedures for increasing consumption. The available compensatory measures for adjusting consumption

downward would vary considerably in their effects. For example, a spendings tax probably would reduce disposable income less than it would increase consumer saving.

34. Hansen, *op. cit.*, p. 199.
35. Sweezy, *op. cit.*, p. 136.
36. Hansen, *op. cit.*, pp. 198-200.
37. *Ibid.*, p. 200.
38. Sweezy, *op. cit.*, p. 875.
39. *Ibid.*, p. 877.
40. *Cf.* footnote 22 above.
41. See, e.g., pp. 217, 247, 258.
42. I could hardly do better at this point than quote from Dr. Smullyan's pertinent comments on Dr. Sweezy's review. "It is not Pierson's thesis that any predetermined amount of investment is necessary for full employment, or that the decision as to the amount of consumption to be guaranteed should be determined by the consideration of inducing an amount of investment adequate to offset the amount of savings that would occur in the absence of compensatory fiscal measures. Rather, it is proposed that the volume of public investment be primarily determined by what is desired for its own sake, and that the volume of private investment be allowed to adjust itself naturally to the guaranteed level of consumer spending. The latter element would be the variable. It would be set at *whatever level was believed necessary*, in conjunction with the intrinsically desirable public investment, and naturally occurring private investment, to bring about full employment." (Emile Benoit-Smullyan, "Rejoinder," *American Economic Review*, December 1944, p. 879.)
43. Higgins, *op. cit.*, p. 146. (Quotation beginning, 'full employment without inflation,' is from another author.)
44. *Ibid.*, p. 146, footnote 2.
45. Hansen, *op. cit.*, p. 197, footnote.

17. POINT FOUR, DOLLAR GAP, AND FULL EMPLOYMENT*

When in the future some historian takes time to plot the many different roads leading to Point Four, he will undoubtedly find much to interest him in the first session of the Preparatory Committee of the United Nations Conference on Trade and Employment which took place in London in the autumn of 1946.

This meeting was in many respects extraordinary. The economies of the eighteen geographically scattered nations represented on the Committee were widely dissimilar. Their interests, therefore, and, indeed, their practical necessities illustrated most of the theoretically possible combinations. A great effort was made to harmonize these differing points of view in a constructive manner. The range of the effort was enormous. Measured by the number and importance of the general principles at stake, not to speak of the complexity of the attendant detail, it is doubtful whether there had ever been an international economic conference of comparable scope. The draft document which emerged began to suggest--bearing in mind the charters of already going concerns such as the International Monetary Fund, the International Bank for Reconstruction and Development, the Food and Agriculture Organization, the International Labor Organization, and the United Nations itself--the distinct possibility of evolving a coherent overall world economic code.

London, 1946

For present purposes, the most interesting aspect of this International Trade Organization preparatory conference was the way a particular set of partly competing, partly complementary principles began to fall into place, or at least into some sort of relationship to one another. There

---

*Reprinted by permission from The Annals of the American Academy of Political and Social Science, Vol. 270, July, 1950.

was a kind of classic simplicity about the accommodation process at this early stage.

First, delegates from a number of economically advanced countries and others said that their governments could not bind themselves to refrain from imposing trade restrictions unless they could be assured against another depression in the United States. The economic stability of nations all over the world was dependent, they said, on what happened to employment and effective demand in the major industrial nations, especially the United States. They hammered the point that the most important issue before the conference was full employment.

At this juncture a delegate from one of the underdeveloped countries said that full employment was all very well, but that it offered no solution for the problems of his country. What was needed there was not just full employment, but productive full employment; not just elimination of unemployment, but elimination of underemployment. In short, what was needed was economic development, modern technology, industrialization.

These sentiments were thereupon echoed all around the horseshoe table. It turned out that almost all the delegates present considered that the countries they represented were underdeveloped. The draft agenda for the conference was altered forthwith to provide for separate consideration of the subject of economic development. An extra committee was set up to deal with that subject. The extra committee proceeded to draft a new chapter containing several important articles--the nucleus of what was later to become "Chapter III: Economic Development and Reconstruction" of the Havana Charter.

Thus, from its initial focus on the general need to reduce trade barriers, attention was forcibly shifted to the need to retain the contingent right to increase certain of these barriers if circumstances (for example, recession in a country like the United States) caused demand to fall off and created balance-of-payments difficulties for other countries. From the importance for the rest of the world of having full employment in the United States, the spotlight moved to the inadequacy of any underdeveloped country's own full employment unless it was productive employment--to the need for economic development, and not trade barrier reduction alone, to make that employment productive. Also, by parallel sequence, it moved from the desirability of full employment to the undesirability of maintaining it by means of a persistent export surplus--to the desirability of as much export surplus as would correspond to productive foreign investment to assist the development of the underdeveloped or the war-torn countries.

This oversimplifies, of course. There were disagreements, not always fully resolved, about interpretation of the various points here recited, not to mention disagreements on other points, such as the extent of permissible trade restrictions in the interest of economic development. But men's minds were here engaged in constructing a working relationship between full employment, Point Four (as it had not yet been called), and trade barrier reduction. Perhaps the main thing lacking in this connection was a sense of the proportions of the world trade disequilibrium--the dollar gap problem. Considered it certainly was: exceptional trade restrictions were admitted if necessary to protect a country suffering from balance-of-payments difficulties; countries were urged to maintain full employment without leaning on the crutch of a so-called "favorable" balance; and provision was made for consultation if balance-of-payments difficulties should persist. But the chronic nature and the real magnitude of the dollar gap problem were not apparent at that time.

Our Policies Should Be Integrated

The campaign for economic development took on momentum and became a world-wide crusade. After President Truman's dramatic pronouncement in Point Four of his inaugural address in January 1949, which had the quality of a statement ushering in a new era in human affairs, it appeared that the question about economic development was no longer Should it be done? but rather How is it to be done?

Admittedly, the crusade for economic development of underdeveloped areas was so widely supported and so deeply motivated that it could not have been stopped in any case, regardless of the position taken by the United States. Moreover, deciding on the contribution the United States Government and American private capital will actually make toward action so peculiarly hard to define, or at any rate delimit, has proved to be a time-consuming process. Still, viewing the matter broadly, it seems fair to say that the Point Four goal has now been accepted here as well as abroad, and that the dominant preoccupation is with that practical question, How is it to be done?

This is harder to answer than might at first glance appear. Many of the best minds in government, business, finance, agriculture, labor, education, medicine, science, engineering, and other fields are helping to find the answer, and no one would claim that we have reached the point where good ideas about how to proceed are no longer at a premium.

Yet, with all the need to push this highly practical and immediate line of inquiry, it is permissible to ask whether another question of a somewhat different order, which seems to be getting rather less attention, is not equally vital for the United States, and equally timely. I refer to the question of how we are to establish the right relationship between Point Four and other major economic policies.

This second type of question, since it has to do with over-all perspective, seems to be no one's business in particular, and thus tends to be neglected. The result of such neglect is that we do not have a unified economic policy, with all the major parts organically related. Instead, we have a collection of separate policies which are forced into some kind of fit, good or bad.

Looking over the economic field, what is it that we really want? It may be assumed, for one thing, that we want to close the dollar gap. We also want to close it in such a way that exports and imports will balance at a high level, rather than at a low level. We want to help other countries to improve their lot by raising their productivity and their standards of living. We want to keep on raising our own living standards. We want our economic policies to help us hold our friends and allies abroad and win us new friends and allies if possible. We want to enhance our national security through assuring supplies of needed materials. We want to strengthen the United Nations. We want customers--a full-employment market. Without sacrificing flexibility, we want our various economic interest groups to be safeguarded in appropriate degree. On top of all this, we want to avoid excessive governmental controls.

Can such a heterogeneous lot of economic objectives be reduced to simpler terms? Well, here is a shorter list that seems at any rate to take account of all the aims just enumerated: (1) the Point Four Program for economic development; (2) a closing of the dollar gap--as far as possible by expansion of imports rather than by reduction of exports; (3) domestic full employment; (4) national security; (5) a maximum of individual freedom and initiative.

To say that successful integration of these five aims would go a long way toward solving the problems with which the United States is confronted today is not, of course, to be certain that the means of integration are at hand. It does appear, however, that much might be gained if serious attention were given to studying how to integrate three of these major elements--Point Four, the dollar gap, and full employment. The remarks that follow will be addressed to this subject, with also some incidental reference, where possible, to the other major elements in the picture.

Point Four and Dollar Gap

The dollar gap is financed by the American taxpayer, and involves foreign grants and loans which tend to confer a charity status on the recipient countries. Since neither of these conditions appears permanently desirable, the question of closing the gap arises. Point Four is often spoken of as one of the best ways of closing the dollar gap. Let us try to evaluate this claim.

The elements tending to support it are two, each with its own time cycle. First, while the international investments are being made--or, rather, for as long as the current flow of dollars going abroad exceeds the return flow of earnings and repayments--the dollar gap requiring official action to finance it is smaller by the amount of this net investment. Second, when the programs of economic development have reached the stage of yielding results, the countries whose production has been increased in this manner are in a position to earn more dollars through larger exports, while at the same time they and perhaps third countries as well, being less dependent on us for some of their traditional imports, are in a position to save dollars, if they will, by importing less.

These two effects, it will be noted, are quite dissimilar. What may be called the net investment effect does not narrow the export-import gap, but automatically reduces the amount of the gap that has to be filled by compensatory official financing. The increased productivity effect, on the other hand, can, if consciously directed to that end, actually help to narrow the export-import gap as such.

The increased productivity effect obviously will not become noticeable in any given case until some time after development programs are initiated. From a global point of view, of course, some of this beneficial effect is likely to overlap a still favorable net investment effect, each then reinforcing the other until further time has elapsed.

One of the big uncertainties in the picture is the question as to how long the foreign investment process can be kept up before earnings and repayments turn the net flow in the other direction, making the dollar gap problem harder to manage, rather than easier. The answer is not easy to find. Much will depend on the proportions between equity capital and loans and on the rates of amortization applied to the latter, as well as on the magnitude and time-shape of the original capital movement as a whole.

The other big uncertainty has to do with how much of the increased productivity effect will be retained to raise living standards in the countries being developed, in fulfillment of what is the major purpose of Point Four, and how much, on the other hand, will be used to improve their export-import position. It may indeed be hard to balance world trade while some countries are so unproductive that they have little to offer in exchange, but it does not necessarily follow that when those countries grow somewhat more productive, this in itself will make the attainment of world trade balance a simple matter.

On the whole, the immensity of the field waiting to be opened up by technical assistance and international investment suggests that Point Four can make solution of the dollar gap problem substantially easier, at least potentially. The fact that the net investment flow may eventually turn in the "wrong" direction is not an immediate worry. On the other hand, the size of the dollar gap at the present time, the very obvious difficulties of creating the confidence needed to get a vast amount of investment going, the delays before development programs pay off in sufficiently greater productivity to make a marked improvement in the underdeveloped countries' export-import balances possible, and the great need on the part of those countries not to think only of their export-import balances but rather to enjoy as much as possible of the benefit from that greater productivity internally--all these things warn us that Point Four, far from being the whole answer as far as the dollar gap is concerned, will prove for that collateral purpose too little and too late.

Dollar Gap and U.S. Full Employment

It is one of our declared national policies to make every reasonable effort to maintain conditions in which there will be afforded useful employment opportunities for all who are able, willing, and seeking to work. Aside from what the chance to work means to our own people, all the evidence shows that our success or lack of success in this endeavor is one of the crucial tests by which both the merits of our economic system and the value of our friendship will be judged abroad.

The essence of the relation between the dollar gap problem and the problem of maintaining full employment in the United States is that closing the gap will make maintaining full employment somewhat more difficult--or, to put the same thing more constructively, will make it more obviously necessary to work out a fundamental solution of the full employment problem. This follows from the fact that closing the gap will, taken by itself, tend to reduce the overall size of the market for American products.

There seems to be a fairly prevalent belief--very likely a reaction against the excessive claims of those who ask for protection against imports--that the aggregate demand for American products will be reduced only if the dollar gap is closed by reduction of exports, and not if (or to the extent that) it is closed by expansion of imports. This belief appears to be without foundation. Expansion of imports--even where the imports are commonly thought of as "noncompetitive," being high-grade raw materials for industry, or luxury goods like French lace, or "invisible" (service) items like travel abroad--will correspondingly reduce the purchasing power that might otherwise have been used to buy American goods and services. Thus American production and employment levels are bound to be affected, by way of the demand side of the equation, regardless of whether export-import balance is achieved at a low level or at a high level.

It does not follow, however, that aggregate demand for American products will be equally affected by increased imports on the one hand and loss of export markets on the other. On the contrary, it seems fairly clear that the adverse effect will be quantitatively less if imports are increased than if exports are reduced. For this there are several reasons.

In the first place, the direct effect, on aggregate demand for American products, of a loss of $1 billion of export markets is minus $1 billion; whereas the direct effect of an additional $1 billion of imports is almost certain to be minus less than $1 billion, since some part of the purchasing power used up to buy the new imports would otherwise not have been spent at all--these dollars being, so to speak, tempted away from savings.

In the second place, if we are talking about sudden, large-volume changes, the indirect or derived effects are also likely to be less unfavorable when imports are expanded than when exports are contracted. This follows from the fact that certain of our industries are so heavily dependent on exporting (machinery, iron and steel products, motor vehicles, cotton, tobacco, and apples, to name some examples) that a major reduction in export totals might create difficulties that would spread far and wide and bring about substantial secondary losses of income and purchasing power. To be sure, some of the new competition from a major rise in import totals would likewise pinpoint on particular industries and particular localities. But, on the whole, it seems likely that the impact from even a sharp rise of imports (for example, imports of rubber, oil, wool, and a wide range of manufactured products such as textiles, china, glassware, chemicals, or watches) would be more evenly distributed and have less severe secondary repercussions than would a major reduction in exports.

The points just brought out do not, of course, prejudge whether or not the Government has an obligation to assist business and labor to make such readjustments as may in fact be necessary if import competition, aided by a lowering of import barriers, forces real retrenchment in particular instances. What they do suggest is that expansion of imports is likely to complicate the problem of maintaining full employment somewhat less than it will be complicated by the loss of export outlets.

This conclusion, based on the probable over-all size of demand in terms of dollars, is reinforced by the further consideration that expansion of imports is likely to mean more production and more employment for even the _same_ aggregate dollar demand, because it will result in lowered costs and keener price competition. When it is realized, in addition, that a stepped-up interchange of commodities and services could help to knit the world together, that standards of living are raised when goods move freely about the world without hindrance or subsidy in accordance with comparative efficiencies, that our national security requires that we stockpile essential raw materials and in general retard the depletion of our own natural resources, and that an expansion of imports involving a reduction of trade barriers would tend to lessen governmental controls here and abroad whereas a forced contraction of exports would necessarily tend to intensify such controls, the case for trying to make the major adjustment through larger imports is very clear.

To achieve that result will require great efforts, however. It may be truly said that the loss of export markets is no less unwelcome to those immediately affected than the loss of domestic markets which are captured by foreign competitors. Unfortunately, if barriers keep imports out, then, unless the Government holds the gap open at taxpayers' expense, inability of foreigners to buy will drag our exports down, regardless.

However, to come back to the main issue, the attainment or preservation of full employment will be somewhat complicated by closing the dollar gap, regardless of which way this is done. Since the gap is about $6 billion wide at the present time, the probable impact from closing it--or, let us say, the impact from closing the part not likely to be covered by foreign investment under Point Four--deserves respectful attention.

One conclusion might be that the dollar gap should not be closed at all, or even narrowed. A better conclusion would be that we need domestic policies, consistent with our various other national objectives, to assure the maintenance of sufficient aggregate demand to support prosperity and full employment. We need such policies, of course, not merely to absorb the impact from closing the dollar gap. Obviously, a shortage of markets may develop from causes quite unrelated to foreign trade. But such a shortage, then, in addition to its other disadvantages, will multiply the difficulties of dispensing with our export surplus. Clearly, if the dollar gap needs to be closed, it is essential to create conditions, through sound prosperity policies, in which the effort to close it will not be frustrated by pressures to keep imports down and exports up.

Point Four and U. S. Full Employment

The argument is sometimes heard that we must aid the underdeveloped countries for the sake of our own prosperity; in a word, that full employment requires Point Four. This claim has been known to be made by representatives of underdeveloped countries, as well as by citizens of the United States. Since we have already examined the relation between Point Four and the dollar gap, and between the dollar gap and United States full employment, we should now be in a position to complete the triangle by assessing the merits of this further claim.

The first thing our previous analysis shows is that any help we obtain from Point Four in maintaining production and employment in the United States must come from the net investment effect and not from the increased productivity effect obtained in the "results" stage; that is, it must come from the temporary avoidance of the necessity to eliminate the export surplus, and not from its actual elimination. Point Four can promote better export-import balance in the world, or it can facilitate our full employment; but it cannot do both simultaneously. (Of course, it seems likely to keep our qualified technical experts pretty fully employed in any case! But what is under discussion here is our over-all employment level.) The fact that developed countries are better customers than underdeveloped countries shows that Point Four can make world trade expand, but not that it offers a magic formula to banish our "overproduction" worries. Unless the underdeveloped countries' exports increase still faster than their imports, Point Four will not, as we have seen, make any permanent contribution toward closing the gap. If it does make such a contribution, we shall be all the more thrown back on the necessity of perfecting domestic full employment policy. We cannot have it both ways.

In the net investment stage, Point Four can undoubtedly ease our internal problems more or less, depending on the size of the net investment outflow. Private savings going into foreign investment spare the budget the necessity of comparable or greater expenditures or tax reductions that would be required for maintaining the same volume of demand for American products. Heavy-goods industries geared to large export markets need not so suddenly contract. Farm surpluses need not pile up so fast. Readjustment processes are moderated or postponed. Time is gained to work out more lasting solutions. This may well mean that when exports and imports are brought into reasonable balance later on, the balance struck will be at a higher level than could be hoped for, in the face of the natural tendency for our exports to gravitate downward to the level of our imports, if the export surplus had to be squeezed out immediately. If so, this will mean that the postponement not only spreads out the impact felt by our economy, but actually lessens it somewhat in total magnitude, for reasons already discussed, and assists in gaining the other advantages of high-level two-way trade.

More than this can hardly be said. Indeed, what needs to be emphasized most is that any claim that Point Four can actually solve our full employment problem is entirely wrong. To think that Point Four is a *sufficient* condition for full employment in the United States is to cherish an illusion. For an American to think that it is a *necessary* condition is to cherish a very dangerous illusion indeed, because such ideas tend to block efforts to find real solutions of our fundamental economic problems.

A vital connection, all too often overlooked, between Point Four and United States full employment runs in the reverse direction. If we can maintain full employment, and especially if we can be sure of continuing to maintain it, that will undoubtedly help Point Four. If a business recession develops, or even, it may be, a threat that the level of demand will not keep rising so as to justify the expansion necessary to take care of increased productivity and a growing labor force, wise action will become doubly difficult. In such circumstances the pressure to economize by cutting off assistance to foreign countries, including the underdeveloped countries, will be second only to the mounting pressure to keep imports out and increasingly subsidize our exports. By contrast, the wealth and the good will flowing from a solidly based full employment will be a major factor in promoting development programs all over the world, because they will allay doubts that we can afford to give generous and continuous aid.

Conclusions

These considerations invite, I think, the following general conclusions:

Point Four will help to postpone the necessity of entirely closing the export-import gap and will facilitate, within limits and for a time, the maintenance of prosperity and full employment in the United States. A sound domestic full employment program, however, is essential to a proper perspective on Point Four, and to adequate funds for carrying it out, as well as essential to a closing of the dollar gap, especially at the desirable high export-import level.

Point Four should be supported for its own sake, and not for specious or extraneous reasons.

Sound considerations of national security are, of course, never specious or extraneous. The amount and the distribution of the aid we can render today may not correspond exactly to what would be indicated in a world in which the foundations of peace had been securely laid, a world in which all types of constructive co-operation under the general guidance of the Economic and Social Council and its affiliated agencies could move ahead with enormous strides to fulfill men's hopes. Even so, it still appears to be true that an approach dictated by a due regard for certain intrinsic functional relations between the major considerations other than defense is likely also to strengthen defense itself by winning allegiance to our cause. Such an approach, as it applies to Point Four, may be summarized here as follows:

Give profound consideration, sparing neither sympathy nor critical judgment, to the needs of the countries requesting aid for their development. Do this not merely for the sake of the people of those countries, but also for the sake of our own interest in a peaceful world in which the ideals by which we set store can be practiced, can flourish, can further evolve. Avoid a parsimonious attitude. Equally avoid any tendency to degrade Point Four by forcing its pace from ulterior motives, such as the hope of getting full employment for ourselves at bargain rates as a lucky by-product. This long-term job--the job, as President Truman put it, of "making the benefits of our scientific advances and industrial progress available for the improvement and growth of underdeveloped areas"--should be done for its own sake. It is well worth doing.

18. ON UNDERWRITING CONSUMPTION AND EMPLOYMENT*

The purpose of this note is to amplify one aspect of my earlier proposal for underwriting full employment in the United States[1]--the part having to do with techniques for boosting consumption when it would otherwise fall short of the target. It is probable that the subject of full employment will claim the spotlight again when and if the world situation permits major reductions in armament expenditures, and it is at least possible that a policy of assured full employment in this country, if we had such a policy now, would help to hasten that day.

The question of feasibility depends, I have argued, on whether or not aggregate consumer spending is underwritten in addition to aggregate employment as such. Without that feature, a policy of guaranteed full employment could involve the government in so large a degree of direct responsibility for the creation of jobs--such as expansion of public works, and perhaps wholesale subsidies to, and/or control over, private production--as to compromise the essentials of our private-enterprise system. Because of that risk, such a policy (as contrasted with contracyclical policy in a more limited sense) is not likely to be voted in the United States in the foreseeable future. That risk disappears if aggregate consumer spending, too, is underwritten and maintained at a proper level, one high enough to keep reliance on supplementary public works within reasonable bounds.[2] The risk of an unbalanced budget remains, but this--a corollary of the danger of oversaving itself--is not, as the other risk is, one that our system of private enterprise cannot bear.

I have elsewhere suggested a number of alternative procedures for enlarging consumers' incomes directly when personal consumption expenditures would otherwise--even at a full-employment level of income payments--fall below the underwritten level.[3] For some time I was inclined to stress

---

*Originally published as a Communication in The American Economic Review, Vol. XLV, No. 4, September, 1955. Reprinted by permission.

tax reductions or offsets. Here I wish to bring into consideration a different method, involving the use of what might be called Consumer Sales Premiums (CSP for short). This method would provide not only additional purchasing power but an actual inducement to spend. Where an income-tax rebate, for example, would not favor consumer spending relative to consumer saving, but rather would tend to raise the level of both, CSP would be distributed only in connection with consumer spending as such and hence would establish a direct incentive to spend more, both out of normal income and out of the premiums when cashed. Thus the target level of consumer spending would be reached at smaller cost to the government.

Certain other general characteristics of the CSP method may also be briefly noted here. It would not noticeably reduce anyone's incentive to work--a charge sometimes loosely leveled against consumer transfer payment schemes in general but actually valid in special cases only. It would be perfectly flexible as to the amount of "lift" to consumer income it could provide. And it would be reversible into a special sales tax,[4] with a minimum of difficulty or misunderstanding, in the event the problem shifted to one of avoiding an inflationary rise of consumer spending above its guaranteed ceiling.

CSP would take the form of small coupons or stamps, in convenient denominations, which would be used as follows: (1) The Treasury would distribute them to banks and designated post offices throughout the country. (2) Banks and post offices would pass them along, when authorized by the responsible agency in Washington, to "retailers"--stores, service establishments, independent professional practitioners such as doctors--in ratio to their certified current volume of consumer business.[5] (3) During periods declared to be "pay out" periods, retailers would give them to individual consumers as premiums on their purchases (value of purchase, times authorized percentage, figured to the nearest penny). (4) The individual consumer would redeem his CSP for cash at his bank or post office before the expiration date marked on the stamp's face. (5) Banks and the U.S. Post Office Department would return the CSP in bulk lots to the Treasury and would receive face value plus suitable compensation for their services as agents.

The administrative problems connected with such a scheme do not appear unduly formidable. The burden on retailers would be roughly like that of a sales tax--slightly more for bills mailed, since these upon payment would require a return receipt transmitting CSP. While there might be a number of CSP agents in a community, each retailer would normally have to choose one source of supply, and all lists of applicants would be cross-checked to prevent duplication. Each consumer would likewise normally deal with a single bank or post office selected by him. As a convenience and further precaution he probably would have a blank book issued to him, identified as his, to the pages of which his CSP would have to be affixed to be eligible for redemption in cash.

A numerical example will illustrate the effect on the economy as a whole. Assume aggregate consumer spending in year X underwritten at $300 billion, with the top limit set at $306 billion. Ignoring here the seasonal factor in sales, at least $75 billion should then be spent each quarter, or $25 billion each month. Assume that, after six weeks, the preliminary forecast for the first quarter showed only $72 billion. The responsible agency might then authorize CSP to be issued on all retail sales at a 10 per cent rate during months 3, 4 and 5. If monthly rates of consumer spending rose from $24 billion in months 1 and 2 to $27.3 billion in months 3, 4 and 5 (let us suppose that the inducement of obtaining CSP raised "ordinary" spending to $25 billion; add $2.5 billion CSP converted to cash less $200 million of extra saving from this extra cash), this would bring the five-month total to $129.9 billion, as against a target minimum of $125 billion, and the responsible agency might order termination of CSP payments at that point. The premiums might have to be issued again at the same or a different percentage rate, later in the year. Or, if conditions changed markedly and total consumer spending for the year threatened to exceed the $306 billion limit, the responsible agency would bring into play the special sales tax or other agreed device for curbing a spending excess.

Notes

1. See my "The Underwriting Approach to Full Employment: A Further Explanation," Rev. Econ. Stat., Aug. 1949, XXXI, 182-92. Also my "The Underwriting of Aggregate Consumer Spending as a Pillar of Full-Employment Policy," Am. Econ. Rev., Mar. 1944, XXXIV, 21-55; other papers collected in Full Employment and Free Enterprise (Washington, 1947); and "Employment the Key," Christian Science Monitor, July 23, 1949, mag. sec., pp. 2, 12.
2. See "The Underwriting Approach...," op. cit., pp. 184-

-85, for my theory of the "correct" level of aggregate consumer spending. Briefly, (1), estimated full-employment GNP, minus (2), the sum of (2a) expected government purchases of goods and services, including all public works approved "for their own sake," (2b) expected gross private domestic investment (probably, as a general rule, the anticipated cyclical-average level), and (2c) expected net foreign investment, equals (3) the level at which personal consumption expenditures should be underwritten. Thus one may advocate, as I personally do, rather generous regular appropriations for public works, but the amount included in (2a), and hence reflected in (3), depends on the will of Congress. A foreign-trade balance, plus or minus, similarly affects, and is accommodated in, (3) because it registers in (2c) and, where due to foreign aid, etc., in (2a). Actually my proposal calls for setting, not a single target figure for aggregate personal consumption, but a range between a guaranteed floor and a guaranteed ceiling, the leeway allowed being possibly of the order of 2 per cent. A summary statement on how minimum and maximum levels both of aggregate consumption and of aggregate employment would be likely to be established and administered in practice, i.e., the respective roles of Congress and the Executive and the requisite amendments to the Employment Act of 1946, appears in "Employment the Key," *op. cit.*; see also *Full Employment and Free Enterprise*, *op. cit.*, pp. 163-70.

3. See "The Underwriting Approach...," *op. cit.*, pp. 187-88. It is important to note that such measures--indeed, all *compensatory* measures under this plan, whether they be (a) such measures, taken in relation to current rates of consumer spending, to expand or contract consumer income directly, or (b) measures, taken in relation to current levels of employment, to expand or contract public works (and, incidentally, hold income payments at the full-employment level)--are viewed as *supplementing and in no sense substituting for basic or long-run policies*, a primary function of which is to make compensatory measures less necessary. The more that basic fiscal and other measures (high wages, a tax system that is progressive but encourages risk-taking, prevention of abuses of monopoly power, etc.) can do to strengthen production incentives and broaden the distribution of purchasing power, the better.

4. I am opposed to giving sales taxes, with their regressive character, any disproportionate emphasis in our tax system. However, if a special sales tax were linked with CSP in a two-way compensatory mechanism of the type here considered, the usual objection need hardly apply. The effect would be as progressive during periods when it was necessary to boost purchasing power as it would be regressive when necessary to hold purchasing power down; or more so, assuming sales tax exemptions for necessities.
5. Purchases for business account would sometimes masquerade as consumer purchases. However, "leakage" in either a real or a statistical sense (in reduced leverage value for the economy, or in excess of transactions included for CSP over transactions included in the personal consumption expenditures aggregate) should prove relatively minor.

19. AN INTERNATIONAL ECONOMIC CODE: A SUGGESTION*

I

In the economic sphere, expectations play a particularly important part, both in capitalist and in socialist systems. A mainspring of positive action is the anticipation that favorable conditions will be, or can be made to be, present. A question arises as to whether the economic work of the United Nations could at this time do more to apply the same general principle internationally on a worldwide basis. The effects would be economic and, indirectly, political, the two spheres being so closely linked.

It is widely conceded that the material welfare of the have-not nations could be substantially advanced by economic means if only political tensions could first be relaxed. This consideration is of great importance but, of itself alone, it seems to assign to economic means only a secondary and dependent role. It is also widely believed that poverty tends to breed war, so that economic means that help to reduce poverty already help to lessen political tensions and the chances of war. It is indeed necessary to act on this premise but, unfortunately, in present circumstances, if peace must wait until poverty has been eradicted, it must wait a long time. Is there no way out of these delays and frustrations?

A way might perhaps be found if it were possible to draw to a greater extent on expectations to supply what present reality cannot. That is, the attempt might be made to build up hope and begin to allay fear by somehow introducing on a worldwide basis a greater measure of favorable assurance about future economic conditions--long before national and international action had been able to diminish existing poverty to any really gratifying extent.

The way to do this on the grand scale--always assuming, of course, that it were possible at all in conditions as

---

*Reprinted by permission from Kyklos, Vol. XIII, 1960, Fasc. 2.

we find them today--would be through the promulgation of an International Economic Code. Such a "Code" or charter need not be (it will be argued below that it should not be) a convention binding on governments, since a considerable measure of favorable assurance would most likely be obtained without enforceable commitments. It would be better, potentially, than piecemeal international agreements about this or that aspect of international economic relations, valuable though these, too, would be. For example, it would be better, potentially, than a charter on trade such as the General Agreement on Tariffs and Trade (GATT) already provides, plus some regional Common Markets, plus a charter on foreign investment. This is so, partly because it would be more far-reaching than any imaginable series of such limited-purpose agreements, and partly because, in matters of this kind, the whole is greater than the sum of its parts. Putting it more colloquially, professional negotiators know the virtues of a "package deal."

The latest attempt at such a Code was the Havana (International Trade Organization or ITO) Charter, signed more than ten years ago in 1948 but not ratified. Since any parallels that might be cited from earlier periods of history would certainly be far from complete, we may call that also the first or pioneer attempt. Numerous reasons have been assigned for its failure to win the acceptance of the legislatures of governments. Two rather compelling reasons were that the Havana Charter undertook to contain binding commitments on governments, and that it began by taking the reduction of trade barriers--an excellent objective but not the main need of the postwar world--as its pivotal point.

II

Since nations are differently circumstanced they naturally espouse different and only partially consistent principles. In their necessity to live and prosper as best they can, they must obviously behave in this mutually inconvenient manner. Thus, a main problem in all international negotiations is to decide which principles should give way to which others--and to what extent.

What should be the relationships among, for example, the following important economic principles, each of which has its advocates in various parts of the world:

(1) that a country should not be prevented by international commitments from using domestic means to maintain

full employment;

(2) that a country should receive some protection against the "export" of deflation, or of inflation, by other countries;

(3) that its exports of goods and services should not be discriminated against by other countries;

(4) that even non-discriminatory barriers against its exports should be reduced where they are high and should be on a basis favoring the efficient economic competitor (i. e., a tariff rather than a quota basis);

(5) that an underdeveloped country should for the sake of its economic development be accorded exceptional rights to erect trade barriers;

(6) that major primary commodity prices should by special arrangements or agreements be prevented from fluctuating widely;

(7) that private foreign investment, and private enterprise in general, should be given encouragement and protection;

(8) that adequate foreign capital should be made available to the underdeveloped countries without strings for purposes to be determined by the recipients;

(9) that foreign trade should be conducted (or should not be conducted) by the state;

(10) that competitive enterprise should be protected against unfair practices of private cartels and uneconomic behavior of government trading organizations;

(11) that competition in international trade should not take place on the basis of substandard labor conditions;

(12) that countries should not seek to promote their export trade by competitive currency devaluation?

The list, while it includes many of the major principles espoused by various governments, is of course not exhaustive.

It would be premature to undertake to answer the above question here, but some general comments may be offered on it. In the first place, the relationships among the various principles in any Code capable of carrying a sense of conviction and serving as a guide to action would obviously have to be somewhat subtle and intricate, though perhaps less so than would appear on the surface. In the second place, we can safely assume that to frame a binding convention with regard to such difficult subject matter would still be an impracticable undertaking.

In the third place, even a Code conceived of as only a body of principles representing the "best thought" or "conscience" of humanity on this subject--principles not backed by sanctions other than the force of world opinion--could probably not be worked out successfully unless some definite and at the same time generally acceptable "orientation" could be given to it from the beginning. That is, there would first have to be a decision that the various principles involved should be mutually related in a manner calculated to uphold one or more master principles recognized by nearly everyone as being of pivotal importance. Here, probably, is the crux of the problem.

Fortunately, viewed from this angle, the situation looks far from hopeless. There are, certainly, master international principles that nearly all thinking persons are now coming to recognize as being, by necessity, of pivotal importance. We may call these master principles the principle of greater international accommodation ("harmony" would be perhaps too strong or ambitious a word), and the principle of higher and more equal economic development.

One other important element, referred to earlier, is the need for a fair degree of inclusiveness in the subjects to be covered by such a Code. The bigger the "package," the greater the opportunity for countries to make concessions on points not deemed to be absolutely vital to their interests. Such points, if negotiated on separately (the conditions that should govern foreign investment, for example, or those for commodity agreements), will naturally be the subject of the sharpest bargaining, each one separately to the limit.

Thus the rather lengthy list of principles given above may in fact need still further expansion for best results. For instance, the case for special regional trade arrangements might require formulation as a positive principle rather than as a mere exception to the previously mentioned principle of non-discrimination in trade. And the question of immigration policy, which could well be regarded as the ultimate question in this entire field, might turn out, in this day of explosive population increases, to be better included than ignored altogether.--If so, its inclusion might possibly be by way of a principle relating immigration quotas in some degree and manner to population growth rates in the countries of origin.

What has been said up to this point is that an International Economic Code might be possible, given the following conditions: (1) no binding commitments on governments, hence no need for detailed, legally conceived and drafted safeguarding clauses; (2) a decision to seek to recognize <u>all</u> the major international economic policy needs or motivations; and (3) a decision to examine them all together from the point of view of certain overriding <u>objectives of the world community</u>--namely, greater international accommodation and higher and more equal economic development.

III

What the master principles could be expected to do is to make it possible to get a far larger measure of agreement than could otherwise be had about the circumstances in which (to put it abstractly) A should take precedence over B, and B over C, and about those other circumstances in which in turn B or even C must, in a practical sense, be considered paramount.

With self-interest as the starting point and international accommodation and economic development as the added master principles, it can be broadly deduced, for example, that the principle against the "export" of deflation (No. 2 in the above list), the one against preventing the use of domestic means to maintain full employment (No. 1) and the one for lowering tariffs and avoiding quantitative restrictions or quotas (No. 4) stand, as a general proposition, in that order of priority. ("Priority" here means breadth or inclusiveness of interpretation; no implication of chronological sequence is intended, since all principles are assumed to be in effect simultaneously.) However, a small industrial country suffering from balance of payments difficulties and incapable of exerting much deflationary influence beyond its own borders might be conceded a top priority for principle No. 1, and a major industrial power might, on the other hand, be asked to limit its definition of "domestic" means under principle No. 1 in such a way as to give higher priority to the obligation expressed in principle No. 4. This, of course, is a much over-simplified illustration.

In practical terms, this approach undoubtedly implies concessions to the underdeveloped or have-not nations at various points. That is, all nations would have obligations but the degree of obligation would tend to vary directly with their wealth, power and influence--the reverse of the jungle law. The industrialized countries would not need to become poorer; on the contrary! However, they would need to cooperate in making the underdeveloped countries go forward at a relatively faster pace. This, it should be pointed out, is not something that could be realistically attributed to the Code, since it appears to be rather a condition for maintaining the modern world as a going concern. What the Code, if it existed, would do would be to recognize the actual situation overtly in a formal and orderly way.

It must be apparent that restraint and good will would

have to be exercised by governments when judging whether or not to approve a Code of this kind. Too narrow or extremist a view, expressed in the form of unworkable amendments, could injure or destroy its prospects. For example, one country might be tempted to insist that private investors should simply dictate the terms on which their capital would be exported for development purposes, while another country might be tempted to demand formal codification of the right to nationalize and of the proposition that the prices of primary commodities must go up in relation to the prices of manufactured goods. If such positions were to be taken up and were not overridden by a more balanced, world-embracing view, the Code could become a travesty of the concept with which it began.

This reference to political considerations by no means denies their importance or value but rather suggests that success would depend not only on the Code's substance but also on the process by which its text might be developed. Early public debate--say on the composition and terms of reference of a commission of experts to be appointed to do the drafting--might easily cripple the undertaking from the start. On the other hand, by the methods of analysis, consultation with experts and quiet diplomacy open to the United Nations Secretariat for doing the job assigned to it under the UN Charter, it seems reasonable to suppose that a suitable document for adoption by the Economic and Social Council might be evolved.

IV

If it be said that such a Code would create jurisdictional conflicts with the Specialized Agencies--in whose fields of responsibility much of the Code's far-ranging subject matter would undoubtedly lie--a two-fold answer might be given. There is no reason why existing charters with detailed rules and provisions for enforcement should not co-exist with a new declaratory Code of broader scope, designed for the purpose of getting the world forward by fitting the various pieces of the picture together and creating favorable expectations. Secondly, in seeking to end the compartmentalization of economic policy and construct an integrated approach, the United Nations would be exercising just the kind of leadership of which it alone is capable.

If it be said, on the other hand, that a declaration of general principles without binding and enforceable commitments is worthless even if signed by many governments, no decisive answer can be given. However, it must equally be admitted by the critics that no means of making progress on the international relations front have yet been discovered that can be called infallible. In this situation, the exact relation between moral and legal forces becomes unclear, and what remains is a strong imperative to develop and use the potentialities of both.

20. A "FREEDOM BUDGET" AND GUARANTEED FULL EMPLOYMENT

It is encouraging that two hundred leaders of civil rights, religious and labor groups and other prominent progressives have endorsed a proposed program under which poverty could be virtually abolished in America in the next ten years. Their call to action appears in the pamphlet, *A "Freedom Budget" for All Americans*,[1] conceived by A. Philip Randolph and shaped by the hand of Leon H. Keyserling. This document deserves many readers, for its panoramic view and its detailed analysis alike. I would only urge the need for a more definitive approach to guaranteed full employment. But I will come to that later.

I

The authors correctly state that abolishing poverty in this country has become a moral problem. Economically, there is no longer any real obstacle. Sociologically, personal deficiencies of the poor or the unemployed should not be mistaken for the main issue, any more than personal weakness would be considered the main cause of fatalities in a shipwreck, especially if too few lifeboats were provided.

The economic point--familiar but crucial, and cogently presented here--is that we are now able to eradicate poverty because of our wealth and our growth potential. By liberating that growth potential and also using the resources idle today, the authors estimate that we could carry out the necessary additional measures and could finance the Federal budget cost ($185 billion in 1964 dollars over ten years) with some room to spare, doing this *without raising tax rates, even if we must continue to enlarge our national defense expenditures substantially at the same time*. Nor need it cause inflation, if we will put first things first and cut only nonessentials. (The same reasoning applies in the last analysis to the balance-of-payments problem, which the authors do not discuss.) In other words, it would be wrong to postpone the war on poverty until the end of the war in Vietnam.

Skeptics will come forward to attack the basis for this arithmetic. The authors have estimated that our gross national product, which was $663 billion (1964 dollars) in the year 1965, could be raised to $1085-1120 billion by 1975, creating a $2315-2442 billion "economic growth dividend." (By this they mean the excess over what the GNP would hypothetically add up to by remaining constant at its 1965 level.) This growth dividend, enabling us to afford the war on poverty without retrenching elsewhere, presupposes an increase in productivity or output per man-hour in the private sector of about 3 1/4 to 3 3/4 per cent a year. The result, with a growing labor force, would be an economic growth rate of about 4 1/2 to 5 per cent a year, after an initial two years of still faster growth (apparently about 8 per cent a year) caused by rapid elimination of the existing unemployment.

Viewed as prediction, this could well be over-optimistic. Yet these growth rates are in line with some other carefully developed estimates of what we could and should aim to achieve. Skeptics and "gradualists" should moreover take note that, while the authors certainly consider such expansion feasible, and strongly urge it--since then all income levels would gain--they do not predict it. Instead they say this: should we fail to use our reserve productive powers and our full growth potential, thus diminishing somewhat the extra yield obtainable in future from present tax rates, the war on poverty would still deserve top priority and should in that case be partly financed by raising tax rates and making them more progressive.

To achieve results, their argument continues, we must have time schedules and an integrated, balanced program that will weave together in a mutually reinforcing way (1) the maintenance of full employment, (2) the obliteration of "private poverty," both of workers and of those who, for reasons of age or other valid reasons, cannot and should not work, and (3) the elimination of the "poverty in the public sector." For (2) we need higher minimum and other wages, policies tending toward parity for farm incomes rather than for farm prices, more adequate Social Security and welfare programs, with social insurance also financed in part from general Federal tax revenues, and progress toward realizing the guaranteed annual income concept for all. For (3) we need a great stepping-up of our programs concerned with education, health, transportation, natural resources, air and water pollution, distressed areas, rural communities in general, and above all urban renewal, which should especially emphasize slum clearance and much more construction of low-income housing.

The authors stress that Federal leadership is essential to get the job done, and that the Federal budget is the most powerful single instrument of national economic and social policy. This does not mean, however, that they want the Federal Government's spending to rise at the expense of private enterprise, or of State and local government. On the contrary, the "Freedom Budget" pictures State and local spending as rising more than Federal spending, and the prevailing total-government, private investment, and private consumption shares of GNP as being maintained. (The supply side of the equation is discussed too--or at any rate structural questions such as what the Office of Economic Opportunity, and training for needed skills, and general education could do to help create a more perfect labor market. But the emphasis throughout is on aggregate demand and its various components, as the subject indeed requires.)

The authors identify full employment--"opportunity for year-round employment to all of those able to work and wanting to work, including those whose abilities need lifting through training and education"--as by far the most important single approach to the eradication of poverty. Allowing for involuntary part-time workers and also for some who are just too discouraged by scarcity of job opportunity to continue searching for work, they attribute 40 per cent of all our poverty directly to full- or part-time unemployment (not counting unemployment's indirect effect in depressing wages), 20 per cent to substandard wages, and the other 40 per cent to the fact that some households simply do not have anyone in them who could or should be employed. They also consider full employment an imperative end in itself. A guaranteed annual income on a nationwide basis--yes, as a supplement to a nationwide full-employment policy. By no means would they agree with the thesis that automation has brought us to the point where the system of income distribution needs a divorce from the system of production and jobs.

II

On pages 4, 12, and 64 of A "Freedom Budget" for All Americans it is stated that the Federal Government should "guarantee" full employment. On page 32 an "unqualified commitment" to sustained full employment is advocated. Elsewhere (e.g., page 23) the word "assure" is used. The great majority of the signers must have meant this to be taken literally. My comment, offered in the same spirit, is that the guaranteeing of full employment is essential but is not practicable by the means proposed in this pamphlet. But it would be practicable to guarantee full employment if one more element were added--and I hope that the sponsors of the "Freedom Budget" can be persuaded of this.

Let me say at once that for maximizing employment the program as it stands has two great strengths: its size in terms of aggregate demand is auspicious, and its heavy stress on elements like housing construction and slum clearance would structure the employment pattern somewhat away from automation-sensitive kinds of work and toward work that the labor force can do. There are more jobs per extra dollar of final demand in city rebuilding, and in other parts of the proposed program such as resource conservation and replenishment, than in many of the things the individual consumer would buy if he were given the extra money through tax reductions. A massive attack of the kind proposed could contribute enormously to job creation and could certainly create periods of full employment.

Indeed everything coincides to bless a program like the proposed attack on slum ghettos: the fact that it goes to the very heart of our social needs today; the dubious value (stressed by Galbraith, for example) of some of the things that might be done alternatively with the same money, such as produce still more unneeded gadgets for still more affluent consumers; and finally, the excellent employment effect. Surely, that program is a must!

The only trouble is that it and the other good programs proposed cannot as they stand be combined into a total program that assures full employment. It might be so on paper, but not in the actual legislative process in which the President in his annual Economic Report or at other times makes recommendations for action to maintain employment, and Congress approves or amends the President's recommendations, or takes the initiative itself. Suppose that President Johnson were to present the "Freedom Budget" as a Great Society program without changing a line of it. Would Congress necessarily also give it blanket approval? To ask this question is to answer it in the negative. Quite apart from such direct opposition as might arise on various points of substance and intent, there are also too many incidental cross-currents. Consider as just one example the religious issue bedeviling Federal aid to education.

Lest this be taken as criticism of Congress, let me ask the signatories of the "Freedom Budget" this question: Would you recommend it to the President or to Congress without changing a line of it? You are on record as "in broad agreement with its basic objectives and broad outlines," "while not necessarily endorsing every detail." Fair enough. But where does it leave guaranteed full employment?

Of course the authors do not need to be told that the details will change in the give-and-take of discussion, or that the rate of growth itself will depend on "the feasibility of various ranges of policy endeavors and popular attitudes." What they count on, therefore, is that the Federal Government would "continuously lead in organizing and financing enough job-creating activities to close the gap between full employment and employment provided at other public and private levels. None of the Federally-created jobs," they add, "need to be made-work, because our unmet needs in the public sector are large enough to absorb beneficially this Federal effort." (page 4)

One might wish it were otherwise, but surely there still is good reason to believe that an open-ended commitment to provide jobs on public works and services to those who fail to find jobs elsewhere is impracticable in this country, unless coupled with a further assurance effectively limiting the weight this commitment might have to bear. Made-work versus filling unmet needs in the public sector is not the main issue. The main issue is that it would be thought by some to embody too serious a threat to our private enterprise system. This is not a new story. When the Employment Act of 1946 was being drafted and redrafted, the preamble at one stage contained a strong commitment in general terms along the line now again suggested, while at the same time the arrangements envisaged in the operative clauses were strikingly weak. Needless to say, this conflict was resolved by deleting the strong commitment.

But there is no reason for pessimism. I would repeat that full employment can be guaranteed under the "Freedom Budget," in my opinion, by adding to it one element it now lacks. That element is a guarantee of aggregate consumer spending--coupled with the guarantee of full employment itself, which could then no longer be thought by anyone to threaten a possible Federal take-over of the economy. Both guarantees would be given under an amendment to the Employment Act that would call on Congress to express its employment policy year by year in the form of specific commitments. To suggest this approach is not to put more emphasis on private consumer spending and less on slum clearance or on anything else needed to end poverty in the public sector; it should not be so construed. The suggestion aims rather to insure that Congress would not be in the position of chipping away at full employment if it voted against some of the specific items, favored by the author of this note as much as by the authors of the pamphlet, that might be proposed by the President.[2]

In brief outline, this would work in the following manner. Let us say that the President in his Economic Report would present the program of the "Freedom Budget." He would among other things spell out its quantitative implications in terms of a full-employment GNP: (a) so much proposed total government spending for goods and services, (b) so much expected private domestic investment, (c) so much expected net exports (worth separate attention for trade policy reasons, in spite of its small size), and (d) so much private consumer spending needed to round out the total. That amount of (d), and the level of jobs that the President regarded as corresponding to full employment, he would ask Congress to guarantee. But at the same time--and this is the crux--he would point out that, if Congress chose to cut back (a), it would need to increase (d) correspondingly; or slightly more, if (d) would clearly be less labor-intensive than (a).

Congress would then have a choice of <u>proportions</u> between government spending and private spending (which indeed it should have) but not of over-all levels of demand and activity in our economy (which it would not need, full-employment levels having been already called for in principle as far back as 1946). Congress would also give finality to the working (statistical) definition of full employment for the year ahead, and would designate in advance the type of means to be used, without further debate, to raise or lower consumer purchasing power on the one hand or publicly sponsored employment on the other if the official (i.e., Congressionally approved) indexes of consumer spending or jobs strayed appreciably from the target rates. The phrase "raise or lower" is used because, in order to make the system operate equally strongly, and on equally unmistakable signals, against inflation, not only a floor should be guaranteed but also a ceiling--possibly about two per cent above the floor. Finally, if Congress remained in virtually continuous session, it could also give the expansion or contraction orders in response to the mandatory signals it had arranged, although surely that task had better be discharged by the Executive Branch.

What means consistent with social justice <u>could</u> be specified for raising or lowering consumer purchasing power when necessary, i.e., in those periods when the interaction of all domestic and international events and all the "Freedom Budget" measures and other basic policies currently in effect demanded, by flashing the agreed signal, that type of compensatory action? I suggest three alternative plans:

Plan A. Since income tax variations have already won wide public recognition as a useful tool, introduce the nationwide guaranteed annual income idea in the form of a negative income tax plan that would pay out allowances partly closing the poverty income gap of all poor families and unattached individuals. Then raise those allowances or negative taxes, and lower positive income taxes, when necessary to increase total purchasing power, and raise positive income taxes, preferably without lowering the allowances, when necessary to decrease it.

Plan B. Adopt a reversible or two-way sales tax/sales bonus at the Federal level and use this to achieve the needed variations in purchasing power. Just as most sales taxes are regressive, hurting the poor man most, this particular scheme would be predominantly progressive, and all the more so if sales tax exemptions were granted for necessities in the periods calling for contraction. In the more frequent periods calling for expansion, everyone buying anything at retail would get coupons or stamps which would be redeemable in cash if presented within a reasonable period at a bank or post office, those agencies being in turn reimbursed from the Treasury.[3]

Plan C. Provide for reductions in income taxes for those who pay them, coupled with an appropriate equivalent for poorer households, e.g., a stamp or coupon plan or even cash payments considered as a partial refund, rebate, or offset to the largely hidden taxes they do pay to Federal, State, and local tax jurisdictions. After all, a substantial part of their small incomes--possibly as much as 30 per cent on the average--goes to pay those hidden taxes now. In periods requiring contraction, raise income tax rates only.

* * *

To sum up, I should like to re-emphasize two points. First, a "Freedom Budget" is imperatively needed, to accelerate the war on poverty and give it focus. The sooner we get it the better. Second, the "Freedom Budget" in its present form cannot yield guaranteed full employment because guaranteed full employment does not come as a by-product but needs in addition its own kind of envelope plan or insurance policy operating in part by way of control over aggregate purchasing power.

I would urge on the authors of the "Freedom Budget" that everything they have said about the need to assure sustained full employment is true. And more besides: in particular, it is this alone that can remove the perennial fear of a shortage of markets, and thus provide the basis for a sound U.S. international policy on trade and aid, helpful to the developing countries and others. Fortunately, guaranteed full employment can be more than a figure of speech: it can be made a reality now.

Notes

1. Subtitled _Budgeting Our Resources, 1966-1975, to Achieve "Freedom from Want."_ A. Philip Randolph Institute, New York, October 1966. 84 pp. The "Freedom Budget" is an adaptation and up-dating of the "American Economic Performance Budget" which Dr. Keyserling and the Conference on Economic Progress have been advocating for several years.
2. The proposal summarized here is explained at length in my _Insuring Full Employment: A United States Policy for Domestic Prosperity and World Development_, New York: The Viking Press, 1964.
3. For further details on Plan B, see my _Insuring Full Employment_, _op. cit._, pp. 38-39, and my "On Underwriting Consumption and Employment," _American Economic Review_, September 1955, pp. 645-47.

21. POVERTY AND THE GUARANTEED INCOME PROPOSALS*

In the thirty years since the Great Depression, the "one-third of the nation ill-housed, ill-clothed, ill-fed" has shrunk to one-fifth. In his sobering book, The Other America,[1] Michael Harrington spoke not long ago of 40 to 50 million "internal aliens" in our society, which would be about one-fourth. But subsequent government estimates, now used by most analysts, show slightly under 20 per cent of the population as "poor" today. While non-whites, large families, and families whose head is aged or female or not in the labor force are hardest hit, other groups are not spared.

In round numbers there are officially estimated to have been, as of 1964, 34 million poor persons altogether, in 12 million poor households--a figure composed of 7 million families and 5 million "unrelated individuals." Any definition of poverty in terms of a particular level of money income is bound to be somewhat arbitrary, of course. Where exactly should the line be drawn? How well in any case will the best-drawn line fit different kinds of people? The Council of Economic Advisers, in its Annual Report of 1964 which heralded the drive against poverty, set the poverty line at $3000 for all families of two or more (before taxes and in 1962 dollars) and at $1500 for unattached individuals. The Social Security Administration refined this measure by distinguishing between families of different size, using weighted averages of the "market baskets" believed to be needed by different demographic groups, and deriving a poverty index by applying a multiplier of three to the Department of Agriculture's "economy" food budget (in prices of 1964).[2] This index, which is now used by the Office of Economic Opportunity and other government agencies, yields the estimates

---

*This report was written in 1966 for the Foundation for Voluntary Service with a view to its incorporation as a chapter in a book planned to be issued by the Foundation on the poverty problem in the United States.

of the extent of poverty cited above. For non-farm households it draws the line at $3130 for families of four and $1540 for single individuals, with gradations between and above. The farm-household line is lower--currently by 30 per cent--to allow for home-grown food and for housing owned or occupied by farmers at relatively small cost.

This index of poverty, and consequently the calculations based upon it, have come in for their share of criticism. Some experts have challenged the contention that it is possible to live on the "economy" food budget for extended periods of time without serious damage to health; or have doubted, given all the evidences of extensive poverty in rural areas, that so much lower a cash standard for farm families is actually warranted; or have proposed multipliers other than three for deriving a total budget from a budget for food. A fairly slight change in concepts or methods could, moreover, change the estimates by a wide margin. For example, if the Agriculture Department's more generous "low cost" food budget had been used instead of its "economy" budget, the poor would have numbered 50 million in 1964 by the same calculation, instead of 34 million.

There is much to be said for views such as those of Alan Haber who finds the poverty lines as drawn by the Social Security Administration too low, for several reasons combined, and concludes by saying: "When a family does not have enough for a healthful, self-respecting mode of living, then it is poor. One can bicker about how poor, and the levels of deprivation might suggest different social policies, but the semantic refinements do not change the reality of social isolation and inequality."[3] Nevertheless we can hardly do better than to use the official definition as providing the current measure of poverty in the strict sense of that term, especially since the critics of this definition have no agreed alternative to offer.

1. The Poverty Income Gap

There were, then, in 1964, by official estimate, about 34 million poor persons in the United States, and 12 million poor households, counting 5 million unattached individuals as well as 7 million families, large or small. These totals were obtained by the Social Security Administration by constructing and applying a poverty index according to which the dividing line between poverty and non-poverty was $1540 for (non-farm) individuals, $1990 for two persons, and so on up by somewhat irregular increments to $3130 for families of four and, finally, $5090 for families of seven or more (non-farm) persons. Farm households were considered to need less cash--though an original differential of 40 per cent has since been lowered to 30 per cent--because of the food and housing income they receive in kind.

It is easy to find fault with any specific income index of poverty, and some of the objections to this one have been noted already. A further point, illustrating again that such formulas should not be taken too seriously except as operational tools, is that they are normally based on personal income before taxes rather than on actual disposable income. More than 600,000 persons who would not have been counted by the Social Security Administration in 1961 under its subsequently developed formula, because they were not poor on a before-taxes basis, are estimated to have fallen below the poverty line when they paid their income and Social Security taxes. Of course, a budget used for the poverty index could already contain the necessary allowance for those levies. But in that case any rise (or fall) in income or payroll tax rates would automatically make a "correct" standard be "incorrect" afterwards.

In view of unavoidable complications and ambiguities such as those mentioned here and above, there is little to be lost and something to be gained by calculating the implications of various negative income tax plans on the basis of some formula which is approximately equivalent to, but simpler than, the one devised by the Social Security Administration. This will be done in this chapter, following the example of Professor Robert Lampman, one of the leading proponents of negative income taxation,[4] and of Christopher Green, whose recently published book, Negative Taxes and the Poverty Problem,[5] contains the most comprehensive exposition of the subject available. In their convenient, round-numbers formula, the poverty line starts at $1500 for the unattached individual and simply adds $500 for each additional person in the household, up to a top of $5000 for families of 8 or more. Thus $3000, for example, is the amount for a family of 4.

Together with these technical preliminaries, a point of substance needs to be noticed here; namely, that the mere existence of a guaranteed income plan would undoubtedly increase the number of poor appearing in the statistics. Had such a plan been in effect in 1964, for instance, the totals under the same definitions would have been somewhat higher than given--possibly 37 million persons and 13 million families or unattached individuals--because many of the "hidden" poor who were living doubled up in other families just to make ends meet would then have split off and claimed their separate allowances from the Federal Government. According to the Social Security Administration there were 2.8 million such hidden poor in 1964--poor individuals or members of "subfamilies" composed of married couples with or without children, or of one poor parent with one or more children--living in families that were above the poverty line. (On the other hand, there were also perhaps 500,000 aged families and individuals who would no longer have been counted as poor had it been desired to tighten up definitions by treating the assets of the aged as convertible into additional consuming power during their remaining expected years of life.)

Finally, then, we reach the financial measure of the extent of poverty--the concept of the poverty income gap. A family's income deficit or poverty income gap equals the poverty-line income for a family of that size minus its actual income. Using Census data and aggregating all units and groups, it appears that the nation's poverty income gap in 1964 amounted to slightly over $12 billion--the poor needed $29.1 billion to cover basic requirements, but they had only $16.8 billion, so they still lacked $12.3 billion. Thus the gap came to about $360 per poor person and $1000 per poor family unit on the average.

Adding the hidden poor (as defined just above) would raise the total to about $13 billion. This $12-13 billion figure is of interest as an *ex ante* measure of the width of the 1964 poverty income gap but, as Green and others have emphasized, it substantially understates the cost of *closing* that gap, because simply to distribute that much money according to the deficiency pattern would have affected incentives in such a way as to cause work and earnings to fall and total costs to rise further. (Mainly for this reason a number of the transfer-by-taxation plans do not seek to guarantee incomes high enough to close all of the poverty income gap but only a part.)

So much for the statistical dimensions of the problem in the recent past; what of the future? Because of the growing productiveness and wealth of our society, it is usually supposed that the number of poor and the size of the poverty income gap in real terms if not also in dollars will tend to decline, so that poverty will gradually cease to be a major problem in the United States. This supposition appears reasonable, barring serious mismanagement of the employment situation and the economy generally. Average per capita income should continue to rise, and the incomes of the poor, too, can be expected to rise. That is, some of the poor will gain from the prosperity directly through higher wage incomes or even through higher incomes from their small equities in land and stocks, etc., and many others will surely gain indirectly as the general prosperity arouses the social conscience. For example, we can expect to see increased Social Security benefits in 1967 and presumably at intervals thereafter through higher rates, broader coverage and possibly new programs (and this, in spite of the contributory features, will entail some income redistribution in favor of the poor); and we can also expect upward and outward adjustments of minimum wage standards, as well as the institution or expansion of various antipoverty or economic-opportunity measures designed not so much to alleviate poverty at the moment as to strike at the stubborn social and individual roots of residual poverty and give the poor a better chance to compete.

How fast this will take place is, of course, a question without an answer today. At the slow pace maintained since the end of the Second World War, poverty might not be substantially liquidated for half a century more. This will certainly not do. Calling for a radically different tempo, the authors of *A "Freedom Budget" for All Americans*[6] have urged a many-sided campaign to eliminate poverty almost entirely--all but about 2.25 million persons--by the year 1975. This, they believe, could be done by means of full employment and rapid economic growth which would yield such an "economic growth dividend"--in other words, would so expand the gross national product--that the whole program could be carried out without sacrifice and the Federal Government's contributions to it could be readily financed. That is, the government spending could be financed--*if* we really use our reserve productive resources and our *full* growth potential--from the larger yields obtainable from the growing tax base without raising tax rates, even given the necessity to enlarge our military and space expenditures substantially at the same time.

The authors of this set of proposals attribute 40 per cent of poverty in the United States directly to involuntary full-time or part-time unemployment, 20 per cent to substandard pay, and the other 40 per cent to the fact that some people "cannot or should not be employed." Their program calls for progress toward a guaranteed annual income as a matter of right, "*supplementary to rather than in place of a nation-wide full-employment policy*" (emphasis in original). A main objective is the elimination of "poverty in the public sector" through acceleration of efforts in the fields of education, health, transportation, natural resources, air and water pollution, distressed areas, rural communities generally, and above all slum clearance and the construction of low-income housing. This kind of planning, with specific targets and time schedules, could be of undoubted interest and importance.

A rising gross national product will no doubt contain an element of price increase along with its basic component of rising real output. Hence any given poverty lines as expressed in dollar terms will presumably need to be revised upward from time to time to keep the standard from depreciating in real terms (not to speak of revisions likely to be called for as changed ways of living cause the very composition of the market basket to change). This does not affect the presumption of a favorable, downward trend in poverty. What might on the other hand upset the presumption would be (1) redefinitions of the poverty standard, (2) cyclical economic instability, or (3) a secular decrease in the demand for labor resulting from technological progress, especially from the advance of automation. Some comment is therefore in order on each of these subjects.

(1) A long-term rise in average per capita income may lead to occasional upward revisions in the poverty standard which will tend to keep the number of "poor" and the "poverty" income gap from declining. That is, real conditions will be getting better but without any corresponding reduction in the cost to the government. If society wants its economically disadvantaged members not just to satisfy a more or less fixed, physiologically given "minimum" need but to "keep up" with the general procession--sharing in the growing bounty of life and avoiding the stigma of being deprived or too different in their consumption habits--there is no way of telling how many might continue to be classed as being poor, or as being at any rate below socially tolerable standards. For example, it might some day well be decided to eliminate not only poverty (in the sense of, say, 4-member family budgets below $3000) but also "deprivation" (below $5000); even a "modest but adequate" budget (now visualized as $6000) might eventually be made the minimum standard.

Perhaps the most likely, and also most desirable, outcome will be that public opinion will consider poverty as being in some degree a relative concept and will therefore demand some upward revision of standards as time goes by but not enough to cause the poverty lines to rise as fast as average incomes. In that case there will still be a secular downward trend in the number of the poor and the extent of the poverty income gap but this trend will possibly be gradual.

(2) If we fail to prevent future recessions, then ob-

viously poverty could become a more serious problem at times, financially as well as otherwise. According to official statistics, unemployment averaged 4.8 million or 6.7 per cent of the civilian labor force in 1961 as compared with slightly under 3.9 million or 4.6 per cent in 1964. (Peak monthly jobless percentages were 7.0 per cent in the 1960-61 recession, 7.5 per cent in the previous dip in 1958). Also, more persons could find only part-time work in 1961; 8.0 per cent of labor force time is estimated to have been lost through unemployment plus involuntary part-time work in the former year, 5.8 per cent in the latter. If 1961 economic conditions had prevailed in 1964, raising unemployment by say one million and forcing say 500,000 more persons who wanted full-time jobs to work only part-time, how much larger would the number of poor persons and size of the poverty income gap have been than the 34-37 million persons and $12-13 billion referred to above?

Among the unemployed at any given time are many who are single, but let us suppose that the additional unemployed and involuntarily part-time employed would have had two dependents each on the average. If we then take the unrealistic extreme assumption that <u>all</u> of them and their dependents would have become poor (i.e., none of them being poor and none substantially above poverty beforehand), the number of poor persons would have risen by 4.5 million and the poverty income gap would have widened by about $1.6 billion. Far more likely, however, some of the added unemployed and short-time workers and their dependents would have been poor already, many others would have been saved from poverty--at least for some time--by receiving unemployment compensation and/or drawing down savings, and still others would have been sustained by work relief programs or other special anti-recession measures adopted by Congress. Assuming one-half (or even two-thirds) thus preserved from falling into poverty, the number of the poor would have risen by 2.25 (or 1.5) million, while the poverty income gap--if we make some additional allowance for the fact that the families already below the poverty level would have been driven down still further--would have widened by something like $900 million (or $600 million).

These calculations make no pretense at refinement. But at least one may conclude that a guaranteed income plan--which by paying out more in bad years than in good would itself tend to have some countercyclical effect--would not be rendered financially unworkable by a recession no deeper or longer-lasting than those in recent memory.

(3) Some writers expect automation--or, more broadly,

cybernation--to reduce the available work to such an extent that joblessness piles up secularly and the present system of income distribution, closely linked to production and especially to work performed, becomes untenable. This is Robert Theobald's position.[7] According to him and those who agree with him, this revolutionary development should be seen as a triumph and not a disaster. Now that man's age-old dream of abundance has come true, we should make the other great dreams of justice and freedom come true also by simply distributing, to all, the incomes needed to buy back the products of abundance. Reduced to its simplest terms, the economic problem is consumption, not production. "They also serve who only stand and consume!"[8]

Opponents of this thesis rely for the most part on four arguments: (1) Statistical investigations (such as the one conducted recently by the National Commission on Technology, Automation and Economic Progress)[9] do not show increased unemployment arising from automation. (2) We will continue the well-established trend to longer education, earlier retirement (desirable if it is not a device for just pushing older workers out of the labor force into poverty!), a shorter work-week, and ampler vacations, thus reducing the work sought and gaining the benefits of rising productivity without a concomitant rise in involuntary unemployment. (3) Public works and services--in such comparatively neglected fields as slum clearance, housing and urban redevelopment; rural area development; health; education and retraining; scientific research; conservation and anti-pollution--can and should be greatly expanded to take up the slack caused by labor displacement from the more automation-sensitive lines of work. (4) The private sector itself holds virtually limitless possibilities of generating more employment in the provision of nonstandardized services, no matter how far automation may go in eliminating jobs in mass-produced services and goods.

This controversy is not likely to be settled for some time. In my own view, the first of the above arguments is over-optimistic, failing to take adequate account of snowballing or compound-rate effects which will naturally be much less obvious at first than later;[10] the second and third arguments are generally valid; and the fourth is valid within limits but finally, if pushed too far, becomes a trifle absurd. I would conclude that the Theobald school is more nearly correct in its sweeping views of where we are headed than many economists are as yet ready to concede, but also that what this school predicts is a little farther off in the future than it would have us suppose, and consequently that to jump to the solution it proposes would be premature.

If these conclusions are correct, the disemployment caused by the advance of automation--in the face of considerable inertia and some active resistance--need not cause any net loss of jobs or job income over the next decade, given reasonably good economic management. Hence the cost of closing the poverty gap need not expand. (A rise should be expected in the cost of normal public works and services, but that is another matter.) Naturally the poverty gap will tend to widen if and when displacement by automation does get ahead of re-employment. Even then the increased productive efficiency which caused the machines to be substituted for men in the first place should, in principle, hold down the aggregate real cost burden--as distinct from the amount of income redistribution. But the latter would have to rise, to enable the disemployed to continue to buy the products of the economic system.

2. Some Ways of Closing or Narrowing the Poverty Income Gap

During the Second World War, Lady Juliette Evangeline Rhys-Williams took a leaf (we may suppose) from the book of the Utopians by proposing that all state-operated welfare services in England should be combined into a single comprehensive system with benefits payable each week to all citizens--in principle--regardless of need. Since the existing unemployment insurance system was held to be creating work disincentives, however, the able-bodied unemployed who refused to accept jobs offered to them were to be excluded. This "social dividend" was to be tied directly to the income tax and financed by a proportional tax of 7 shillings 6 pence to the pound (i.e., nearly 40 per cent). In a quite separate section of the income tax, a surtax on incomes above 600 pounds sterling would raise the revenues needed for the regular functions of government including defense.[11]

Green reviews briefly[12] the proposals of some postwar writers--C. E. Ayres, Robert R. Schutz, D. B. Smith and Eveline Burns--who have similarly advocated social dividends for all. A slightly different approach is that of Theobald and some others including Edward E. Schwartz: their guaranteed minimum income concept would if adopted involve deciding how much income is enough to avoid a condition of poverty and then raising all too-low incomes up to those levels. Still other writers--notably Milton Friedman and Robert J. Lampman--have favored the much more modest and less expensive offshoot of social dividend taxation under which a negative income tax would in itself raise the incomes of the poor only part way toward such target levels.

Thus the guaranteed income proposal may be said to have two main variants--a periodic payment to everyone (or "universal demogrant"), and a periodic payment to the poor. In the former case the rich would no doubt receive their payment only as a credit which reduced their taxes, or the principle of universality might be breached in practice by excluding those above a certain income level altogether. Again, a payment only to the poor might be enough to eliminate their poverty income gap or it might be only some fraction of that.

Before going further into details, however, it seems best to locate the guaranteed income concept in the broad spectrum of ideas as to economic means of promoting both general prosperity and individual welfare. Combatting poverty is not the only reason that has been urged for having governments distribute extra income; and distributing extra income, through the tax system or otherwise, is obviously not the only means by which governments can and do combat poverty. Setting the guaranteed income schemes themselves aside for a moment, we may consider briefly some of the other proposed ways of increasing the incomes of the poor, whether that result would follow as a direct effect of a frontal attack on poverty or as an important side-effect of achieving some other large purpose (admittedly the one is not always sharply distinguishable from the other). For practical purposes it seems useful here to deal separately with (1) aggregate demand proposals, (2) proposals for expanding the existing kinds of transfer payments, and then (3) guaranteed income plans as such.

(1) Aggregate demand proposals

If aggregate demand is continually maintained at high enough levels (and other sensible economic policies, be it said, are also followed, not forgetting job training), then the poor among others will *ipso facto* be helped to have more jobs, better wages, and higher social insurance benefits. Thus the aggregate demand proposals are at the same time important proposals for narrowing the poverty income gap.

In calling the roll of those who have insisted that steady prosperity is impossible if special steps are not taken to maintain demand, the underconsumptionists such as J. A. Hobson and Major C. H. Douglas in England, William Trufant Foster and Waddill Catchings in the United States, and the organizers of the social credit movement in Canada should not be forgotten. According to them, however, there is an inherent financial flaw in the economic system which continually prevents it (because of savings) from distributing enough purchasing power to buy back the goods produced. Their thought is often elusive, and baffling at points where it becomes more precise.

John Maynard Keynes, in his incomparable diagnosis of the workings of an expanding-contracting economic system, stressed the role of the "investment multiplier." Thus he showed how an addition to investment spending would produce a considerably greater addition to aggregate demand because it would put out new income, most of which in turn would be spent (the exact proportion depending on the "marginal propensity to consume"), leading again to further investment and further consumption in a series of diminishing circles. Going on from there to less solid ground, he and most of his American followers in the New Deal period concluded that more public investment was the only remedy worth considering for insufficient aggregate demand and the attendant unemployment.

Certainly there is need for substantially enlarged public investment--fields obviously demanding it have already been mentioned in the previous section. It should be mainly put on a permanent or continuing basis, but with provision also for acceleration and deceleration (the reserve shelf principle) to offset private investment fluctuations or, more precisely, cyclical movements in the level of employment as a whole. However, if full employment is to be guaranteed in an economic system having the American "conventional wisdom" and practices, there remains a further need for direct adjustments in aggregate income and spending at the private consumer end. While these should not be used to keep public investment from growing, they <u>should</u> keep it from being the subject of a commitment under which, in order to fill all gaps, it might have to grow beyond the point of feasibility and general consent. What I suggest, therefore, is an insurance approach--both to full employment as the objective and to purchasing power as precondition for acceptability of the full-employment guarantee. First, a working decision can be reached at the beginning of each year on the level of aggregate consumer spending that is necessary, given the expected size of the other components of gross national expenditure (government purchases of goods and services, gross private domestic investment, and net exports). Then, more purchasing power should be put out if and when current statistics show that that level of aggregate consumer demand is not self-sustaining; and, conversely, some purchasing power should be withdrawn (by means of higher taxes), in order to avoid an inflationary over-demand, if and when the agreed level of consumer spending is being exceeded by more than the pre-arranged safety margin.

For putting out more purchasing power, when necessary, I have indicated without commitment a rather wide range of means (reductions of taxes and/or additions to transfer payments) that might be used. I have suggested, however, particular consideration for (a) a reversible federal sales tax/sales bonus at the consumer level, which would operate with progressive (anti-regressive) incidence in payout periods through Treasury Department coupons or stamps made convertible into cash; or else (b) income tax reductions--accompanied, however, for low-income groups, by a stamp or coupon plan or by cash payments considered as a partial refund, rebate, or offset to the very substantial although largely hidden taxes they pay to federal, state, and local tax jurisdictions.[13] As will be seen later, the machinery of a negative income tax could also be used, secondarily, for the latter part of (b).

(2) Proposals for expanding the existing kinds of transfer payments

It should first be noticed here that income in cash and income in kind are alternatives. You don't have to buy food if you raise it, or pay rent if you live in your own house. To increase income in kind is thus tantamount to lowering the (cash income) poverty standard and reducing the poverty income gap. Income distributed in kind--as in the case of health benefits under Medicare, rent subsidies, universal free public education, and certain forms of public relief--is clearly already an important supplement in this country to income in cash. The bulk of what is provided under the Economic Opportunity Act might also be cited here. Proposals for broad extensions of medical care for the non-aged, rent subsidies to broaden the supply of low-cost housing, and school lunches for children find many supporters. In principle, at least, the income-in-kind approach might even be extended to designating certain consumer goods as "non-scarce" and offering those goods to everybody free of charge.[14]

Clearly, however, cash is the most flexible and least paternalistic form in which extra income can be distributed. Theobald puts the case forcefully: "To be poor is to have too little money. The immediate need is not moral uplift, cultural refinements, extended education, retraining programs or makework jobs, but more money."[15]

A vital source of income to the poor is transfer payments--notably social insurance benefits, military pensions, and direct relief--payments remote from current production and more like negative taxes. Only quite recently so important, transfer payments now constitute about 8 per cent of total annual personal income in the United States--as much as interest income, or as rents plus dividends. The total has lately been climbing to $40 billion a year (using slightly different definitions, the Council of Economic Advisers and Social Security Administration publish slightly different totals), and roughly half of this goes to the poor--roughly half of whom, again, get some of it. How much the existing transfers mean to the poor can be seen from Green's analysis based on data extracted from the Survey of Consumer Expenditures made by the Bureau of Labor Statistics in 1960-61. In that fiscal year (no comparable later study exists) the roughly $14 billions of transfer payments that the "before-transfer" poor received added nearly 50 per cent to the other income they had, closed more than three-fourths of what would otherwise have been their total poverty income gap, and lifted one-third of them out of poverty altogether.

The total array of transfer payments can be made sufficiently protective even it it still resembles a patchwork quilt.[16] In fact, most of what is required for a guaranteed income plan could well be provided by a strengthened Social Security system. However, without some changes in form that system would have difficulty in providing all the income-guaranteeing machinery needed. That is, neither social insurance nor public assistance as each is known at present looks like the right vehicle. The specifically antipoverty--and in that sense economical--public assistance programs administered today by welfare departments are so notoriously humiliating and otherwise objectionable that they should clearly be curtailed rather than expanded. The social insurance schemes, with all their recognized advantages, are nevertheless debarred by their terms from reaching all needy groups, and constitute furthermore an uneconomical means of attacking poverty, since much of their benefit goes to those who are not poor.

Take public assistance first. Although public assistance to specific categories of poor persons (to families with dependent children and no breadwinner, to the aged, to the blind, to the permanently and totally disabled) helps less than one-fourth of the poor at any given time, this set of programs does now distribute some $4 billion a year, not counting administrative costs or expenditures on medical assistance for the aged and vendor medical payments. Furthermore, well over 90 per cent of the money goes to those who are poor. This approach stands increasingly condemned, however, in the eyes of virtually everybody. The means test is degrading, even brutal, in its application. The residence requirements cause great difficulty. The small army of welfare workers has to spend most of its time checking up on eligibility and administering the financial arrangements. Not only are the payments too small to eliminate poverty but the interstate inequalities are extreme.

On top of all other objections, these public assistance programs necessarily kill off the incentive to work because they in effect levy a 100 per cent tax on extra income by reducing the assistance they give dollar for dollar as other income rises. This could become a really serious matter in case more persons capable of working were made eligible for such assistance. What might indeed be done on the positive side is to provide Federal Government financial contributions to the non-categorical "general assistance" programs conducted by the States and localities--a step which seems long overdue. "General assistance" could even be converted into a system of payments with mandatory federal standards and without the usual means test, thus becoming in most respects except actual administration very like a negative income tax plan.

Social insurance, with its philosophy of contractual rights, obviously provides a far more acceptable base on which to expand. This is particularly true because the system is still underdeveloped in the United States by the standards of other industrialized countries; thus, as Walter Reuther has said, we more than any other highly industrialized nation neglect "those who are too old to work and too young to die." In dollar terms, too, the social insurance base is much more substantial; the Old Age, Survivors, Disability and Health Insurance program (OASDHI) alone pays out more than three times as much as public assistance. Some widely advocated and desirable amendments would double minimum payments to the aged, "blanket in" a million aged persons not now covered, extend medical care to all age groups, and strengthen unemployment compensation by raising benefit levels, broadening coverage, and postponing or abolishing the limit on the period of payments. Several of these desirable measures would, to be sure, necessitate considerable subsidizing of the system by the Federal Government out of general tax revenue, and would thus weaken considerably more the system's claim to be pure insurance. But a clarification like that should be regarded as progress.

On the other hand, the majority of the present recipients of social insurance benefits are not poor before getting these transfer payments, so that merely raising benefit levels is a relatively inefficient way of striking at poverty as such. Conversely, many of the actual poor are in households with no present or past earner, or with an earner whose pay has been so low that the insurance benefits cannot do very much to alleviate the poverty. It has been said that nearly all of the aged, disabled, widowed and orphaned could on their part be guarded against poverty by a not impractical strengthening of OASDHI. Still, this would be an expensive undertaking; according to one estimate, it would take a $10-11 billion increase in the program, two-thirds of which would go to the non-poor, to bring one-half of the aged poor out of poverty. Careful, detailed calculations would thus be required to show, for example, to what extent the Administration's current proposals for a payroll-tax-financed $4 billion strengthening of that main arm of the Social Security Act will reduce poverty if adopted in their present form.

If we now look beyond immediate experience in this country, we encounter several possibilities that verge on, or that could be incorporated with, an actual negative income tax plan. One, known to social insurance systems elsewhere, is a "partial demogrant" for dependent children. Experts have frequently cited as a striking omission from our system the absence of any scheme of such family allowances. If that omission were to be repaired, as Daniel P. Moynihan and others have urged, moderate allowances financed out of general revenues, as in Canada, would appear preferable to the French system of high allowances with a heavy employer payroll tax, a combination that seems to have had a depressing effect on wage rates and on the incentive to work. Since a high proportion of American children are in non-poor families, the problem in this country would be to avoid excessive cost--as well as undue encouragement to further enlargement of already large families--on the one hand, and too-small allowances on the other. This might perhaps be done by abandoning the principle of universality and paying the allowances only to families whose incomes are less than the value of income tax exemptions and deductions, and then only for a stipulated maximum number of dependent children.

Another possibility is an arrangement that might be called the all-tax credit. On the basis of studies by Richard Musgrave for 1954, Green concludes that the effective total tax rate on the poor, counting especially the indirect taxes they pay such as sales and excise taxes, must be close to 30 per cent on their income. He then estimates that a very substantial proportion of all poor families (say 3.3 million) could be lifted out of poverty if their money incomes were raised 30 per cent through a cash tax credit costing the Government about $4.5 billion. The main disadvantage which Green cites is that a plan using as its basis a percentage of income (rather than a percentage of deficiency of income) would automatically give the "poorest" poor the least and the "best off" poor the most. This criticism would not apply to a nonproportional (flat sum) tax credit such as I have frequently suggested as a possible device for doing approximate justice to non-payers of income taxes at times when, in order to maintain a system of guaranteed full employment, current economic conditions would require income tax reductions for those better off.[17] A mixed verdict is, therefore, perhaps the right one. The indirect taxes which nobody escapes paying do seem to constitute an important neglected weapon in the economic arsenal, but probably they could better serve as a general justification for giving back money through the federal income tax system than as the specific basis determining the amount and form that a negative income tax plan should take.

(3) Guaranteed income proposals

The preceding discussion should help to make clear where the guaranteed income proposals as such fit into the broader spectrum of current and suggested measures. Both the negative tax plans for boosting the income of only the poor and those for giving a social dividend to everybody would operate by distributing extra money income through the Federal income tax system. Even the mildest of the plans in the former category would not only help the individual poor but also in the process help to sustain aggregate demand. A social dividend scheme would go so much farther quantitatively and in its implications for social and economic reform that it could be expected to gravitate toward becoming a scientifically calculated aggregate demand plan as well--i.e., not merely an incidental sustainer, but in the end the precisely calculated regulator, of aggregate demand.

The guaranteed income idea has gained a quite substantial following today. Among organizations that have either endorsed it or proposed intensive study of it are the National Commission on Technology, Automation and Economic Progress, the Democratic Study Group, the Council of Economic Advisers, the Office of Economic Opportunity, and the National Association of Social Workers.

There is no doubt, however, that the various advocates

of a guaranteed income differ widely in what they would support and what consequences they foresee. Some see this proposal as paving the way to a new kind of society.

> As a first step to a new consensus it is essential to recognize that the traditional link between jobs and incomes is being broken. The economy of abundance can sustain all citizens in comfort and economic security whether or not they engage in what is commonly reckoned as work. Wealth produced by machines rather than men is still wealth. We urge, therefore, that society, through its appropriate legal and governmental institutions, undertake an unqualified commitment to provide every individual and every family with an adequate income as a matter of right.... We do not pretend to visualize all of the consequences of this change in our values.... In retrospect, the establishment of the right to an income will prove to have been only the first stage in the reconstruction of our society brought on by the triple revolution.[18]

It will be obvious that at least the more modest guaranteed income schemes, aimed at helping to bridge the income gap of the poor, could be adopted as a supplement or complement to improvements in the social insurance system and other antipoverty measures. Even public assistance through welfare departments, though it would be largely superseded by a negative income tax, would presumably not be eliminated entirely but would rather be rendered more effective as a small residual system.

In the theory of full-employment policy it is useful to distinguish between policies that are "basic" and those that are "compensatory" in the economic sense. (Elsewhere in this book, "compensatory" is used in the different, sociological sense: the deprived individual rather than the improperly functioning economy is compensated.) Basic economic policies are adopted "for their own sake," i.e., for reasons other than economic stabilization at full employment, while compensatory economic policies are used to adjust the level of operation of the economy up or sometimes down in the light of conditions as they emerge from the interaction of all domestic and international events and all the basic policies that are currently in effect. From this point of view a plan and mechanism to guarantee individual incomes (as distinct, for example, from a plan and mechanism to guarantee <u>aggregate</u> consumer demand) would clearly represent a continuing, basic economic policy if adopted.

3. The Negative Income Tax Plans

A guarantee that no family and no unattached individual would have less than a certain stipulated money income would imply the existence of some specific method of giving families and individuals money when their total income from all other sources fell short. Such transfers might possibly be made via the Social Security Administration, as previously implied, but the present discussion like most others assumes that they would in fact be made via the Internal Revenue Service by tying any negative income tax scheme into the law and procedure governing the individual income tax. Further evolution of the cooperation between the SSA and the IRS must naturally be presupposed in any case.

The key point is that households with incomes below the guaranteed levels would no longer have to forfeit their self-respect in obtaining assistance, as they commonly must under relief procedures today, or risk an adverse discretionary decision by some welfare worker, but would receive the extra income as a matter of right. They would not be asked why their incomes were so low. Both the determination of eligibility and the transfers of funds would be handled in an essentially impersonal, private, and quasi-automatic manner.

How much money a poor household would get would depend on two features of the particular plan adopted: (1) the level below which no household (of that size) was to be allowed to fall, even if it had no other income whatever, and (2) how fast the subsidizing of income by means of an allowance was to be tapered off (to hold down the cost of the scheme) above that minimum level when a household did have other income. The tapering off, which would be tantamount to a tax rate on the allowance, would eliminate the allowance entirely at some "break-even" point. Given the minimum level and the tax rate for other income, the break-even point would be automatically determined. Or, given the minimum level and the chosen break-even point, the tax rate for other income would be automatically determined. Green shows[19] that all systematic income-subsidizing plans, different as they may appear on the surface, have in them the three variables just mentioned, any two of which mathematically determine the third.

A tax rate (for other income) that was close to 100 per cent would tend to kill off the incentive to earn other income, since there would be little or nothing gained by making the effort to earn it. On the other hand a rate close to zero per cent (i.e., no tapering off at all) would very much increase the cost of the plan, since few if any households would fail to get a subsidy. Suppose, then, that the minimum level for a family of four were to be set at $1500, and the level at which it would no longer be given any extra income at $3000, and (accordingly) the tax rate for other income at 50 per cent. It if had earned, say, $1600 on its own, it would in effect keep $800 of that and have a total income of $2300. In reality, of course, no such tax would be levied on those earnings of people in poverty; rather, this family would keep all the income it earned but its allowance would be cut from $1500 to $700. Whichever way the matter is looked at, however, it comes to the same thing.

What would count as other income? Green rightly stresses that, in principle, it would be desirable to use a comprehensive measure of money income from almost all sources. Certainly the measure should be broader than "adjusted gross income" as defined for tax purposes today, since this omits most public transfer payments such as social insurance benefits that often determine whether a family is in fact poor or not. Hence the "adjusted gross income" definition would make the plan discriminate in favor of such transfer payments as against earned income; worse still, some "poor" families upon receiving their negative-tax allowances would be lifted above some "non-poor" families not entitled to receive allowances. On the other hand, unless the plan were one designed to close the poverty income gap entirely, public assistance and free will private gifts (other than scholarships) probably should be excluded from "other income"; they could then serve as the residual form of aid, reserved in the end for a comparatively small number of special cases.

Thus, if a four-member family under the same rules as before had $2600 from OASDHI benefits and a veteran's pension, it would receive in addition $200 as a negative-tax allowance (i.e., $1500 minus 50 per cent of $2600 or $1300) and would end up with $2800. If it had instead been getting $800 in unemployment compensation, it would now have $1900 (i.e., jobless pay of $800 plus an allowance of $1500 minus $400). Or, if it had been living on nothing but $1600 in welfare money, it could now expect to receive the full $1500 in negative-tax allowance with no questions asked, plus some amount of public assistance--surely more than the $100 needed to keep it from being worse off financially than it was before.

TABLE 1. CHARACTERISTICS AND COSTS OF SELECTED NEGATIVE INCOME TAX PLANS

Type of Plan	Per cent of Poverty Gap filled	Estimated Total Costs ($billions) in 1964 under three assumptions A	B	C
Negative rates plans				
1. Guarantee 50% of poverty-line[a] income. Tax[b] 50% for household's other income. Break-even point comes at poverty line.	50%	6.1	8.0	6.3
2. Guarantee 25% of poverty-line income. Zero tax for other income up to 50% of poverty line, 50% tax thereafter. Break-even point at poverty line.	39.7%	4.9	5.4	4.7
3. Guarantee 50% of exemptions and minimum standard deduction; double for aged. Tax 50% for other income. Break-even point at EX-MSD line.	56.3%	6.9	8.8	7.1
Fill-the-gap plan				
4. Guarantee 100% of poverty line income by simply making allowances equal to household deficits. Other income is in effect taxed 100%.	100%	If poor do not react by reducing earnings, costs will be: 12.3	16.1	13.8
		More likely, poor will reduce earnings anywhere from 25% to 100%; costs will then be: 14.6-25.1	18.4-25.3	16.1-23.0

Social dividend plan[c]				
5. Guarantee 100% of poverty line income. Tax 50% for other income. Break-even point at 2x poverty line ($6000 for family of 4).	100%+	31.2	33.1	30.8

Source: Derived from tables in Green, *op. cit.*, based on Census data for 1964.

a. Poverty lines as defined by Lampman, *i.e.*, $1500 per head of household or unattached individual, $2000 for 2-member family, $2500 for 3, $3000 for 4 ... $5000 for 8.

b. In this context, "tax" means reduce the allowance granted.

c. Only a modified social dividend plan is shown. The pure form, under which the tax for other income would be zero so that even the biggest taxpayer would receive an allowance (reducing his net liability to the government), is here omitted, as it has been from Green's comparative tables.

Assumption A: Public Assistance is treated as part of income in calculating allowances. Moreover PA is not reduced, so that the cost of the plan is also the net cost of introducing it.

Assumption B: PA is excluded from income in calculating allowances, thus widening the income gap and raising the cost. Cost of plan per se is shown, disregarding any reductions in PA.

Assumption C: PA is excluded from income in calculating allowances. In consideration of the negative income tax plan, PA is reduced. The net cost of the plan to the Federal Government is shown, assuming 50% of the total PA cost reduction accrues to it, 50% to the States.

The characteristics and costs of various plans

Table 1 summarizes some representative negative income tax proposals. The plans fall into three categories. First come several so-called negative rates plans that provide an income floor well below the actual poverty line and a formula for reducing ("taxing") allowances when families or individuals have some other income. Next is shown a plan which simply fills the poverty income gap for any poor family without offering allowances to any of the non-poor. Very likely this is the plan that the term "guaranteed income" in conjunction with the idea of fighting poverty suggests to most people. Last comes a social dividend plan. Actually it is a modified social dividend plan: while no line is drawn between the poor and the non-poor, this "demogrant" is not really universal, since the allowances have been tapered off in relation to other income by a formula that eliminates them entirely at a certain point well above the poverty line.

What is shown for each of these plans is, first, the percentage of the total poverty income gap it would fill and, second, how much, under some of many possible assumptions, the plan would cost. It would carry us too far into technicalities to explain here the derivation of all the figures, let alone the alternative assumptions that might lead to results somewhat different from those shown, but even the casual reader should notice in passing a few of the salient points.

Plan 1 forms a base line against which to measure others. It lets nobody fall below half of poverty-line income; it taxes away the equivalent of half of other income; and it fills just half of the total income gap. This gap, it will be recalled, was \$12.3 billion (disregarding the hidden poor) in 1964, the year used for the Table 1 figures. Plan 4, which simply fills all gaps, is therefore shown (under assumption A) as costing \$12.3 billion at an absolute, purely theoretical, minimum, and Plan 1 is shown as costing one-half of that, or \$6.1 billion. Plan 5, the modified social dividend plan, paying dividends to many who are not poor but have incomes ranging up close to the national median level, would cost upwards of \$30 billion on a net basis (i.e., would redistribute that much; the gross amount of the dividends has been figured at about \$155 billion). Going back to No. 4, which would close the gap for the poor but not give anything to anyone else, this plan could also turn out to be expensive, costing not merely the \$12.3 billion which a first glance at it would suggest but more like double that amount. The reason is that under such a plan, unless it included a provision denying eligibility to those able but unwilling to work, they could give up their other income and still have just as much to live on, because they would then get a correspondingly larger allowance. This would certainly have a markedly adverse effect on work incentives, and the table suggests a range of possible results. (Incidentally, there could also be some reduction of efforts on the part of those just above break-even levels of income. The table probably underestimates costs somewhat in making no allowance for that.)

This leaves Plans 2 and 3, two rather interesting variations on Plan 1. Plan 3 dispenses entirely with a separately calculated "poverty" line as key to the allowance formula and bases itself instead on the line of the "EX-MSD"--which is convenient shorthand for the personal exemptions and minimum standard deduction found in the income tax today. Exemptions and deductions were originally established with a view to not taxing away any really necessary minimum income, and even now the EX-MSD line is not altogether unlike the poverty line discussed herein. The former gives $900 for one and $700 for each additional family member, while the latter gives $1500 for one and $500 for each other member. Thus for four-member families both formulas yield the same result ($3000), but for unattached individuals and small families the EX-MSD formula is substantially less favorable and for large families it is more favorable than the poverty-line formula. Some of the hardship that the EX-MSD formula would otherwise entail for one- and two-member families could be corrected by allowing double exemptions and deductions to persons 65 years of age and over, as is done in figuring their tax liabilities today--and in Plan 3. Plan 2, finally, has been included here to illustrate the possibility of taxing (reducing allowances) for other income at progressive or at regressive rates instead of at a flat rate--50 per cent or any other. In the progressive-rate scheme shown in the table the stress has been put on furthering the incentive to earn at least some income; this is done both by making the allowance small in itself and by "delaying" the tax, i.e., not reducing the allowance at all for the first quite considerable block of income earned. Several kinds of variation on the flat-rate theme should evidently be carefully examined if or when legislation to provide for a negative income tax is being framed.

Some problems of negative income taxation

This discussion should not end without some further attention to the problems that the introduction of negative income taxation would raise. We may here briefly consider:

(1) the "notch" problem, (2) the relation to the present tax law, (3) the filing of declarations (allowance claims), (4) timing the allowance payments, (5) minimizing adverse incentives, and (6) the cost burden.

(1) Some too-simple plans for giving cash allowances to the poor would create a so-called notch problem. That is, they would raise the income of at least the best-off households eligible for allowances above that of the worst-off households not defined as poor and hence not eligible. This would be not only unfair but pernicious in its effects, giving those households near the bottom of the non-eligible category an inducement either to earn less income or to conceal from the tax authorities some of the income they did earn.

The notch problem would arise, for instance, under a plan designed to close all poverty income gaps and also give an allowance premium for other income in order to avoid the strong work disincentive from a 100 per cent tax (noticed in the discussion of Plan 4, just above). Thus, if a family that was guaranteed $3000 and earned $2000 were allowed $1000 to fill its income gap, and were also allowed say a 20 per cent premium on its earnings, or $400, it would have $3400 altogether and would be better off than a family that earned $3200 and was consequently ineligible for any allowance.

The solution for notch problems lies in graduating the tax for other income and extending eligibility to households with incomes somewhat above the poverty line or other guaranteed base level. For example--disregarding the technical refinements--if the family that earned $3200 were given an allowance of 10 per cent, it would end up with $3520 and would thus remain ahead of the other family. Thus, solving the notch problem makes the break-even point rise, and consequently also the cost of the given plan. (In other words, after Plan 4 had been modified to reduce work disincentive and also avoid the notch problem, it would again cost more than its minimum theoretical estimate of $12.3-13.8 billion. It would also in principle become indistinguishable, then, from a modified social dividend plan such as Plan 5.)

(2) It would be hard (although not altogether impossible) to devise a negative income tax plan that would simply dovetail into the present tax law without conflicting with it in any way. There may be some disadvantage in this. The fact that the definitions of income and tax unit would almost certainly need to be different (unless the present law were to be reformed first) should cause no special problem. Somewhat more troublesome, however, although still not of major moment, could be the difficulty of arranging for so-called *mutual exclusion*, i.e., avoidance of overlap between the

positive and negative rate schedules, so that no person already required to pay a tax would also be entitled to receive a net allowance.

These, too, are rather technical points and can only be touched on lightly here. The mutual exclusion issue has a bearing on the question whether it would be better for a negative income tax plan to use a special poverty-line formula, as do most of the plans shown, or a formula based on the value of exemptions and the minimum standard deduction in the income tax (EX-MSD), as does Plan 3. Mutual exclusion might be managed in the latter case but generally not in the former.[20] An EX-MSD formula would doubtless gain readier acceptance for the idea that the plan merely involved extending the present income tax system to the very lowest income households by means of negative rates. It would also give less incentive for family fragmentation than the poverty-line approach, because the financial advantage in leaving a family and emerging as a single person would be only $200 ($900 minus $700) as against $1000 ($1500 minus $500). On the other hand, the poverty-line approach would be more equitable in relation to family size, and especially in avoiding the EX-MSD bias against single persons; it would by definition pinpoint the attack on poverty somewhat more efficiently; and it would give less incentive to poor families to have a large number of children. On which side the balance of advantage would lie is not easy to say at present. If, however, the existing law were to be amended to allow a larger exemption-deduction to single persons and the head of a household, a decision in favor of the EX-MSD formula would seem to be indicated.

As for definitions, it may be recalled from our previous discussion that equity and workability both require that <u>income</u> in a negative income tax should mean, approximately, total money income, rather than "adjusted gross income" (let alone the still narrower "taxable income") as construed under present law. The <u>tax unit</u> should also be defined differently. Consistency with the anti-poverty objective would necessitate putting greater emphasis on the basic family in the sociological sense (although other persons who were obtaining more than half their support from members of the basic family unit would continue to be included with it). Consequently, in order to prevent an unwarranted proliferation of claims for allowances, it would probably be necessary to enforce joint filing by spouses for negative income tax purposes, and to deny to children under 19 and students under 22 years of age the right to file separately.

(3) If a negative income tax plan were adopted, tax

forms--positive or negative--would have to be filed by or for everybody. The resulting great increase in the number of forms need not in itself present any major problem in a computerized system. But time, attention, and administrative expense would certainly be demanded for obtaining valid income declarations from the poor.

On the one hand, the Bureau of Internal Revenue or some other agency acting on its behalf would have to provide a large corps of tax-form advisers. Every precaution should moreover be taken to see that these officials did not impose a new kind of means test by the manner in which they treated ignorant or illiterate persons. On the other hand, it would be necessary to obtain from the Social Security Administration, the Veterans Administration and perhaps other sources information which is not at present given out on the transfer income paid to individuals. At the same time the under-reporting of certain other kinds of income such as sporadic earnings and farm, interest and rental income would doubtless remain a widely prevalent problem.

(4) The timing of allowance payments would probably constitute the most difficult problem in administering a negative tax scheme. An annual settle-up date like 15 April of the next year would leave the poor, or at least the newly poor, without current resources. Quarterly or monthly payments, the converse of current withholding of positive taxes, would solve that problem at the cost of creating awkwardness by requiring forecasts of the year's income at the beginning. Many errors would have to be corrected or compensated subsequently for households with fluctuating incomes. (The introduction of an income averaging procedure--designed, in this case, to prevent too favorable treatment for fluctuating incomes--seems rather unlikely.) Too optimistic a forecast could leave a household virtually stranded until it was revised. Too pessimistic a forecast, as in the case of someone who was unemployed and without job prospects at the time the calculations were made but later got a job and held it, could lead to major overpayments. These would then have to be paid back or worked off at a later date--by no means a simple remedy in the case of poor people.

Still, these difficulties could hardly be regarded as insuperable. The overpayment problem, for example, arises occasionally for OASDHI beneficiaries under 72 years of age whose earnings increase unexpectedly, and is resolved by a money refund or by the withholding of benefits to a corresponding extent in the following year. Presumably a plan with frequent payments, linked to a systematic up-dating of forecasts quarter-by-quarter or month-by-month, could create a workable basis.

(5) In introducing any new type of income distribution, care must obviously be taken to avoid inadvertently creating or significantly strengthening incentives to do things of which soci-

ety disapproves, such as cut wages, fragment the family, have large numbers of children at society's expense, or refuse to work. The last two of these evidently constitute especially significant dangers in the present context. Clear guideposts would be useful here but, since in both cases the results of such empirical studies as have been made are largely inconclusive for a negative income tax plan as such, one is thrown back on speculation and common sense.

A good deal has already been said in the preceding section about the incentive to work, and particularly about how the terms of a negative income tax plan could be adjusted so as to reduce if not eliminate the work disincentive. Several further points might be made here. Many of the poor are not in a position to work or to be supported by a worker anyway; for them this incentive issue is, therefore, irrelevant. Most of the others seem unlikely, in our consumption-oriented economy, to be deflected from trying to get other income just because they receive an allowance, especially if that allowance brings them only part way up to the poverty line standard. Of those who are so deflected, some will no doubt be consciously using the bare security provided by the allowance to think and live creatively and develop their own potential.

Taking all considerations into account, it seems possible to dismiss as unwarranted the fear that a well-constructed negative income tax plan would have materially damaging work-incentive effects. (For some less well-constructed plan, the verdict would seem to depend pretty much on one's view of human nature, as witness these two conflicting statements, both from the same book:[21] (1) "A psychology of abundance produces initiative, faith in life, solidarity...man by nature is not lazy.... People might prefer not to work for one or two months, but the vast majority would beg to work, even if they were not paid for it." (Erich Fromm) (2) "Those who believe that men will want to work whether they have to or not seem to have lived sheltered lives." (William Vogt)

Would negative income taxation, by providing allowances that varied with family size, cause the poor to treat children as a cash crop and have more of them? In the case of some poor people, and to some extent, very likely it would. A partial safeguard would be to taper off the allowances when families grew beyond a certain specified size, and to avoid discriminating against the poor in this by applying the same principle to the exemptions for dependents under the positive tax system. The basic answer, of course, is that the attack on poverty must include far more than the giving of cash allowances. Nevertheless, as Alvin L. Schorr has well said of income maintenance efforts in general, "Balancing any small effect [toward a higher birth rate among the poor], a substantial income-maintenance program should significantly improve the circumstances of many families. In their children's generation, at least, it may provide the competence and climate to achieve the family size that that generation genuinely wants."[22]

(6) Whether or not a negative income tax would create an appreciable burden of cost for positive taxpayers would depend, of course, on the kind of plan adopted. One of the leading proponents of this negative tax approach, Milton Friedman, sees it as not only a means of limiting governmental intervention in economic life but also as an economizing measure, to be instituted in place of virtually all other welfare measures, including not only all Social Security programs but even farm subsidies and public housing.[23]

One need not agree with Professor Friedman on that score to realize that at least such plans as Nos. 1-3 in the table would be inexpensive enough for our economy to take in stride under conditions of continuing prosperity. The annual net cost of plans in this range would be of the order of \$5-\$7 billion. This is less than the amount by which federal tax revenues will now increase automatically from year to year at constant tax rates, given stable conditions somewhere near the full-employment level, simply as the result of the way economic growth produces more total and per capita taxable income. Actual tax reductions granted during 1964 and 1965 amounted, it may be recalled, to about \$16 billion.

If it were a question, however, of using negative taxes to close the poverty income gap entirely (Plan 4), or to provide a kind of social dividend (either under Plan 5 or under Plan 4 modified to reduce work disincentive, as explained earlier), the orders of magnitude would definitely change. What would now be in question would be annual net costs running anywhere from \$20 billion to \$30 billion or higher.

Naturally, if the rate of expenditure on national defense (now projected at \$73 billion for fiscal year 1967-68) could even be cut in half, that in itself would cover this expanded requirement. Furthermore, according to the previously cited <u>A "Freedom Budget" for All Americans</u>, it would even be possible to continue to enlarge defense expenditures and yet finance \$185 billion of additional federal expenditures on needed domestic programs in the next ten years.[24] But that plan contemplates many objects of expenditure that could hardly be set aside in favor of social dividends without entirely changing the production picture. Moreover the estimates presuppose a degree of effort at drawing in unemployed manpower and continuing to push economic growth that may well not be forthcoming. Therefore, on all counts, it is safer to assume that, barring arms reduction, the introduction of a fill-the-whole-gap or social dividend type of negative income tax plan would necessitate putting heavier burdens on taxpayers in the middle and upper income brackets.

4. Conclusions

The question to which this chapter has sought an answer is this: should a program for the early abolition of poverty in the United States include as one feature a guarantee of family and individual income which would be implemented by means of a negative income tax? My own answer, based on the findings set forth in the preceding pages, would be yes--elaborated and qualified as follows:

1. The principle of the guaranteed income should definitely be endorsed.

2. A relatively modest negative income tax plan to give effect to that principle by supplementing the incomes of the poor should also be endorsed.

3. Whether this should be a "small" plan (i.e., of the general order of $6 billion a year, with the income floor set at around one-half the poverty-line level) or an "intermediate" plan (assuring more like two-thirds of poverty-line income, at a cost in the general neighborhood of $10 or $12 billion) is at this stage a tactical rather than a fundamental issue. (Today I would start with the presumption that support of a "small" plan--just so it puts a standard nationwide floor under incomes--is tactically better. But the situation and hence the presumption could easily change.)

4. A plan for a negative income tax to close the whole poverty income gap, whether with or without the added feature of social dividends to some or all of the non-poor, should definitely not be endorsed.

To summarize here the reasoning on which these conclusions are based--it starts with the consideration that to attack poverty with a combination of long-range measures and current services is not enough. Something must also be done to maintain money incomes.

Might that "something" not be composed of elements such as improved Social Security programs, stronger minimum wage legislation, and a more effective full-employment policy, thus making it unnecessary to add a new, untried approach? Probably in a practical sense the answer to this is no. All those things would be highly desirable, but no one of them could eliminate altogether--at a cost that society would be likely to want to pay--the cause or causes of poverty for which it is the specific partial remedy.

Full employment would still require some frictional unemployment--possibly a full-time unemployment rate a little under 3 per cent of the civilian labor force. (In a system of guaranteed full employment, the allowable frictional unemployment would of course be a definite percentage or quantity--the one approved by Congress, agreeing with or modifying the President's recommendations in his Economic Report.) Minimum wage laws can be of great help to the working poor, who benefit rather little from present transfer programs; but they cannot cure the low pay that results from voluntary part-time work, nor could they under normal private enterprise quickly raise all low rates of pay without creating additional unemployment. Social insurance and public assistance (welfare) programs exist to compensate for lack of connection with the labor market, including here also temporary unemployment or incapacity. The complete elimination of poverty among those involved would, however, be very expensive by means of higher social insurance benefits, covering as these do so many non-poor as well. And it would be highly undesirable (if somehow, miraculously, feasible) by the demoralizing methods of public assistance; indeed, to get rid of those methods should itself be a major aim of public policy.

Even on negative grounds, therefore, one could certainly favor adding a new income-raising device--with carefully constructed controls built in to prevent political manipulation--that would operate through the federal tax machinery and be free of the particular objections and limitations that apply to the more familiar methods. To my mind, however, the real reasons for endorsing the principle of the guaranteed income as a matter of right, and a modest negative tax plan for implementing the guarantee, are positive and fundamental.

In the first place, it seems to me highly desirable to establish now the principle that there is a right to some income by virtue of membership in our national society--a right that does not depend on having a present or past link to work or production or, alternatively, on proving that one is suffering from some conveniently categorized disability. Vested interests, in liberal and labor ranks as well as elsewhere, can be expected to oppose this change. But the march of technology seems eventually bound to affect the demand for labor to such an extent as to make it impossible to continue to maintain that really legitimate income must depend on production. I believe it is none too soon to introduce into our system an element that can later by expansion be given the larger role it is likely to have to play some day in order to save the situation.

In the second place, quite apart from that longer-run issue, a decision to use the income tax machinery for distributing negative taxes could pay large returns in the immediate future. Any guarantee of full employment would require the availability, for economic compensatory purposes, not only of a reserve shelf permitting public works and services to be accelerated or decelerated but also of some convenient means for quickly expanding or contracting private purchasing power directly. Once a negative income tax were installed to help effectuate a basic, continuing antipoverty policy, the income tax system as a whole would become available also as a comprehensive compensatory device in the economic sense. Then by prearrangement it could be made an effective instrument for temporarily increasing income (by lowering positive taxes and raising negative taxes, i.e., increasing the allowances) and for temporarily reducing income (by raising positive taxes, with or without a lowering of negative taxes). Because the income tax is a familiar and, to the general public, no doubt a reasonably popular device, this might be the most readily acceptable way of solving the problem in question. The solution of that problem is important not only because the assured maintenance of full employment is a major value in itself but also because assured full employment would make a great contribution to the elimination of poverty.

If this sufficiently establishes the point that some kind of negative income tax plan for putting a floor under the incomes of the poor ought to be endorsed, it certainly does not speak for endorsing any radical, really expensive plan that would in effect declare a divorce between income and the necessity for all who can work in the existing production system to do so. On the contrary, such a step would be highly premature.

Objectively, automation does not yet warrant the view that jobs cannot be had or that society does not need everyone's effort as a basis for further increases in national wealth. It is much too soon to relax. (Even if America were already rich enough, which is not true, there remains the great challenge, scarcely acknowledged as yet, of helping the vast numbers of people in the underdeveloped countries to escape from their poverty.) Subjectively also, an abandonment of the old concepts would be quite unwarranted. The evidence is overwhelming that people, by and large, want work and would not be satisfied with just income.[25] It will in any case take time for the positive sense of obligation to society and to community to grow to the point where the sanction of work-related income can be simply dropped.

Certainly it is clear that establishment of a society free from work obligations in advance of the firm establishment of continuing full employment (the assurance of work to all able, willing, and seeking to work) would create an odious new kind of class system in America. Those who had jobs could keep them if they liked; those who had not succeeded in obtaining jobs would of necessity form the core of the new leisure class. It is obvious that nobody wants this--least of all, probably, those who have been unsuccessfully looking for work as a basis for income and self-respect.

There is, to be sure, some risk at the other end of the scale of making guaranteed income seem altogether too undramatic and too ineffective a means of lifting the poor out of their poverty. Is it really worth while to go to the trouble of introducing a new kind of income supplement that will neither close anyone's poverty income gap completely nor make it possible to terminate the public assistance programs of welfare departments? This is the case against modest plans such as No. 1 and No. 3 in the table. (Nor would they fully end the means test; but of course, only a universal social dividend scheme could do that.) They would partly replace public assistance and admittedly they would have their own advantages of keeping work incentives alive and, by paying allowances only to the poor, not costing very much. By the very fact, however, that they would reduce the allowances 50 cents for every dollar of other income received, they could never by themselves alone bring any poor household's income more than half way up from the position it was in to the poverty line or (perhaps better, as already explained) the EX-MSD target level.

There would, I believe, be much to be said for adopting if possible a somewhat more ambitious plan--something intermediate between Nos. 1 and 3 on the one hand and Nos. 4 and 5 on the other. It might, for example, be desirable to keep the 50 per cent tax for other income but set the floor at two-thirds instead of one-half of EX-MSD or of poverty-line levels as herein defined (thus enabling a family of 4 to be sure of at least $2000 instead of $1500, assuming its poverty line to be at $3000); this would raise the break-even point to $4000, making some families with distinctly limited means but not actually "poor" also eligible to receive allowances. The cost might then be nearly double that of Plan 1. Or some other intermediate-cost plan might be preferable. Given that much additional income for the poor from negative taxes, it would be possible to cut back public assistance substantially more, and some other antipoverty programs could perhaps be dispensed with as well.

On the other hand, it might as a practical matter turn out to be possible to secure early enactment of a small guaranteed income plan but not of an intermediate plan. This is perhaps the outlook at present. Apart from the momentary situation, it would seem unwise in almost any circumstances to limit endorsement to an intermediate plan only. Even a small plan would facilitate a useful sorting out and eventual simplification of the complex battery of antipoverty measures, besides having the two fundamental advantages discussed above. Sound tactics would, therefore, avoid jeopardizing the chance of gaining those advantages, which could prove of inestimable permanent value to the poor, just for the sake of trying to put a somewhat higher floor under all poverty incomes right from the start.

Notes

1. Michael Harrington, The Other America: Poverty in the United States, New York: Macmillan, 1962.
2. The basic studies are by Mollie Orshansky, reported in "Counting the Poor: Another Look at the Poverty Profile," Social Security Bulletin, January 1965; "Who's Who among the Poor: A Demographic View of Poverty," Ibid., July 1965; and more recent articles in the same journal.
3. Alan Haber, "Poverty Budgets: How Much Is Enough?" Poverty and Human Resources Abstracts, Vol. 1, No. 3, May-June 1966, Institute of Labor and Industrial Relations, Univ. of Michigan-Wayne State Univ., Ann Arbor, Mich.
4. Professor Lampman is the author of a number of papers on the subject, including "Negative Rates Income Taxation" and "Preliminary Report on a Plan for Negative Income Taxation," unpublished reports for the Office of Economic Opportunity, 1965.
5. Published by the Brookings Institution, Washington, D. C., 1967. This study in preliminary manuscript form provided invaluable assistance for the writing of the related sections of this chapter. Mr. Green's book can be expected to serve as a handbook if negative income taxation becomes a legislative issue.
6. A. Philip Randolph Institute, New York, September-October 1966. This report was sponsored by more than two hundred leaders of civil rights, religious and labor groups and other prominent liberals. The economic analysis and statistical computations were supplied by Leon H. Keyserling.
7. As stated in his book, Free Men and Free Markets (New York: Clarkson N. Potter, Inc., 1963) and in a number of subsequent papers and articles. Incidentally, Theobald permits himself to call full employment an obsolete goal, apparently ignoring the fact that full employment means absence of (more than a small amount of) involuntary unemployment. That goal is clearly a major objective in the kind of society he envisages as well, even though the labor force would shrink as a result of voluntary withdrawals. It surely

serves no useful purpose to caricature the concept of full employment, which is correctly given in the Employment Act of 1946 as the existence of "useful employment opportunities, including self-employment, for those able, willing, and seeking to work."

8. Quoted from Meno Lovenstein in The Guaranteed Income: Next Step in Economic Evolution?, edited by Robert Theobald, (New York: Doubleday & Co., 1966), p. 114.

9. Technology and the American Economy, report of the National Commission on Technology, Automation and Economic Progress, Vol. 1, (Washington: Government Printing Office, February, 1966).

10. One of the most striking analyses of the speed with which automation is developing and could affect the economy is in Irving E. Kaplan's report on "The Projected Effect of Automation on Future Navy Personnel Requirements," an unlimited-distribution research memorandum (SRM 67-3) issued August 1966, U.S. Naval Personnel Research Activity, San Diego, California 92152. In Part II, dealing with the Navy's environment, i.e., the economy as a whole, Kaplan states his own conclusion (p. 25) that "By 1972, allowing one to six years to design and build automated production systems, a large majority of the nation's jobs now in existence will be obsolete."

11. Lady Rhys-Williams, Something to Look Forward To (MacDonald, 1943); details were developed further in her Taxation and Incentive (New York: Oxford University Press, 1953).

12. In Negative Taxes and the Poverty Problem, op. cit.

13. See my Insuring Full Employment (New York: Viking, 1964); the reversible sales tax mechanism is discussed on pp. 38-39 and also in American Economic Review, September 1955, pp. 645-47. A number of alternatives were noted in articles from 1944 on and recapitulated in "The Underwriting Approach to Full Employment: a Further Explanation," Review of Economics and Statistics, August 1949, pp. 187-88.

14. Starting, for example, with foods such as bread and milk. This idea, which may be of theoretical interest, was once advocated by the "market socialist" group in Germany and has recently been suggested for study by Erich Fromm in The Guaranteed Income, op. cit., pp. 181-82. Pushed to the limit, this approach could greatly simplify the administration of income transfer, enabling the government to pay just the key distributors instead of millions of consumers. But that ad-

vantage would not be gained in the earlier stages.

15. Article in Renewal, May-June 1966, p. 16.
16. The phrase and some of the data in this section are taken from Alvin L. Schorr's "Alternatives in Income Maintenance," in Social Work, July 1966. Of course the patchwork effect becomes even more striking when the federal antipoverty effort is viewed as a whole. According to the Task Force on Economic Growth and Opportunity (in its First Report: The Concept of Poverty, Chamber of Commerce of the U.S., Washington, D.C., 1965, pp. 1, 23), Secretary Celebrezze of the Department of Health, Education and Welfare counted 42 programs at the federal level that "have a fairly direct application to poverty," and the National Catholic Coordinating Committee on Economic Opportunity listed 53 such programs, costing $31 billion in 1964.
17. See previous discussion and footnote 13. For example, in Fiscal Policy for Full Employment, a report sponsored by the Labor Committee of the National Planning Association (NPA Planning Pamphlets No. 45, May 1945), I included (p. 37) some rough calculations, mainly based on estimates by Helen Tarasov, showing a per capita indirect tax burden of about $100 a year at that time, and suggested that it might reasonably be postulated, for purposes of tax offsets when needed, that no one paid less than one-third of the average per capita amount, or $33.
18. Statement on "The Triple Revolution" (the reference is to revolutions in cybernation, weaponry, and human rights) sent to President Johnson on 22 March 1964 by the 37-member Ad Hoc Committee on the Triple Revolution; here quoted from p. 10. The Committee included Robert Theobald and was organized by W. H. Ferry, Vice-President of the Center for the Study of Democratic Institutions, in Santa Barbara.
19. In Negative Taxes and the Poverty Problem, op. cit. The present section is particularly indebted to Green's study for data and, where indicated in the text, for analysis. His text and tables should be consulted for a wide range of specifications of different negative income tax plans which cannot be included here--other variant forms, more complete and precise treatment of assumptions, elaborate breakdowns comparing different plans as to their effect on families of different sizes, etc.
20. Mutual exclusion is provided for also under a more complex formula suggested by James Tobin in "Im-

proving the Economic Status of the Negro," *Daedalus*, Vol. 94 (Fall, 1965), pp. 889-95. This plan would grant a basic allowance of $400 per capita and would set the tax for other income at 33 1/3 per cent up to the point where the allowance had been reduced to zero, after which the present tax schedule would apply. The cost would be about double that of Plan 1.

21. *The Guaranteed Income*, *op. cit.*, (1) pp. 176-178, (2) p. 157.
22. "Income Maintenance and the Birth Rate," *Social Security Bulletin*, December 1965, p. 30.
23. Milton Friedman, *Capitalism and Freedom* (University of Chicago Press, 1962), pp. 191-194.
24. See Footnote 6 and related text.
25. Some examples of this evidence: the already cited views on jobs and income of the civil rights-labor-liberal-religious sponsors of *A "Freedom Budget,"* *op. cit.*; the comment of the Chamber of Commerce-sponsored Task Force on Economic Growth and Opportunity, p. 12 of *The Concept of Poverty*, *op. cit.*, that "For those with potential to escape poverty, it is a harsh fate to be guaranteed a minimum income by the rest of society and to be cast aside without opportunities to help themselves"; the remark of Commissioner of Labor Statistics, Arthur M. Ross, in a recent speech (before the W. E. Upjohn Institute for Employment Research, October 6, 1966) that "Under all these circumstances there is a real possibility--a real danger--that the unemployed in the slums and ghettos will be put on a dole."

22. GUARANTEEING FULL EMPLOYMENT IN THE UNITED STATES*

I have two quite simple propositions that I want to make. The first is that we ought to guarantee full employment in the United States. And the second is that it can be done.

Before I really get started, however, there is one detour that I have to make. What do we mean by full employment? Most people seem to be quite clear about it, but one of our most interesting panelists, my friend Mr. Ferry, the other day said he was not in love with full employment--that full employment and steady jobs are nice to have but are not adequate for personal or national purposes. Well, I agree with much that Mr. Ferry said and a hundred percent with the second part of that particular statement. Full employment is not an adequate personal or national purpose. As he pointed out, besides work there is also play, and politics, service, and contemplation. President Hamilton put it very well when he said that beyond earning a living there is the question of living the life we earn. I couldn't agree more with those thoughts. But when Mr. Ferry said in the first part of his statement that full employment is merely "nice" to have--instead of essential to have--I suspect he was using a sort of private definition according to which full employment means jobs for everybody whether they need or want jobs or not. Back of this would be the moral judgment that everybody *ought* to work.

But *that*, of course, is quite a different matter. It is certainly not what full employment has meant to all the people who have been concerned with it for 25 years or more. The Employment Act puts it very well. The Act doesn't use the term "full employment," but advocates employment opportunity--useful employment opportunities, including self-employment, for those able, willing and seeking to work. That is what full employment means. There is nothing wrong with

---

*An address delivered at the Governor of Hawaii's Conference on Human Resources, Honolulu, February 2, 1967.

voluntary non-participation, but *involuntary* non-participation *would be* eliminated by full employment--except, of course, for a minimum amount of frictional unemployment.

Governor Burns in his very fine keynote address said the same thing. He said we are committed to providing jobs for those able and willing to work, and we also want to provide help to those who would like to become able. This is surely the concept, and it is important. We should keep our eyes on the stars--on things that are beyond employment--but meanwhile let's keep our feet on the ground and get this very practical question of employment settled in the right way.

The reasons why we need full employment are so often spoken about that perhaps it is gratuitous for me to mention them again. Still, let me remind you of some of them. First and foremost, when you are unwillingly deprived of the opportunity to participate, it amounts to nearly total frustration. It completely ruins your legitimate pride. You can't really have a life.

Then there is the fabulous amount of waste that goes with unemployment and non-utilization of our resources. The Council of Economic Advisers now uses a figure just over a quarter of a trillion dollars to measure our national loss in the years 1958 to 1965. Just think what we could do with a fraction of that money in combatting poverty!

A third major reason comes out when we consider the problem of equal rights. Whatever other elements are in that picture, it is clear that unless there are enough job opportunities, the Negro is going to have an extra hard time to get one. And this is not just a matter of justice--it is a matter of the cohesiveness of our whole society. There are, of course, other groups besides the Negro who should also have justice. There are the older workers, now often pushed out of the labor force to make place for others. There are the younger people, who aren't helped very much as they come along to get their first jobs. There are also the women, who are discriminated against in the labor market, especially when jobs are scarce. And, of course, there are minorities such as the American Indian and so on.

Now, what I have been saying so far is completely familiar. However, I want to go further. I believe that it is not enough just to have full employment, or approximately full employment, in some particular period of time. In addition to that, we need to be sure that we are going to have it indefinitely. The assurance of the future maintenance of full employment is as important as the having of it right now.

(I noticed in a column by Joseph Kraft, in the *Adver-*

tiser a week or so ago, a very nice phrase. He said, if you mention a guaranteed income, you are apt to get a fight, and if you mention Social Security, you are apt to get a yawn. I wonder what you're apt to get, according to him, if you mention guaranteed full employment!)

Now let me tell you why I am convinced that we have to be sure we are going to maintain full employment. There are two major reasons, one domestic and the other international. Both of them seem to be absolutely fundamental for everything else that we want to do. The domestic reason is that, in the absence of any assurance of continued prosperity and full employment, all the interest groups in our society are bound by their obligations to their constituents to push a little too vigorously from the standpoint of the good of society as a whole. In Mr. Jack Hall's paper he mentions that organized labor's first responsibility is to the members it represents. The same thing applies, of course, to employer organizations, farmer organizations, and others.

Take for instance the 35-hour week issue which came to a head a few years ago. Labor was pushing for it very hard, although the Administration said no, that is not the best thing. But as George Meany remarked, pointing to years of excessive unemployment, "It's only a goal because nothing else has been done." I have talked to a number of labor people in the past who have said things like, "Well, if you let the textile industry in New England down, where are those people going to get a job? If we could be sure they would be able to get a job somewhere else, and that society was also taking care of the problem of transition, it would be possible for us perhaps to be a little more statesmanlike."

You just can't ask labor, or business, or the farmers to be more statesmanlike if the Federal Government isn't being statesmanlike by doing its job of keeping the total framework of society up. Now take business, for instance--the big-business area where prices are administered. If I were administering a price in a business organization, I would want to be sure that the price was set high enough so that I would make enough profit in good times to take care of me in the next recession. And that is exactly what big business does. But if you aren't going to have recession--or at least no recession in the economy as a whole--then you can afford to set lower prices, which will be beneficial all around.

Or take the farmers. Farmer organizations for decades have been driving the State Department's trade liberalization advocates to despair by their policy of fighting for markets by dumping agricultural products abroad and shutting out agricultural imports.

As I said, all these powerful interest groups are doing what they have to do. Only if the Federal Government comes in and provides the assurance that there will continue to be an ample total market and jobs for all, so that there is no longer any necessity to ask for too much now as a hedge against the next dip--only in those conditions can we really expect to see a package bargain struck that will be adequate and satisfactory to society as a whole.

What about the international side? Mr. Thompson said, I think, that an injury to one is an injury to all. The poet Blake said that no man is an island unto himself. Through my own experience I have had an opportunity to see how the interests of other countries are affected by the presence or absence of domestic prosperity and full employment in the United States. Years ago when the ITO--International Trade Organization--charter was being negotiated, I happened to be a member of the U.S. negotiating team. When we got to London for the first meeting, my colleagues in the State Department, who could think of nothing except lowering trade barriers, were in for a surprise. All the other major countries--in this case the western industrialized countries--said: we don't care so much about that; what we want to know is, are you going to have full employment in the United States, so that you will keep up the demand for our goods?

More recently, and in a more sophisticated form, you get the same thing over and over in the economic committee of the United Nations General Assembly, and in the summer debates of the Economic and Social Council in Geneva. The reasoning is absolutely correct, in my opinion. The less developed countries by and large are never going to be able to develop unless they are allowed to export manufactures--after, of course, first learning to produce manufactures efficiently. The cards are stacked against the possibility of their ever developing strictly as agricultural nations or exporters of raw materials.

Now we in the United States have in recent years spoken very sympathetically of that desire on their part. We have tried to urge our friends in Europe to relax their trade barriers, and successive administrations have tried to get us to lower our own barriers sufficiently. But there have been limits set by the fear of a shortage of markets. You may remember that a few years ago half of our cabinet in Washington and the chairman of the Council of Economic Advisers went over to Tokyo to hold talks on various matters of mutual interest, largely in the economic field. You may also have seen some dispatches written by Mr. Rosenthal of The New York Times which made the U.S. position in those talks very clear. We sympathize (our team said) with your desire to open up larger markets. We know that you have to have them--Japan has to have larger export markets in order to live. But you on your part should realize that we can't do much about this because we have an unemployment problem.

The point I am making is that, in tomorrow's world, we need to be able to maintain full employment and ample markets for our producers regardless of whether we have an export surplus or not. As a matter of fact, as we grow more mature we ought to act like a mature creditor country and accept an import surplus eventually. Today we have the problems of trade and aid. In the immediate present we need especially to extend aid, more aid than we have been extending to these less developed countries. If we had achieved continuously assured prosperity we wouldn't need to feel that we couldn't afford to do it. We wouldn't need to feel that we were helping somebody in Asia at the expense of some poor people in Appalachia, because it would be obvious that we could do both.

But in the longer run these countries want to get off the hook of aid. They don't like to be in a position of dependence, any more than we would. They want to pay their way by trade. And as soon as they can really get going, they will be in a position to export if the advanced countries of the world including America will accept their goods. But, with the best will in the world, we won't be able to pledge ourselves to a policy of accepting substantial amounts of additional imports from the rest of the world, unless we are sure that, as compensation for that, we can develop additional markets through additional purchasing power at home. So, our international position as well as our domestic situation is going to require the insuring, or the guaranteeing--I don't care which--of full employment and of a level of demand consistent with full employment.

* * *

Now, my second proposition--that it can be done. How do we do it? I think we all are, or want to be, practical people. I would say that part of the answer to the question as to how we do it has been given by this Conference. It would be quite needless for me, and presumptuous besides, to talk in Hawaii about all the things the state Administration is doing and is planning to do. All of this detailed planning work has to be done here. Most of it is on what would be called the structural side of the full employment question.

I am going to talk about the other side, the Washington end--and not all of that, since on the structural side Washington must also be active, helping you, for instance, to set standards and providing you with some of the necessary finance. My subject here, however, is mainly the aggregate demand. I am hopeful that you will not misunderstand my meaning. I think we have come beyond the point where we need to argue as to whether unemployment is a structural question or a question of aggregate demand; it is obviously both. Others have dealt, much better than I possibly could, with the structural aspect. I want to talk about the Federal Government's responsibility for maintaining enough draft to keep the fire burning brightly--enough aggregate demand. This fits with the other. It should fit the other as a glove fits a hand, but it is not supposed to be the same thing.

If we have in fact come beyond the point of major controversy over whether our unemployment is due to structural causes or to insufficient aggregate demand, I still think there is a certain knack even about the aggregate demand side that hasn't yet percolated through to Washington. I am not quite as sanguine as Dr. Hitch seemed to be about that, if I understood him correctly, even though we must certainly all agree that the shortages of demand don't pinch us as badly now as they did thirty years ago.

Let me then begin by saying that I think we could come a very long way with the kind of approach that puts together a package of demand made up of the different things that we badly need in our society. The best recent example of that that I have seen is contained in a document entitled A "Freedom Budget" for All Americans, put out by the A. Philip Randolph Institute on the basis of statistics and economic analysis by Leon Keyserling. Some two hundred civil rights, labor, liberal, and religious leaders sponsored this program. It is essentially an antipoverty program with full employment treated as the principal one of many means to be used.

The authors of this document believe that in ten years we could add an economic growth dividend--or cumulative increase in our gross national product over present levels--amounting to considerably over two trillion dollars. The Federal Government's share of that, just keeping the same taxes we have now, would be of the order of half a trillion dollars. The program they advocate, to spearhead the antipoverty movement, would cost the Federal Government, for its part of the job, 185 billion dollars in those ten years. But this would not mean that the Federal Government would become bigger in relation to either State and local government or to private enterprise; in fact it would become a little smaller in the process in relation to State and local governments, as well as no bigger in relation to private business. These projections are all predicated by the authors on a national rate of growth, over most of the decade, of four and a half to five per cent a year, involving some growth of labor force and an increase in productivity or per man-hour output in the private sector of about three and a half per cent a year. The authors further indicate that, since the Federal Government's added take during this period would be roughly five hundred billion and the antipoverty expenditure only 185 billion, the program would be perfectly compatible with a substantial simultaneous expansion of defense expenditures should that prove necessary.

Their program consists first of all, as I said, of full employment. Secondly, it has in it various ways of raising private incomes by way of Social Security, higher wages, broader coverage of minimum wages, a shift in emphasis away from support of farm prices to support of farm incomes, and, as they say, progress toward a nationwide guaranteed income as a matter of right. This last they advocate, not in substitution for, but as a supplement to, guaranteed full employment. Thirdly, this program calls for elimination of what they call "poverty in the public sector." Here, too, I think they have made a very good case for what I personally believe strongly in, that is to say a great expansion in some activities very necessary for society's welfare--slum clearance and low income housing, education, health, transportation, conservation and development of resources, antipollution, help for depressed regions like Appalachia, help for rural communities in general, and so on.

This would obviously require federal leadership, but, as I said, not a bigger federal piece of the pie, since the pie would be made to grow larger. Moreover the growth rate figures underlying this program are not above what we have sometimes managed to achieve, and not above some other reputable estimates, even though a cautious estimator might judge them to be a little high.

Now I think this program is good. But I also think that a question could be raised as to whether it would ever be possible to push a complicated package like that at all quickly through Congress. Suppose the Administration accepted the whole thing, lock, stock and barrel; could they get it through Congress? I think this is a fair question.

There would be in Congress any number of people who would disagree on some of the particular details for one reason or another. Some might disagree in principle, others for possibly extraneous reasons like, say, the Church-State issue which acts as a drag on federal aid to education. Well, the President might be able to get eighty per cent of it through. Yet if he didn't get a hundred per cent through, then, assuming the program was calculated to produce full employment, the full-employment target would be missed unless Congress were willing to allow all gaps in employment to be filled by additional expansion of programs that it had approved. (To be accurate about it, over-saving could make such additional expansion necessary even when income payments had been pushed up to the full-employment level to begin with.)

However, some members of Congress would probably object to that on the ground that they didn't want the Federal Government to grow bigger in that way. Having held the public sector to a total of so much, they wouldn't want those gaps filled since that would still make for a bigger government sector in relation to the private sector. I am not saying the majority would argue that way but some members probably would. There would no doubt even be those unreconstructed souls who would question the good faith of those who were putting the proposition forward--people who would say that the government wanted to stack the deck and get business into an agreement, and then perhaps create unfavorable conditions through tax policy, or antitrust policy, or price policy, or something like that, that would make business not come through with its share, and then the government would have to fill the gap and government would take over more territory.

Actually, it is not just business interests that might be worried about it. You might also get labor worrying, in the sense that obviously if you have to rely on the possibility of a really large expansion of the flexible public works program to take up the slack, the question arises of the administrative or organizational feasibility of it. Certainly there are people who wouldn't want to find out that they were being eased out of the labor market, and put on a dole, so that they wouldn't any longer figure among the unemployed. Hence they wouldn't want to get into the kind of a situation where, in order to meet the full-employment guarantee, that kind of adjustment might come up for urgent consideration.

I have some doubt along these lines myself--doubt about the feasibility of really guaranteeing full employment by this method alone, considering how the executive and legislative branches work on a normal piece of legislation. So why not look for something a little simpler, surer, and better? What I suggest is that the "Freedom Budget" should be retained but that, in order to get a real commitment to full employment much more quickly, the guarantee on the part of the government to fill all gaps in employment should be accompanied and made more acceptable by adding a further guarantee of aggregate consumer spending. This would give business a satisfactory target to shoot at. Any business firm could still lose customers to its rivals, but, with the total market at the consumer end pegged at a certain size which was determined to be adequate, there could hardly be a general or a cumulative downturn in business.

For example, if we were going to have a gross national product of 800 billion by maintaining full employment, then more than 500 billion would be in consumer spending, if we kept to the proportions that are customary. But the amount to be guaranteed would actually be derived as follows. You could get an estimate of what the total volume of private investment would be, on the assumption of continuing full employment; and an agreement from Congress for certain public expenditure programs; and also an estimate of that small but internationally strategic item, the export surplus. Adding these three you could then get by subtraction what was needed for consumer spending to yield a total demand, made up of the four components, that should be adequate.

Using this approach, the President in his Economic Report might ask for the total "Freedom Budget." But now in effect he would in addition be saying to Congress: "If you will accept this whole program, then say 520 billion of consumer spending is enough. But, if you find yourselves unable to agree with all of these proposed public expenditures, then you will need to raise individual consumer spending correspondingly. These are the proportions between the private and public sectors that I think society in our day and age demands. But if you don't go along with me on that--and there can of course be reasonable differences of opinion about it--at least we won't let the total economy down. For in that case it will be necessary to up the figures that I have given you for the private consumer spending total."

What would be needed to implement this suggestion I am making is an amendment of the Employment Act--from the drafting point of view a very simple amendment. The fundamental nature of it would be to put responsibility on Congress. At present there is no responsibility on Congress under the Employment Act to do anything in particular. There is a general national policy, and the President has the responsibility of putting forward his specific proposals. Congress, then, through its Economic Committee in the first instance, goes over those proposals. What seems to be missing is the obligation of Congress to state its own position on the levels of activity necessary for the economy, either agreeing on this with, or specifically amending, the proposals of the President. That is, Congress should itself come out with what it regards as a legitimate target for total employment--75 million jobs or whatever it might be for the year ahead--a target which we should not fail to achieve, and with, secondly, a target for total consumer spending. The latter would testify to the intent not merely to maintain full employment (as Congress would finally define it) in disregard of all other considerations, but to maintain it in accordance with the consensus that had been reached by Congress itself as to how much of the economy should be public and how much should be private. In other words, this technique would separate the issue of public versus private activity from the issue of maintaining the right overall rate of operation.

Congress, therefore, under this amendment, need not agree on more program details than it wished, but it would be obliged to come up with figures at which total employment and total consumer spending would each be pegged, and to instruct the President and his Administration to see that those levels were maintained. If at any time there were not enough jobs, new items would be taken off the public works shelf. If at any time consumer spending was not being maintained, method "x" or method "y" or "z" would be called into use for boosting it.

It is very important, I think, that Congress should now assume this kind of responsibility. This is the missing piece in our economic management. Responsibility, of course, is something that cuts in more than one direction. Anyone like myself who advocates guaranteed full employment has the responsibility not to ignore either the danger many people see of overheating the economy by inflation or the balance-of-payments danger. Well, as regards inflation, I would say that this approach would be quite helpful, for two reasons. In the first place, it would set a target ceiling as well as a floor--for example, not less than 75 million jobs but also not more than 76 1/2 million jobs during the year ahead, and similarly with consumer spending. Those upper limits would help at least in a mechanical way to keep any kind of spiraling inflation from happening.

But more fundamentally, it should be possible with this approach to get a real sense of agreement to avoid inflation from labor, business, and all other parties concerned. In view of this assumption of responsibility by the Federal Government, I believe there could be an acceptance, for instance, of some kind of wage-price guidelines. Labor would be getting the thing it most needs, the assurance of jobs. Business would be getting the prospect of a stable, adequate market for its products. Avoidance of excessive claims should thus become possible on what is really a political level, quite apart from the helpful mechanical checks I mentioned a moment ago.

The balance of payments problem is, of course, a related issue. I cannot go deeply here into that very technical subject, but there are several things to be said. [One is that a continuously strong economy attracts funds. Another point is that most of the industrial countries are committed in one way or another--some of them more deeply than we have been so far--to a policy of continuous expansion; and when everyone is going forward in step, one country is not so apt to lose funds to the others.] Probably, too, we could make more sophisticated use of our interest rate policy than we have in past. Furthermore it seems reasonable to suppose that out of those long-drawn-out discussions now going on among the monetary experts will emerge a better and less worrisome international monetary system--one that will give us both more protection against speculative raids and also larger total reserves.

Privately I myself would think it was not beyond the bounds of human ingenuity to devise an international mechanism that would take foreign aid out of consideration as a balance-of-payments problem. When we supply large amounts of foreign aid, we today accentuate our balance-of-payments problem, unless the funds are spent to buy our own goods and services. Thus there can arise a conflict of interest: we want to help people in other countries, but we don't want to worsen our balance-of-payments problem. I think, as I say, that it should be possible to devise a safeguard against that--a way of measuring the part of the balance-of-payments difficulty that arises from foreign aid and then neutralizing this through the international payments apparatus.

But finally, assuming that all these things should prove inadequate for solving the American balance-of-payments problem, then I think we would have to face the fact that we were up against the question of our scale of values. There has to be some point where you finally come to that. In this case the question would be whether it was more important to maintain our full-employment policy or to allow American citizens and American dollars to go freely wherever they wished without any check on them at all. It seems to me that the tone of this conference has shown a vivid appreciation of the importance of doing things for full employment, for people, and for welfare. Therefore--according to this view, which I share--if it eventually proves necessary to temper slightly some of the other rich freedoms that we have enjoyed so carelessly, well then, it will have to be done.

Now--to go back to my main proposal--you might well ask me how we could maintain consumer spending if we had the guarantee and if the current rate of spending was running too low. As to this, we fortunately have learned a good deal in the last several decades about the uses of tax policy, and it has by now become quite accepted by the public that you can sometimes lower the income tax. Much more thought is also being given these days to transfer payments, which are virtually negative taxes. So, this question is now a little less formidable than it used to appear. Nevertheless, just lowering the income tax, when you find that you need to give a boost to purchasing power, doesn't help the poorer members of society who don't pay income taxes. Hence some other way must be found in order to complete and equalize the operation.

One pretty good way, I believe, of solving this problem would be to establish as a new device a federal sales tax or sales bonus--alternatively one or the other, depending on conditions. Most of the time it would presumably be a bonus, but if the spending level was getting out of hand it could be a tax. In other words when, according to the Congressionally established target, we were not getting enough consumer spending, a pay-out period would be declared and everybody who bought anything would get coupons convertible into cash at the bank or post office. Since a sales bonus would be progressive rather than regressive, the usual objections to the sales tax would not apply.

However, perhaps a better way still is suggested by the current discussions of a guaranteed income implemented through a negative income tax. The real trouble with using income tax variations as a regulator of the level of demand today is that we don't yet have the negative part of that instrument, and so--if I may just repeat this point--you can't benefit the lower income groups by reducing income tax rates. I myself happen to believe that we should in any case adopt the principle and practice of a guaranteed family or household income on at least a moderate scale as a matter of right. The Social Security mechanism isn't going to do the whole job of raising up incomes that are below the poverty line; it can't because it doesn't reach all groups, and does on the other hand reach a great many people who are not poor. Minimum wages can be extended--I hope they will be--but they too have their limits and are obviously not the whole answer. As for public assistance, there are so many things wrong with the welfare programs as presently administered that everybody knows they should be curtailed rather than expanded. On these somewhat negative grounds alone, therefore, a good case can be made for a negative income tax. But I would say there are two more fundamental reasons why such a plan should be adopted.

The first is the progress of cybernation. I don't myself believe that the cybernation revolution is right upon us in the sense of causing us to lose employment opportunities in a catastrophic way in the next decade. But I do think, from the studies I have read, that there is a lot more going on under the surface than many people realize. Moreover this will be a snowballing process, and eventually we will come, I believe, to the kind of situation where we will pretty well have to divorce income from work.

Let me say that I would be completely opposed to substituting the idea of the guaranteed income for the idea of guaranteed full employment. In the first place we haven't reached that stage. We are not too rich yet. There are lots of things that we can do to wage war on poverty at home even if the United States in an average sense is adequately affluent, as some writers have suggested. Then there is the rest of the world; we certainly want to help the majority of mankind, living in the less developed countries, to get out of their poverty. So, on the objective side, I am sure we haven't reached the point yet where people cannot be used productively. Surely it is highly premature to think that we have. Again, turning now to the subjective side, it is equally obvious that people today don't want to be given a handout instead of work. They want a job. And as long as any substantial numbers want a job and can't get one, their involuntary unemployment is in conflict with the concept of full employment.

Indeed, if we were to establish a guaranteed income before establishing guaranteed full employment, I don't see how we could fail to be setting up a new and pernicious kind of class system in this country in which the people who already had jobs could hang on to them, and the people who hadn't been so fortunate could never get in but would have to live instead on some kind of dole. On the other hand, to take this step together with, or immediately after, establishing guaranteed full employment would be, I think, very useful, providing us with a mechanism that we are eventually going to have to use quite heavily.

In the meantime, also, the guaranteed income would provide the other half of the income tax mechanism which could be used to serve the quite different purpose of maintaining the level of aggregate consumer spending about which I have just been speaking. That is, in periods when we were faced with insufficient purchasing power and consumer spending, we would be able not only to lower the taxes of the positive income tax payers but also to enlarge the periodic payments to the non-taxpaying households. This would seem perfectly fair for everyone--a balanced way of maintaining our common prosperity.

I would just like to say again in conclusion that guaranteed full employment is bound to be partly a matter of structural measures, using that term very broadly, and partly a matter of aggregate demand. On the structural side, while the Federal Government has a substantial part to play in providing funds, other assistance, and standards, most of the detailed spadework has to come at the State and local levels from people who really know the situation. When we turn to the maintaining of aggregate demand, this is a matter of federal fiscal policy, a part of the picture that necessarily fits with and supports the other.

Actually, I would hope that Hawaii's Administration, and your Commission on Manpower and Full Employment, would not only be able to show how this local part of the job should be done in Hawaii, but would even be able to go beyond that and find formal or informal ways of helping the Administration and the Congress in Washington to recognize and do their part.

23. BEST CURE FOR INFLATION — GUARANTEED FULL EMPLOYMENT*

The "trade-off" is not an immutable law of our economic life. America has not run out of easy ways of doing things. If these are heresies, it can't be helped.

What Chairman Paul McCracken of the Council of Economic Advisers was talking about before the Joint Economic Committee of Congress was obviously not the international political scene (where everyone knows that there have been no easy ways to run out of for many years) but only our domestic economic quandary caused by the rise of inflation. And what I mean as to his comment on that[1]--and I say this with much respect for McCracken's skill, his values, his tone, and his right to use an expression like that rather loosely in order to make the point that he wanted to make at the time--is only this: that the easy ways that the country may have had of doing things were not doing the thing that was fundamental; that the way of doing <u>that</u> is not altogether easy, naturally, but is not so hard either; and that we have not run out of it. But I do mean that much.

The underlying concept of the trade-off came into vogue as the concern over our inflation spread. There is nothing complex about it in principle. Business and labor both like to charge what the traffic will bear, and so the high demand, piled higher for several years by huge military spending, bid up wages and prices. Eventually, in fairness to fixed-income receivers if for no other reason, there had to be a decision to apply the brakes and check the demand--direct fiscal brakes of less spending and more taxing, indirect monetary ones of fewer bank loans at higher rates of interest. But this sort of braking action, while at first it might seem to be having practically no effect whatever, is bound in due course to slow production too in some degree and cause some workers to be laid off. Hence the conclusion is drawn that some sort of trade-off between major

---

*Reprinted by permission from <u>The Commercial and Financial Chronicle</u>, May 8, 1969.

desiderata is inevitable: if we want more price stability, we must also--so it is said--accept more unemployment.

Two Approaches

How much more? Well, figuring out just how much more unemployment we are going to have to have in order to buy just how complete a slowdown in prices how soon is quite another matter. No one really knows the answer, though many feel impelled as usual to act as though they did. (Don't just stand there--forecast something!) McCracken and the Nixon Administration, showing a keen awareness of what is at stake for the disadvantaged groups in our society, have undertaken to apply the brakes as lightly, gradually, and experimentally as may be possible. The other school of thought has all along offered a tougher prescription: if you don't face up to the need to kill off the inflationary psychology and inflation now--and of course that will increase unemployment somewhat temporarily--your softness will most likely bring on a recession that will really destroy jobs.

Yet, differ as they do on strategy, there is nothing to suggest that either school questions the trade-off concept as such. Both begin their reasoning by taking it for granted. Economic news writers have made that abundantly clear. Eileen Shanahan for one showed it with particular clarity when she wrote in The New York Times (Dec. 8, 1968): "That some sort of compromise must be made between the objectives of full employment on the one hand, and price stability, on the other, is beyond argument.... Modern economic theory and policy has yet to find an answer to [render unnecessary] some decision about 'the trade-off'."

Here I must beg to differ. Economic policy does have, in my opinion, a better answer than that. I also venture to say that it is too late in the day not to use the best answer that we have. But, in order to do that, we will need to discard the whole traditional trade-off approach and embrace a different concept, that of guaranteeing the continuous maintenance--paradoxical as this may seem--of full employment.

What is full employment? By my definition it is "useful employment opportunities, including self-employment, for those able, willing, and seeking to work." (Employment Act of 1946, sec. 2). But "those" must clearly mean "all those," and in addition--either as an integral part of the definition itself or as an essential accompanying policy: it makes little difference which--people who are willing but not able, and so might be too discouraged to keep on "seeking," must be helped to become able. This is where training programs are especially important, and our manpower policies generally, including regional programs like Appalachia. This is the main specific remedy for so-called unemployability or true hard-core unemployment.

It does appear that anyone professing confidence in the conventional trade-off doctrine must be a little uneasy. What is the nature of all that reasoning about the percentage of unemployment needed to keep the percentage rise in prices within tolerable limits? Speculative in the extreme. What is the goal of the policy? Something, I submit, hardly worth the trouble involved in reaching it. Unless, that is, we must pessimistically conclude that in economic policy we lack up-to-date ideas entirely (whatever our ingenuity may be in other fields) and so must be satisfied with inherently very unsatisfying solutions.

Heritage of Depression Era

The trade-off is a concept deriving from the days of our great depressions. When one of those "acts of God" occurred (a way of expressing ignorance about the in-any-case frowned-on art of controlling the demand), workers by the millions were thrown on the street and businessmen found their markets absolutely flat. Wages and prices certainly came down. Today, while shunning a return to such conditions, the economic doctors are still preoccupied with the thought that a milder dose of the same old medicine will be just enough to hold prices reasonably steady. Pressure on people but not too much pressure. Just a slight twist of the arm. The bull fight without really killing the bull.

But the foundations of that hope are extremely shaky, to say the least. Statistics?--the evidence cannot help but be inconclusive, although the fact that prices continued to climb throughout the recession of 1957-58 while unemployment went up to touch 7.5 per cent (seasonally adjusted rate) might be cited as evidence against the thesis. Logic?--here the case for the trade-off is especially weak. Why expect our powerful unions to knuckle under in their wage demands if unemployment rises moderately? A response of that kind seems no more probable in the world of today than persistence of upward wage pressure coupled now with rising pressure for more unemployment relief and larger welfare payments. Ultimately, to be sure, and at certain levels of unemployment and shrunken demand, a real economic squeeze would be bound to produce its intended results, ending the inflation. But what does that mean: hard times of what duration and to what extent--and expectable under what political auspices? Consider also this haunting question: how can anyone say with confidence how much unemployment would still have to be retained as a permanent warning after the shake-down was over?

It only remains to be observed that the effects of even a fairly small rise in unemployment could be dire enough. The mayors of our bigger cities will testify that we will not succeed in creating a better society by going in the direction of making life economically more difficult for Negroes. This point has been made very well by McCracken himself--as, for example, in a speech during late Johnson days to the National Industrial Conference Board, in which he remarked that "Those marginally positioned in the labor force, and therefore the first casualties of unemployment, are also heavily those in the ghettos with whom an awakening national conscience is increasingly concerned. We are not apt to accept many tenths of a per cent increase in unemployment to gain ground on the price-level problem." Exactly so.

There Is an Alternative

To disparage the trade-off approach to policy would be a great pity if there were no better alternative. Fortunately, however, there is one. That better alternative, I submit, is to grasp the nettle firmly by guaranteeing full employment at all times, meanwhile negotiating a suitable understanding with labor, business, and farm leaders. By "suitable understanding" I mean one in which it was agreed that the *quid* for the *quo* of guaranteed full employment and continuously adequate total demand for goods and services was the acceptance by those leaders of some kind of reasonable guideposts, guidelines, or frame of reference for the processes traditionally followed in establishing their selling prices.

One can hear the objection that such an understanding could not be negotiated, and possibly the further objection that the leaders of labor, business, and farmers could not prevail on their constituents to follow their lead. I firmly believe that the understanding could be negotiated, for reasons to be stated in a moment. As for the second objection, admittedly in this individualistic country the kinds and degrees of influence exerted on their constituents by leaders of farm organizations, trade unions, and the organizations and individual giants of the business world will fit no simple formula. Some of their constituents--one thinks, for example, of the widely scattered craft union locals in the building trades--can probably indeed be counted on to try to be fiercely independent.

Nevertheless I believe it is fair to say that, in one way or another, the leaders of our big national economic interest groups (these three groups and also others) could be expected to keep a degree of control adequate for the purpose.

But how can one be confident that an understanding along such lines could ever be negotiated with them in the first place? The answer to this seems to me to be relatively simple: because the leaders of the major economic interest groups in our society are, by and large, realists. As realists they must know that the vigor with which their constituents look after their own exclusive interests can affect the national interest--that it is even possible for excessive demands for pay or profits to impair the viability of our economy. And, secondly, any realist is bound to recognize that continuously assured full employment and adequate overall demand would be an unparalleled economic blessing.

The assurance of jobs for all those wanting and able to work would obviously solve the problem that is pivotal for labor--incidentally in the process doing more to improve race relations than any other one thing at this point in our history could. The governmental policies required for effectuating such an assurance would also be enormously beneficial to business, inasmuch as those policies would have to include the maintenance at all times of a sufficiently large market for business output in general. Farmers would gain in both ways: many of them as businessmen would be helped to find better markets for their produce, while some others, situated closer to the margin, would see a decent opportunity at last to make a living outside of agriculture.

Notice, however, the catch. It would be only the confident expectation of those results, created by the Government's guarantee, that would make it possible to negotiate the understanding. At least I do not myself see much logical or historical reason to suppose that the leaders of labor, business, and farmers would give their pledge in exchange for a mere hope. It seems to come down to this: if the Government in its proper sphere would undertake to assume the necessary degree of responsibility for our economy, why should they not do likewise?

Unused Areas of Employment

Evidently, then, the prior issue is whether--and how--a guarantee of full employment could be given and made good. Not in any figurative sense, but really.

Could we, for example, have a plan made up of decently large programs in all those fields where there is wide agreement, backed up by expert analysis, that as a nation we are not doing nearly enough? Let us say in health, education, low-cost housing, urban redevelopment including mass transport, pollution control, conservation and development of resources. Carrying out such programs would be mainly up to the private sector, or to State and local government, but Federal Government partnership and initiatives and Federal spending would be essential too. There is so much catching-up to be done in these areas--and the things needing to be done would furthermore embody such a high proportion of labor, much of it requiring very little training or skill--that an approach like this could, if followed, provide us with a balanced kind of full employment for many years. Comprehensive plans in at least outline form are not lacking either. The National Planning Association, a private organization in Washington, has been publishing such plans for a long time. In 1966 the A. Philip Randolph Institute of New York put out a striking plan along similar lines in a pamphlet entitled _A "Freedom Budget" for All Americans_.

Such an organized, many-sided attack on our "public poverty" would certainly have the enthusiastic support of millions of people, this writer included. If we can have peace in Vietnam, surely the time to launch it will be at hand. Nevertheless a little reflection will show, I think, that this approach _by itself alone_ is inherently insufficient as a method of guaranteeing full employment. Why? Not for lack of things needing to be done but because of differences of opinion about doing them and because of the way in which our national economic policies are formulated and carried out.

Bypassing Conflict between the President and Congress

The division of powers between the President and the Congress and the cleavage between left-wing and right-wing views--essentially the "creeping socialism" issue--just cannot be left out of account. Let us suppose that President Nixon were to recommend in an annual Economic Report to Congress a section-by-section composite program along the lines just described--one that would, if followed, maintain full employment for the ensuing year. He would plainly not be in a position to guarantee that result, since the various parts of his program might for any number of reasons be cut down by Congress and the resulting gap might not be filled by anything else. Clearly, even in periods when policies and current conditions may be largely favorable to expansion, full employment cannot be actually guaranteed unless the Federal

Government itself stands ready to become the employer of last resort. And this is something that, in present circumstances, any President has reason to know that any Congress may very possibly not agree to.

This is why the composite program method, although sometimes advocated as the road to assured full employment, is insufficient by itself alone. Fortunately, however, its limitations can be overcome by broadening the approach. Under a suitably broadened approach, Congress could be enabled to guarantee full employment without having to risk creating a larger public sector than it thought the country should have. And the President, in recommending a series of specific programs, would then not be staking full employment on the willingness of Congress to authorize them all or others of equivalent weight. In short, the issue of public *versus* private activity would have been cleanly separated--*by the* very nature of the different approach I am talking about--from the issue of maintaining the right overall rate of operation of our economy.

Mechanics of Suggested Program

Since we are now no longer on generally familiar ground, let me take a moment to explain how this would work. (Parenthetically, the enabling amendments to the Employment Act of 1946, though momentous, could be brief and rather simple in form.)

To begin with, the President in his annual Economic Report, prepared as usual with the help of his Council of Economic Advisers, would include *two* proposed guarantees--(1) of the level of employment, and (2) of the level of consumer spending. The level of employment chosen by him as corresponding statistically to the full-employment concept would reflect his judgment of how much unemployment was reasonable in the light of manpower policies and labor mobility at the time. (I would myself suppose that such "necessary frictional unemployment" would amount to 3 percent of the labor force or less.) The level of personal consumption expenditures chosen would be derived by a process of estimating a full-employment level of gross national product or expenditure and subtracting from it its three other components, i.e. estimates of (a) government purchases of goods and services, (b) gross private domestic investment, and (c) net exports.

Two further essentials: First, in order to make the crucial allowance for the possibility that Congress would not agree to all the items in his public expenditure program (a major part of the "(a)"), the President would also indicate, either by means of a series of paired figures or by some more general statement, by how much in his view the consumer spending guarantee should be raised or lowered if that public program were in fact to be reduced or enlarged. Second, in order to minimize the risk of inflation, he would include not only recommended floor levels for employment and consumer spending but ceiling levels for both as well.

Some time after receiving this Economic Report, Congress, advised by its Joint Economic Committee, would agree or disagree with what the President had recommended. In any case, however, Congress would under this proposal be responsible for establishing its own guaranteed levels for employment and consumer spending, and also for deciding in advance what methods of adjustment were to be used when, as, and if those levels proved to be not self-sustaining. That is the crux of the matter.

In regard to the levels, Congress might for instance decide that the employment target (floor) during the year in question--in other words, that year's authorized operational definition of full employment--should be 79.5 million jobs, seasonally adjusted, whereas, let us say, the President had proposed 80 million. Or it might trim $10 billion off the President's proposed program of public expenditures on goods and services--but in that case the logic of the situation would require it to raise the private consumer spending target correspondingly. Or if, on the contrary, Congress should decide to increase public spending, it would then be logically obligated to lower private consumer spending.

In regard to the adjustment methods, the chief novelty would lie in the devices that might be selected for directly raising, as well as lowering, the level of consumer spending. (Perhaps it needs to be underscored that maintaining full employment would not always in itself also indirectly maintain the indicated rate of consumer spending, since either too much or too little of that income flow could be channeled into saving.) Two of the most promising available alternatives would probably be the following: (a) A reversible sales tax/sales bonus at the Federal level: in periods calling for expansion, everyone buying anything at retail would get coupons or stamps which would be redeemable in cash if presented within a reasonable period at a bank or post office, those agencies being in turn reimbursed from the Treasury. (b) A negative income tax plan, enacted to give effect to the widely discussed anti-poverty proposal of a nationwide guaranteed annual income: these allowances or negative taxes could be raised, and the positive income taxes lowered, when necessary to increase consumer spending, and conversely the positive income taxes could be raised, preferably however without lowering the allowances, when necessary to decrease it.

Two Important Aspects

As to implementation, two aspects will bear emphasizing here. Action would not be triggered by forecasts, since all adjustments of taxes and/or of the "last resort" jobs program would be made only when the accredited national consumer spending and/or employment series of statistics showed that the economy was in fact failing to meet the Congressionally set standards. The adjustments would, however, be made promptly in the prearranged manner then--rather than at the end of long-drawn-out, uncertain, and partly self-defeating political struggles such as have preceded our compensatory tax changes until now.

Here then can also be summed up the second reason why guaranteed full employment would actually make it easier to ward off price inflation, rather than harder. The approach described would automatically call for scaling down consumer spending when the latter would otherwise rise above the level set at its safe upper limit, and would automatically call for putting some public works back on the reserve shelf when total employment would otherwise rise above its pre-established ceiling. In other words, in addition to the negotiated restraint on cost-push inflation which was emphasized earlier, there would also be a twofold prearranged check on inflation from the side of demand.

Our Foreign Status Would Be Helped

Our balance-of-payments problem, which partly derives from our price inflation but also in large part does not, is beyond the scope of this discussion. I must, however, say something about the way that the burden of this discussion bears upon our position in the world at large. For the advantages of a policy of guaranteed full employment over a policy of trade-off would lie not only in the domestic sphere but also in the sphere of foreign economic relations. In particular, the substantive basis for our policies in regard to foreign trade would be transformed for the better.

The difference would be that the perennial fear of a shortage of markets would be permanently eliminated. That is because one of the elements used in calculating the level of consumer spending to be guaranteed would be, as already noted, our net foreign market or export surplus. Hence whether we faced a continuing export surplus or--in due course, at the right time--a more or less even trade balance, or an import surplus, would not affect our ability to guarantee full employment and a sufficiency of total demand, domestic and foreign combined. Thus we could in particular be more helpful to the developing nations--not only by being generous with well-considered forms of aid but also (since we ourselves could not run short of markets at any time in the foreseeable future) by encouraging them to export more goods to us, including manufactures, so as to move "from aid to trade" as soon as they were ready for it.

Those who speak for liberal trade policies would then still be contending with the inevitable protectionism of certain private interests; but they would not any longer be up against, in addition, the conscience of the legislator who has the public interest at heart and is genuinely worried about an impending lack of markets and jobs for Americans. It is hardly too much to say that America would have found the key to the puzzle of how to be the good neighbor it desires to be.

To return finally to the main thesis of this article, there is the possibility of using full employment itself--rather than unemployment--as a sort of trade-off against inflation. This is so because there is a practical method of putting full employment on a guaranteed basis. If I am right about this, then statements to the effect that we have to compromise between the objectives of full employment and price stability are clearly wrong.

One way to find out if this very different sort of trade-off will work would be to try it.

Note

1. "The basic fact we find is that the country has run out of easy ways of doing things." McCracken testifying before the Joint Economic Committee, quoted by Hobart Rowen in International Herald Tribune, February 18, 1969.

24. A NOTE ON THE BUDGETARY IMPLICATIONS OF GUARANTEED FULL EMPLOYMENT

The writer has described elsewhere[1] a method that could be used to guarantee full employment[2] in the United States. One of the questions of interest to legislators and others is: what would this plan cost?

It would not necessarily cost anything. The proposal is for insurance of the economy by compensatory fiscal action against difficulties that might materialize or again might not, and, if they did, might result in either positive or negative budgetary cost.[3] The factors that would determine the outcome can, understandably, all be subsumed under the savings-investment relationship; for purposes of exposition, however, it will be convenient to distinguish (a) that relationship in purely domestic terms from (b) the effect of the foreign-trade balance, and at the same time to consider both (c) that relationship as calculated in advance and (d) the net result of non-offsetting miscalculations.

The proposal under reference is to the effect that the President should include recommendations in his annual Economic Report, and that Congress should then decide and should give firm commitments, on the following:

(a) that a level of aggregate employment not less than g, or more than g + h million persons (Department of Labor seasonally adjusted monthly figure)[4] would be maintained in the year ahead--any point within this range being officially regarded as corresponding to full employment;
(b) that a rate of personal consumption expenditures (Department of Commerce series) not less than m or more than m + n would be maintained in the year ahead--this being regarded as the adequate, non-inflationary range of consumer spending in a full-employment GNP (in which the proposed government component would be assumed to be determined by considerations partly or wholly independent of employment);
(c) that method (methods) x would be automatically invoked whenever necessary to raise or lower aggregate employment so as to keep it within its target range; and

(d) that method (methods) y would be automatically invoked whenever necessary to raise or lower disposable personal income so as to keep the rate of personal consumption expenditures within its target range.

A few words of explanation may be added to this summary statement on each of these points.

The numerical employment target in (a) would naturally be meant to provide "useful employment opportunities, including self-employment, for those able, willing, and seeking to work" (Employment Act of 1946, sec. 2); i.e. the intention would be to meet the employment needs of the labor supply in its short-run definition. The proposal also envisages, however, that training programs would stand ready to help anyone to become able who wanted to be but at the moment was not. Practically speaking, the President and Congress would be estimating the size of the labor force and deducting what they regarded as a reasonable catch-all allowance for prevailing "frictions" (between-jobs turnover, delays in accommodating new labor-market entrants). Misjudgments would certainly be possible--for example, wrong guesses at the outset as to how many persons would be seeking to work now who were too discouraged by lack of job opportunity before--but such errors could soon be corrected since the proposal envisages a new quantative definition of full employment each year in any case.

The critical aspect of the estimating called for under (b) would concern the government component of GNP, especially its Federal sub-component. The decisions that establish the regularly approved level of government purchases of goods and services will probably always, under our political system, be influenced by many considerations. Employment itself may be urged as one of the most important considerations at times, but it can seldom if ever be expected to override entirely such other explanations of the final outcome of Congressional debate as differing opinions about the intrinsic value of particular budget items, strong personal biases for or against bigger government or social programs in general (commonly the most important consideration of all), and chance combinations of events. Consequently, whenever--under the proposal--Congress disagreed with the President's recommendations for Federal spending on goods and services, it would be logically obligated to estimate the net effect of its disagreement on the total of government spending for goods and services at all levels of government combined and, other things being equal, adjust the consumer spending target appropriately in the opposite direction. "Appropriately" need not mean equivalently, since the marginal demand for labor might be different (presumably it would be higher) in the public projects in question than in private consumer-goods production.

An estimate would also--under (b)--be needed of business spending, i.e. gross private domestic investment. Although its cyclical swings would be dampened down, or even in the end practically obliterated, by the virtual elimination of fluctuations in the economy as a whole under the continuous full-employment, adequate-demand policy postulated, they might well carry over, diminishing in amplitude, into the early years of the policy. It might thus at that time be thought best, in the interests of stability in the construction industry, to allow for business spending at its anticipated cyclical-average level rather than at the level actually expected in the year ahead. In the former case, that is, the residual private-domestic-investment cycle would be counteracted mostly by means of opposite movements of final, employment-balancing public investment rather than by anticipatory opposite variations in the consumer spending target.

Coming here to (c), it is self-evident that a commitment to hold aggregate employment within a pre-announced range would require the Federal Government to stand ready to act as the employer of last resort, i.e. to hire more workers on its own payrolls or under its own contracts and/or to finance State or local governments (or possibly non-profit organizations) prepared to do that extra hiring. The commitments and action under (c) would thus be within the general frame of the concept of a reserve shelf of public works and services. From this "shelf" additional jobs would be drawn when necessary by accelerating work or starting up new projects, and to it some jobs would be "restored" when necessary by decelerating existing work or suspending or terminating certain projects.

There would be a considerably wider choice of methods under (d) than under (c), since many different ways can be imagined of raising or lowering taxes on consumers and/or lowering or raising transfer payments to them, so as to adjust disposable income <u>directly</u>. To the writer it has seemed that a study of the available alternatives might lead to the choice of either (i) enacting a reversible sales tax/sales bonus at the Federal level, or (ii) adding flexibility to a negative income tax plan enacted as the mechanism for giving effect to the guaranteed income proposal. Under (i), everyone buying anything at retail would--in periods calling for expansion of consumer spending--get coupons or stamps that would be redeemable in cash if presented with reasonable promptness at a bank or post office, those agencies being in turn reimbursed from the Treasury.[5] Under (ii), the allowances or negative taxes would be raised, and the positive income taxes lowered, when necessary to increase consumer spending, and conversely the positive income taxes would be raised, and the allowances lowered (but never below their base level), when necessary to decrease it.

* * *

Since the proposal envisages two separate operational targets, each of which might tend to be overshot, undershot, or squarely struck, there would evidently be nine imaginable combinations as regards the cost of taking the compensatory fiscal action needed for fulfilling the guarantees once they had been given. Let a minus sign stand for a tendency to create a budget deficit (positive cost), zero for a tendency to create a balanced budget (no cost), a plus sign for a tendency to create a budget surplus (negative cost), C for consumer spending, and E for employment. The alternative conditions and the budgetary results of compensating for the tax changes or government spending changes would then be:

conditions	results of compensatory action
1. C above target, E above target	+ +
2. C " " E on "	+
3. C on " E above "	+
4. C " " E on "	0
5. C above " E below "	+ or 0 or -
6. C below " E above "	+ or 0 or -
7. C on " E below "	-
8. C below " E on "	-
9. C below " E below "	- -

In short, three hypothetical situations can be distinguished in which fulfilling the commitments would tend to cause a Federal budget surplus; three others in which it would tend to cause a deficit; one in which it would be neutral in its effect on the budget; and two in which the result could go one way or another, depending on the relative weights of the factors involved. That is, in operating a policy of this kind the government might sometimes (in principle, at least) have to expand jobs and cut down consumer spending at one and the same time, or vice versa. (One question would be whether, with employment held on target, consumer spending would tend to stay within the range deemed correct *a priori* and established as its own target; and a separate question would be whether, with consumer spending held on target, employment would tend to stay within the range officially designated as "full.")

But fulfilling the commitments by invoking compensatory adjustments ex post would of course be only part of the story. The budget result in toto would reflect not only the effects of compensating for tendencies to miss the target, but also the positioning of the targets in the first place. To take an example--the consumer spending target might, in some year, (a) be set high and then achieved by deficit-creating compensatory action which was found necessary ex post; or (b) it might be set high and be nevertheless achieved "automatically," thanks to a deficit-creating tax reduction engineered ex ante which left more income at consumers' disposal; or (c) it might be set lower, in consideration of an ex ante decision to enlarge government purchases of goods and services, a deficit being however created in this case by that new government spending (not financed by new taxes).

Thus, if we try to identify causal relationships, we find ourselves on treacherous ground. Cases (b) and (c) show as much budget deficit, other things being equal, as case (a), but what if the dominant motive in (b) were tax reform, and the dominant motive in (c) were the conviction that the country needed the new government spending program for the sake of its product, i.e. the resulting goods and services, rather than for the sake of the jobs? Evidently the politically interesting question--"what would the plan cost?"--needs rephrasing into something like "what would be the state of the budget if the plan were in operation?" On this clearer basis a meaningful, even if qualified, answer ought to be possible.

Essentially the answer is that the state of the budget would depend on whether the economy itself was dynamic or sluggish, and that would be reflected in the current savings-investment relationship. This is not a matter of playing with words. Formulating the problem in such terms is a way of answering ill-considered objections to full-employment policy. If budget deficits were associated with full employment, the blame should be laid on the general tone of the economy at the time, which means on producers and consumers generally; or possibly on the government for hampering producers, i.e. if it did, say by unwise tax policies; but not on the full-employment policy or on the government for sponsoring that policy.[6]

Instead of budget deficits, however, (or, to be sure, the special case of an exactly balanced budget) there might very likely be budget surpluses. There might be, that is, an actualized full-employment surplus--the manifestation of a condition not inevitable or necessarily permanent (as some discussions would seem to imply) but at any rate clearly possible and, in circumstances resembling those apt to be found in the near future, highly probable. Urban rebuilding combined with factors like population growth and mushrooming consumer credit could easily raise investment far above savings. In the context of the present proposal--with consumer spending and employment both held on target--that would mean that the Federal budget when presented on a national income accounts basis would have to run a surplus. The surplus would arise out of (a) decisions that kept taxes above spending *ex ante*, or (b) compensatory action in the form of extra taxes, required to prevent over-shooting of the consumer spending target, or (c) compensatory action in the form of reduced public-works spending, required to prevent over-shooting of the employment target, or (d) the algebraic sum of two or more of those possibilities.

On the other hand, circumstances could also conceivably be quite different, with business depreciation charges, etc., plus undistributed profits plus personal savings exceeding private investment. In that event, the Federal Government would have to engage in deficit financing in its national income accounts budget--in some combination of ways opposite to those just mentioned--to keep consumer spending, or employment, or both, from falling below their target levels.

One possible explanation here might be a general lack of restraint in monopolistic pricing--let us call this a low *moderation-extortion ratio*.[7] Whenever there is little moderation and much extortion, savings will tend to be high as a result of the maldistribution of income arising from the concentrated monopoly profits. At the same time, investment will tend to be low in view of the restrictions on output which represent the other face of the coin of unduly high prices. Thus, under the present proposal, *if* the moderation-extortion ratio were to be low, a consumer spending target high enough to induce full-employment production would tend, other things being equal, to be difficult to achieve without deficit financing, either by prearrangement *ex ante* or by compensatory action *ex post*.

The conventional price-wage spiral would, however, be absent. In this spiral the sequence of events seems usually to have been more or less as follows: (1) as productivity increases, profits rise; (2) administered prices are raised, for still larger profits; (3) workers demand higher wages, in order to catch up--or more than catch up--with the rising cost of living (and obtain a share of the profits announced on the financial pages of the newspapers); (4) the resulting enlarged consumer buying power initiates a rise in competitive prices as well, besides making it possible to raise administered prices again, this time to offset--or more than offset--the higher labor costs; (5) - (n) and so on. Under the proposal, however, the automatic ceiling on total consumer spending--reinforced by the automatic ceiling on jobs, which guards against over-full employment--would at least interrupt this process at stage (4).

Actually, the probabilities are that effective restraint would be imposed not only on the demand factor in price inflation but on the cost-push factor (stages (1), (2), and (3) above) as well. Under the proposal the government would be undertaking to see that labor's most important requirement, adequate job opportunity, would always be met, and equally so the prime condition for the prosperity of industry and agriculture, an adequate total market. Why should not business, labor, and farm leaders be willing, by way of counter-commitment, to accept some kind of reasonable guideposts, guidelines, or frame of reference for the processes that are followed in establishing their selling prices? This point has been dealt with at some length elsewhere.[8] Three propositions are involved: (a) that business, labor, and farm leaders can not be expected to show the requisite degree of self-denial and social responsibility merely because of exhortations and the expressed hope that full-employment prosperity will be maintained; (b) that they could be expected to do so in exchange for firm guarantees; and (c) that they could also be expected to exercise a reasonably adequate degree of control over the pricing behavior of the interest groups they lead.

If our reasoning on this whole aspect of the subject has been valid, we can conclude that the moderation-extortion ratio would not after all be apt to exert much influence in the direction of an excess of savings over investment under guaranteed full employment as proposed. The Government could probably without much difficulty hold the general price level steady (or let it rise very slowly, if that were preferred) and could therefore safely estimate a full-employment GNP, and the derived consumer spending target, on a stable-prices assumption.

The discussion up to this point might to all appearances have been of a closed economy. But external trade could turn out to have real budgetary significance under the rules of the game as proposed. In particular a trend away from past export surpluses to future import surpluses could exert substantial influence towards the reduction of full-employment surpluses or the generation of full-employment deficits. Net exports, the final component of GNP requiring to be taken into account (together with government spending and business spending, already discussed) for purposes of establishing the necessary rate of consumer spending, will of course always represent an additional market if positive and a subtraction from the aggregate market if negative. Moreover if saving equals income minus consumption, an export surplus can be equated to increased consumption and hence to reduced saving, and an import surplus to decreased consumption and hence to increased saving.

The main practical significance here stems from the fact that the less developed countries will some day have to have export surpluses--through the export of manufactures as well as foodstuffs and raw materials--in order to be able to "move from aid to trade." This implies that the United States, as the leading industrialized country, will have to learn to behave like a "mature creditor" nation and willingly accept import surpluses. The proposal under analysis would clearly permit such a development to occur without sacrifice of American prosperity and full employment, since the consumer spending target would be raised pari passu with any expected "worsening" or the export-import relationship. There would, however, be a corresponding "deterioration" in the budget position because of that need to assure domestic production a larger domestic market, to compensate for the smaller net foreign market.

Coming finally to the budgetary implications of miscalculation--i.e. miscalculation in setting up the consumer spending target--it can be seen that this would not be a factor separate from, or additional to, those already discussed. When a compensatory adjustment was needed to bring consumer spending on target, that could indicate either miscalculation or a deliberate preference for letting the savings-investment relationship (or general tone of the economy) reveal itself instead of trying to guess it too closely in advance. Such a wait-and-see attitude would indeed be quite appropriate, once fiscal management had shifted over from essentially a forecasting to essentially an insurance basis.

Miscalculations could evidently occur in: (1) the size of a full-employment GNP (which would depend not only on the price trend but also on the technological trend, composition of output, and any other factors influencing the labor-capital "mix" in production); (2) the level of gross private domestic investment; (3) the level of net exports; and (4) the level of government purchases of goods and services itself. That is, State and local government spending might add up slightly lower or higher than Federal estimators expected; and the Federal Government's own spending intentions might as heretofore be somewhat unclear at the advance estimating stage, or else, even if perfectly clear then, they might still have to be revised before the year was out.

An unforeseen military emergency, certainly, could make revision necessary. To the extent, then, that a large unexpected increase in national defense expenditure went for payments to military personnel or to workers in defense plants, the proposed policy could in all likelihood absorb the impact through the prescribed compensatory action (automatic ceilings) on total employment and/or total consumer spending. On the other hand, a very large unexpected increase in military procurement might so greatly expand "guns" production as to necessitate an arbitrary downward revision of the consumer ("butter") spending guarantee originally given, or even suspension of the whole policy--nothing to wonder at, after all, in such a national emergency.

In more normal circumstances, however, the fact that miscalculations would be bound to occur in the course of the statistical exercise by which the consumer spending target would be established should not be considered as constituting a serious problem, whether in its budgetary implications or otherwise. For in the first place, the individual miscalculations would frequently tend to cancel one another out, and it would be only the net miscalculation remaining that would signal the need to take compensatory action. In the second place, moreover, the taking of compensatory action would in any case be a normal part of the system and not an evidence of defect in the system. Putting this differently, the primary reason for including the consumer spending (floor) guarantee in the proposal is not to try to establish that advance estimating has become a science or even a fine art--dubious proposition at best--but rather to make it possible, given the constraints of American political and economic life, nevertheless to reach the goal of continuously guaranteed full employment.

Notes

1. See, e.g., Insuring Full Employment: A United States Policy for Domestic Prosperity and World Development, New York: Viking, 1964. A recent statement was in a series of articles under the general title "Some Guidelines for a Rational Economic Policy," in Monterey Peninsula Herald, Mar. 2-7, 1970, especially the last four numbers. Among early discussions in American Economic Review were "The Under-

writing of Aggregate Consumer Spending as a Pillar of Full-Employment Policy," Mar. 1944, 21-55, and "On Underwriting Consumption and Employment," Sept. 1955, 645-47. From that period see also "The Underwriting Approach to Full Employment: A Further Explanation," Review of Economics and Statistics, Aug. 1949, 182-92.

2. Whatever might be the possibilities of achieving a theoretically satisfactory definition of full employment in an imperfectly competitive world, its attainment or non-attainment could be verified unambiguously in practice by having the President annually propose and Congress decide on a level of employment that would be treated as "full" during the ensuing year. See text.

3. Except as otherwise noted, the argument herein can be applied to either the national income accounts budget or the ordinary budget. The broader question of social costs (and benefits) is beyond the scope of the discussion, although that question of course provides the basic arguments against tolerating involuntary unemployment and the attendant under-utilization of other resources.

4. Alternatively it might be decided that the figure for unemployment (or possibly the one for labor force time lost) would be maintained at not more than j or less than j - k per cent of the civilian labor force (or available labor force time).

5. This plan was discussed in some detail in "On Underwriting Consumption and Employment," op. cit.

6. Indeed--and speaking here more generally--to the extent that government policies are responsible for raising production and employment levels, the government will almost always deserve credit for improving its budgetary position, since revenues will rise, with the rising tax base, while added expenditures for public works are likely to be little if any larger than subtracted expenditures for various forms of relief, etc.

7. "Monopolistic" here stands broadly for all departures from pure competition--the whole range of situations in which sellers possess some significant degree of control over selling prices, which they consequently "administer," singly or in concert with others. Use of the pejorative term "extortion" is not intended to deny that there are cases where a departure from the hypothetical results of pure competition is desirable, even essential. (E.g., a labor-saving device may be

introduced which, under pure competition, would not only displace workers but have the further short-run effect of forcing certain wage rates below socially acceptable levels.)

8. In "Some Guidelines for a Rational Economic Policy," *op. cit.*, and in "Best Cure for Inflation--Guaranteed Full Employment," *The Commercial and Financial Chronicle*, May 8, 1969.

25. SOME GUIDELINES FOR A RATIONAL ECONOMIC POLICY*

1. The Guaranteed Income Approach to the Abolition of Poverty

Poverty can be eradicated in America. Not only that, but the time is almost at hand when a guaranteed minimum household income might become a politically possible means towards that end.

The sooner the better. There could be a wrong way to go about it, however, and there is even some danger that we might take too restricted a view of our situation and choose the wrong way. That wrong way would be to guarantee a minimum income without also making the pivotal decision to guarantee the opportunity to work.

Imagine the irony of an America where "opportunity for all" meant you could count on being able to consume but not on having a share in the action of production!

Many people are not of working age and capacity, of course, and some who are quite able to work will still prefer not to. But that does not mean that participation in society's business is unimportant to able-bodied people in general. Who wants only to be kept comfortably alive?

For that matter, who wants to see a permanent division between all those who have sufficient advantages to be able to get and keep jobs and those unlucky ones outside the system who must somehow learn to endure a life on the dole?

There is no real doubt that hunger, at least, can be ended in America quickly, given the political will to do it. Surely we cannot in conscience delay where feeding hungry children is concerned, now that the facts have come to light.

---

*These four articles are reprinted by permission from the Monterey Peninsula Herald, where they appeared originally in a 6-article series, March 2-7, 1970. The last two articles have been omitted since they were essentially an abridgment of Chapter 23. The author's original headings for these articles have been restored.

Then beyond that, well within this decade of the 1970s, everyone's income can be raised above poverty levels.

Let it be granted that that will not in itself kill off entirely the sociological and psychological roots of the poverty problem: The folkways and attitudes of poverty will no doubt persist and regenerate here and there to some extent. But that is another story, less interesting at the moment than the income story, especially to those who are most immediately concerned.

The number of Americans living in poverty has been progressively declining--from 39.5 million to 25.4 million between the end of 1959 and the end of 1968 (from 22 per cent to below 13 per cent of our total population) according to the official definition and count. This trend was expectable, given a reasonably prosperous situation for the country as a whole.

As our economy has grown more productive, average per capita income has risen, and <u>some</u> of the gain has accrued even to those at the bottom. Some poor people have had more work at better wages; others have benefited because our general prosperity (not to mention Michael Harrington's book on <u>The Other America</u>, or militancy among the blacks) has aroused our social conscience. Many at the lower end of the income scale have profited from the upward drift in income from Social Security, for instance, even though the insurance benefits go largely to the nonpoor. And the 1964 declaration of war on poverty brought the Office of Economic Opportunity into being to try in various ways to give the poor a better chance to compete.

Real progress has been made, even though many of the escapees from poverty are still "near poor" and many of those left behind are less well equipped to sustain the recent trend.

Richard Nixon will go down in history as the president who gave official recognition to the government's responsibility for eliminating poverty in America. Since urgency is implied, however, that requires an all-out attack, which he has not so far proposed.

He <u>has</u> proposed a better attack than we had before. The starting point is the abolition of the main part of our welfare system (aid to families with dependent children) in its present form. In place of that humanly degrading and economically counter-productive system we will soon have quite a different set of arrangements if the President's Family Assistance Program is enacted.

Personal certifications of income supplemented by spot checks will take the place of the indignities of the present eligibility investigations. A work incentive will begin to operate, through "retention of earnings"; i.e., relief payments will no longer be reduced dollar for dollar for income gained by taking a job.

(For the first $720 of earned income no reduction is proposed, then 50 cents on the dollar. Allowances stop at an income level of $3,920 for the customarily cited family of four.) Families will have an incentive to stay together, too, since states will no longer be able to deny relief, as half of them do now, to those dependent poor children who have a visible father as well as a mother.

These provisions should more than double the number of persons able to obtain some money to relieve their poverty. Moreover under this plan the federal government will put a floor under relief payments all over the country--at $1,600 a year for a family of four, higher than 20 states now pay--and so will narrow the unjustifiable differences between life on relief in New Jersey, New York or Massachusetts and in South Carolina, Alabama or Mississippi. This same family could also get $720 worth of food stamps free.

All of these things will unquestionably help. So will the increases in unemployment compensation and in public assistance to the aged, the blind, and the disabled which carry the administration's endorsement, as well as the proposed rise in the level of personal exemptions under the income tax. In short, Nixon's program does promise to speed the antipoverty program up.

But time is passing and it is only sober reporting to say that the total result from what the President has proposed is going to be too small. The program does not measure up either to the practical necessities imposed by rising racial tension or to the idealistic values now coming more into prominence as young people and others take stock of what they want our country to become.

What then is missing? It would be a mistake, I think, to conclude that the inadequacy of this program in its present form could be cured by just upping the payments which it proposes to give to many of the poor--insufficient though those allowances do indeed appear.

Rather, the main problem seems to lie in two limitations stemming from the general philosophy which has so far governed the approach. First, that the program misjudges the spirit of the times and studiously avoids being a guaranteed income program (some press comment to the contrary notwithstanding). Second, that in tackling the neglected problem of the "working poor" it misjudges also the native spirit of America by choosing to combine work incentive with work requirement instead of with work opportunity.

It is not difficult to see why this has happened. You--or your family provider--must work if you want to eat: at least the Protestant-Judaic ethic says so, and indeed that dictum arises out of practically the whole of mankind's hard struggle to wring a subsistence from nature. Thus in his election campaign Nixon appealed to workers themselves in the following terms:

"Nobody has a greater motive to get the out-of-work to work than today's worker.... One [thing on his mind] is to protect what he has, which is human enough; and the other is to resent the fellow who he believes is taking a free ride on the taxes that he, the worker, pays."

According to this view, we should stay away from a guaranteed income, which rewards nonworkers as well as workers and, in the process, undermines the incentive to work. So President Nixon has been at pains to emphasize that his nationwide floor under relief payments is not a guaranteed income plan.

Indeed it is not, though it can be said to point in that direction. Guaranteed income plans give income unconditionally, as a matter of right. This program on the other hand imposes definite conditions. Money is not to be paid to single unhandicapped adults less than 65 years of age; or to married couples with no dependent children; or to able-bodied parents who do have dependent children but refuse to accept job-training or work if suitable jobs are available locally, or transportation to such jobs.

(Mothers of preschool children, however, if they do not want to go to work and use the proposed newly funded day-care centers, can stay at home.)

What is wrong with this, in principle? Not a great deal, I think, except that it looks too much to the past and not enough to the future. But that in itself is a serious shortcoming.

With the onward march of technology, production shortages should continue to recede and the civilian output to rise, the drain from wars and military buildup permitting. So much so that it will be necessary to spread the work by progressively shorter work weeks, longer paid vacations, extended education and training, sabbatical periods, and so on.

Seeing this, some people have tended to push the panic button, envisaging the early displacement of man by machines in all production. According to them, automation has already made the system of income distribution based on contributions to production, and especially on work performed, wholly untenable. "We don't need people as producers," someone said (one wonders about the "we"), "we just need them as consumers."

Drawn in this manner, the picture is undoubtedly overdrawn. The need for continued hard work, not only to create a decent America but also to help raise up the pitifully low living standards in the under-developed parts of the world, is much greater than this view would have us suppose. Let us not, therefore, announce the demise of the present income distribution system too far in advance.

Nevertheless the time is coming when the realities of production will enforce frank recognition of the need for at least a hybrid system of distribution. And leadership in our present time of momentous changes should recognize that fact. Political leaders have to deal with what people really believe and want.

The newer "life style," less addicted to work, is the case in point here. Since this new outlook rests on the underlying changes in technology--whose dependence on past work is, of course, irrelevant--it is solidly based and will not go away. Hence it cannot well be ignored.

2. The Guaranteed Income Approach (continued)

From technological and sociopsychological facts which are readily available to all observers the conclusion has here, in the preceding article, been drawn that America is basically about ready for a guaranteed income plan. For a system, that is, with built-in financial work incentives as heretofore (you get <u>more</u> income if you work than if you stand aside)--but with also a reasonable minimum of income guaranteed to everybody as a matter of right.

Under such a system one can well imagine that the great majority of able-bodied people of working age would still be glad to toil to increase their income in order to partake more liberally of all that the advertising industry suggests that they ought to have.

Some others would not so earnestly care to work but would nonetheless be nudged into working by social pressure.

Others again would refrain from work for extended periods, making use of the bare security provided by their minimum income allowance to think and live creatively and develop their potential. (To them we should be at least conditionally grateful.)

Finally, certain people would successfully resist the idea that they should do anything but have a free ride at society's expense. What of it? Seriously, with a technology as productive as ours, why is their case so important?

If in principle we ought to have a guaranteed income program, in practice we face the two interrelated questions of the level of generosity and the technical formula. As point of departure we have this: The official upper limit of actual poverty, which is calculated by the Social Security Administration on the basis of the Agriculture Department's very tight "economy" food budget (multiplied by three), is now about $3,600 a year for a nonfarm family of four. And the sum of all estimated income deficits below the poverty line for households of all sizes throughout the country is slightly under $10 billion--or was in 1968.

Clearly the answer does not lie, however, in having the government simply guarantee to bring all incomes up to the poverty line. There would then no longer be any advantage at all, if you were poor, in earning any income: The less you had to begin with, the more you would be given. Earned income would therefore fall off, allowances would have to increase, and the taxpayer's cost would turn out to be much more than $10 billion.

Yet the addition of a work incentive, say an extra allowance equal to a percentage of earned income, would not be the whole answer either. For this would make some households originally just below the poverty line end up with more income than some just above it.

So, to avoid this other unjust and demoralizing result (which would perpetuate one of the many evils of the present welfare system), the percentage allowance for earned income would need to be graduated and costs raised again a bit more by extending allowances to households with incomes already somewhat above the line.

In other words, care has to be taken in constructing the income guarantee formula. But that is certainly no valid reason for inaction. Various technically sound formulas do by now exist on paper, formulas that would be free of obvious injustices, would largely eliminate disincentives to work or to save or to limit the number of children, and at the same time would leave little risk of an unexpected cost overrun such as we now almost take for granted in military procurement.

James Tobin, for instance, has developed a formula which ties in especially neatly with the positive income tax, and this has been used in one of the Brookings Institution's studies of the subject to elaborate four illustrative negative income tax plans ranging in estimated net cost from less than $5 billion to more than $40 billion a year.

The real issue, then, is not technical feasibility but

level of generosity. President Nixon's proposed non-universal guaranteed minimum of $1,600 a year for a family of four, estimated to cost some $4 billion dollars a year near the start, plus food stamps at say $1.5 billion, might politically speaking be considered the lower end of the scale.

The universal guaranteed minimum of $5,500 for a four-member family which was favored by the White House Conference on Food, Nutrition and Health would no doubt be close to the upper extreme if conceived of as applicable immediately.

Sen. Harris and others have now introduced as a Democratic alternative a plan assuring to all families of four a minimum income which would rise to the poverty level ($3,600) after three years, with the allowances set in this case to taper off at the $6,300 income level.

By the third year under this proposal the states would be relieved of all welfare cost, and the federal expense might run, it is said, to $20 billion a year.

There is meanwhile also the Children's Allowance approach, long advocated by Daniel Moynihan and recently brought into new prominence by the chairman of the Senate's Select Committee on Nutrition and Human Needs; according to Sen. McGovern's proposal, payment of $50 to $65 a month would be made for every child in the country. This plan differs from guaranteed income proper in that it misses some people altogether but on the other hand seems to avoid drawing any line between the poor and the rest of society.

Available for consideration too is the $2,400 federal guarantee for a family of four proposed as a first step by the President's Commission on Income Maintenance Programs (Heineman Commission), which was appointed by President Johnson and submitted a thorough report within recent months to President Nixon.

This plan, again, would allow 50 per cent "retention" of other income, so that any family of that size with less than $4,800 would get some income supplement. Any with as much as $2,400 of other income--from wages or old-age and survivors insurance or a veteran's pension or workmen's compensation or property ownership or supplementary state relief payments (in the richer states) or any combination of these or other sources--would be lifted above today's poverty line right from the outset.

The total annual net cost of the plan taken by itself would be about $6 billion, with the states saving $1 billion and the federal government paying $7 billion. Later, if that modest beginning were to be made, economic growth would let the allowances be raised with a constant fraction of revenues at the same tax rates, i.e., even without presupposing an increase in generosity on the part of the rest of society.

To a cash scheme at this level could be added a liberal food stamp plan, as was done after due consideration by President Nixon. Depending on the details of the cash plan itself, the stamps might perhaps cost $2 to $4 billion a year additional.

Certainly as a general proposition (admitting of course the necessity for certain exceptions in short-supply fields like housing and medical care) it is better to avoid paternalism and give income supplements in cash rather than in kind or in hybrid form. Hence the food stamps should be phased out as soon as possible and replaced by more generous cash allowances.

All the same, hasty action in that direction could be damaging. In Let Them Eat Promises, Nick Kotz has shown how a switch from a surplus commodity distribution program to a generally speaking superior food stamp program can sometimes do more harm than good: When that switch occurred in Mississippi in the winter of 1967, scores of thousands of blacks who had been thrown out of work by a wave of mechanization were just too poor to afford the stamps.

So could a switch from stamps to cash actually tend to increase hunger so long as the poorest people in the country still lack the means to buy enough good food and meet their other essential needs at the same time.

It is certainly tempting to simplify our hodgepodge income-support arrangements. Some writers have urged that a guaranteed income program should be adopted but only in place of practically all other transfer payments to individuals, and even some benefits in kind.

That is an attractive idea for the future. A well-integrated approach could lower the costs and increase the returns. But probably we should agree to live a while longer not only with food stamps but with most of the rest of our "crazy quilt" system as well. The real point is not the elegant look of the quilt but whether it keeps you warm.

In short, our income security system as a whole could abolish poverty even if a newly enacted income guarantee by itself alone did not. If a rather modest guarantee plan were to be adopted, some families and unrelated individuals would find that their guaranteed minimum allowances in combination with their income from wages, social insurance benefits, or other conventional sources would lift them above the poverty line. Others would still be below it. (Apparently in 1968 about half of the estimated 686,000 poor families of four had less than that $2,400 of "other" income referred to above.)

For them to cross the line too, the existing forms of relief including the food-stamp allotment would need to be liberalized if other income transfers were not, or some new basis for last-resort aid could be created within the relief system if that should be regarded as desirable.

3. The Pivotal Role of Guaranteed Full Employment

The preceding article noted the point that a guaranteed income plan may provide allowances which are insufficient to eliminate poverty by themselves alone. That, in fact, seems rather likely at first, nor should such a start be scorned.

Various nonrelief forms of income will then close the remaining gap for many poor households, and other categories of relief in cash, kind and food stamps can help the rest.

The main source of additional "other" income is the increased earnings obtainable by the poor through more job opportunity and a stepped-up campaign against substandard pay. Certainly many poor households have nobody in them who can or should work; indeed, persons 65 years of age and over constitute with their immediate dependents about one-fifth of all our poor, and families headed by the mothers of children under 18 perhaps another one-seventh.

Even so, the poverty gap could be more than half closed if we had (1) the assurance of "useful employment opportunities, including self-employment, for those able, willing, and seeking to work," coupled with a strengthened program to help willing but not-so-able persons to become able; and (2) higher pay at the lower levels, both directly through improved minimum wage legislation and indirectly through the influence that the full employment itself would exert on the labor market.

Full employment defined as above admits, of course, of a reasonable minimum of frictional or between-jobs unemployment. It is suggested in the next article that the question of how to construe "reasonable minimum" should be decided by Congress on the annual occasions when it would set up its specific guarantees.

In a report submitted to Congress a year ago, former Secretary of Labor Willard Wirtz urged the extension of minimum wage coverage to some eight million additional workers, largely found in small retail and service establishments, in domestic service, and on farms, and also the raising of all minimum rates to $2 an hour over the next half dozen years.

These measures would tremendously increase the earnings of the working poor, assuming, as seems to be likely, that a carefully phased program along that line would cause no substantial disemployment.

Not as obvious but at least as great is the potential increase in earnings from guaranteed full employment. The disappearance of excess unemployment in the usual sense would of course raise the annual earnings of many more persons than are out of work at any one moment of time.

Also eliminated would be that considerable portion of part-time employment (with low earnings) which is involuntary too. There are apparently, moreover, at least half a million other persons in the country who would be counted as additional unemployed today were it not that they have become demoralized by the difficulty of getting a job and have stopped "seeking to work."

(An undercounting of population in the 1960 census may, finally, give our unemployment figures yet a further downward bias.) With continuous opportunity to get a decent job, however, plus a way to train and become qualified for it, most of the now discouraged, ill-equipped people would become employed earners.

In the second place, there is full employment's effect on earnings by way of wage rates: it is much easier to exploit poor and unorganized workers by paying substandard wages when jobs are hard to get than when they are plentiful.

As long as President Nixon's program makes a work requirement the basis for relief eligibility without assuring work opportunity, it cannot capitalize fully on labor earnings for narrowing the poverty gap. Involuntary unemployment (full-time and part-time) will not be greatly affected by just insisting that people train for jobs, since the main question is in the jobs available once training is completed.

There is also a real danger that the aims of the program may be perverted in some parts of the country in a deliberate effort to hold wages down. By decentralizing of the responsibility for job training to the states and metropolitan areas, local authorities are given the power to decide what constitutes a "suitable" job that must be taken on pain of forfeiting relief.

Experience in other contexts provides ample warning that that power could be used to beat down wages and break strikes, especially among poor minority workers in rural areas.

This discussion shows something that is frequently forgotten, thanks no doubt to what the "new economics" has achieved already in making the return of catastrophic mass unemployment all but impossible.

Even in terms of earnings alone--of what the additional opportunities to work would directly and indirectly contribute toward the raising of money incomes above the poverty level, and so toward the ease and the true economy with which a guaranteed income program could be carried out--an assurance of really full employment would be enormously helpful. But, of course, it would also accomplish far more than that.

One aspect of its basic human importance was mentioned at the beginning of the first article: Any definition of opportunity that leaves out the opportunity to work is simply not good enough to fulfill the promises implicit in the American dream.

Inadequate employment opportunity has furthermore been widening our ominous social divisions. We have all along been suffering, subconsciously at least, from internal strains caused by unduly keen competition for scarce jobs.

The symptoms are familiar: a little too much pressure on older workers to retire before they wanted or could afford to, a little too little consideration for young entrants into the labor market, and above all the fact that blacks have always been the last to be hired in a boom and the first to be let go in a recession.

Today this last phenomenon--not just the fluctuations, but the whole continuing deficiency of Negro, Indian, Puerto Rican and other minority job opportunity--has become so notoriously intolerable that the war against job discrimination has finally begun to be mounted in earnest.

That entire effort for equal employment opportunity is certainly a fine thing. But the fact has to be faced that the movement is bucking a strong current, because the available total opportunity is too small.

"Insufficient but equal" faces a troubled future. Only when the day arrives when job opportunity no longer has to be rationed can we know that the most sincere movement for job equality will meet with full success.

The social values to be gained through guaranteed full employment are matched by the economic stability it would provide. Here--in its economic connotations, that is--"full employment" may be after all an inadequate term, since it seems to suggest a rather specialized subject for those interested in labor matters.

Actually, maintaining assured full employment would involve achieving an unprecedented situation in which recessions would be impossible and inflation highly unlikely. That would evidently be in the interests of practically everybody.

Exception should naturally be made of those members of the financial community who make all their money precisely out of the economic ups and downs of the market, and perhaps also for some theoretical economists overspecialized in bravely forecasting business cycles.

4. Guaranteed Full Employment (continued)

Beyond question the bulk of the additional employment needed in this country for years to come should be provided by filling those huge and now widely publicized gaps in pollution control and environmental improvement (conservation and development of natural resources), urban redevelopment and mass transit, low-cost housing, health, education. Undoubtedly this is how we should reorder our national priorities, and many persons have convincingly pointed that out.

Current services are needed as well as capital investment. For example, many municipal services (street cleaning and sanitation, police protection, mail delivery, parks and recreational facilities, clinics and hospitals, etc.) are very much undermanned.

Moreover these services too use a good deal of relatively unskilled labor, the kind whose outlook is the most precarious today.

Much of this socially essential work should be carried out by the private sector, and much of the rest by state and local government, largely with funds obtained on a revenue-sharing basis from the federal government--a highly desirable new method of financing already offered for trial by President Nixon in his antipoverty program. The implied federal partnership and initiative will certainly have to be supplemented, however, by direct federal spending as well.

In fact, it is self-evident that a real guarantee of continuing full employment can be given only if the federal government stands ready to act as the employer of last resort--understanding this phrase to include the possibility of its financing local governments and even perhaps nonprofit institutions to do some of the actual hiring.

Right here lies the crux of the problem of putting full employment on a guaranteed basis. With power at the federal level divided between the President and Congress, and the nation divided more or less between liberals and conservatives, it is not a simple matter to obtain agreement that the government will always step in to support employment to any necessary extent.

The solution of this problem, however, is suggested by the conditions themselves.

To state very briefly some points that will be elaborated in the final article*, the President in his annual Economic Report to Congress should specify not only (1) the level of employment that in his view will be "full," and (2) the federal public program that he favors, but also (3) the level of private consumer demand (based on Gross National Product calculations) necessary to maintain full employment if that public program is adopted, and (4) the degree to which consumer demand should be expanded if the public program is reduced, or vice versa.

Congress should then go beyond what the Employment Act now provides and should take the final aggregative decisions and give the related final commitments for the year ahead. First, that is, Congress should endorse or modify the President's statistical full-employment definition.

Second, it should decide the basic size of the federal public program it wants. (This may be recognized as a variant of the kind of spending limit already instituted by Congressman Wilbur Mills.)

And third, it should spell out in advance the methods to be used for adjusting total publicly generated employment and total consumer incomes. Reference here is to the methods to be used if and as such up or down adjustments are shown in fact (not by forecast) to be required in order to hit the statistical employment target, on the one hand, or the consumer spending target, on the other. Both of those targets, of course, should allow a workable range between bottom and top.

The built-in commitment to adjust down in case of either consumer overspending or over-full employment is one of the two reasons why this approach would offer strong resistance to inflation.

The other reason is that a part of the process of undertaking a governmental guarantee of full employment and continuously adequate demand for goods and services in the economy as a whole would logically be the negotiation of a suitable understanding with labor, business, and farm leaders. They should agree to be so guided in establishing their selling prices as to restrain "cost push" inflation.

Such an understanding seems, however, quite out of reach unless the government assumes responsibility in its own proper, overall sphere.

It should next be recognized that the advantages of guaranteed full employment would be not only domestic but international as well. This follows from the fact that our foreign trade balance would logically be one of the factors (one of the components of GNP) to be taken into account in

*This article is here omitted; see note on p. 312.

estimating how much consumer spending was required to arrive at a basically adequate total demand for domestic output as a whole.

Hence we would be equally able to maintain full employment with an export surplus or an import surplus. Freed from any compulsive, economic-self-defense need to force our exports abroad or stop imports from coming in, we could begin to use our economic foreign policy much less as a weapon and more as an instrument of good will than we have in the past.

Take, for example, our relations with the developing countries. Not only could we (confident of continuing prosperity) easily afford to be more generous to them with well-considered forms of international aid, but we could also encourage them to export more goods to us, including manufactures, as they have to do in order to be able to move "from aid to trade" as soon as they are technically able to make that transition.

Or take trade barrier reduction more generally. Our free traders would still be opposed by protectionists, as usual. But our legislators at least could now resolve the issues on their real merits, with no need to worry any longer about a possibly impending lack of markets and jobs for Americans.

It is hardly too much to say that America would have found the key to the puzzle of how to be the good neighbor it desires to be.

Naturally, all of our main economic policies are interconnected--for better, if we will, or for worse. The relationship between guaranteed full employment and guaranteed income would not be one-sided but reciprocal. The former would help in the attainment of the latter, as has been shown.

The latter, by the very fact that it would regularly channel additional spending money to the poor, would help to keep consumer spending up to its underwritten level without much need for auxiliary devices. Not only that, but it could itself provide a very convenient auxiliary device for use when necessary.

Today a lowering of the income tax will boost consumer spending but obviously not the spending of those too poor to pay any income tax. The other taxes which the poor certainly do pay could nevertheless be rebated to them to a comparable extent on some roughly estimated basis--in periods, that is, when actual consumer spending was falling below guaranteed consumer spending.

Or a reversible sales tax-sales bonus could be instituted at the federal level, and in periods calling for expansion all buyers of goods and services in the retail market would get coupons made redeemable (unlike food stamps) in cash. Possibly the most convenient mechanism of all, however, would be a negative income tax such as might be used for effectuating a guaranteed income plan. Here the allowances (negative taxes) would simply be raised, and the positive taxes lowered, when necessary to increase consumer spending.

Conversely, the positive income taxes could be raised, but preferably without lowering the allowances, when necessary to reduce consumer spending.

Consider, finally, certain parties at interest including the worker who, as President Nixon has suggested, resents having to carry the loafer. The guarantees of income and employment in combination could do a good deal toward sorting out in a natural, individually determined way just where in society people want to belong. True, the minimum income paid for out of taxes would keep nonworkers from starving. It would be up to the democratic process to decide, however, how high in relation to each other the minimum income allowances and minimum wages ought to be set.

At the shop level this sorting-out could continue. Along with strict enforcement of nondiscrimination in hiring, and with a really adequately funded program for upgrading the employability of anyone seeking that help, could go a new insistence that no employer had to hire anyone not willing to do the work and not either able to do it or in process of training himself so as to become able.

Or take the case of a teen-ager who might work just long enough and often enough to "get by" (by having something more than his minimum allowance to spend)--preferring to do other things than work most of the time. Or the case of an older worker who might have formed the habit of taking extra days off whenever that suited him. Both of them could easily be making the right decisions for them.

At the same time, the new situation would offer an unusually good opportunity for employers and unions to make some adjustments in their rules on temporary work and absenteeism, having in mind both the problems of management and the just claims of the steady, productive worker.

26. MORE NEWSPAPER ARTICLES

1. Economic Insurance*

To the Editor:

Your May 18 editorial "Dubious Economic Insurance" says that "Insurance against recession is needed, but both the nature and the timing of the President's latest fiscal dividend appear questionable." May I make three observations.

Insurance against recession is indeed very much needed, not only for domestic prosperity and full employment but also as essential support for a constructive United States economic foreign policy on trade and aid. The domestic and the international issues involved are so important that it seems time to stop juggling this (insurance against recession) as a phrase and instead establish it as a system.

Second, your editorial criticizes the nature of the President's latest fiscal dividend (cuts in excise taxes), saying that undue reliance is being put on tax cuts and too little on higher spending. I agree in general with your view but, precisely because we need the economic insurance, I cannot agree unconditionally.

Personally I strongly favor, as you do, meeting those "unfulfilled demands for public services--schools, hospitals, transportation--that only increases in spending can satisfy." This should be done because of the values involved and to some extent also because it is easier to get a quick employment lift that way than through tax cuts, as Leon Keyserling and others have pointed out.

But insured full employment does not depend on getting Congressional acceptance for any particular volume of public works and services. Consumer spending can still be raised by means of tax cuts to fill the residual gap.

Finally, your criticism of the timing of the President's move tends to confirm the great difficulties of economic prediction and hence the desirability of following an insurance

---

approach rather than a forecasting approach. Without going into details here, the distinction would hinge on establishing separate targets for employment and (tied to expected domestic investment and the trade balance) for consumer spending; adjusting taxes--possibly through a reversible sales tax/sales premium arrangement--whenever consumer spending actually misses by more than the agreed margin; and stepping up or slowing down public works and services whenever employment, in spite of the supposedly adequate total effective demand, actually strays from its own target.

John H. G. Pierson
Riverside, Conn., May 18, 1965

2. Guaranteed Income and Guaranteed Job*

Hunger can be ended in America quickly. After that, well within the '70s, everyone's income can be raised above the poverty line. A key move in that direction would be a guaranteed minimum household income. The technical problems have been solved on paper. Politically it could soon be possible.

Nevertheless, to guarantee incomes without guaranteeing the opportunity to work would be a mistake.

President Nixon's welfare program is a big step forward, but it falls short on both of those counts. It does not, as it stands, assure a minimum income to all Americans (with or without dependent children) as a matter of right. It does not make sure that everyone always has a chance for a decent job.

Though the work incentive feature is fine, the work requirement aspect is dated, considering how productive our technology has become. Work opportunity is what should be stressed today instead.

The guaranteed minimum should also, if possible, be set higher than Nixon's $1,600 for families of four, plus his say $720 in food stamps. Even a modest beginning, however, would still permit all incomes to be raised above the poverty line (about $3,600 for families of four) by drawing on other income sources too. Moreover, it is important to keep the

---

*Reprinted by permission from the Honolulu Advertiser, March 27, 1970.

minimum allowance in proper relation to minimum wages.

Cash allowances are the main thing. But food stamps should still be continued for as long as the poorest people in the country lack the means to buy enough nutritious food and meet their other basic needs at the same time.

What about those "other income sources?" Many poor persons (the aged or disabled, mothers with young children) obviously cannot or should not work. Nonetheless, work could still be the main source of additional income for the poor as a whole, assuming two things.

First, full employment, for more jobs. Second, higher pay at bottom levels, which can be brought about partly by improved minimum wage legislation and partly, again, by ending job scarcity, the condition which always tends to undermine wage levels, especially among poor, unorganized rural workers.

Besides helping the poor to have more income, guaranteed full employment is needed from a social standpoint to make opportunity real in America, and to reduce racial tensions. For equal-employment-opportunity efforts to succeed, the total opportunity has to be sufficient. "Insufficient but equal" faces a troubled future.

From the overall economic standpoint, guaranteed full employment would make recessions impossible and inflation highly unlikely, paradoxical as that may seem. Internationally, it would enable America to be a good neighbor. First of all, we Americans should and could be generous with aid to the developing countries. But, since our own prosperity would be established as totally independent of export surpluses, we could also buy their goods, including manufactures, to help them make the transition "from aid to trade."

As many people have pointed out, a reordering of domestic priorities is essential today, with emphasis on pollution control and environmental improvement, urban redevelopment and mass transit, low-cost housing, health, education, municipal services. Fortunately, this can also help to secure full employment.

But unfortunately it cannot--by itself alone--actually assure or guarantee full employment. Not because of any lack of things needing to be done, but because of differences of opinion about what should be done (the "creeping socialism" issue, for one thing) and because of the way our national economic policies are formulated and carried out.

Guaranteeing the level of consumer spending--together with the level of employment itself, naturally--would solve that problem. If Congress then wanted to modify the President's proposed Federal spending program, it could do so without sacrificing a full-employment gross national product, by simply moving the consumer spending target in the opposite direction.

Maintaining the right overall rate of operation for the economy, which is non-controversial, would have been cleanly separated from the controversial public-versus-private-sector issue.

Finally, what about inflation? First of all, the employment and consumer spending guarantees would have ceilings as well as floors, to restrain inflation from the side of demand and prevent the price-wage spiral.

Secondly, because the government was offering those guarantees, it would be in a position to persuade business, labor, and farm leaders to agree to follow some reasonable set of guidelines in establishing their selling prices, so that "cost push" inflation would be restrained too.

Here lies the explanation of that seeming paradox--the reason why the outright guaranteeing of full employment, far from representing a "well-intentioned but impractical" goal, would itself provide the best cure for inflation. The implications of this may be startling. It collides with the generally accepted "trade off" doctrine, according to which there is supposed to be an immutable inverse relation between inflation and unemployment. But that is an unduly pessimistic idea. It could and should be forgotten.

3. Another Approach*

The current talk about an "incomes policy," just given new impetus by Fed Chairman Burns, clearly assumes--often too smugly, I feel--that business and labor should learn to be responsible to the rest of us or else must be made to be. Period.

Some form of suasion or even outright price and wage control may indeed be necessary to choke off the present inflation. A better answer will be called for soon, however. The real key to governmental leadership on the wage-price front and to curbing the misuse of business or labor market power surely does not lie in either admonishing or forcing

---

*A letter to the editor of The Washington Post, printed May 26, 1970. Reprinted by permission.

business and labor to practice self-denial and responsibility--not in that alone, at any rate--it lies in first or simultaneously assuming the government's own proper responsibility.

That is to say, it lies in having the government guarantee the opportunity to work and the level of aggregate demand for goods and services which is a requisite for that continuous full-employment condition. If the government would in this way do its own part in maintaining a healthy economy, why should not labor and business agree to do likewise?

Those "cost-push" pressures toward inflation would then abate. Not only that but the mechanism essential for continuous full employment in a country with our traditions would provide for ceilings as well as floors on the number of jobs and on the rate of private consumer spending, so that inflation would also be restrained from the side of demand. (These conclusions, of course, run counter to the prevailing "trade-off" theory, that the price of less inflation is more unemployment.)

The political feasibility of giving such a guarantee arises out of the insufficiently appreciated fact that maintaining the right overall rate of operation for the economy, which is non-controversial, can be separated from the controversial public-versus-private-sector issue. If Congress wanted to modify the President's proposed federal spending program it could do so, without sacrificing a full-employment gross national product, by simply moving the consumer spending target in the opposite direction.

John H. G. Pierson
Washington

4. Are Permanent Controls on Prices Needed or Not?*

Addressing the Fabians in England, John Kenneth Galbraith stated again the other day that permanent wage and price controls are essential if we are to have high employment without intolerable inflation in future. The key word is "permanent." This is not the temporary "quick freeze"

---

*Reprinted by permission from the Honolulu Advertiser, November 30, 1970.

idea advocated by Congressman Henry S. Reuss and others for stopping inflation now.

"There are," says the next president of the American Economic Association, "no alternatives." Keynesian fiscal and monetary management simply cannot stand up any longer against the power of big unions and big corporations. "At any near approach to full employment, unions can seek and win wage increases much in excess of productivity gains, because...corporations can retrieve wage increases and something more."

He adds that the necessary "forever" controls are technically feasible in the U.S. because our economic structure is such that "only a few hundred unions and a couple of thousand corporations need be touched."

What about it? Are these conclusions prophetic or premature?

My view is that this positive suggestion is much to be preferred to the fashionable negative opinion that there is just no way of having full employment and price stability both (the "trade-off" philosophy, sanctified statistically by the "Phillips curve"). Galbraith may be right, too, that legal controls are the only answer. Certainly this cannot be disproved as of now.

But is cannot be proved yet either. Before we treat it as though it were, I suggest that we first try a different approach: a "quick freeze" now, then the offer of a firm guarantee of permanent full employment, in exchange for which business and labor leaders should agree to abide by some reasonable set of price and wage guidelines.

Under this proposal, which I have elaborated in books and articles, there would also be a further inflation-stopper in the form of a ceiling on aggregate private consumer spending. That is, under an amendment to the Employment Act of 1946, Congress would each year set top and bottom limits to consumer spending as well as to employment itself.

This system of "Economic Performance Insurance" would be politically possible because the public-versus-private-sector issue would be automatically disentangled from it. The current consumer spending target would be set in the light of how much government spending for goods and services Congress actually favored--and also (another story) in the light of an internationally sound policy on imports and exports, so sadly lacking today.

To get our national priorities right we obviously need a big expansion of certain public services; at least I join with Galbraith and no doubt millions of others in so asserting. But if a presidential plan along that line were trimmed down in Congress for any reason, we would still, under my proposal, accomplish the super-priority of full employment (without inflation).

According to Lee Cohn in The Washington Star of Nov. 10, Chairman Paul W. McCracken of the Council of Economic Advisers now favors a "social bargain" under which the government would stimulate vigorous economic expansion if labor and business would curb wage and price increases. This sounds like at least a faint echo of the proposal which I have re-stated above.

But why be ambiguous about it? Surely the time for ambiguity or timidity in facing our bigger social and economic problems is now past. Let our national leaders--in one party or the other or both--come out flatly for guaranteed full employment, and negotiate with big business and big labor with that offer as the heart of the deal.

If Galbraith is right, this wouldn't work. Very well; we could then adopt his system of controls. But as things stand today, the burden of proof still seems to be on those who despair of business and labor ever cooperating with society unless literally forced to do so. Let the government offer them a solid commitment to permanent non-inflationary full employment, and personally I think they would want to go along.

5. Full Employment Need Not Generate Inflation*

The confrontation between fear of inflation and fear of unemployment ought to be resolved before it fires up racial conflict and youth revolt to destroy our society.

We are told that there has to be a "trade-off": if we want greater price stability, we must put up with more unemployment. When rising demand has squeezed most of the slack out of the goods and labor markets, business and labor

---

*Copyright 1971 by The New York Times Company. Reprinted by permission from the Op-Ed page of The New York Times of January 23, 1971, where it formed Part III of a series on Wages and Prices and ran under the editor's title, "A Comprehensive Plan to Balance Our Economic Life." A few sentences from the original manuscript which the Times copy eliminated for reasons of space are here restored.

have the power to make prices and wages spiral upward.

In this spiral, profits and prices tend to rise first, while union wage demands often far exceed productivity increases. The whole process bristles with warranted recriminations.

Many people wonder, since there's so much that obviously needs doing (take pollution control, urban redevelopment, low-cost housing, health, education, municipal services), why intelligent social planning under government leadership couldn't solve the whole problem. Workers would have the jobs. And if prosperity were definitely here to stay, big business could charge lower prices because excess profits would no longer be needed against future recessions. Government revenues would soar even if tax rates were lowered.

Doubtless the main obstacle to acceptance of this approach has long been--and may still be today--a fear of a creeping-socialist effort to take the economy over on the pretext of keeping it going.

Be that as it may, our experts consider the trade-off as axiomatic, and focus on what sort of trade-off to make and how to maneuver. Some economist may advise stopping inflation at any cost. When seeking election or re-election, one probably thinks first about stopping the rise in unemployment.

Now a narrow political view of this matter could be tragically inadequate. That sort of compromise won't do at all. Even to attain full employment is not enough; its continuation has to be assured. What we need is a policy that guarantees that everyone seeking and able (or trainable to become able) to work will hereafter always have that opportunity.

We need this because universal opportunity to have a bona-fide life is what America is supposed to be all about. We need it because the racial problem is practically insoluble without it. We need it for ending poverty in this country --the extra wage income, to make cash and food-stamp allowances less expensive, depends on our having full employment to give more jobs and minimize chances of paying substandard wages. (On improved minimum wage laws as well.)

Our international position, too, is at stake. We need guaranteed full employment to become the good neighbor we want to be. Not only must we feel able to assist poorer countries that ask economic aid, but also be able to stick to liberal trading principles--because assured of a permanently adequate total market for our own products--and help them move "from aid to trade" as they become ready for it.

But what of inflation? Justice to fixed-income receivers demands that we stop inflation, and so does our need to remain internationally competitive, to protect our balance of payments. Is there really a way out of the impasse?

I submit that there is, and that a solution (described in detail elsewhere) can be broadly envisaged along the lines set out below. It would be "economic performance insurance," guarding against both deflation--too little demand for goods and labor--and inflation--too much demand. It would fully support our private enterprise system and the traditional division of powers between Congress and the President. Let me briefly explain.

(1) Assurance against deflation: Full employment would be defined and guaranteed each year in practical statistical terms. It would then be achieved by in effect pegging total demand (GNP) in advance at the presumptively right level, with the government coming in as employer of last resort (and disemployer of "first resort") to compensate up or down in case of significant net error in the calculations.

(2) Acceptability to private enterprise: Business would be assured of an adequate market for which to compete, and against unwanted expansion of the public sector at the expense of the private sector. This would result from combining the job-level guarantee with a guarantee of the level of private consumer spending, calculated from the GNP goal after noting how much government spending for goods and services was actually endorsed by Congress. (Also noted would be State and local government spending, private domestic investment, and--with implications already mentioned--net exports.)

If private consumer spending should tend to fall short of or exceed the promised rate, adjustment would be mandatory through taxes and/or transfer payments (social insurance etc.) vis-a-vis individuals. A negative income tax such as could evolve from President Nixon's welfare reform program would provide an especially convenient although not indispensable mechanism.

(3) Avoidance of inflation: The guarantees of employment and consumer spending would have ceilings as well as floors. Two powerful brakes would thus act against upward spirals. Besides, on the strength of those governmental guarantees, including the brakes, labor and business leaders could be expected to support some system of wage and price guidelines to reduce "cost push" pressure.

My thesis clearly does not depend, however, on the validity of this expectation, which some will consider unrealistic. For an "incomes policy" has to be evolved in any case. Beyond the "quick freeze" urged by a number of Democratic leaders, probably desirable as a temporary measure, we might even need the permanent legal controls on wages and prices which Galbraith sees as essential for non-inflationary "high" employment in future. (I would doubt that need, however, considering the different approach envisaged.)

(4) The relationship between the President and Congress: No unreasonable element would be introduced. Congress would not be asked to rubber-stamp a Presidential spending program or give the President wide discretionary powers.

The President's annual economic recommendations under the Employment Act would henceforth include: (a) a full-employment target, (b) a consumer spending target consistent with the recommended government spending program, (c) procedures for adjusting the job total up or down if its target was being missed, and (d) similarly contingent methods for adjusting consumer spending. The vital amendment to that Act would be this: Congress would be obligated not to rest content with criticism but to establish final decisions for the year on those same points. The policy being thus set, execution of adjustments (c) and (d), when actually called for by the current showing of the chosen statistical series, would logically rest with the President.

Questions of prerogative are involved but also questions of commitment, and it is commitment--the willingness to assume appropriate responsibility--that is really essential here.

6. Remedy for the New Mercantilism*

To the Editor:

Congratulations on your July 29 editorial on "The New Mercantilism." America has, as you point out, become a "mature creditor" nation--one that receives a large and growing return flow of interest and dividends from past foreign

---

*Copyright 1971 by The New York Times Company. Reprinted by permission from The New York Times, August 7, 1971, where it appeared under the heading "Approach to Inflation Control." The author's original heading has been restored.

loans and investments, while the traditional surplus on merchandise trade declines. This in principle need not be as frightening as many congressmen of both parties have reportedly found it.

Basically, as you say, our response should not be to adopt "mercantilist" subsidies for exports or protectionist measures such as import quotas. Instead we should learn to avoid damage to the American economy as these fundamental international shifts occur. It is stronger domestic economic measures against unemployment and inflation that offer the right solution.

The crux of the problem, however, is this: how can we in fact avoid damage to our own economy as our export surplus shrinks or even vanishes? One must answer this question.

In general terms the answer is that we must learn to control the aggregate of the huge domestic components of total expenditures for domestic output, and purposely move that aggregate up (or down) as the relatively tiny export surplus goes down (or up). In practice this means that the personal consumption expenditures component of G.N.P. needs to be so adjusted; the other two components--private domestic investment and Government purchases--are bound to obey other laws.

Aggregate consumer spending can be perfectly well controlled and adjusted to the needs of full employment in the light of the trend in the export balance (and the current view of the desirable size of the Government's own role). This is so because Congress can, by slightly amending the Employment Act of 1946, assume the responsibility of at last going beyond mere criticism of the President's annual economic report and can decide each year at what level consumer spending, as well as employment itself, is to be held.

This approach also clearly brings inflation control within reach, for two reasons. First, it envisages ceilings to employment and consumer spending as well as floors. Second, such an assumption of responsibility by the Government is the natural psychological precondition for expecting business and labor to act responsibly on prices and wages. If that sounds unrealistic, let me phrase it differently: this approach will minimize the element of compulsion in the "incomes policy" of which we undoubtedly now stand in need.

John H. G. Pierson
Washington, July 29, 1971

7. Insuring a Stable Economy*

The problems that by their and our very nature hold our attention are not economic (technical)--they are social (human and moral): how to preserve our planet and live in decent friendship and cooperation with our fellow men of every age, race, and creed. Ecology, Vietnam, racial discrimination, poverty, the revolt of youth.

Nevertheless, we have to solve the problem of economic performance--which we are obviously failing to do at this time--in order to gain even the chance to solve some of our most pressing human problems. We have no choice but to attend to the economic foundations of our social structure.

An approach has been developed which does--that is, would--solve the problem of economic performance in this country and also as far as the economic relations of America with the rest of the world are concerned. This approach I will call "Economic Performance Insurance" (EPI).

Economic Performance Insurance would prevent recessions and would also prevent inflation. On the one hand, it would guarantee the continuous maintenance of full employment--no unemployment in excess of the amount decided on in advance by reasonable men as constituting "necessary frictional unemployment." On the other, it would rule out spiraling prices by curbing both demand-pull and cost-push inflation.

Excessive demand-pull would be checked because the EPI mechanism would set not only floors but also ceilings to aggregate employment and to aggregate consumer spending. Excessive cost-push would cease because the government's commitment to EPI would provide a sound basis for reasonable counter-commitments on their pricing policies by business and labor. (In short, in this kind of "incomes policy," the responsibility would be mutual, as it should be.)

Some corollary benefits would be: restoration of opportunity for all as a cardinal American principle; help in solving the race problem by making equal employment opportunity efforts able to succeed; help in eradicating poverty, both by increasing the amount of paid labor and by creating labor market conditions that would tend to wipe out substandard wages; help in having good-neighbor economic policies, especially by establishing that export surpluses would no long-

---

*Reprinted by permission from the Honolulu Advertiser, August 14, 1971.

er be needed as a condition for our own domestic full-employment prosperity.

The key to the feasibility of instituting EPI lies in the fact that this approach responds to the existing division of economic powers between the President and Congress and to the existing division of views in the nation on the public-versus-private-sector issue. The noncontroversial problem of maintaining the right level of operation of our economy would be kept quite separate from the ongoing struggle to decide on the size of the government's own program.

In terms of legislation what is required is a comparatively simple amendment to the Employment Act of 1946 which would establish a clear congressional responsibility in this field, to be exercised year by year in specific terms after Congress has received and studied the President's proposals as set forth in his Economic Report.

27. THE EMPLOYMENT ACT REVISITED*

The candidates are setting their economic sights too low. When the Democrats fault the administration for giving us inflation and unemployment both at once, and promise to do much better themselves if granted the chance, that is not enough. Also needed--and also possible--are some solid assurances or guarantees.

The American economy can no longer afford the luxury of reacting defensively to every inflationary or deflationary pressure that happens to develop. Without forcing the economy into rigid controls, it is possible to devise a system of "performance insurance" procedures to maintain guaranteed full employment without inflation.

Such a system could be built around annual estimates--submitted by the President and legislated by Congress--of acceptable ranges of total employment and consumer spending for the next fiscal year. The procedures that could be established to carry out such a system would control the overall amount of economic activity while in general leaving the individual producer free.

Certainly this proposal does give conventional thinking a wrench. Some of our institutional machinery would have to be strengthened to put it into effect. In short, it raises several practical problems. Why not? For this is not a question of patchwork but of shaping the economic core for the social regeneration of America that is now, one hopes, on the way. The main point is that an approach is possible with, not against, the grain of tradition, so that under good leadership the practical problems raised can perfectly well be solved.

New Ground Rules

A full-employment guarantee is perhaps implicit in

---

*Reprinted by permission from The Washington Post, where it appeared May 14, 1972 under the title, "Full Employment without Inflation: A Proposal."

what some presidential candidates have sometimes proposed. Thus, Sen. Edmund Muskie has said: "It is time to commit our nation to the right to a job." Sen. George McGovern: "If I were President of the United States, I would set as the first order of business the creation of a decent job for every American." Sen. Henry Jackson: "As far as I am concerned, the Employment Act of 1946 means what it says...that the Federal Government under any administration, Republican or Democratic, must be prepared to use all the powers at its command to see that people have work." Sen. Hubert Humphrey: "Employment is a right for every American--like freedom or due process. Government has an obligation to fulfill that right as the first matter of policy."

Such statements would, I believe, be more frequent and more explicit if it were wholly clear how a guarantee of the chance to work would really, if given, be implemented. Some will recall that the 1968 Democratic Party platform promised that "For those who cannot obtain other employment the federal government will be the employer of last resort, either through federal assistance to state and local governments or through federally sponsored projects." But without an explanation of how it can be accomplished this does little more than widen the credibility gap.

Once the focus shifts from merely reducing unemployment to actually guaranteeing full employment, without going against the grain of tradition, some new ground rules have to be observed.

The first rule is that the approach must not threaten to have the public sector undermine private enterprise. An ironclad governmental pledge to serve as employer of last resort up to full employment might be construed as posing such a threat if offered all by itself. Such a pledge is indeed essential, but it needs to be supported by a further pledge that the market for the output of private producers will be sustained at a level high enough to maintain full business prosperity and preclude excessive reliance on the last-resort work programs.

This is one side of the question. Yet a basic problem in our society today is its obvious need for greatly expanded services (and capital investments) in the public sector, to counterbalance our overemphasis on the production of gadgets for the more or less surfeited rich. Both our cities and our backward rural areas cry out for attention. Health, education, low-cost housing, anti-pollution, mass transport--the fields starved for funds are well known. Those expenditures, partly governmental and partly private, should be made for their own sake, and clearly some initiative must come from Washington. An extra advantage is that many of them would produce more jobs dollar for dollar, especially jobs for less-skilled and less-educated workers, than would additional private spending.

In this sense the government should, as Michael Harrington recently put it, serve as employer of first, not last, resort. There is an imperative to so reorder our national priorities--a social imperative, like the need to narrow rather than widen further the income gaps between our rich and our poor. But the necessity for the government to serve as employer of last resort is also there, and this--the stabilization question--is essentially an economic matter. Two different issues, separate but complementary, are thus involved. Strong action of the first, socially motivated kind would undoubtedly reduce the need for the second, the stabilization action, but the second too is indispensable, like a latch on the door.

A Pledge on Spending

As for maintaining the market for the output of private business, the government should also guarantee an appropriate rate of aggregate consumer spending. Calculating this is a technical matter, for the President's Council of Economic Advisers in the first instance. However, what is essentially involved is: (a) to estimate the total overall expenditures for goods and services (GNP) necessary to justify production at the full-employment level; and (b) to subtract the anticipated government and business and (plus or minus) net export components. This gives (c) the rate of consumer spending to be announced and pegged.

The second ground rule is that guaranteed full employment must also not heighten inflation. Here we should distinguish between the grave dangers of inflation and whether full employment should be cast in the villain's role. Unfortunately this subject has been much obscured by preoccupation with the concept of an inevitable trade-off between inflation and unemployment, based on the "Phillips curve." Serious inflation can obviously occur far short of full employment. On the other hand, no modern government is going to use unemployment for really keeping inflation stopped, because the extent of unemployment, misery and repression required would be utterly out of harmony with present ideas of social justice. In short, a different, positive approach is needed--one in which some sort of incomes policy has a big part to play.

But luckily, that is not all. Actually, a program of guaranteed full employment would not feed inflation but could greatly help in the control of inflation. The mechanics of such a program would halt upward spirals, since ceilings as well as floors would be set to employment and to consumer spending. Thus "demand pull" would be kept in check, as would much of the "cost push" that stems from workers' efforts to keep up with a rising cost of living. Besides that, with the government at last assuming its proper responsibility for underwriting the continued health of the economy, the psychology would be right for business and labor leaders to agree to cooperate by abiding by some reasonable set of price and wage guidelines and thus minimize the need for measures of compulsion.

The third main ground rule is that guaranteed full employment must not be sought by means that disregard the traditional relationships between the President and Congress. There could be little future in any plan that expected Congress either to rubber-stamp the President's program or to grant him unduly broad discretionary powers.

The Role of Congress

Let me now show specifically how the Employment Act of 1946 could be amended so as to guarantee the opportunity to work to all Americans. The act provides that the President, guided by his Council of Economic Advisers, shall each year by Jan. 20 transmit to the Congress an Economic Report; this report is now required to include a statement of the levels of employment, production, and purchasing power needed to carry out the policy of achieving "useful employment opportunities, including self-employment, for those able, willing, and seeking to work."

That passage should be amplified by addition of the words "including specifically the minimum and maximum levels of employment recommended in the light of that policy, and the minimum and maximum rates of aggregate personal consumption expenditures deemed consistent with that policy in view of the program of Federal Government purchases of goods and services recommended to be undertaken and the anticipated other demands on the national product." The point is to tell Congress how the President proposes to define full employment and in what proportions he recommends having the country's economic activity divided between the private and public sectors.

It is in section 5(b)(3) that we are brought face to face

with the basic weakness of the act. At present the Joint Economic Committee, after it has studied the President's Economic Report and reached its own conclusions, is merely required "as a guide to the several committees of the Congress dealing with legislation relating to the Economic Report...to file a report with the Senate and the House of Representatives containing its findings and recommendations with respect to each of the main recommendations made by the President in the Economic Report." But surely the annual economic exercise should not end by disappearing this way in thin air. Rather, the JEC should be empowered and required to file its report "together with a draft Joint Resolution for the consideration of the Congress as provided for in section 6."

This new section 6, presumably entitled "Congressional Action on the Report of the Joint Economic Committee," could for brevity be phrased approximately as follows: "Sec. 6. As soon as practicable after the filing of the report of the Joint Economic Committee, the Congress shall by joint resolution of the Senate and the House of Representatives set forth its decisions with respect to: (a) the minimum and maximum acceptable levels of employment throughout the year in question; (b) the minimum and maximum acceptable rates of aggregate personal consumption expenditures throughout the year; (c) the preventive action to be taken by the President if employment should at any time tend to fall below its minimum, or rise above its maximum, acceptable level as defined in (a); and (d) the preventive action to be taken by the President in case personal consumption expenditures should at any time tend to fall below their minimum, or rise above their maximum, acceptable rates as defined in (b)."

How It Would Work

What this means is, first of all, that full employment would have a clear-cut statistical definition which would change from year to year. From the estimated labor force must always be subtracted some amount of unemployment deemed reasonable in the light of production shifts, manpower policies, and labor mobility at the time (the allowance for "necessary frictional unemployment"). Having considered the various factors, the President might in some year--this is simply an illustration--propose a minimum or 86.5 million jobs in terms of the seasonally adjusted monthly total reported by the Labor Department. He might also state that, in his view, anything over 87.8 million jobs would represent too tight a situation in the labor market, with too much upward pressure on pay scales and on total income payments. (Some such "band" between minimum and maximum is necessary--how wide is another question, not dealt with here--to keep from having to balance the economy on a razor edge.) Congress on its part, acting under the proposed new section 6(a), could disagree quantitatively on various grounds if it wanted to--technical estimating grounds or a difference in point of view about the percentage of unemployment consistent with "full" employment. But in any case it would have to assume the responsibility of arriving at definite decisions of its own.

Suppose then that, in spite of a favorable general outlook buttressed by the assured maintenance of enough consumer spending, employment as reported by the Labor Department started dropping below its congressionally established floor. What would be done? Obviously the government would have to step in as employer of last resort, accelerating some ongoing public works and services and taking other projects off the reserve shelf. Congress would have written the specifications for this under section 6(c)--what sorts of works and services were to be included (federally financed state and local government projects would certainly be, but could private nonprofit projects qualify?); the formula for apportionment by states; and so on. Execution would rest with the agencies designated by the President.

If an opposite situation should arise, with employment going through its ceiling, projects would be decelerated or discontinued entirely and put back on the reserve shelf, again under rules laid down by Congress in section 6(c).

Adjusting Consumer Spending

In the case of consumer spending, the proposed procedures would, to begin with, resolve the impasse that occurs now when Congress is less impressed than the President is with the need for new governmental leadership in social programs, or vice versa. Suppose that the President, keen on reordering the nation's priorities, were to recommend a number of spending programs that would, in sum, raise the percentage of GNP represented by the government's own purchases of goods and services. The majority in Congress might agree, or go even farther. On the other hand, perhaps the majority would favor maintaining the existing GNP ratios instead. Thus, to illustrate, Congress might some year decide--under 6(b)--that the acceptable limits to consumer spending would be $765 billion and $780 billion, whereas the President, with different GNP proportions, more heavily weighted on the government side, in mind, had recommended a range of only $745-760 billion.

Suppose this time that it was consumer spending, in terms of the seasonally adjusted annual rates reported each quarter by the Commerce Department, that tended to get out of line. In spite of continuous full employment it might do so, in either direction. What would be the remedy? In making the applicable rules for this eventuality, under 6(d), Congress would have had numerous options. It might have decided that any necessary adjustments should be made through variations in the personal income tax and the addition or termination of certain payments to low-income households. Or, if welfare reform had led to the adoption of a plan guaranteeing a minimum income to all households as a matter of right, and of a negative income tax as the pay-out mechanism, Congress might have accepted a presidential recommendation that the income tax itself (positive and negative) should be the only instrument used.

Or perhaps congressional economists would have concluded that spending by consumers might still (even with booms and slumps ruled out) fail to respond sensitively to adjustments in their disposable income, brought about by methods like those just mentioned. In that case Congress could choose a method that would cut direct to the goal, such as a federal sales tax/sales bonus at the retail level, with the bonuses operating via stamps convertible to cash. During periods when the tax aspect had to be called into play to keep consumer spending from going too high, this tax would automatically lower the amount received, net, by business, that being then designated the amount required to be held below the established ceiling.

Self-Sustaining System

Under the approach proposed, since our whole forward-looking system is geared to expectations, consumers and producers would behave in ways tending to make the economy inherently more self-sustaining. Gone, for example, would be such deflationary influences as the oversaving and overpricing due to the fear of the loss of jobs and income in a future slump.

The regular committee system of Congress would function as it does now. Tax reform decisions in the Ways and Means Committee, for instance, would not clash with the standby tax adjustment mechanisms, but would only--since they would alter after-tax income and its distribution--affect the likelihood that those mechanisms would have to be called into play. In fact, considerable legislative feedback could be expected. An unduly large or frequent need to use adjustments for shoring up employment or consumer spending would spotlight the urgency of improved legislation relating to distribution of income, enforcement of competition and/or regulation of monopoly, or other factors strategically affecting the self-balancing capacity of the economy.

The "automaticity" of this approach would certainly not eliminate the need for good operational judgment, especially in deciding when to start and when to stop taking compensatory action. Gearing up for fast action would certainly be required, and agreement on how long employment or consumer spending could without prejudice remain at "unacceptable" levels, outside the prescribed band. The preparation of an adequate reserve shelf of public works and services would be a major task but not as difficult by any means as it always has been in the absence of a firm national commitment to, and understood means of maintaining, full employment.

How does this bear on the immediate problem of reducing unemployment from close to 6 per cent? If the proposed plan with its built-in restraints on inflation were already on the legislative drawing boards, unemployment could probably be brought down to 3 per cent--or to whatever other level Congress would want to stipulate--more quickly than discussions today suggest. But there is no point in attempting the impossible. In the transition period it might well be decided to move up to full employment in a series of quarterly steps and reach it, say, in the second year.

One of the especially striking advantages of the proposed plan lies in the area of foreign trade policy. An increase of net exports, through import restrictions and other means, has often been sought in the past as a solution for our unemployment, even though other countries might suffer from the action we took. That indeed is exactly the escalating danger today. The approach here proposed would turn the relationship around and call for an expansion of the domestic market (via consumer spending, which would be pegged higher) when the foreign market (net exports) was projected as declining. Consequently this approach would allay fears of a shortage of markets in the overall sense, and so would help to maintain a liberal foreign trade policy based on the widest interpretation of national self-interest. The less-developed countries, for instance, could then be extended a generous helping hand in their efforts to move "from aid to trade."

Foreign trade; society's claims vis-a-vis those of business, labor, farmers, and other interest groups; the problems of blacks and other minorities--these and other basic issues of the times all show that what is really needed is not just less unemployment but full employment on an assured basis. The opportunity to work is fundamental in America and in a real sense it is necessary to sustain all other forms of opportunity. Certainly even a reduction of present unemployment would be very welcome. The extra wealth from the extra production could then--together with any resources shifted from defense to peace--be devoted to making more rapid headway in fighting poverty and rescuing the environment. But we can do much better than that. The candidates are setting their economic sights too low.

INDEX